A Gentleman of Pleasure

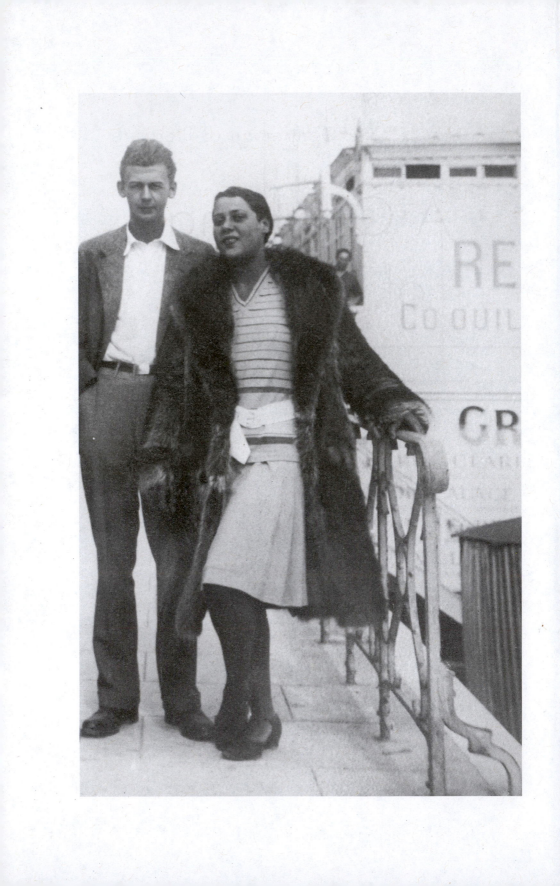

A Gentleman of Pleasure

One Life of John Glassco

Poet, Memoirist, Translator, and Pornographer

BRIAN BUSBY

McGill-Queen's University Press   Montreal & Kingston • London • Ithaca

ISBN 978-0-7735-3818-4

Legal deposit first quarter 2011
Bibliothèque nationale du Québec

Printed in Canada on acid-free paper that is 100% ancient forest free
(100% post-consumer recycled), processed chlorine free.

This book has been published with the help of a grant from the Canadian Federation for the
Humanities and Social Sciences, through the Aid to Scholarly Publications Program, using
funds provided by the Social Sciences and Humanities Research Council of Canada.

McGill-Queen's University Press acknowledges the support of the Canada Council for
the Arts for our publishing program. We also acknowledge the financial support of the
Government of Canada through the Book Fund for our publishing activities.

Library and Archives Canada Cataloguing in Publication

Busby, Brian John
A gentleman of pleasure : one life of John Glassco : poet, memoirist, translator,
and pornographer / Brian Busby.

Includes bibliographical references and index.
ISBN 978-0-7735-3818-4

1. Glassco, John, 1909–1981. 2. Authors, Canadian–20th century–Biography.
3. Pornography in literature. I. Title.

PS8513.L388Z67 2011   C811'.54   C2010-906218-3

Frontispiece: Glassco and Sibley Dreis on the boardwalk at Nice, 1929.

This book was designed and typeset by studio oneonone in Adobe Garamond 11/15

In Memorabilia Mortis
PROFESSOR LAWRENCE P. NOWICKI
1930–1995

"Run, don't walk ..."

Contents

A Gentleman of Pleasure

We end, in other words, by loving him as much for what he really was as for what he tells us he was, and discover that the two characters complement each other and make an intelligible whole. In this way we grasp the truth that man is not only a living creature but the person of his own creation.

John Glassco on Giacomo Casanova,
Memoirs of Montparnasse

Introduction

John Glassco was, in his own words, "an accomplished liar," "a great practitioner of deceit."[1] These talents, cultivated at an early age, served well his art and public persona. Among his greatest powers were those of mimicry and self-transformation. In private, they not only aided his survival but also allowed for the pursuit of relationships and interests not spoken of in polite company. His life and work were made fuller through deception, fabrication, and fantasy.

Nowhere are these talents more evident than in *Memoirs of Montparnasse*, the untrustworthy keystone under which one must pass when considering Glassco's story. This engaging and intriguing account of youth has been variously described, praised, and denounced. Malcolm Cowley, perhaps the foremost chronicler of the expatriate experience, considered the book "the most accurate picture of Montparnasse."[2] To George Woodcock, it was both "a strange projection out of time"[3] and a work of "glittering freshness."[4] In the introduction supplied by Glassco's friend Leon Edel, the work is compared to other memoirs of the time and place and is praised as "more immediate – possessing almost the effect of 'instant' memory, total recall."[5]

During the decade that spanned publication and Glassco's death, the veracity of *Memoirs of Montparnasse* went largely unchallenged; the many anachronisms, inconsistencies, and improbabilities contained in the work all but escaped critical notice. Indeed, the author's gestures toward the truth, his hints that things might not have been quite as depicted, were ignored. With remarkably few exceptions, those writing about the memoirs received the work as presented: the chronicle of a young man's adventures in the Paris of the late 1920s and early 1930s. It was not until the years following Glassco's death that the curtain began to be pulled slowly aside, exposing the memoirs as a response to others, composed with an eye on the bestseller lists in late middle-age. Glassco himself aided in this unveiling by leaving behind journals, notes, inscriptions, drafts, and widely scattered correspondence in which his intentions are clearly laid out.

Since his death, there has followed a re-evaluation that has at times seemed harsh. Fellow Montreal poet Louis Dudek, the earliest critic to express doubts as to the veracity of Glassco's memoirs, was nevertheless an early champion of the book. However, as the decades passed, and the extent to which Glassco had fabricated became more evident, Dudek came to consider the work as a collection of "irresponsible claims."[6] He wrote that he could not reread so much as a page and cautioned: "*Memoirs of Montparnasse* is a great little book, but only if you remember that it is not a memoir, it is not a history, it is a work of imagination and fantasy."[7]

As is often the case in the memoir, a genre influenced by self-interest, self-censorship, and the limits of memory, truth lies somewhere between history and imagination and fantasy. There can be no doubt as to Glassco's presence in Montparnasse during much of the period claimed, nor can it be argued that he was not acquainted with many of its figures, among them Louise Bryant, Gwen Le Galliennne, Yvette Ledoux, Caridad de Laberdesque, Hilaire Hiler, Jimmie "The Barman" Charters, Bricktop, Ethel Moorhead, Edwin Lanham, Archie Craig, the Dayang Muda of Sarawak, and of course Robert McAlmon and Kay Boyle. Contemporary letters penned by McAlmon, Moorhead, and Glassco's McGill University friends Doug Adam, Leon Edel, and A.J.M. Smith confirm several of the events described in the memoir.

Glassco himself described *Memoirs of Montparnasse* as a "loose and lying chronicle," and it is with this in mind that the work has been approached here.[8] For the purposes of this biography, unless corroborated – in contemporary publications, correspondence, or in other memoirs – many of the anecdotes and encounters found within the work have been ignored. While some may receive consideration within these pages, they have not been accepted as historical fact.

The composition of the memoirs is in itself worthy of a book – and indeed one has already been written: Philip Kokotailo's *John Glassco's Richer World: Memoirs of Montparnasse*. With this work, I recommend the essay

"Memoirs of Montparnasse: 'A Reflection of Myself,'" by Thomas E. Tausky, and, in particular, Michael Gnarowski's critical introduction and notes found in the 1995 Oxford University Press edition. Professor Gnarowski spent more than a decade in pursuit of what he has described as "the knowable truth" concerning Glassco's Montparnassian years.[9] His work greatly changed the way the memoirs are viewed. This biography benefits greatly from his research.

For the most part, other work discussed in this biography is not readily available. This country has not treated Glassco well. His important translations of Hector de Saint-Denys-Garneau's *Journal* and collected poems were issued in small editions, received little notice, and slowly drifted into that sad status we refer to as "out of print." Glassco's own verse has fared ever so slightly better. Of the five volumes published during his lifetime, only *Selected Poems* received a second printing. When, in 1997, Ottawa's Golden Dog Press published *John Glassco: Selected Poems with Three Notes on the Poetic Process*, Glassco's verse had been out of print for nearly a quarter-century. The 2001 Golden Dog edition of *The English Governess* is the only edition of Glassco's international bestseller to have been published in his native land.

The Canadian reaction to Glassco's pornography has been typically one of ignorance, indignation, and silence. In this area it is foreign publishers who, recognizing significant commercial potential, have shown the greatest dedication. *The English Governess*, *Harriet Marwood, Governess*, *Fetish Girl*, and his skilled completion of Audrey Beardsley's *Under the Hill* are all available through publishing houses in England and the United States. *Squire Hardman*, the least common of all his titles, can be found in *Punitive Poetry*, an anthology of "disciplinary poetry" published by a small press located in Bexhill-on-Sea, East Sussex.

The disregard demonstrated within this country has even extended to Glassco's best-known work, *Memoirs of Montparnasse*. When resurrected in 2007 under the New York Review of Books imprint, it had been out of print for nearly a decade. There is no Canadian edition.

The intent of this biography is to not only raise awareness of Glassco as a unique figure but to draw attention to his writing and his role in furthering translation and to correct the many varied misconceptions and misunderstandings about his life.

Forty years ago, Louis Dudek began his review of *Under the Hill*:

> The way we arrange it, most good writers live in obscurity and die in oblivion. Later the myth grows. We imagine how wonderful it must have been, art being the one true greatness. Actually it was mostly solitude, neglect, poverty. The best live among us in disguise.[10]

There was solitude and neglect in Glassco's life; though born into wealth, poverty was one of his "lifelong terrors."[11] Glassco was a man of many disguises, some he discarded, others he maintained until his death. Yet, he chose to leave behind documentation that he knew fully well would expose his masquerade. In death, he laid bare not only his own myth but also the calculation and purpose under which it had been crafted. In this sense, it was the ultimate act by a man who, tormented by chronic doubt as to his artistic capacity, was given to self-flagellation. Ever ready to dismiss his abilities, he wrote of himself as a "trifler, dilettante, *petit-maître*."[12]

Glassco told a central truth when he described himself as an accomplished liar; he took delight in deceit. But he lied, however unintentionally, in dismissing his talent.

We have here a stylist who was as comfortable and accomplished in writing what has been taken to be Victorian erotic prose as he was imitating poetry of the early nineteenth century. Glassco's completion of *Under the Hill* reveals not so much as a seam between the Beardsley's words and his own. His poetry received several honours, including a 1971 Governor General's Award. The existence of the John Glassco Translation Prize reflects not only his own work as a translator of French-language poetry and prose but his key role in laying the foundation for what was to become modern Canadian translation. Added to this we have *Memoirs of Montparnasse*, which has been described as "the best book of prose written by a Canadian."[13] No trifler, no dilettante, no *petit-maître*. John Glassco created a most eclectic and unusual body of work.

It is, of course, an unnecessary observation that one whose life spanned the greater part of the twentieth-century lived through a period of great change. Montreal, the city in which Glassco was born and raised, is no longer the largest in the country, nor is it the financial centre. Though it continues to hold its place as Canada's most beautiful metropolis, its looks have been greatly diminished by demolition, development, and Drapeau.

Readers with some knowledge of Montreal may take exception to the use of the term Golden Square Mile, a neologism that was only beginning to be used at the time of Glassco's death. The term is employed here for the simple reason that it better reflects the affluence and power held within its boundaries than does the original "Square Mile." I rush to add that neither designation was in use during Glassco's youth, when he was a resident of the area.

Similarly, with few exceptions I have employed the appellation French Canadian, rather than Québécois, throughout the text. The former was not only preferred by Glassco but it was the term used with near exclusivity until the final decade of his life.

ONE | 1909–1928

The small, unhappy boy, impatient in his youth –[1]

John Glassco wrote that he'd been born in a magnificent house, a mansion among many on a beautiful shaded street in Montreal's Golden Square Mile. It had been the home of his grandfather, Edward Rawlings, founder and president of the Guarantee Company of North America, a man of affluence and influence in what was then the largest, wealthiest, and most powerful city in the Dominion. A Victorian mélange of verandas and conservatories, dormers and dressings, the Rawlings mansion was constructed almost entirely of wood, and so appeared peculiar and out of place in a city of cut stone and brick. It rested on the southern slope of Mount Royal, just above Sherbrooke Street; Alexander Mackenzie, the second prime minister, had been a neighbour. Once the setting of great activity, by the time of Glassco's birth, the expansive grounds – the flower gardens, the pear orchard, the tennis courts, the stables – having suffered years of neglect, were slowly returning to nature. All lay within the shadow of the Unitarian Church of the Messiah, a magnificent, massive, grey structure built in the English Gothic style. To have begun life in such an elaborate and unusual house seems somehow so very appropriate for one who would go on to live the most extraordinary, idiosyncratic life in Canadian letters.

In truth, Glassco was born several blocks away at his parents' home on the northeast corner of St Luke and St Matthew streets. It was a perfectly respectable address, perhaps a touch modest for the daughter of one of the city's most affluent men, but was most certainly a more grand, more impressive address than what one might expect of her husband, Archibald Patrick Stinson Glassco – A.P.S. – a structural engineer with the Quebec Bridge Commission.

A Hamiltonian, A.P.S. was the son of John Thomas Glassco and Charlotte Stinson Glassco, the third in a family of four children. Theirs had also been a large house – with two live-in domestics, both named Agnes – one of a number of similarly comfortable Glassco households in Hamilton. Through business and sport, the surname had achieved a certain profile within the city, beginning with the arrival in 1843 of William Henry Glassco and his young family. The grandfather of A.P.S., William Glassco, had been a Toronto furrier with a profitable wholesale and retail business; it was said that much of his success stemmed from lengthy annual treks into Rupert's Land in order to barter directly with native trappers. While relocating forty miles to the west may have made these journeys slightly shorter, William Glassco most certainly sought other benefits in trading his prime retail location on Toronto's King Street for one on the identically named thoroughfare in Hamilton. He would have recognized great advantage in a younger, thriving community with no existing furrier. Within three years of the Glassco family's arrival, their adopted town had doubled in population and had been incorporated as a city. Between journeys west, William Glassco began to diversify his interests, creating a conglomerate of sorts. In 1861, with his sons John and Henry, he established W.H. Glassco, Sons and Company, a concern that incorporated several businesses, among them Globe Straw Works, manufacturers of "men's and women's straw goods of all descriptions."[2] Three years later he was one of the founders of the Board of Trade of the City of Hamilton and later became its president. Before his death in 1899, sixteen days short of his eightieth birthday, William would serve as a director and shareholder in the Hamilton Provident and Loan Society, the Hamilton, Guelph and Buffalo Railway Company, the South Ontario Pacific Railway Company, and a commercial steamship line, the St Lawrence Navigation Company; all, ultimately, to the benefit of his descendants.

In 1897, in the days surrounding his seventeenth birthday, A.P.S. followed his elder brother John to McGill University and, four years later, obtained a bachelor's degree in electrical engineering.[3] After graduation he remained in Montreal, working first as a designer for the Dominion Bridge Company, before moving on to continue his work in bridge design for the Grand Trunk Railway.

A.P.S. married well. Although it was true that the Rawlings family had been present in Canada a much shorter time than had his own – by four generations, in fact – it had risen to a height far above that of the Hamilton

Glasscos. Edward Rawlings, the patriarch, had landed in Montreal in 1863 as a twenty-three-year-old charged with establishing and managing a branch of the European Life and Guarantee Company. He was said to be part of a family that had once been great landowners in Ireland. Indeed, it would one day be claimed that Rawlings was a successor of the Irish Earldom of Carhampton, which in 1829 had gone into abeyance. However, his true beginnings, while perfectly respectable and decent, were considerably less impressive. Rawlings was born in 1839 London to a wholesale merchant and a rector's daughter.[4] Though raised in the city of his birth, he'd received at least a portion of his education in France; as a consequence, Rawlings was perhaps overqualified to conduct business in Montreal, where English was considered very much the principal language of commerce. In every way, the island city was dominant in British North America, and the time at which Rawlings landed was particularly propitious. The expansion of the St Lawrence canal system, combined with the deepening of the channel to Quebec City, had ensured its place as the pre-eminent port city, a position Montreal would hold for a further century. Industrialization was beginning to draw workers from the rural parts of the province. Even the civil war in the republic to the south was proving beneficial as British military presence swelled and displaced Confederates took refuge in the city. But above all there were the ever-present railways – the Montreal and New York Railroad, the Champlain and Saint Lawrence Railroad, and the Grand Trunk Railway – which had made Montreal a major hub. The years leading to Rawlings's arrival had seen reckless expansion, to a point at which capacity far exceeded need. The three-year-old Victoria Bridge, considered the eighth wonder of the world, began to be spoken of as a folly. And yet, through merger and acquisition, the rails remained active, their shareholders convinced that great profit lay in the future.

Rawlings's posting in the New World would have never taken place had it not been for the intervention of Sir Alexander Galt, who, as director of the Grand Trunk Railway, was frustrated with his company's inability to secure bonded employees and had encouraged the European Life and Guarantee Company to set up a branch in the Canadas. Rawlings knew the business well: more than one relative was working for European Life and Guarantee, and he had himself been employed by the firm since the age of fourteen. As resident secretary and manager of the Canadian branch, the newly arrived Briton worked with a six-member board that included politicians George-

Edward Rawlings in 1864, the year after he arrived in Montreal.

Étienne Cartier, John Ross, and Charles Joseph Alleyn, as well as Thomas Cramp, the president of the Board of Trade, Charles John Brydges, managing director of the Grand Trunk Railway, and Henry Thomas, the director of the Bank of Montreal.[5] The Canadian offices Rawlings established at 69 and 71 Great St James Street flourished, filling needs fuelled by the colony's rapid growth. Within two years the European Life and Guarantee Company's Montreal branch was reporting an annual premium revenue of 300,000 pounds. In the old country, however, the situation was quite different. The London office had undertaken a number of unstable investments, projects that would certainly have met with disapproval by the prudent and ever-cautious Rawlings. When, in 1868, the London office collapsed, Rawlings took his clients to Sir Hugh Allan's Citizens' Insurance Company of North America, at which he established and managed a life and guarantee department. Though successful, the move failed to satisfy Rawlings, and in 1872, together with his friend Galt, he established the business that would come to be known as the Guarantee Company of North America.[6] Under Rawlings's management the company expanded quickly. Within a decade it was firmly positioned as the largest fidelity guarantee company in both Canada and the United States. The transplanted Londoner sat with J.P. Morgan, George Pullman, and Asa Potter on the board of directors of the United States Guarantee Company, the US subsidiary he'd established in 1890.

Rawlings served ten years as vice-president of the American Bankers' Association, was a director with the Montreal Telegraph Company, and a governor of the Montreal General Hospital. In late nineteenth-century Montreal, this son of a merchant wholesaler stood beside the miller's son Alexander Walker Ogilvie, who had been responsible for much of the city's industrialization, and Sir William Cornelius Van Horne, the former telegraph boy who had become president of the Canadian Pacific Railway, very much a part of the establishment. Rawlings had become an enormously wealthy man, "known for his kindness of heart, for his charity and for his nobility of character."[7] He was twice president of the St George's Society and a member of Montreal's Metropolitan Club, the Mount Royal Club, the St James Club, Forest and Stream, the Royal Montreal Golf Club, the Montreal Hunt Club, and the Lawyers' Club of New York. A neighbour of the future head of the Quebec Superior Court, Rawlings also served as a justice of the peace for the Province of Quebec.

During summer 1866, while visiting the British Isles, he courted and married twenty-year-old Lucretia Carter. The ceremony was conducted by the bride's father, the Reverend Henry Carter, DD, at Ballintoy Church in Northern Ireland, after which Lucretia left Mount Druid House, the Georgian rectory in which she had been raised with her eleven siblings. Life in Montreal would prove more luxurious. The Simpson Street mansion belonging to Edward Rawlings may have been constructed of wood, but it was otherwise typical of the grand homes of the Golden Square Mile. In stark contrast with the houses of the wealthy found in London and New

York, these were sprawling structures often set on many acres of land. The upper class families so blessed as to live within the boundaries of the Golden Square Mile – Mount Royal to the north, Dorchester to the south, Atwater to the west and Park Avenue to the east – held seventy percent of the country's wealth. It was home to the Molsons, the Birks, the Holts, the Redpaths, Lord Strathcona, and, of course, Alexander Ogilvie and William Van Horne.

Within these luxuriant surroundings Edward and Lucretia Rawlings raised six children, the youngest of whom was the beautiful Kathleen Mabel Beatrice. Born 10 January 1884, she was raised in privilege, comfort, and formality; young gentlemen wishing to call on the three Rawlings daughters were expected to consult *Dau's Society Blue-Book for Montreal* for the appropriate day and hour. How Beatrice met her future husband has been lost to history, though the connection between Edward Rawlings and the Grand Trunk Railway, then the employer of A.P.S., may provide something of an answer.

Beatrice was twenty-one years old at the time of the marriage, three years her fiancé's junior. The wedding of heiress to engineer took place late in the damp, cheerless afternoon of 19 September 1905 at the Church of England's St James the Apostle, the Rawlings family place of worship on the corner of St Catherine and Bishop Streets. Elaborate arrangements and adornments were described, somewhat inelegantly, in the early edition of that day's *Montreal Daily Star*:

> The decorations of the church will be carried out in white and green, palms, white asters and chrysanthemums being used. The bride, who will be given away by her father, will be gowned in white Bruges lace over white taffeta veiled in white chiffon, the skirt having frills of accordion pleated chiffon under the lace.
>
> The bodice of Bruges lace embroidered in peards [*sic*] has a girdle form d [*sic*] of folds of white satin, the same decoration appearing on the elbow sleeves which are finished with ruffles of real Valenciennes lace. The tulle veil will be caught with orange blossoms, and a bouquet of roses and lilies will be carried. The bride's only ornament will be the gift of the groom, a brooch in wreath design of pearls and diamonds.[8]

The reception, held at the Rawlings mansion, three blocks from the church, was well attended. Guests included the Simpsons, the Ogilvies, the Stewarts, and Brooke Claxton, Sr, father of the future Liberal cabinet minister. After changing into her travelling clothes – a blue moiré gown and cloak of Rajah – Beatrice left with her groom for Toronto, Niagara Falls, "and points further west."[9] It was not a long honeymoon. Within a month, the newlyweds had returned to Montreal and, after a brief stay with a family friend, had moved into 49 St Luke Street. Their first home together, it was furnished almost entirely with wedding gifts provided by the Rawlings and Glassco families. The address was not nearly so humble as their yet-to-be-born son John would one day claim. A large house, it provided accommodations for two live-in servants and was just a few minutes walk from the Rawlings mansion, well within the bounds of the Golden Square Mile. Surrounding homes were quite grand; the mansion of James Johnston, an importer and retailer who had been of some significance in nineteenth-century Montreal, was located just one block over.

The union of A.P.S. and Beatrice produced two sons and one daughter. The future poet and pornographer was the second to be brought into the world. Edward David – David – the eldest, was born in April 1908; the arrival of their only daughter, Beatrice Mary Lucretia, lay far in the future; just a few months shy of her parents' twentieth wedding anniversary, in fact.

John Glassco's birth, shortly after midnight on 15 December 1909, a relatively mild Wednesday, was announced by way of a lone notice in that afternoon's *Montreal Daily Star*:

GLASSCO – On December 15th, to Mr and Mrs A.P.S. Glassco, a son.[10]

No further announcements were placed in the city's other English language dailies, nor did the family send out cards heralding the new baby's birth. Their second son would one day write that he was neither planned nor wanted. What can be said with certainty is that Glassco's early years weren't at all unusual for someone of his class. He was cared for not by his parents but by a series of nursemaids; the first, perhaps, being Nellie Gee, in whose arms he was photographed as an infant on the veranda of the family's summer house. The 1911 Canadian census records two domestics – nineteen-year-old Jenny Mitchael and thirty-year-old Neal Marthe Russell – as living in the Glassco home. It is certain that one of these women, perhaps

David and Buffy Glassco with nursemaid Phoebe Trenholme, Pointe Claire, 1910.

both, cared for the young sons of A.P.S. and Beatrice. Of all these women – and it would seem there were many more – Glassco said that his favourite was Hester Marryat, to whom he would dedicate his best-selling work, *Harriet Marwood, Governess*, an erotic romance of dominance and submission written in the Victorian manner.[11]

It is only a slight exaggeration to claim that the future writer was known as John Glassco only on paper. To very nearly all who knew him, he was

Buffy, a name that lasted from the evening of his birth until the afternoon of his death. This unusual, feminine-sounding sobriquet originated with his brother David, who at age two struggled with the word "brother" and spoke of his "baby buffy." As there was no birth certificate, one might say Buffy was his first name, his true name. It wasn't until a family trip to Hamilton, at the age of ten months, that he was christened John Stinson Glassco; the proper ceremony performed by the Right Reverend John Philip DuMoulin, the bishop of Niagara, at Christ's Church Cathedral.

"At that time," Glassco would write, "my parents were living on a modest scale, being wholly dependent on my father's earnings as a structural engineer; but there was an atmosphere of affluence in the house at all times due to my maternal grandfather's great wealth which formed a kind of background for everything."[12]

On the morning of 12 December 1911, this background was brought forward with the death of Edward Rawlings, three days short of his grandson Buffy's second birthday. Though he'd remained the head of the Guarantee Company, this once persuasive and dominant figure had spent much of his last decade in eccentric solitude, puttering about the top floor of the decaying mansion in which he would die. His final weeks had been spent bedridden, surrounded by his wife and children.

To his shareholders, Rawlings left an ever-prosperous company with annual surpluses of over $1 million. A new, larger head office on Beaver Hall Hill – which the company would incorrectly trumpet as Montreal's first skyscraper – had moved beyond the planning stages.[13]

Edward Rawlings's considerable wealth was divided by seven; each of the five children, Beatrice Glassco among them, received a share. Two of the seven parcels were left to Edward's widow, with the proviso that upon her death what remained would be invested and held in trust for the grandchildren until each reached the age of twenty-five.

It is possible that Beatrice's sizeable inheritance, which included a stock portfolio estimated at $1 million, prompted A.P.S. to set up his own business; that same year he established himself as an independent contractor and consulting structural engineer. The success of this new venture may be measured by the fact that within five years he was working as an insurance inspector under his brothers-in-law Henry and Walter at the Guarantee Company.

Beatrice Rawlings Glassco, c. 1911.
Glassco kept no images of his father.

These changes in employment had no effect on the indulgent lifestyle in which Beatrice had been raised. With her husband and two boys, she continued to summer on the West Island of Montreal, in what was then the Town of Pointe Claire. The area was popular among monied English Montrealers, offering escape – if only minimal – from the heat and humidity of the city. The family's summer house was located on Golf Avenue, far within the stone and iron gates of the exclusive Beaconsfield Golf Club, opposite the impressive clubhouse. It belonged to Beatrice, a "glamour girl" whose interests, her son

Buffy would claim, extended no further than "golf, social life and fashion magazines."[14] In 1914, Beatrice would serve as the president of the club's Ladies Branch and two years later became Ladies' Club champion.[15] The balance of the year the family lived in one or another in a series of large rented houses and spacious apartments within the Golden Square Mile.

This comfortable, semi-transient lifestyle came to an end in 1914 when – following the death of her mother, Lucretia – she and her family moved to the Rawlings mansion. Half a century later, Glassco would remember it as "a magnificent three storey house, with innumerable verandas and greenhouses, but in rather poor repair, and full of the vestiges of my grandfather: the whole top floor had been his sanctum for the last ten years of his life, when he became increasingly eccentric, bibulous and estranged from his wife and family, and was crammed with a fantastic assortment of books, papers, chemical apparatus, broken clocks etc. The whole house and grounds, with their mixture of splendour and decay, have remained in the background of my consciousness."[16]

This lingering image of his grandfather's mansion would not always remain in the background of consciousness; knowingly Glassco carried it forward into his fiction, where it served to inspire similarly elaborate, sad structures. The once grand family home in gentle, gradual decline would become a ubiquitous feature in the landscape of his imagination.

The death of Glassco's grandmother came within months of the beginning of the Great War. At the outset, A.P.S., a thirty-three-year-old married professional with two sons, chose not to enlist. When he did volunteer, in September 1916, the war was in its third year. His service was anything but noteworthy. Although he was made a lieutenant with the 245th Battalion of the Canadian Grenadier guards, and stated his willingness to take part in the Canadian Over-Seas Expeditionary Force, he remained in the country. In April 1917, he was granted a one-month leave during which he resigned from service.

Five months after the armistice, A.P.S. was made secretary and bursar of McGill University, an appointment that may very well have been aided by Herbert Molson and others of the board of governors who had had business dealings with Edward Rawlings. In his new position, A.P.S. was second only to the principal and vice-chancellor, roles filled in 1920 by Sir Arthur Currie. The Great War general had been a participant in every major Canadian action and had conceived the seemingly inconceivable with the Allied victory at the Battle of Vimy Ridge. The unorthodox selection of the aloof Currie, a somewhat disreputable insurance broker and realtor with no postsecondary education, a man who had lived his life outside the walls of academe, was a controversial one. The appointment was criticized by many, but not A.P.S., whose correspondence indicates that he was very much in awe of a man whose military service was so very different from his own.

McGill had been greatly damaged by the war. Enrolment dropped and university coffers had been depleted as several hundred students left their studies to fight in the conflict – more than two hundred would be killed overseas. For years its buildings had been neglected, and its equipment and laboratories had been worn through military research. Postwar, the university was forced into a crucial and costly period of renewal and expansion, something for which A.P.S., as an engineer, appeared well suited. During the next decade he would oversee the construction of several new buildings and the remodelling of others, including the Arts Building, which in 1926 was completely rebuilt behind the original facade; all would be in place before the enrolment of his second son.

The relatively brief academic career of Buffy Glassco had begun at the age of four under a Miss Derrick, who ran a private kindergarten located in a house a few blocks away from the Rawlings mansion. It was there that he fell in love for the first time. The object of his affection, a little girl named Lorraine Morgan, did not return his feelings, causing distress so considerable that in his sixth decade he still remembered her name.[17]

By the age of six he had followed his older brother into Selwyn House, a private boys' school located on Mackay Street in what had once been a family residence. It was an institution with high self-regard, but little history. Originally named Lucas School, Selwyn House had been established in 1908, largely through the support of Herbert Holt – president of the Royal Bank of Canada, future knight bachelor – a man, who, as the head of the monopolistic Montreal Light, Heat and Power Company, appeared omnipresent in the lives of the city's residents.[18] In helping to found the school, Holt had ensured that the entitled sons of the Golden Square Mile were educated close to home. No longer would they be obliged to interact with boys from less wealthy families at Westmount's Wickham House, or those of St John's (soon to be renamed Lower Canada College).

Entering Selwyn House, Buffy Glassco, grandson of Edward Rawlings, joined classmates with surnames like McConnell, Birks, Drummond, Van

Horne, Molson, and Thetford and under the eyes of English masters received what he would always consider "the best education imaginable."[19] Though younger than the others in the first form, Glassco excelled. He shared in the affection and respect of the other boys for their headmaster, a Cambridge man named Colin Campbell Macaulay. Austere, with the appearance of a "retired major from the Indian Army," Macaulay's popularity with the students of Selwyn House is perhaps at least partly explained through his reluctance to employ the switch.[20] Punishments were sporadic and rare, occasioned only by the most extreme acts of disobedience. Glassco's one-time claim, that the headmaster frequently warmed his bottom with a special ruler "swung with great expertise," was written in late middle-age to a fellow author of flagellantine literature and, if not untrue, is at the very least an exaggeration.[21]

If A.P.S. perceived a flaw in the education provided by Selwyn House, it was most certainly found in the lack of emphasis the school placed on athletics. Sport, he believed, played an important role in molding a well-rounded young man. As an adolescent A.P.S. had seen two cousins play for the Hamilton Tigers football club, one of whom, E.S. "Bonnie" Glassco, would become Canadian tennis champion. A.P.S. himself had spent three seasons as halfback for the McGill Collegiate football team and, in 1921, played third when the Royal Montreal Curling Club won the Governor General's Trophy. Yet he had sent his sons to a school entirely lacking in athletic facilities. Twice a week Buffy, David and the rest of the student population were obliged to troop through city streets for an hour of games at the Montreal Amateur Athletic Association grounds or the Coliseum skating rink.

Glassco, a man who in adulthood had a complete disregard, whether participant or spectator, for sports outside the equestrian, would make some grandiose claims as to his athletic accomplishments at Selwyn House:

I was captain of the Senior hockey team at Selwyn House School (it's the closest thing to Eton in Montreal!) and we were never beaten in 2 years. "John Glassco is a demon stickhandler, with a shot like a bullet. This baby-faced kid from swank SHS has real class." (Montreal *Gazette*, Feb. 3, 1921). We played all over Montreal and even beat the tough French kids from Point St Charles. I played right wing, and we had a beautiful fast front line: I remember their names, Tyron Nichol at centre and "Butcher" Hutchinson at left wing. And we had a rock-like defence with Donald Meagher and Dickie Molson; our goalie is now in Trudeau's cabinet at Ottawa, as President of the Treasury Board and still blocking shots.[22]

Like similar, less detailed assertions concerning his abilities in cricket and as a swimmer, the story from which Glassco quotes is of his own invention. It is doubtful that the school, with an enrolment of something less than one hundred, had a senior hockey team. The school holds no records of a team playing during the years in which Glassco was a student, nor is there mention of a Selwyn House team in the rather extensive sports reporting of Montreal's English-language newspapers. One week after the date given for Glassco's fabricated story, *The Gazette* reported that the Montreal Inter-School Hockey League junior championship had been clinched by an undefeated team from Westmount High School. The team representing Lower Canada College was later declared senior champions.

The 1923 Selwyn House School Sports Day on the Montreal Amateur Athletic Association grounds. Glassco stands on the top row, seventh from the left.

This detailed invention, written at the age of sixty to his friend Geoffrey Wagner, an associate professor at the City University of New York, is unusual in that he shared so very little about his childhood with friends and acquaintances. In the few published reminiscences of early life, Glassco has a tendency to look away from his family, choosing instead to focus on the city in which he was raised. Within each we find fleeting glimpses of his mother: she considered the affluent suburb of Outremont the home of "the more respectable French"; she was saddened by the disappearance of an ornamental iron deer that accompanied the demolition of the Sherbrooke Street gates to the Linton mansion.[23] The only family memory Glassco cared to repeat was that neither his mother nor his father understood a word of French, a claim that made his future accomplishments as a translator all the more impressive.

The longest and most candid recollection of his early life is found in his "Autobiographical Sketch," a dense five-page document he wrote in middle age while convalescing at the Royal Edward Laurentian Hospital. It is a most curious piece of work. Following a format not shared in his other writing, it contains something of a legal flourish, ending with his signature beside the date and place of composition. In it he writes: "until my eleventh birthday I was outwardly a normal and even conventional boy, though subject to the most cruel and unremitting nightmares which were always connected with the idea of being unable to *trust* anyone."[24]

He attributed his nightmares to the "extraordinary treatment" received at his father's hands: "for many years, from as far back as I can remember, he had inflicted the most savage and shameful beatings on us. Even to record this now fills me with a disgust and anger. There is no doubt that my father was a sadist, of the kind that is absolutely unaware of his propensity. The whole ritual of punishment, the barring [*sic*] of the buttocks, the shameful position to be assumed on a bed, the period of *waiting* to be so endured before his own arrival (often as long as half an hour), the slow and protracted severity of the punishment itself, the loathsome ceremonial of forgiveness and kisses afterwards, – all these properly belong in some work of flagellantine pornography."[25]

Such were the boys' cries that they were heard by the young Cecily Hallowell, David's future wife, who lived next-door to the Glassco family's summer home on Golf Avenue.[26] Beatrice did nothing to prevent the beatings; indeed, however unintentional, she may have encouraged the abusive behaviour of her husband. In his sketch, Glassco writes that his mother once admitted that sounds of the punishments inflicted on her sons had excited her sexually.

The abuse the boys suffered reached far beyond their father's hand and cane, extending to his invention of two rival sons. "Bill and Jim" lived in Notre-Dame-de-Grâce, not one mile to the west, and were sons from an imagined previous marriage. These older boys were everything A.P.S. believed his true sons not to be: honest, heroic, and athletic. While David thought the stories A.P.S. told about Bill and Jim were true, his brother Buffy recognized the lie, just as he did the contradiction: "Perhaps the most notable result of my father's severity towards us both, combined with his constant emphasis on the virtues of courage and truth-telling, was that by the ages of eight and six we were physical cowards and expert and incorrigible liars."[27]

Glassco could not remember a time at which he had not hated his father. Toward his mother he felt little more than indifference. He would record something of their roles as parents in "The Whole Hog," a poem written from the vantage point of middle age:

When I was very young my mother told me
That my father was the strongest of men
(Not in words at first, of course – but I knew);
Later I learned he was the best and bravest;
And during my adolescence (a difficult
Time for us all) I had her whispered word for it
He was the wisest parent in the world.

Long ago I put aside the question
Of her motive in this matter …. Perhaps
A sense of guilt for the disloyalty
Of a too-clear, too-wifely valuation
Of his man's-worth, was expiated so …[28]

In 1922, the upkeep proving increasingly expensive, Beatrice and her siblings sold their parents' mansion and grounds, splitting the proceeds. The great wooden Victorian house and stables were razed, the orchard and tennis courts were levelled, and Chelsea Place, an impressive, if mildly inelegant complex consisting of dark brick town homes was constructed. Buffy Glassco saw nothing to regret in the destruction. Of it and the other mansions that had once belonged to Montreal's financial and merchant princes – Strathcona, Drummond, MacDougall, Lyman, and the others – Glassco would write: "These houses were simply expressions of their wealth, optimism and complacency (each, also, with an air of somehow being designed for a royal visit), and once the builder had died and the visit, if any, had been paid, the house lost its *raison d'être* and became little more than a monument to shrewdness and greed. No one, certainly not his heirs, wanted to live on in such an ornate pile, with its crushing load of taxes and its heating, servant and maintenance problems: the natural thing was to tear the whole thing down and sell the land."[29]

With her share of the sale, Beatrice and her husband purchased a new home on Cedar Avenue facing Mount Royal Park. An enormous house, modest only in comparison to the Simpson Street mansion, Glassco thought it "a monstrous castle."[30] Selwyn House was much preferred to this assemblage of "dark-panelled walls, leaded windows, thick stair-carpets, 'period' chairs and all the rest of the opulent, fake furnishings."[31] However, the following spring, the refuge provided Glassco by school and Colin Campbell Macaulay was disrupted by academic success: Glassco graduated at the top of his class. Curious as to the potential of his foremost student, the headmaster had Glassco write the junior matriculation exam for McGill University. At the age of thirteen, he managed a passing grade. Glassco held out hope that he might be allowed to spend a year in private study under Macaulay, after which he would take the senior matriculation and enter McGill in autumn 1924. A.P.S., however, believed his son much too young to entertain thoughts of university and instead sent him to join David, who, having been expelled from Selwyn House, was attending Bishop's College School in Lennoxville. A boarding school, 150 kilometres southeast of Montreal, Bishop's would provide Glassco with his first experience living apart from his parents.

Glassco described the school as a "waking nightmare" – a cliché to be sure, but one that captured accurately his experiences.[32] Rather than being placed in the top form, in which he would be preparing for the junior matriculation he had already passed, Glassco was enrolled in the lower fifth form, so as to be in the same year as his brother. It wasn't long before the younger Glassco drew the ire of his classmates, whom he so easily bettered academically. His relative youth only compounded the animosity, and he soon learned to hide his intelligence. It was not a tactic he would always follow – Glassco played the leading role in the Dramatic Club's production of Eugène Labiche's nineteenth-century comedy *Le Voyage de Monsieur Perrichon* – nor did it save him from torment. His stammering speech made him an object of ridicule. Slight, fair, and delicate, with a somewhat feminine look, he became an easy target for the school's bullies and predators.

Nearly four decades later, in middle age, the nightmarish experiences at Bishop's College School remained clear: "The six months I spent in this place still remain with me as a memory of homesickness, physical suffering, fear, shame and unutterable boredom; this was also when I had the first experience of being forcibly sodomised, an experience which was disgusting but not really painful."[33]

Glassco sought an out and discovered it one April day in 1924. While in the infirmary with a badly cut finger, he spotted a discarded dirty bandage and used it to poison his wound. The infection quickly spread, first to his other hand, then his face. By the end of Easter vacation, the sepsis was such that A.P.S. asked Doctor Herbert Stanley Birkett, the former dean of McGill's Faculty of Medicine, to examine his youngest son. Birkett advised that the fourteen-year-old remain at home. Thus, Glassco's Bishop's College School education came to an abrupt end. The following September, he was sent to Lower Canada College in Notre-Dame-de-Grâce, the chief rival of Selwyn House. Glassco could not escape the boredom he had experienced at Bishop's. Once again, he was going over familiar academic ground. He lost interest and was incapable of applying himself. Now an adolescent, and a bored one at that, he turned to drink. He developed friendships with boys many years his senior, pushed the bounds of the curfew imposed by his father, and began frequenting houses of ill repute. His virginity, he would claim, was lost at the age of fourteen in a brothel on rue Jeanne-Mance.

These acts of rebellion coincided with a time of great change on Cedar Avenue. Fifteen years after the arrival of Buffy, her previous child, Beatrice was again pregnant. In June 1925, at the age of forty-one, she gave birth to a daughter whom she named after herself.

A few months later, A.P.S. agreed to allow his younger son's entry to McGill. Glassco tells us that his interest in academic life was all but dead. He quickly developed disgust for the university, finding nothing within the curriculum that would advance his desire for a career in letters. This opinion of McGill was no doubt tempered by the fact that it was in so many ways his father's domain. The younger Glassco held disdain for Currie, the man under whom his father worked, the man his father held in such very high regard. The freshman believed that Sir Arthur, the hero of the Great War, "had brought to McGill his army leadership and a very good high school education," but nothing more.[34] Though enrolled in the Faculty of Arts, Glassco's reading had everything to do with his own interests and bore little resemblance to course lists. He did little work, rarely attending classes, and barely passed his English examinations.

His greatest connection to the university came through his nearly imperceptible movement "on the edge of literary and intellectual circles at McGill."[35] Glassco never attempted an explanation of his literary tastes and interests, nor does his breeding provide a suggestion. It was true that Edward Rawlings had been known to put pen to paper, but that pen had been "wielded in the interests of pure commercialism."[36] Within the insurance industry, he had been known as "the author of a paper containing suggestions as to how defalcations by bank employés may be averted, which has been highly praised by ins. and business men generally all over the Continent."[37] His father's public writing consisted of a lone forty-eight-page booklet, *McGill University Centennial Endowment: A Greater McGill*, co-authored with Walter Vaughan, biographer of Sir William Van Horne. Generously illustrated, it was nothing more than an overt appeal for money in the Campaign for a Greater McGill. The writing it contained was straightforward but holds interest when the authors turn from the world of academe to that which they know best: railways: "The average salary of a professor in McGill at the present time is $3,000, very much less than the annual earnings of a locomotive engineer, while the instructor can only look with envy upon the wages of the mechanic and the artisan."[38] Glassco once quoted his father, whose own reading consisted in the main of reports and mystery novels, as having said that the family had never before had a boy with "literary aspirations."[39]

The origins of Glassco's interest in literature are a matter of speculation. One source may be found within the "fantastic assortment of books" his grandfather had amassed in the Simpson Street mansion.[40] It may also have sprung from the fine English education he'd received at Selwyn House with Macaulay's masterly recitations of Shakespeare; and then there was the popular C.T. Antsey, a mathematics instructor who held literature above all other subjects, and would talk of having visited Tennyson as a young child.

Glasscо's personal library, now housed at Queen's University, provides no clues; at his death it held only one book from his boyhood, a copy of the Bible in which was pasted "Let the child speak to You," a "Christmas Message of the Reverend George H. Donald."[41]

Near the end of her life, Beatrice wrote with pride on the occasion of her son having won the Quebec Literary Competition for the manuscript of *A Point of Sky* – what would become his second collection of poetry. She recalled an early poem, perhaps his first, composed one summer during what was then the long drive between Pointe Claire and Montreal:

I always remember your little poem about the nun
who was sad & glum
because she had a boil on her upper gum![42]

A slightly more mature piece of verse is found, undated, in his surviving Selwyn House notebooks:

"MOUSE'S" FIRST MOUSE[43]

I
Now shall I tell in form of song
Of a dog so small that we called him "Mouse"
His legs were short and his tail was long
And he slept in a basket in this house.

II
But in the house *real* mice were there,
Who stole and nibbled and much harm did,
And these quite safely 'neath the stair
In holes and burrows were well hid.

III
But in the daytime one ran by
Our valiant "Mouse" who, from his place,
Pounced on and squeezed till it did die
The small mouse with the whiskered face.

Moving about the edge of the university's literary and intellectual circles, Glassco encountered, but did not befriend; the warm relationships he shared with A.J.M. Smith, F.R. Scott, and Leon Edel would not occur until middle age. Of these and other writers, he would become close to only one, Graeme Taylor, with whom he would share much of the next three decades of his life.

Four years Glassco's senior, William Graeme Taylor had grown up in the comfortable middle-class community of Montreal West. His father, Samuel J. Taylor, was a Presbyterian clergyman. A graduate of the University of Toronto and Presbyterian College in Montreal, the reverend had spent the early years of his ministry in Western Canada. In Glassco's memoirs, Taylor is quoted as having said that his father never had a church and that "he went out on horseback converting the Indians in the Yukon."[44] In fact, Samuel Taylor had spent much of the 1880s in what were then the southernmost districts of the North-West Territories. His first two children, Margaret and Helen, were born on land now part of the Province of Saskatchewan – quite likely in Moose Jaw. In addition to his duties as a minister, he served for a year on the Board of Education for the North-West Territories. In 1892, Samuel Taylor was made secretary of the French Mission Board, a body designed to bring French Canadian Catholics to Presbyterianism, and the family relocated to Montreal. There, he and his wife, Christina, had seven more children. Graeme, born 28 December 1905, when his father was fifty and his mother forty-five, was the last. He followed a baby, James Hamilton Taylor, who had died in 1903 at the age of three months.

Glassco was in his first semester at McGill when he met Taylor; he'd not yet celebrated his sixteenth birthday. Late in life, Leon Edel, the future magisterial biographer of Henry James, cast his mind back to the cafeteria of the Student Union "one winter afternoon in 1925" when he was first introduced to Glassco and Taylor by mutual acquaintance Doug Adam.[45] To Edel, Glassco and Taylor were "two flowery youths":

Glassco was a bright-faced youth of about sixteen with the look – because of his receding chin – of an eager faun that had got lost somewhere in the Roman landscape and turned up among the snowdrifts of Sherbrooke Street. I can still see him, blond and handsome like some English lordling, spasming the ash off his cigarette, among the teacups. His companion, Graeme Taylor, had a high forehead and reddish hair and sat as if in chronic boredom; it may have been my own youth, but I found myself put off by his aggressive stare … Buffy and Graeme used phrases like "he's a stout fellow" or "it's sound, very sound." Or they giggled – it was in reality half giggle and half derision.[46]

These affectations and half giggles, what one might expect in a precocious sixteen-year-old, seem at odds with Taylor's character. Edel paints the elder student as "a trifle superior and aloof," more mature than his fellows, possessing "a quiet dignity and often an aggressive directness."[47] It is only in the company of "Young Buffy Glassco" that the frivolous side of his nature surfaced.[48] Half a century after their initial meeting, Edel remembered Taylor as a man who "wrote well" – a reconsideration to be sure: in letters composed in the 1920s, Edel places Graeme Taylor beside A.J.M. Smith and Leo Kennedy as one of the foremost Canadian writers of his generation.

Edel had only just turned eighteen when he met Taylor, and like Glassco, was swayed by the elder Taylor. To this self-described unsophisticated, untutored boy from the prairies, Taylor was "the embodiment of wisdom … serious, sophisticated, sarcastic" – carrying the appearance of "a young nobleman in an Oscar Wilde play."[49]

Early in their acquaintanceship, perhaps at that first meeting, Glassco told Edel of a story he intended to write:

I remember the glitter in his eyes, the eager juvenility of his description of a story he planned to write. It would be about a young man like himself who fell in love at a ski lodge with a fashionable young girl in her beautiful ski clothes; he dwelt on her boyishness and glamour; and then how deglamorized she seemed when she descended the stairs in a dress, quite feminized and usual. He promptly fell out of love with her. Glassco was already obsessed by his androgyny and the masculine women who figure, whip in hand, in his delicately written Krafft-Ebing fiction.[50]

It's entirely possible that, in relaying the outline of this unwritten story, Glassco recognized Edel's influence at *The McGill Fortnightly Review*, "an independent journal of literature, the arts and student affairs edited and published by a group of undergraduates at McGill University," which had published its debut issue that very same semester.[51] Founded by F.R. Scott and A.J.M. Smith, then graduate students, the *Fortnightly* was never intended to focus exclusively on things literary, yet it is for the writing in this area that it is best remembered. Smith used its pages to promote modernism and argue for a break with the Victorian. Edel wrote for the *Fortnightly* and, through his presence on the editorial board, oversaw the publication of much of the most innovative Canadian poetry of the day. Glassco's initial contribution, published in the issue of 22 March 1926, was more modest in style and range:

SEARCH[52]

What is it we seek? Is it Beauty? Is it honour? Is it happiness? The bubbles go racing through the wine and vanish. We raise it to our lips …. Through the window we see the yellow leaves of the plane-tree, drifting in the autumn breeze. Soon the tree will be stripped and bare. Another will hold the self-same cup, will ask the self-same question: What is it we seek? One after another, things pass away …. But there is something there, and we cannot find it.

The small, unhappy boy, impatient in his youth – he wants to be a man, or perhaps an engine-driver. He is an engine-driver. Is he satisfied? No; the stations and the signals flash by. The day finishes and starts again. He peers ahead, still seeking the elusive answer. Moments come when, blinded by beauty and ecstasy we have found it. But alas! They pass. This is not what we are looking for …. These are but pinpricks in the vast carcase of our being. So we go on, searching, backwards and forwards, up and down. We listen for sounds and portents. We peer into the eyes of our fellows. Do they know? Have they found it? No; they are peering into ours for the self-same reason. They cannot find it. They, too, are searching and waiting. The priest is talking of God, and we nod knowingly. The philosopher repeats something he has read in a book written by a Greek three thousand years ago, and we say: "Yes. Well?" The scientist dissects a beetle, and makes something go faster or slower, and we murmur, "Wonderful, wonderful!" The artist throws the shadow of his various calf-loves on the screen, and we applaud him, because for a moment he diverts us, and gives us a vague hope that we may stumble across it. Whatever it is, it must be the most wonderful thing in the world, because it is so intensely believed in …

This prose meditation credited to "J.S. Glassco," written the previous year, was the sixteen-year-old's first published work. What some might consider a rather accomplished piece of juvenilia, Glassco came to dismiss as "rather silly and priggish."[53] As with nearly all of his early work, it was all but disowned; he kept no copies.

"Search" had been published in the final issue of the *Fortnightly* for that academic year. Two months later, having written his final exams, Glassco felt relief at having been liberated, albeit temporarily, from McGill, the very university he'd so desperately wanted to attend three years earlier.

If Glassco is to be believed, the summer that followed was a memorable one. Now sixteen years old, he'd taken to going out on the town "in the company of young men of over 20" – a habit A.P.S. could not abide.[54] In his "Autobiographical Sketch," Glassco writes that Beatrice, seeking some level of peace in her Cedar Avenue home, gave him $500 so that he might spend the summer in Paris. It was a most unlikely solution to the escalating tension between her husband and youngest son. One wonders that A.P.S., who had imposed a curfew of ten o'clock each evening, would deem a solo trip to Paris at all acceptable. However, there is nothing in the vague outline Glassco provides of the summer adventure that might discredit his improbable story. Glassco writes that he sailed on the *Alaunia*,[55] of the Cunard line, where onboard, he met "a wealthy young homosexual."[56] He disembarked early, travelling with his new friend to Hoddom Castle in Kirkcudbrightshire, Scotland, just miles from the English border, where the two engaged in "homosexual relations."[57] Though Glassco claimed that he took no pleasure in the sexual aspects of their relationship, he continued to spend time with the unnamed aristocrat and lived off his friend during a month-long stay in London. It was in that city that Glassco discovered what he described as "the great attraction I possessed for homosexuals."[58]

Glassco fails to record the end of his association with the "wealthy young homosexual." He writes that he travelled alone to Paris, summing up his entire time in the city of lights with a single sentence that approaches cliché: "I fell in love with Paris at once and forever, and when I left for home in the fall of 1926 was only thinking of how I could return."[59]

It is somewhat telling that Glassco does not describe the adventure at Hoddom Castle as his *first* homosexual encounter. In all probability, this had already taken place with one of the "young men of over 20," a list of unknown length that included Graeme Taylor.

Back in Montreal, now in his sophomore year at McGill, Glassco was drawn ever closer to the clergyman's son. Although there was most certainly a sexual component, it would be incorrect to describe their relationship as strictly homosexual. Edel, who saw a fair deal of the two young men, was the only member of their group to so much as touch upon the friendship. Writing shortly after his friend's death, Edel depicts Buffy Glassco as one untroubled by his sexuality, a youth who had accepted peculiarities within himself, as he did the quirks of others. The relationship and *relationships* that Glassco and Taylor shared, in Montreal, in Paris, and in Nice, led Edel to think of the young Buffy as "a faun ready to make friends in some enchanted woodland with man or woman."[60] He observed that Glassco was "a bit frightened by certain kinds of women and nearly always delighted if he could establish a triangle. He then liked best as a kind of untragical Oedipus, a male companion and a woman to be shared between them."[61]

Of Glassco's McGill acquaintances, Edel saw more and knew more of the bursar's son's activities and preferences. The others may have found his proclivities mysterious, perhaps they felt a need for privacy; whatever the explanation, only Edel would write of Glassco's sexuality, the element of his being that had so dominated his work: "I think Buffy felt that a male companion defended him against predatory females; he could then all the more enjoy the latter, for – to judge by the forms of his fantasies – he could, given the right woman, be comfortably bisexual."[62]

What A.P.S. and Beatrice made of their youngest son's relationship with the elder Taylor, Glassco did not record. It is almost certain that their view was hampered by an extreme naïveté. Glassco once dismissed his father's knowledge of sexuality as extremely elementary and claimed that neither parent had any knowledge of the existence of homosexuality.

Glassco considered his friendship with Taylor to be more important than anything else he experienced at McGill. It was a rather obvious distinction. Although he studied with greater discipline in his sophomore year, Glassco was still unable to muster the great passion for academic life experienced at Selwyn House. Where he'd so admired the youthful masters of his former school

– Macaulay, Anstey, and L. St George, the object of a boyhood crush – he found McGill's professors old, fatigued, uninspiring, "wheezing pedants."[63] Accompanied by Taylor, Glassco met often over tea and cigarettes in the Student Union cafeteria with various members of McGill's literary circle but dismissed the vast majority of his fellow students as a "commonplace tribe."[64]

He found a forum for his frustration in "Collegiana," a weekly "penetration of college yokelry" published within the pages of *The McGill Daily*.[65] Started the previous February by Lew Schwartz, one of the associate editors, the column was an assemblage of trivial titbits culled from university newspapers from across North America. As "L.S.," Schwartz prefaced these often amusing glimpses of student life with his own wry comments and observations.

In October 1926, with the academic year still fresh, Schwartz began the column anew in collaboration with another writer initially known as "J.S.G.": John Stinson Glassco. The contrast between the "Collegiana" of the previous academic year and that of the new semester was jarring. The polite restraint of L.S. had been replaced by a full-out assault on McGill with its cowardly professors "mouthing shopworn platitudes, transmuted into profanity with pollysyballic [*sic*] alchemy" to a student body that was likened to "an atavistic growth."[66]

From the start, the bursar's son dominated this new, unforgiving "Collegiana." A week later, sans L.S., he returned to the pages of the *Daily*:

The youth of a country is generally its most redeeming feature, as in Canada, but in the United States the matrons are procreating a horde of Young men (i.e, college men) who might be compared to the arboreal mammals from whom they perseveringly deny they descended, particularly in the state that is called Tennessee. And yet the points of comparison between the two species are ridiculously clear: they behave like monkeys, they look like baboons (the football players, at any rate), and they conduct their petty copulations in the manner of anthropoid apes ....[67]

This crude attack on US youth, which drew much from the Scopes Monkey Trial, was the last column written under his initials. Glassco was setting his sights elsewhere and would require a less transparent cover.

Published under the name "John of Anjou," Glassco's third "Collegiana" begins with "Trivium," an F.R. Scott poem that had been published anonymously in the most recent *Fortnightly*:

> Masses heard the great Houdini,
> Masses shouted for the Queenie,
> Did you ever see such asses
> As the educated masses?[68]

The great escape artist Harry Houdini had visited McGill three weeks earlier to deliver a lecture on his debunking of Canadian-born Boston medium Mina "Margery" Crandon, the "Witch of Beacon Hill." Two days later, a student named Joscelyn Gordon Whitehead challenged the showman's strength by sucker punching him in the stomach. The blows aggravated an undetected case of appendicitis, and on Halloween Houdini died of peritonitis. The death, seemingly brought about by one of their own, may have been the talk of the university, but it was the visit of the "Queenie" – Marie of Romania, and her children Princess Ileana and Prince Nicolas – that Glassco chose to address:

> While she is spraying her sticky molasses of democratic ideals and foul sentimentality over the women's section of the leading newspapers, the half of the Roumanian population which is not in jail (as political prisoners) is so cowed by the flagellation of its own shame that it is merely looking for an empty rain-barrel to cover its lacerated buttocks.[69]

Standing as the most political of all Glassco's writings, the target of this atypical rant was not limited to the monarch Marie but reached the entire McGill establishment, those who had extended such a warm welcome to the Romanian queen and her children. In so doing, Glassco was criticizing his own father, the role he'd played as an organizer of the highly wrought visit, and his unbroken deference to aristocracy and class. Employing the very same imagery that would one day suffuse his erotica, Glassco had linked A.P.S., the flagellator of his own frightened sons, with violence on a much greater scale.

Of all the writing published during his days at McGill, whether in the *Daily* or the *Fortnightly*, this was the single piece Glassco elected to keep. While the reactions of Sir Arthur Currie, the bursar, and the other gracious hosts of the Romanian royal family to this particular "Collegiana" are unknown, it is perhaps telling that "John of Anjou" was not heard from again. Glassco quickly adopted a new pseudonym, "Euphorian," under which he continued his assault on McGill and its "educated masses," advising undergraduates who fancied themselves rebellious to "read the McGill Fortnightly Review in the Prince of Wales Hotel."[70] All was done in the name of "anti-'bloody-respectability.'"[71] The best of these columns, a "scourge" on the Puritanism Glassco thought prevalent at the university, ends with his first published verse, a couplet "which, although metrically and euphoniously wretched, nevertheless expresses the spirit of the crusade":

Lift up the sword of Rabelais
And smite the squirming Y.M.C.A.[72]

As the fall semester drew to a close, and the Christmas break approached, Schwartz returned to "Collegiana" to announce with certain defiance that the column would continue; Euphorian would not be silenced. However, the very next column was to be the last. It was replaced two weeks later with "The Goose Step," "A Compendium of Calumny Dedicated to the McGill Intelligentsia."[73] This new weekly discourse was the "Collegiana" of Euphorian taken to the extreme:

The McGill Intelligentsia, the most august body of intelligent persons in the highest seat of the higher learning, hereby announce themselves sponsors of a weekly column to be known as *The Goose Step*. In view of the fact that the purpose of the column is to amuse ourselves we gracefully ignore all requests and dedicate the column to ourselves.

The Intelligentsia of McGill is composed of a few dynamic students, the cream of the university's intellect. We believe in the Supermen because we are the Supermen. We believe in criticism that is destructive. We are vehement in our criticism and exasperating in our attitude. We shall be lofty and disdainful, impatient and irascible.

We shall perpetuate outrages as despicably outrageous as libel laws and a fatherly Student Council permits us. We shall be merciless and ruthless.

We are instituting a reign of intellectual terror at McGill.
Beware ye morons and underdogs!

In his "Autobiographical Sketch," Glassco implies that "The Goose Step" was his own, though it is clearly the work of many hands. It may very well be that Glassco was the compiler, drawing the short essays, poems, quips, and *bon mots* contained from the unidentified he referred to as "the elfin spirits of the Union Cafeteria."[74] Curiously, of the dozens of pieces, only one, a poem by Euphorian, is signed:

QUESTION[75]

Lesbians and lavender men
Do not attract each other:
Why is it?
I have asked the Student's Council
But they do not tell me –
Or they do not know

Why lavender men do not attract
Lesbians ...

With the new column, the attacks on the university begun under "Collegiana" resumed. The value of the Department of Commerce was questioned, the argument being that one could not be taught "the technique of business," and as such a school devoted to this purpose had no place in an institute of higher learning.[76] A second column called for the department to be dissolved; its students were advised to concentrate their efforts on becoming stenographers.

Protests were made to the Student Council. More than twenty students descended *en masse* to the newspaper's offices demanding that "The Goose Step" be killed. One letter writer charged that the *Daily* was printing "huge 'columns of junk.'"[77] Others, including the newspaper's editor-in-chief, A.R.

Harkness, complained that "The Goose Step" contained literary allusions comprehensible to very few; the *Daily*, he asserted, was intended for the average student.[78] Harkness moved quickly against the column, but not before he himself had come under attack in his own pages:

ABOLISH THE MCGILL DAILY[79]

This newspaper is a menace; it stands for everything that the Martlet and the Fortnightly Review do not; it is stupid, uninteresting, poorly written, stultifying, and demoralizing to the student body in general, and there can be no doubt in the mind of every honest, representative student that it should be relegated to limbo.

After publication, Harkness asked Schwartz to discontinue "The Goose Step," a request the associate editor refused. His letter of resignation followed the final column:

ABOLISH THE GOOSE STEP[80]

Once again the intelligent few have been thwarted and outweighed by the dolts and morons of the university. The Goose Step is discontinued at the order of the Editor-in-Chief who has harkened at the complaints that have been made against it. Because the Goose Step has dared to criticize it has been smothered. The people who have criticized possessing the mental equipment of a manicurist or a street-car conductor have taken offence …

The feeble-minded, who are also ignoramuses, claimed that they did not understand the Goose Step. Its words were too long, its allusions were to modern literature, a bad thing. They did not know literature. They were in Arts, or Commerce, or Science, and Medicine, or merely students of Theology and have no use for such nonsense. When they did understand they were grieved to find it so simple and their intelligence was insulted. But the Babbits may now cheer with their McGill yell for the Goose Step has been suppressed.

Though "Collegiana" and "The Goose Step" were gone, Glassco was able to make one final assault on "the dolts and morons of the university." Stealthier in nature, it came in the form of a prank: a review of a nonexistent book he called *Moscow Gold*. This second and final contribution to the

Fortnightly was intended to make fun of Currie's irrational conviction that Communists were intent on infiltrating McGill. Glassco's criticism of this fictitious work by "General Sir Nicholas Hoare KCB, LLD, OUDS, with biographical preface by his son-in-law Marcus Lazaroff," published by "Knapp & Dreme," was the earliest of his many literary deceptions:

> Once more we have the Soviet bugaboo in our midst. It is astounding to the point of laughter to see the trouble that such rabid Imperialists as Sir Nicholas will take in order to show up the "secret hand of Russia." In seven hundred and forty-eight pages, this estimable military man has given a complete, exhaustive and thoroughly biased account of all that Moscow has done, and is doing, to finance the progress of Communism, Radicalism and Anarchism in English, American and even the leading Canadian Universities. Incidentally, it reveals nothing more than is already known by our own Secret Service.[81]

Currie's obsession with the influence of communism upon McGill was common knowledge. The previous year, shortly after the *Fortnightly* had published its second issue, he'd called Scott and Smith to his office and had challenged the magazine on numerous fronts, not the least of which was his concern that content might become "Bolsheviki."[82] Scott, himself, had attended a dinner party at which the principal revealed that he wrote the Intelligence Bureau in Ottawa to ask for records of each and every individual invited to speak at the university.

A.P.S. shared Currie's concern and had even gone so far as to raise the spectre of communism in his fundraising efforts. In his booklet, *McGill University Centennial Endowment*, the bursar warns of the one grave consequence brought on by lack of capital: "In some universities members of the teaching staff, depressed and embittered by their poverty, and despairing of the future, have turned to the heresies of socialism and communism. May this not happen at McGill!"[83]

In deciding to not put his name to the bogus review, Glassco had again demonstrated a clearheaded caution that he would soon abandon. Scott and Smith's reasoned defense of the *Fortnightly* during that early meeting with Currie had in no way resulted in the principal's blessing. The magazine continued to be watched closely with distrust and suspicion. Fearing that his teaching fellowship might be in jeopardy, Edel chose to resign from the editorial board. Allan Latham, the son of George W. Latham, one of the few English professors admired by the Intelligentsia, also had his name removed from the masthead but, with Edel, secretly continued his work with the magazine.[84] Smith did not join in the subterfuge and allowed his name to stand from the first issue until the last, an involvement that, he believed, contributed to the fact that he was never hired by the university.

At very best, Glassco's contributions to the *Fortnightly* can be described as slight; certainly they were no more worthy of notice than those of his friends Doug Adam and Graeme Taylor. The latter also contributed two pieces to the review: "the flow will return," a short story written as "Hans Mann," and a poem entitled the "The Unknown World," which appeared under the curious pseudonym "Jon Grahame."[85] A rather unexceptional work, the latter is Taylor's only published verse, and is atypical of the class of poetry found in the *Fortnightly*:

THE UNKNOWN WORLD[86]

Behind the eye and the ear
    A world is hiding,
Remote, yet incredibly near,
    In the spirit abiding,
A world that the heart and the mind
    Can share in receiving,
A world that no song can enwind
    In its weaving

That spring, as his second year at McGill was drawing to an end, Glassco writes that he experienced a "violent quarrel" with his parents; one which resulted in his leaving the "monstrous castle" on Cedar Avenue.[87] The months that followed, so he claimed, were spent borrowing from friends, moving from place to place, and working on what he described as "a long poem in the manner of Eliot's *Waste Land* [sic]."[88] The estrangement lasted throughout the summer and only came to an end through overtures on the part of A.P.S., who encouraged his son to return home for what was meant to be his third year at McGill. Glassco's attitude toward the university had not changed. Only one course, taught by Clive Harcourt Carruthers, a professor of Classical Languages, captured his attention.[89] Where the Intelligentsia published in "The Goose Step" a manifesto against the classics, one of its member found himself studying with interest Catullus, Tibullus, and Propertius. Decades later, Glassco would later write in appreciation to Carruthers, describing the course as "one of the greatest pleasures of my junior year."[90]

The stay at the Cedar Avenue house was soon brought to an end by a second, more violent argument. Glassco again left home, convinced he would never return. In the "Autobiographical Sketch," Glassco writes that he "lived with and on a number of women and girls"[91] and that he often supported himself through a series of colourful and varied jobs: toy salesman at Eaton's, cabby with the Jewitt Taxi Company, stagehand, and "running the roulette-wheel in the YMCA on Drummond Street."[92] That he was employed at such a great number of positions in such a short period of time may be an indication of his aptitude as an employee, but it is more likely one more example of Glassco's imagination; on two other occasions he writes that he never left home at all.[93]

Late in the autumn semester he'd come to recognize that continuing his studies was nothing but a futile act. Five days before his eighteenth birthday, Buffy Glassco, the bursar's son, dropped out.[94]

He moved with Taylor into a one-room apartment on Metcalfe Street, and two days after Christmas joined his new roommate as a clerk at the Sun Life Assurance Company. Glassco's responsibilities consisted of posting up the weekly premiums for the burial insurance of labourers in Hong Kong. Although a great uncle held a much more senior position in the company's Hamilton office, it is likely that the job came to Glassco through Taylor, who had begun working for Sun Life a few weeks earlier. Each morning the pair would start off on the very short walk through the slush and snow to the company's head office on Dominion Square.

One year later, at the advanced age of nineteen, Glassco would refer to his month and a half of employment in the insurance industry as "the most wretched period of our lives."[95] Glassco wrote twice – in *Memoirs of Montparnasse* and in the "Extract from an Autobiography" from which it grew – of this brief interlude between the musty Student Union cafeteria and the colourful cafés of Paris. Both include details of an arrangement he and Taylor made to sublet their apartment to two friends who used it for evening trysts with, it is implied, a variety of women. In doing so, Glassco and Taylor supplemented their combined monthly income of $170. In the latter account, that found in *Memoirs of Montparnasse*, word of the arrangement spreads, and it is not long before others have struck similar bargains. A.P.S. learns that Buffy and his roommate are "running something very close to a house of ill-repute,"[96] having been informed by Colonel Wilfred Bovey – whom Glassco calls Colonel Birdlime – the director of Extramural Relations and Extension at McGill.[97] According to Bovey, Currie's "unofficial aide-de-camp," the goings on in the Metcalfe Street apartment are well known within the McGill community, a revelation which, if true, would have placed the elder Glassco, as bursar, in a tricky position.[98] With neither discussion nor negotiation, A.P.S. offers his son a monthly allowance of $100, on the understanding that he adopt a more discreet lifestyle. The "Extract from an Autobiography" provides the further detail that the allowance would last for some seven years. If as described, it is likely that this period was intended to stretch until the age of twenty-five, at which point Glassco would inherit his share of Edward Rawlings's fortune. Paris was not mentioned, but it may have come as something of a relief to A.P.S. that Taylor and his son intended to leave the country; the scandal engendered by the Metcalfe Street apartment had spread beyond McGill's Roddick Gates to the St James Club. Subleasers included several sons of the well-to-do, including John Pemberton, who had received the inaugural Lucas Medal, awarded to the Selwyn House boy who, among other things, displays exemplary behaviour. Though Glassco had only just turned eighteen, A.P.S.'s goal of his second son becoming a judge must have already receded to the point of fantasy. Beatrice's dream that her son Buffy would one day be ordained a bishop in the Anglican Church of Canada, possibly serving the Diocese of Montreal, was equally unrealistic. A new goal had been set, that of keeping Buffy out of trouble.

Of the two accounts, "Extract from an Autobiography" is not only the more contemporary – by over four decades – it is the only history that Taylor would have read. Unlike that found in *Memoirs of Montparnasse*, it includes a description of one of several evenings spent at St Catherine Street's Traymore Cafeteria. There, in rather inelegant surroundings, Glassco would plead with Taylor, imploring his friend to accompany him to Paris, trying to convince him that they could both live comfortably on the allowance provided by his father. Taylor's eventual acceptance of this arrangement marked a significant shift in the relationship between the two men; for very nearly the remainder of his life, something approaching three decades, Taylor would be financially dependent on and indebted to Glassco.

The decision having been made, the pair moved quickly. Through a relative, Alistair Fraser, a general solicitor in the legal department of the Canadian National Railway, Taylor received two tickets on the *Canadian Traveller*, a Merchant Marine ship scheduled to leave the port of St John. Although he hadn't been able to contribute financially, Taylor had managed to save the pair some money; he would receive free passage, while Glassco was charged half-fare.

The "Extract from an Autobiography" provides a dreamlike account of the final evening in Montreal, beginning when the pair engages an open sleigh with which they call on a Westmount beauty named Mona McMaster.[99] Although the girl excites Glassco, he plays a detached third. Together, they take this girl, whom Taylor has loved "in a fantastic way" since childhood, for a night on the town.[100] She is treated to an evening of theatre, after which she is ferried to the Venetian Gardens jazz cabaret. Mona's pleasant evening comes to a rather jarring conclusion in the vestibule of her Westmount home, where Taylor ends their relationship and joins Glassco in an awaiting taxi. For his part, Glassco romanticizes the sudden breakup, "envying them their sentimental parting." He writes: "I myself had no one to sentimentalise over, because the only person I loved was coming with me."[101]

In Glassco's two accounts, those of "Extract from an Autobiography" and *Memoirs of Montparnasse*, he and Taylor depart from Bonaventure Station. There is no fond farewell, there is no *bon voyage*; neither friends nor family members are present when they board the train that will take them to St John and the *Canadian Traveller*.

Glassco, who never claimed to be a mariner, described the *Canadian Traveller* as being 950 tons, "slightly larger than a tugboat."[102] In fact, it weighed 5319 tons and measured four hundred feet in length; it was entirely typical of the cargo ships then used by the Merchant Marine.

On 4 February 1928, a cold day with moderate winds, the *Canadian Traveller* left the port of St John, bound for Swansea, via Halifax, a voyage so unremarkable and tedious that, when describing it in *Memoirs of Montparnasse*, Glassco chose to embellish through the addition of a supernatural event: a hurricane in winter.

TWO | 1928–1931

... a dream of Paris ...[1]

The two young men from Montreal, worn out by a prolonged Atlantic crossing, took leave of the *Canadian Traveller* in Cardiff and spent the evening in London. Though Buffy Glassco took an immediate dislike to the city and was disappointed by both Westminster Abbey and Rotten Row, poor planning delayed progress to Paris. He and Graeme would have to remain in London for one more night. In the face of this bleak prospect, Buffy had the idea that they visit George Moore, "the greatest living English writer, greater even than Hardy," at his Ebury Street home.[2]

The above is the account Glassco gives of the first two days that he and Taylor spent in the Old World; and like much of the writing contained in *Memoirs of Montparnasse*, it is both inaccurate and fanciful. The *Canadian Traveller* did not dock at Cardiff, but at Swansea, roughly fifty kilometres to the west. We know that there was no meeting with George Moore; on Valentine's Day, 1928, while the *Canadian Traveller* was at sea, Moore entered a nursing home with a severe case of uraemia, little more than a week before his seventy-sixth birthday. He was not released until 21 April, by which time Glassco and Taylor were well into their Paris adventure.[3]

If there is truth to be found in Glassco's account of this brief passage through London, it most certainly rests with his evaluation of Moore, the author with whom he had been so captivated while at McGill. Glassco and Taylor shared a particular passion for Moore's masterwork *Esther Waters*, the stark tale of a servant girl who loses her position when she becomes pregnant and of her subsequent struggles to raise a child amid hypocrisy and poverty. Decades after its 1894 publication, the realist novel remained popular and fashionable among well-read young college men. For Glassco, however,

Esther Waters was more than an admired literary work; it represented a great victory. Moore had been forced to defend this story of a "fallen woman" against determined attacks by British censors; his success in so doing, led to the bestseller lists and financial wellbeing. The writer appealed to Glassco and Taylor, Leon Edel wrote, "because he acted as if he were on Olympus – as if the literary life were a god-like life."[4] Indeed, Glassco described Moore as his "literary god" and at the age of eighteen was so inspired by Moore's chronicle of youth, *Confessions of a Young Man*, that he began writing his own memoirs.[5] It would not be lost on the Montrealer that his idol had made several revisions to the "confessions" since the original publication.

In his own chronicle of youth, Glassco writes of a dream of Paris that he and Taylor shared. From the very first page of *Memoirs of Montparnasse*, they are a pair "united by comradeship, a despisal of everything represented by the business world, the city of Montreal and the Canadian scene, and a desire to get away."[6] Absent from this list of complaints is family. A.P.S.'s offer of the $100 monthly allowance had been made on the condition that his younger son live a more discrete lifestyle, but the aspiring memoirist and poet had no intention of doing so. He sought escape from the watch of his father, Colonel Bovey, the St James Club, and the judgemental tittle-tattle of the staid establishment into which he'd been born. A great many cities might have provided sanctuary, but not a one could stand with Paris, the city with which Glassco had fallen in love two years earlier. Once the playground of the literary god Moore, in the years that followed the Great War it had become home to many of the world's most forward-looking poets, painters, sculptors, novelists, and composers. Paris was the artistic centre of the West; Montreal, though dominant within the Dominion, might best be compared to a large European provincial city.[7]

Wholly unfamiliar with the works of French Montreal, Glassco's city "scene" was dominated by Stephen Leacock's light Christmas offerings to the book-buying public and the polite get-togethers of the Canadian Author's Association.[8] The latter had been ridiculed by F.R. Scott in the pages of the *Fortnightly* as a group of "unknowns," "Virgins of sixty who still write of passion."[9] The Association's 1926 crowning of Bliss Carman as Canada's unofficial poet laureate spoke to the pervasive Victorianism against which the magazine had fought.[10] But the *Fortnightly* was now gone and so very many of its contributors had left Montreal: Doug Adam had returned to his father's Scottish manse and Arthur Smith was taking up his studies at

John Glassco at age eighteen.

the University of Edinburgh, while Buffy Glassco and Graeme Taylor had arrived in the city where, to employ the words of Gertrude Stein, "the twentieth century was."[11]

Not long after the pair shared their first drinks on the stove-heated *terrasses* of Montparnasse – perhaps within the first month – Glassco had the good fortune to meet Kay Boyle. A struggling US writer of uncertain ability, Boyle had only just settled in Paris – indeed, her arrival in the middle of March had just followed that of Glassco and Taylor – and yet she was already known in the city's literary circles. Boyle's reputation had preceded her. This had nothing to do with her published work – an essay, two book reviews, and an unexceptional excerpt of a novel, all published years earlier – but with scandal and sympathy.

In 1923, Boyle had arrived in France with Richard Brault, a French exchange student she met and married while living in Cincinnati. Within three years, she had left her husband for Ernest Walsh, the co-editor, with Ethel Moorhead, of the literary magazine *This Quarter*. Walsh was handsome, but tubercular. The passionate affair lasted no more than a matter of months before he succumbed to the disease, leaving Boyle pregnant, but by no means alone. She was supported by her suffering husband and Moorhead, who held Boyle's hand during the birth and later perjured herself by registering the baby girl as Walsh's legitimate daughter before the Mairie de Nice.

The story, both titillating and sad, opened heavy doors to the salons of Paris, and Boyle was quick to enter. At her first party, held at the house of Eugene Jolas, publisher of the experimental literary magazine *transition*, she found herself in the company of James and Nora Joyce, Gertrude Stein, Archibald MacLeish, Sylvia Beach, and the surrealist poet Phillippe Soupault.

When Boyle met Glassco, she was living in luxury at the rue Louis-David apartment of her employer, Gladys Palmer Brooke, the Dayang Muda of Sarawak. An eccentric and wealthy woman who counted a life-sized bronze statue of her deceased Aberdeen terrier among her many precious possessions, Brooke had been born into England's wealthy Huntley and Palmer biscuit family. In 1904, at the age of twenty, she'd married Bertram Willes Dayrell Brooke, the Tuan Muda of the Kingdom of Sarawak on the Island of Borneo.[12] Though the marriage had ended in divorce, Brooke retained the royal title of Dayang Muda and a goodly portion of her former husband's wealth. The life of the princess – no doubt extremely interesting – had encouraged the English publisher John Lane to draw up a contract for her memoirs, which in turn had led the Dayang Muda to hire Boyle as a ghost-writer. It was a task made difficult by the princess's memory. As Boyle describes it, "her valiant attempts to relive the memories of all she had been, or had not been, served no purpose except to stun her into silence."[13] The solution to this problem was fabrication and fancy. *Relations and Complications* was derived less from the "Recollections of H.H. the Dayang Muda of Sarawak," as proclaimed in the subtitle, and more from the imagination of Kay Boyle.

At some point during the composition – between April and June 1928 – Boyle had Glassco hired to type the manuscript; and it wasn't long before he joined his new friend in the creative process. By Boyle's account, they were a good team: "During the hours of work Buffy and I … inserted in the mouths of the long-dead great additional flights of repartee and far more brilliant *bon mots* than I had managed to invent alone."[14] Among their inventions, Boyle recalled, was a scene in which Oscar Wilde scandalized a dinner party by relating a "time-worn limerick."[15] Whether explained by Boyle's own faulty memory or the caution shown by John Lane, the anecdote was not included in the published book.

Glassco enjoyed the work but was irritated by the sporadic pay; even when forthcoming the money was only a measure of what was owed. Boyle was witness to the method Glassco used to redress the balance, as it played out before the Dayang Muda and her cousin Cedric Harris, otherwise known as the poet Archibald Craig:

> It puzzled me when, on entering the salon, he took to bowing stiffly from the waist both to the Princess and to Archie, and that now he stood at a distance from them, near the grand piano, nervously refusing to sit down as he had done before. I concluded this must be a belated awareness of the deference a Canadian owes to British royalty, and I felt I must respect this and not discuss it with him. It was only long, long after that Buffy told me he had begun slipping gramophone records from the Princess' collection inside his jacket every day, and he had to move with caution to avoid breaking them. The records compensated for what he had not been paid, and the sale of them in the Quarter was usually enough to buy his supper that night.[16]

In his own writing about *Relations and Complications*, Glassco claims to have been nothing more than the typist; the book is Boyle's alone. While this is not true, the locations of Glassco's contributions remain a mystery. Boyle abandoned the project before it was complete and once wrote to her bibliographer that she'd had nothing to do with the final two of the book's seventeen chapters; her assumption was that they'd been composed by Glassco and Craig.

Questions as to authorship are but indistinct shadows found within the fog that surrounds Glassco's Parisian adventures; little can be said with great certainty. His own recollections often confuse and contradict. In *Memoirs of Montparnasse*, the typing of the Duyang Muda's book is shifted from spring 1928 to some vague date in the latter half of 1930, the year after its true publication. The obfuscation is furthered by Glassco's decision to present his collaborator under two guises: as Kay Boyle, a figure mentioned repeatedly, but whom he never meets; and disguised as Diana Tree, a lively English writer with four novels to her credit. Here, it is Tree who offers Glassco employment in typing *Relations and Complications*, adding that they "have been superbly ghost-written by Kay Boyle."[17] Moreover, it is Tree, not Boyle, with whom he shares a brief romance, a passing intimacy that almost certainly took place.

According to Glassco, it was through Boyle that he and Taylor met Robert McAlmon. Though an American, the thirty-three-year-old writer and publisher had something of a Canadian background; McAlmon's father had emigrated from Northern Ireland to Canada as an adolescent, while his mother was a native of Chatham, Ontario.

McAlmon described his father as a "nomad pastor" – a label that could just as well have been applied to Taylor's own.[18] The Reverend John Alexander McAlmon had spent many decades travelling between the disparate small towns of South Dakota until age and senility claimed his ministry. The family withdrew to Minneapolis and, after the fragile reverend died, relocated once again, settling in Los Angeles. Glassco writes that at their first meeting McAlmon told of how he'd joined – and then deserted – the Canadian military during the Great War. It was a good story, once thought a fantasy designed to support his public image; but like McAlmon's fiction it was planted firmly in truth.[19] On 28 August 1916, while a guest of Winnipeg's Empire Hotel, the midwesterner had enlisted in the 190th Overseas Battalion, only to desert four months later while en route to St-Jean-sur-

Richelieu, Quebec.[20] It is entirely possible that he was in Montreal at the time of Glassco's seventh birthday.

By 1920, McAlmon had made his way to Greenwich Village, where with his friend William Carlos Williams he produced *Contact*, a mimeographed, irregularly published literary magazine devoted to experimental writing. Two months after the debut issue, in February 1921, McAlmon made a decision that would both shadow the remainder of his life and stain his legacy: he accepted a proposal of marriage. His bride was the poet Bryher – Annie Winifred Ellerman – the daughter of Sir John Ellerman, an enormously wealthy English shipping tycoon who was said to be the largest taxpayer in the British Empire. Although McAlmon may or may not have recognized it as such, the union to which he'd committed himself was in every sense a marriage of convenience: McAlmon, a bisexual, had married a lesbian. Indeed, it is almost certain that the marriage was the idea of his wife's lover, the poet and novelist H.D., née Hilda Doolittle. The arrangement was financially rewarding; McAlmon was provided a share in Bryher's allowance and, sometime after the couple's second aniversary, was presented with a gift of approximately $70,000 from an appreciative father-in-law.

By the time Glassco and Taylor encountered McAlmon, the US writer had been living in Paris for seven years. Charismatic, athletic, and only just shy of being strikingly handsome – he bore more than a passing resemblance to John Barrymore – the midwesterner was a popular figure. McAlmon made his many acquaintances and friends while spending freely and generously on drink at the Dôme, La Coupole, the Sélect, the Deux Magots, and the Dingo. He paid Ernest Hemingway's expenses during a 1923 trip the pair had taken to Spain and was helping to support the deathly ill Italian poet Emanuel Carnevali. To James Joyce, McAlmon provided a generous monthly allowance of $150. He bought the Irishman drink, typed his manuscripts, and hawked subscriptions to *Ulysses*. Yet, despite McAlmon's kindness and generosity, after his 1927 divorce from Bryher and the accompanying settlement, he was saddled with the uncharitable epithet "Robber McAlimony." Hemingway, so often offended by anyone who had done him a kind turn, worked to make his former friend into an object of ridicule.

Great things had been expected from McAlmon. Ezra Pound, for one, thought him a writer of tremendous promise. In *The Dial*, the poet praised McAlmon's "considerable determination to present, or at any rate a capacity for presenting, the American small town in hard and just light, no nonsense, no overworking, no overloading."[21] Though a heavy drinker, it was not right to say – as many did – that McAlmon spent much more time at the bar than the typewriter. He ranked among the most productive of the expatriate writers.[22]

Beginning in 1921, McAlmon had been published at something approaching one title a year, all but two through his own house, known variously as Contact Editions and the Contact Publishing Company. The uncharitable claimed McAlmon had set up the company to publish himself, ignoring the fact that his work had been featured with regularity in *The Little Review*, *This Quarter*, *The Transatlantic Review*, and other important literary magazines of the time. While it was true that McAlmon had published most of his own books, he'd also issued titles by Djuna Barnes, Bryher, H.D., Hemingway, and William Carlos Williams. In 1925, McAlmon had brought out *The Making of Americans*, the book Gertrude Stein, forever lacking in modesty, considered the magnum opus of her generation. Completed in October 1911, the manuscript was long and unwieldy; despite Stein's persistent pursuit of publishers, the work had found no home in England or the United States. In this regard, it fit well with McAlmon's stated intent, to issue works "not likely to be published by other publishers for commercial or legislative reasons." When it finally appeared under the Contact imprint, Stein's experimental novel was 925 pages in length. With little interest in such petty details as print runs, promotion, and distribution, it could be said that McAlmon was publishing until the money ran out.

On the evening he first encountered Glassco and Taylor, McAlmon was preparing for publication a book of his own poetry, *North America, Continent of Conjecture*. It was a work Glassco thought worthy of ridicule. He would never be impressed by his new friend's writing; indeed, Glassco dismissed the bulk of McAlmon's oeuvre as "unreadable."[23] Late in life, in answer to a query from the author Hugh Ford, Glassco reflected on the days spent in Montparnasse and his friendship with McAlmon, who was thirteen years his senior: "You must know that as a youth of 17-18-19 I lived only on the fringes of that expatriate epoch insofar as it was of *literary* importance: in fact, I hardly was aware of what was going on, because I was more interested in the people than in what they were writing. McAlmon, for example, was much more vivid as a person than as a writer: I don't think his literary work had any value whatever, and I know he himself suspected it had not."[24]

While McAlmon's attraction toward the two young Montrealers might be explained by generosity or mere amusement – Morley Callaghan, an observer, suggested that it was both – Glassco hinted at something further. *Memoirs of Montparnasse* provides a detailed account of their first encounter, beginning with introductions over drinks at the Dôme. What follows is an evening of activity fuelled by double whiskies, vermouth, brandy, bottles of wine, and double ice-cream sodas. They enjoy *canard pressé* and Moselle at La Coupole, a dinner spoiled by a beery, blustering, bullying Ernest Hemingway, who makes insinuations about McAlmon's sexuality and his relationship with the two new friends. The trio next hire an open taxi in which they are transported to the "mysterious, sinister" rue de Lappe, site of the Bal des Chiffoniers, a homosexual dance club.[25] There Glassco is waltzed around the floor by the Jamaican writer Claude McKay, disguised as "Jack Relief," who offers his lithe partner a Cuban cigarillo spiked with hashish.[26] Quickly overcome by nausea, Glassco is ushered to an anonymous café, where his discomfort is eased with the aid of chicory-laced coffee. From there it is off to the Café Pigalle and, finally, Bricktop's. McAlmon proceeds to insult the clientele and performs what he describes as the aria from his "Chinese opera," "a hideous, wordless, toneless screaming," while balancing with open arms and mouth upon a barstool.[27] The evening winds down back at La Coupole with McAlmon moving between sleep, tears, and curses, as his two young Montrealers eat their breakfasts of scrambled eggs and white coffee. Glassco and Taylor carry the seasoned and soused writer to their studio apartment, install him in one of the two beds, and fall asleep together in the other. "Waking uncomfortably a few hours later, however," Glassco writes, "I found he had made his way between Graeme and me and I began to wonder if he had been quite as helpless as he appeared to be in the Coupole bar."[28]

Yet, the earliest extant draft of Glassco memoirs, likely the first, contains an altogether different conclusion to the evening: "But the final proof of McAlmon's incredible vitality was apparent less than four hours later, when I woke to find him in our bed; now quite nude and pressed against my back, he was sleeping soundly, but the signs of his pleasure were already clotting coldly on my hinderparts."[29]

This original conclusion to Glassco's nocturnal adventures – an evening rendered improbable, if not impossible, by the sheer number of events and locations – speaks to one element of McAlmon's attraction to Glassco, a sexual component that the junior writer was advised to excise from the finished work. The Robert McAlmon of *Memoirs of Montparnasse* is a more fatherly character, something of a mentor, who eases the limited entrée begun under Boyle into the salons, studios, and flats of expatriate Paris.

In *Memoirs of Montparnasse*, Glassco displays great talent in writing of his many encounters with the artists and writers of the day. Nowhere is this more evident than in his description of Gertrude Stein, the solid, commanding figure around whom the US expatriates orbited:

> Gertrude Stein projected a remarkable power, possibly due to the atmosphere of adulation that surrounded her. A rhomboidal woman dressed in a floor-length gown apparently made of some kind of burlap, she gave the impression of absolute irrefragability; her ankles, almost concealed by the hieratic folds of her dress, were like pillars of a temple; it was impossible to conceive of her lying down. Her fine close-cropped head was in the style of the late Roman Empire, but unfortunately it merged into broad peasant shoulders without the aesthetic assistance of a neck; her eyes were large and much too piercing. I had a peculiar sense of mingling attraction and repulsion towards her. She awakened in me a feeling of instinctive hostility coupled with a grudging veneration, as if she were a pagan idol in whom I was unable to believe.[30]

Glassco encounters Miss Stein only once, during a party at her impressive *appartement* at 27 rue de Fleurus. He is, at the time, engaged in an enthusiastic discussion about Jane Austen with Man Ray, whom he calls Narwhal:

> We must have been talking with an animation unusual for one of Gertrude Stein's parties, for several guests had already gathered around us.
>
> "You are talking of Jane Austen and sex, gentlemen?" said a tweedy Englishman with a long ginger moustache, "The subjects are mutually exclusive. That dried-up lady snob lived behind lace curtains all her life. She's of no more importance than a chromo. Isn't that so, Gertrude?"

Robert McAlmon, Glassco, and Graeme Taylor, summer 1929.

I was suddenly aware that our hostess had advanced and was looking at me with her piercing eyes,

"Do I know you?" she said. "No, I suppose you are just one of
those silly young men who admire Jane Austen."

Narwhal had quietly disappeared and I was faced by Miss Stein, the
tweedy man and Miss Toklas. Already uncomfortable at being an
uninvited guest, I found the calculated insolence of her tone and lost
my temper.

"Yes, I am," I said. "And I suppose you are just one of those silly
old women who don't."

The fat Buddha-like face did not move. Miss Stein merely turned,
like a gun revolving on its turret, and moved imperturbably away.[31]

A run-in with Gertrude Stein, a pornographic movie enjoyed in the company of Peggy Guggenheim, and the sipping of wine with James Joyce at
his Square Robiac apartment, each of these events presented in *Memoirs of
Montparnasse* represents a fleeting encounter; a person met, never to be seen
again. There is no evidence that he was so much as in the same room with
even one of these eminent expatriates. His friends, acquaintances, and lovers
are found among the minor personages of *la ville-lumière*, such as the beautiful and exotic Caridad de Laberdesque,[32] who played two small roles in
Luis Buñuel's 1930 surrealist film *L'Âge d'or*. Those with whom Glassco was
most friendly were artists, such as the painter Hilaire Hiler,[33] who managed
The Jockey Club, or the talented sculptor Gwen Le Gallienne[34] and her
Canadian lover, Yvette Ledoux,[35] who shared a studio next to McAlmon's
flat at 147 rue Broca. These are the lesser lights, dimmed further by history.
Among this crowd, McAlmon and Boyle stand out, not only as names that
have in some limited sense lived on but by virtue of the fact that they were
writers. Both would mention Glassco and Taylor in their memoirs, but a
great deal of time would pass before these recollections would make their
way into print.

Of the books on Montparnasse published in the years during and after
their time in the Quarter – indeed, in the three decades that followed –
Glassco and Taylor feature in only one: a 1934 memoir entitled *This Must Be
the Place*. The reference is fleeting:

Two more writers who were great friends were Buffy Glassco and Graham [*sic*] Taylor, both Canadians and fine chaps. They would sit at one end of the bar, their little Scotty between them, discussing serious subjects that I did not understand and being superior to most of the others in the bar.[36]

The man credited with these words, Jimmie "The Barman" Charters, was by far the most popular server of drinks in Montparnasse, having tended bar at the Dingo, the Parnasse, and the Trois As, among other establishments. It is likely that he first served Glassco and Taylor at the Falstaff, which the pair frequented.

A beefy former prizefighter, Charters is a most unlikely memoirist – and, of course, wasn't. *This Must Be the Place*, originally subtitled *Memoirs of Montparnasse*, was written at the suggestion of Hiler. Indeed, it is quite possible that the artist penned the passage in question.[37] The writing duties eventually passed to Morrill Cody, a US journalist who had lived for many years in Paris.

The only contemporary published accounts of Glassco and Taylor's activities in Montparnasse are found in a small number of newspaper columns, titled alternatively "Paris Book Chat" and "Book Chat from Paris; News of New Books And Gossip of Litterateurs," written by Leon Edel.

Some months after Glassco and Taylor crossed the Atlantic, the former *Fortnightly* editor followed, arriving in Paris in autumn 1928. A Docteur-ès Lettres candidate at the Sorbonne, Edel lived for the next three years in residence at the Maison canadienne near the Porte d'Orléans. All this was made possible through a Province of Quebec scholarship, which he supplemented with a column written for *The Montreal Daily Star*.

In one of his very first instalments, Edel writes of "the appearance of one or two Canadians whose efforts are beginning to attract attention," before placing his focus on Taylor.[38] "Graeme Taylor," he writes, "has aligned himself with the group who are associated in producing much of the experimental literary material that English writers are turning out on the continent."[39]

Edel was not the only member of the Montreal crowd to place Taylor above Glassco. In February 1928, as the *Canadian Traveller* was en route to

Europe, A.J.M. Smith wrote Raymond Knister recommending a number of *Fortnightly* contributors: "Three men particularly have been doing some interesting work, though I don't think they have published anywhere else as yet. They are Leo Kennedy, Graeme Taylor and Leon Edel."[40] These three writers were united by more than Montreal, the *Fortnightly*, and Smith's praise, each had expressed his intent to write the great Canadian novel. Their friend Doug Adam was convinced that the masterpiece, when it appeared, would take place in Montreal. In fact, he'd argued as much before Taylor, Glassco, and Edel, convinced that the city's extreme wealth and poverty, its ports and railways, its cultural mix, and prodigious nightlife made the setting inevitable.[41] After Taylor left for Paris, the discussion took on the appearance of a competition; one Edel was certain Kennedy would win. He wrote Smith with a prediction: "Actually, Leo will probably write the GCN first, because mine is not a Canadian novel. It is a people novel. That is to say, Leo will be concerned primarily with Montreal and its influence on people: a Canadian novel. My book is concerned with people and their influence on Montreal: a people novel. There is ample field in this country for two novels about the Metropolis."[42]

Taylor had been planning his great Canadian novel while living at the Metcalfe Street flat and continued the lengthy and ultimately unproductive process after his arrival in Paris. In *Memoirs of Montparnasse*, Glassco makes frequent references to *The Flying Carpet*, a work his companion is forever planning but never writes. Several seasons pass before Taylor abandons the novel, apparently without having so much as set down a word. "'I've been conceiving another book,'" he tells Glassco. "'Much better than *The Flying Carpet*. The great Canadian novel.'"[43]

Yet despite Taylor's persistent planning, he did manage to compose; and, of the two young men, he was by far the more prolific and fired up. The clergyman's son had, in the words of his friend Glassco, "combined a taste for literature with an ambition to make money out of it."[44] This drive, combined with a reluctance to rely wholly on Glassco's allowance, provides the best explanation as to why Taylor was so frequently published while living the expatriate life. It is a rather surprising accomplishment, in that his writings demonstrate little in the way of inspiration and reflect nothing of any "experimental literary" group. The first to be published, a two-page short story entitled "Deaf-Mute," is the most memorable. It concerns a French immigrant, Hector Groux, who purchases a farm in Ste-Anne-de-Bellevue on the Island of Montreal. Groux marries Emma, a farmer's daughter, who comes to him with her deaf and dumb older brother. As the area becomes attractive to the wealthier citizens of the city, Groux sells all but two *arpents* of his land. The lives of those in the household continue with little comment until Groux takes up with another woman, Veuve Charrest, with whom he plays cards in the evenings outdoors under a streetlight. Troubled by the relationship, Emma has her brother carry her bags to the local bus stop, informing him that she will not be returning. When Groux arrives home, he is met by his brother-in-law, who, gesticulating wildly, manages to convey that Emma has left them.

"Deaf-Mute" appeared in the summer 1928 issue of *transition*, the expatriate review's "American Number." Graeme Taylor's name joined those of other contributors, among them Pablo Picasso, Gertrude Stein, William Carlos Williams, Man Ray, Paul Bowles, Katherine Anne Porter, Kay Boyle, and Robert McAlmon. The centrepiece of the issue, if it could be said to have one, was an excerpt of James Joyce's "Work in Progress."

And so it was that, just three months after his departure from the Port of St John, Taylor appeared to be well on his way to fulfilling the grandiose expectations of Smith, Adam, and others. This triumph by "a graduate of McGill" was duly reported by his friend Edel in the pages of the *Daily Star*: "It is of that 'short' short story genre which is becoming more and more popular. Mr Taylor has executed it deftly, there is a mature touch to be found in it, and one can hope, after this demonstration, that more of his work will find its way into print here."[45]

By the time the summer issue of *transition* appeared, Glassco, Taylor, and McAlmon had left Paris for Nice and had taken up residence in Maison Poggi, a small apartment above Restaurant Poggi at 11 avenue de la Californie, just one short block from the beach on the Baie des Anges. While this inexpensive "Italian tearoom *pension*," owned and operated by a Franco-Italian named Alberto Poggi, suited well their finances, there were other reasons for the relocation.[46] According to Glassco, the move was prompted by a desire to escape the summer heat of the city and, in particular, the tourists crowding Montparnasse. Moreover, he and Taylor had found Paris an obstacle in the pursuits of autobiography, poetry, and the great Canadian novel. Taylor complained that the city was "hard to do anything but drinking in,"[47] while Glassco had become "so deeply involved with living" that he had no time to write.[48]

Going by Glassco's own account, his output was indeed slim. After one year living the expatriate life, his completed work consisted of nothing more than a single poem: the surrealist "Conan's Fig," most of which had been composed on the *Canadian Traveller*. A second poem, "Nobody's Fool," created by Taylor after gathering scraps of Glassco's abandoned verse, would at best be considered a collaboration. Both works have been lost or destroyed – that is, assuming that they ever existed.[49]

There is no evidence that Nice provided a better environment in which to work. The limited progress made in writing his memoirs, then called *The Arrow from the Bow*, was hindered by "a plump, black-eyed girl" whom he later hid behind the name "Stanley Dahl."[50] Her true name was Sibley Dreis, and she was, as Glassco has her say, "'A Canadian. From Winnipeg.'"[51] Born in the United States, as a child she had immigrated to Canada with her brewer father. Other than what is contained in *Memoirs of Montparnasse*, the only information that Glassco ever shared about his Manitoban girlfriend is found in a brief annotation in which he writes that she was the goddaughter of the cellist Boris Hambourg, founder of Toronto's Hambourg Conservatory.[52]

Glassco's attraction to the plump, rough, and fun Sibley had much to do with her androgynous nature. Like the girl skier in the unwritten story he'd once shared with Edel, Sibley was made glamorous by her boyish clothing. Had she worn skirts, Glassco admitted, he would not have found Sibley nearly so appealing.

Sibley moved into Maison Poggi with Glassco and Taylor, where they began a *ménage à trois*. In March 1929, Edel witnessed the tricky arrangement when he visited his old friends at the *pension*. His writing about the three is couched, though suggestive. In the introduction to *Memoirs of Montparnasse*, Edel quotes Glassco: "'we remained sunk in greed, sloth and sensuality – the three most amiable vices in the catalogue'"; contrasting this with his own experience: "I was too busy with my own life to notice this, I must confess, but in the evenings I would join the three, either drinking *vin rosé* at a café or watching Buffy whirl Stanley around the floor of some *dancing*."[53]

Playing host to Edel was anomalous. Whether due to simple geography, the intimacies and intricacies of the *ménage à trois*, or other distractions, Glassco and Taylor were drifting away from the group they had known at university. They ignored repeated invitations to submit pieces to *The Cana-*

Graeme Taylor, Glassco, and Sibley Dreis on the boardwalk at Nice, 1929.

dian Mercury, a new magazine being financed by Glassco's old defender and *McGill Daily* collaborator, Lew Schwartz. The "Monthly Journal of Literature and Opinion" featured contributions by names familiar to readers of the old *Fortnightly* – Scott, Smith, Kennedy, Edel, and others – but Glassco and Taylor were not among them. In the latter half of the year, when Doug Adam visited Paris, no doubt a welcome break from his father's manse, he stayed with his old friends and shared drinks at the Dôme and La Coupole. They were joined by Edel in what amounted to a brief reunion of the "McGill Intelligentsia." Many years would pass before the Sorbonne student again met over drinks with Glassco; it is doubtful that he ever saw Taylor again. "I was a rather 'square' student from the Latin Quarter," the biographer once explained, "who occasionally went to Montparnasse to get glimpses of those then committed (as I was not) to creative writing."[54]

Edel never met McAlmon. In March, shortly before the visit, he'd given up his room to Glassco, Taylor, and Sibley – the "three lovebirds" – and had returned to Paris.[55] Before leaving, McAlmon had submitted the first chapter of Glassco's memoirs to Ethel Moorhead at *This Quarter*. The young Montrealer soon received 390 francs for the thirteen-page "Extract from an Autobiography"; its prompt appearance in the spring 1929 issue marked Glassco's debut as a professional writer.

The same issue featured "Extracts from the Politics of Existence" and "Unfinished Poem" by McAlmon, followed by two of Taylor's pieces, "Extract I" and "Extract II," drawn from a novel entitled *Characteristics of the Penroses*.[56] The excerpts concern Reverend Penrose, a Presbyterian clergyman who, like Samuel Taylor, had begun his ministry by travelling throughout the North-West Territories. After the arrival of their children, his wife Christina, a woman of some means, pressures Penrose to settle in Montreal where, using his wife's money, he purchases a large red brick house on the lakeshore in Baie d'Urfé. This background Taylor draws from his own family, using himself as a model for wilful Hugh, whom Christine considers "the most difficult of her children."[57] The long passages reveal a domestic melodrama, one seemingly inspired more by Mazo de la Roche than Sherwood Anderson or any of the other writers who were being spoken of with admiration in the cafés of Montparnasse.

Within days of Edel's return to the Maison canadienne, and immediately after the issue appeared, he received a letter from Taylor asking that Glassco's "Extract from an Autobiography" be mentioned in his *Daily Star* column. Four days later, Glassco himself repeated the request:

> I'm sending you by this same mail a copy of This Quarter, in which Graeme's and my things appear.
>
> I hope you like them, but whether you do or not, don't let that influence any write-up you do for the Star. I'd like you to praise my work as much as possible, and in serious academic vein, because it is very necessary that my family realize what a hard-working and talented son they have. Inasmuch as the stuff in This Quarter is the first I have had published, I want to impress the bursar as favourably as can be. Graeme and I agree that it would be best to give Mr Glassco's work more prominence, as there is more need for it. I know you will do it in your best manner. By the way, Graeme's thing is two extracts from an opus called "Characteristics of the Penroses," and mine from a book called "The Arrow from the Bow." Do mention this. And don't

forget to give me more "prominence," irrespective of whether it is due or not! I'll be enterbally [*sic*] grateful to you for the lift. I see my parents this summer.[58]

It seems rather incredible that Glassco believed "the bursar" would be impressed by the "Extract." In the piece, A.P.S. is portrayed as having no understanding and little control over his son's activities. The arrangement Glassco and Taylor struck to sublet their single-room Metcalfe Street flat is described, as is an early morning visit during which Glassco and Taylor are made to share one bed while a friend attempts to have sex in the other. The bursar's son writes of the "stupidity and pettiness of McGill University," with which he was greatly disgusted, adding an anecdote in which the failings of a former English professor are exposed.[59] The taste of the head of the English Department is shown to be limited and conventional, the dean of the Faculty of Arts is depicted as a preposterous figure and something of a letch. Finally, Sir Arthur Currie, the man A.P.S. held in such high regard, is depicted as a "white-spatted symbol of the Army, attired like the editor of *Vanity Fair*" with "a dozen honorary degrees and a good high-school education."[60]

One can only assume that Glassco believed it unlikely that his father, any other member of McGill's governing body, or any faculty member would take the time to track down, much less read, the Parisian literary magazine. However, Edel, the more cautious, more "provincial," recognized that drawing notice to the "Extract of an Autobiography" would most certainly jeopardize Glassco's monthly stipend and quite possibly his own position as a columnist. A letter in which he stated as much was soon in the post to Nice. Glassco and Taylor were taken aback by their friend's reaction. "Personally I think you are mistaken in believing that it would create any furore," Taylor wrote in return: "I may be wrong in my estimate of the academic sensitivity, but if you read his thing over again you may see where you thought it was nasty it was only funny."[61] Glassco was much more conciliatory and realistic. "You are probablh [*sic*] right about jeopardizing you [*sic*] position," he wrote Edel. "And your advice to me re the bursar may be right."[62] Following the counsel of the "Paris Book Chat" columnist, he contacted Moorhead to ensure that no copies of the issue be mailed to McGill.

Given the history between Glassco and A.P.S., it's clear that his wish to "impress the bursar as favourably as can be" had nothing to do with fatherly approval and everything to do with money. The younger Glassco may have been correct in his assertion, made so convincingly at the Traymore Cafeteria, that the $100 allowance could support both himself and Taylor, but this financial arrangement soon became less comfortable. If Glassco is to be believed, the difficult situation was made much worse when in April 1928, less than two months after arriving in Paris, he received a letter from his father: "As you well know, I altogether disapprove of literature as a futile and unmanly pursuit and one that cannot but lead to poverty and unhappiness."[63] Then, as if to prove his point, A.P.S. continues, "I accordingly advise you that your allowance from now on will be halved."[64] Forever short of funds, often hungry and lacking drink, wherever possible the pair relied upon McAlmon's generosity and support and, for a time, found a good provider in Sibley Dreis.

While Edel had felt it unwise to draw attention to Glassco's "Extract," four months later he exercised his limited influence to the full by devoting an uncharacteristically long portion of "Paris Book Chat" to Taylor's next short story, "Dr Breakey Opposes Union," and the little magazine in which it was published. The column was a calculated effort to please "the bursar"; where the previous year Edel had described his friends as having aligned themselves with the experimental expatriate writers, Taylor was now in much more respectable company:

The long-expected reaction against the radical literati in Montparnasse has at last set in, a reaction against the outpourings of Gertrude Stein, and the idiosyncraces [sic] of the journal "Transition" [sic] in which their work has been published. It has come in the form of another journal "This Quarter," which formerly was equally radical in character, but which has just appeared under new management, bearing a sober cover, and continuing the work of contemporaries who are already well-known in the world of letters.

It is particularly interesting to note, however, that included in this list of names displayed on the cover, which numbers D.H. Lawrence, Hendrik van Loon, Ludwig Lewisohn, Liam O'Flaherty, T.F. Powys, Humbert Wolfe, Richard Aldington, Herbert Read, E.E. Cummings and others is that of a Montrealer, Graeme Taylor, to whose work I have already referred on previous occasions. His contribution to this first [sic] number is a short story, essentially Canadian in character, and dealing with a crisis in a clergyman's household at the time when Church Union was a pertinent and defined issue before the Canadian House. ... "Dr Breakey Opposes Union" is a good story, tersely written, and shows that Mr Taylor has secured a fine grasp of the medium. ... The magazine as a whole is very stimulating, and much more lively and interesting than the recent issues of "Transition," which has been growing decidedly dull and blatant. It is to be hoped that "This Quarter" marching safely down the middle path between downright conservatism in letters on one side, and sheer nonsense on the other, will serve a useful purpose in bringing forward some of the newer writers on this side who have been looking for just such a medium wherein they might express themselves. "This Quarter" is the first rather conservative note to be sounded in Montparnasse, and it is to be hoped that the reaction will be healthy.[65]

The story may have marked, "a most definite advance in the work of this young Canadian," as Edel declared, but Taylor was treading very familiar ground.[66] Published in the July–September 1929 issue of *This Quarter*, the first under the editorship of Edward Titus, "Dr Breakey Opposes Union" tells the story of the Reverend Cyrus Breakey, DD, Minister to the Scots Presbyterian Church. Having married the daughter of one of the wealthier members of his congregation, he leads a comfortable existence, living in a large, luxurious Montreal home of unusual design. It is to this house that the reverend returns one afternoon, not long after delivering an address at a luncheon meeting of the Rotary Club. Breakey enters into a discussion with his wife about the proposed union of the Presbyterian and Methodist churches. Although most of his congregation support the union, Breakey is staunchly against the proposition. Should it proceed, he intends to remain fixed, convinced that if "the union does come about, the Presbyterian Church will be smaller, but stronger."[67] Breakey's wife is allowed few words until she announces her intention to leave Montreal and provide no financial support should the husband lose his congregation. The reverend's opposition to the union has not only revealed his selfishness but has led her to question their marriage. A heated exchange ensues during which Mrs Breakey dies in a fall from an interior balcony. Shortly thereafter, the members of the congregation, moved by sympathy for their recently widowed minister, vote against the union. Reverend Breakey confides in his most steadfast friends that his late wife's family, though churchgoers, were known to let fervour influence their reason.

Edel's promotion of Taylor and the supposedly sober magazine to which he contributed was not the first favour the student columnist had done for the two Montrealers. That April, Glassco had written to Edel: "I have taken the liberty of sending a trunk of mine to you c/o the Maison Canadienne. It will arrive about the end of this month, by the Duchemin Moving Co."[68]

Having run up a significant debt with Monsieur Poggi, Glassco, Taylor, and Dreis had skipped out on their landlord and were due to take a train to Paris. Edel was expected to front Glassco the money for the transport of the trunk.

Back in Paris, the three seemed to have led a rather idyllic life. Inexplicably, in Glassco's account, money is no longer a concern; food is consumed, drink flows freely, and evenings are spent at the Opéra Nationale, the Opéra-Comique, the Cirque Medrano, and the Folies-Bergères. The memoirist writes that this comfortable *ménage à trois* lasted but a few more weeks, before being threatened by Gwen Le Gallienne and her pursuit of Sibley. All is quite cordial, casual, and calm; the two young men watch the seduction with a benign resignation, as reflected in this exchange:

> "I do hope we're not in the process of losing our Stanley," he [Taylor] said that evening as we sat in the little *tabac* drinking Cinzano and waiting for her.
>
> "I suppose we're bound to lose her some time or other. This is almost too good to last. Well, well, here's Morley."[69]

Morley Callaghan was new to the cafés of Montparnasse. On 17 April, the very same day Glassco, Taylor, and Sibley had fled Nice, he'd married Loretto Dee in Toronto. The couple set out immediately for Paris, by way of New York, a journey that was covered in some detail in Canadian newspapers. During the preceeding twelve months Callaghan had very much become a literary figure of note; his first two books, *Strange Fugitive* and *A Native Argosy*, had been published by Charles Scribner's Sons, the prestigious New York publishers of F. Scott Fitzgerald and Ernest Hemingway. Indeed, Callaghan had been likened to the ascendant Hemingway, whom he'd befriended when they'd both worked as journalists at *The Toronto*

Daily Star. In her unenthusiastic review of *Strange Fugitive*, Moorhead raises Hemingway's name throughout and ends with the suggestion: "Scribner's will do well to keep their eyes on other young authors appearing in this Quarter [*sic*]: ... Two more young Canadians: – Graeme Taylor and John Glassco."[70]

Moorhead's two young Canadians met Callaghan through McAlmon, who had been promoting the Toronto writer's work in the little magazines. Glassco and Taylor helped the newlyweds find a suitable hotel and served as guides through the cafés of Montparnasse. That Dominion Day, Glassco introduced the writer to Edel, who later reported in his "Paris Book Chat": "Callaghan says that he is in Paris to observe; and he is watching the Montparnassian scene. He does not speak of his work, although it is understood that he has a new novel under way. All that he wants to do here is to sit in the cafes and casually take things in."[71]

Callaghan had not intended to write of Paris, and before leaving Toronto had gone so far as to wager that he would not.[72] He would lose this bet, and in doing so create one of his most memorable short stories. "Now That April's Here" was inspired by three expatriates of the Montparnasse scene: Glassco, Taylor, and their friend McAlmon. In the story Glassco appears as Johnny Hill, an expatriate American with "a chinless faun's head," who, having read *Confessions of a Young Man*, has been writing his memoirs since the age of fifteen. Johnny is one half of a pair referred to in the cafés of Montparnasse as "the two boys."[73] His companion, Charles Milford, is a writer of short stories whom Johnny supports through a small monthly income. Together the two boys spend their nights in the cafés; their days are exhausted lying together in bed, critiquing those encountered the previous evening, invariably snickering at and making fun of those who have shown them any sort of kindness. Among those whom Johnny and Charles look down upon is the McAlmon character, an "ingenuous heavy drinker" named Stan Mason, who has taken a great liking to the two boys.[74] They follow Mason to Nice, live in grand style, and as had their originals, avoid a great hotel bill by throwing their bags out a window in the early hours of one morning.

Back in Montparnasse, the companions continue their lives of leisure; interrupted briefly by a seven-day trip Johnny makes to England in order to meet with his father. With his friend absent, Charles is lost and is exposed as uninteresting and insignificant. One evening he confides in Mason:

"I hope Johnny has enough sense not to pick up with a girl over in England."

"Why worry? Do it yourself now."

"Oh, I do, too, only I don't take them as seriously as Johnny does. Not that I mind Johnny having a girl," he said, "only I don't want him to have a complicated affair with one."[75]

After Johnny's return, he and Charles stroll along the left bank, looking across the Seine at the Louvre:

Casually Johnny told about a few affairs he had had with cheap women in London, and Charles had understood that these affairs had not touched him at all. It was a warm clear evening, the beginning of the real spring days in April and the boys were happy walking by the river in the moonlight, the polished water surface reflecting the red and white lights on the bridges.[76]

Callaghan leaves this romantic image to introduce Constance Foy, whom the two boys had known in Nice. A "simple-minded fat-faced girl with a boy's body and short hair dyed red," she is, with little in way of disguise, Sibley Dreis.[77] Constance and the boys enjoy something of a *ménage à trois*, which begins to fall apart when she comes to prefer Johnny to Charles. Whether through his own choice, or that of Constance, the physical relationship between her and Charles comes to a sudden end. The triangle now broken, both boys are thrown off balance. They end up together in a bar, unable to speak to each other, Charles on the verge of tears. It is only on the street, as they are walking back to their studio apartment, that he is finally able to confront Johnny:

"What are you going to do about Constance," Charles said.

"If it's all the same with you I'll have her for myself."

"But what are you going to do with her?"

"I don't know."

"You'd let a little tart like that smash things," Charles said, shaking his hand at Johnny.

"Don't you call her a tart."

"Please, Johnny, don't strike at me."

But Johnny who was nearly crying with rage swung his palm at Charles, hitting him across the face. Stan Mason had just turned the corner at the Boulevard, coming up to the bar to have a drink, and saw the two of them standing there.

"What's wrong?" he said.

"I begged him, I implored him not to hit me," Charles said.

"Oh, I hit him, I hit him, I hit him, what'll I do?" Johnny said, tears running down his cheeks.

They stood there crying and shaking their heads, but would not go home together. Finally Charles consented to go with Stan to his hotel and Johnny went home to Constance.[78]

Charles stays with Mason, who is left with the unpleasant task of telling the young man that Johnny is returning to the United States with Constance. The story closes after the departure, with Charles sitting alone in a café, Johnny's influence slowly fading.

By the time "Now That April's Here" appeared, in the autumn issue of *This Quarter*, Callaghan had returned to Toronto; he would not witness the certain humiliation the story wreaked on Glassco and Taylor. The pair were readily identifiable as the models for Johnny and Charles; and yet Callaghan's "two boys" were at odds with the shared image of sophistication and *politesse* that their models had attempted to project. Glassco and Taylor's studied good manners were made light of as mere pretensions. Their snickering and "perpetual scoffing," traits Edel had observed at McGill, were regarded as being key elements in their particular personalities.[79] Moreover, the story served as a notice that McAlmon was well aware that he was a source of amusement for the boys. Indeed, Callaghan had included a scene in which the McAlmon character overhears the two boys tittering through the thin walls of his hotel suite in Nice: "They were talking about him and having a good laugh. Stan Mason was hurt because he had thought them bright boys and really liked them."[80]

Though no direct connection is made, Callaghan's narrator speculates as to how the two boys come to have enough money to visit the Riviera. This is followed by a brief episode, almost certainly based on fact, in which the Glassco and Taylor characters are paid $20 by an "elderly English gentleman, who had suggested, after talking to them all one morning, he would pay well to see the boys make a 'tableau' for him."[81] While these elements were disturbing for the two Montrealers, "Now That April's Here" raised a greater concern: Callaghan had laid bare what he knew of their unconventional relationship.

Edel would always feel that it was Callaghan's irritation with Glassco and Taylor, for reasons both literary and moral, which led to the writing of the story. Without naming either, he offered a mildly disingenuous defense of his friends in the pages of *The Montreal Daily Star*:

> The short story he has written is not a remarkably good effort. It tells of two young men who came to live in Paris with the avowed intention of writing, and who drifted into Montparnasse ways. For one who knows something of life in Montparnasse, it is not difficult to recognize that Mr Callaghan has attempted a satire of one or two well-known figures in the quarter. It is not very good satire, and unless one realizes the satire, it does not stand very soundly as a short story. "Now That April's Here," as it is called, was written during the days last summer when Mr Callaghan could be seen of the afternoon on the terrace of La Coupole taking in Montparnassian life and discoursing amiably with Edward Titus, the Montparnasse publisher. There is a faint suggestion in the satire of his short story that Mr Callaghan was actually annoyed by the people he is attacking. Thus, for the uninitiated, any artistic effect he may have attempted is lost. It reads, in fact, much more like the "human interest" story of a newspaper than a real short story: and that is a criticism one could make of most of Mr Callaghan's short stories.[82]

This harsh critique would not stand the test of time. Interviewed six decades later, Edel had revised his opinion, praising the accuracy with which Callaghan had depicted his two friends:

> A very serious young man, Graeme was. He carried himself with great seriousness, and didn't say very much. And what he said was usually spoken from on high, you know: a dictum, a statement. He was almost a law-giver. Nearly always, Graeme achieved his kind of arrogance by – you would come with an enthusiasm and he would throw cold water on it: "It wasn't the thing to know," "it wasn't the thing to understand," "it really was rather vulgar, wasn't it?" This was the stance

that they took. And this is what Morley Callaghan caught in his story – which I think is a rather cruel story. But he did characterize the two of them. He describes them very well; that is the way they looked, wearing those big hats, which they bought, and sitting around in the cafés, and using language like "stout fellow" and so on.[83]

In his own memoir of Montparnasse, *That Summer in Paris*, Callaghan wrote that his story had been the result of a challenge issued by publisher Edward Titus, but his true motivation lay elsewhere. Near the end of his life, he described the purpose of the composition in a CBC radio interview:

I know – and Buffy admits this – that McAlmon was enormously generous in trying to look after Buffy and Graeme. And Buffy and Graeme used to snicker at McAlmon. It used to hurt me that Buffy would talk about McAlmon the way he did, you know, laughing at him. McAlmon had written a poem – he'd been in Mexico – and he had a line in the poem about ancient Aztec civilization: "Is this the Aztec heart that beats upon the temple floor." And Buffy and Graeme would sit there, and Buffy would say, "Is this the Aztec heart that beats upon the temple floor," and they'd kill themselves snickering. And this used to wound me because I felt I owed a great deal to McAlmon, and I knew that McAlmon never said a nasty thing about Buffy or Graeme. Moreover, what he used to say to me about them was – he'd just smile and he'd say: "Ah, they're just the most amusing little devils that have come around here in a long while." You see a kind of affection. And I thought that Buffy was being rather ruthless about McAlmon. So I did my little story, which I think is a fine story and I don't regret at all."[84]

The satirical tale of Johnny Hill, Charles Milford, Constance Foy, and Stan Mason would haunt Glassco until his death. In 1936, it provided the title of Callaghan's second collection of short stories and was included once again in a later bestseller, *Morley Callaghan's Stories*.[85]

The fight over Sibley, which Glassco considered "the subject of Callaghan's story,"[86] also served as the basis of a similar scene in Robert McAlmon's "thinly fictionalized memoir" *The Nightinghouls of Paris*, written more than a decade after the event.[87] In all likelihood, it wasn't the first

McAlmon work to have drawn inspiration from the adventures of his young Canadian friend. In May 1929, McAlmon completed a short novel, *My Susceptible Friend, Adrian,* he'd been working on at Maison Poggi. He wrote Sylvia Beach: "I think it is the best thing I've ever done, but it is Shocking [*sic*] in what it says and knows, though by no means a fairy story. Only the life of one of several boys about Paris, composite, with other characterizations and episodes therein."[88] Composite or not, one of the boys about Paris to which McAlmon had referred was almost certainly his young friend Buffy. In fact, whether in error or by intent, Glassco makes mention of McAlmon's novel in *Memoirs of Montparnasse* as *Promiscuous Boy.* McAlmon had intended on publishing the short novel, presumably under his Contact Editions imprint, but soon abandoned plans. Though the manuscript was lost, quite possibly stolen, it is not at all improbable that elements were later incorporated in *The Nightinghouls of Paris.* Indeed, by middle age, Glassco had come to confuse the two works, referring to the later novel as "THE SUSCEPTIBLE BOY"[89]

Flawed in structure, lacking a narrative arc, *The Nightinghouls of Paris* was more a collection of randomly placed anecdotes than a proper novel. As such, it was typical of McAlmon's writing, which Glassco came to later criticize as "obviously literal transcriptions of things set down simply because they had happened and were vividly recollected. There was neither invention nor subterfuge; when the recollection stopped, so did the story."[90] This opinion is not unlike that expressed by Gore Vidal, who recognized his father, Eugene Vidal, a boyhood friend of McAlmon, as the model for Gene Collins in the episodic novel *Village: As It Happened through a Fifteen-Year Period.* Indeed, the entire Vidal family is reflected with great accuracy in the work. "I can testify first hand that, as far as my family goes, McAlmon invents nothing," Gore Vidal writes. "He is a literal recorder."[91]

To describe *Village* or any other McAlmon novel as having a foundation in fact is to state the obvious. McAlmon's fiction was, to use the words of his biographer Sanford J. Smoller, "invariably autobiographical."[92]

The Nightinghouls of Paris centres on Kit O'Malley, a US writer whom McAlmon modelled on his idealized self. Possessing good looks, good taste, and enviable talent, O'Malley is the man at the centre of expatriate Paris; as such he serves as an unassailable narrator, watching with amusement the couplings and uncouplings of those around him. At the opening of the novel, O'Malley sits in La Coupole with Hilaria, a beautiful *femme fatale* clearly modelled on Caridad de Laberdesque. What follows is similarly populated by characters based on the figures of the expatriate Paris of the late 1920s: Kay Boyle becomes Dale Burke; Hilaire Hiler is Gaylord Showman; the Dayang Muda of Sarawak is the Princess of Faraway; Forest Pemberton is Ernest Hemingway; and Morley and Loretto Callaghan appear as the Canadian writer Shawin Flannagan and his wife Maggie. However, before any of these figures appear, McAlmon introduces "the boys," modelled on Glassco and Taylor: Sudge Galbraith and Ross Campion. Two young would-be writers from Montreal, they are the characters most present in the novel, second only to the narrator.

The boys are newly arrived in Paris, courtesy of an allowance given Sudge by his father, and have sought out O'Malley after the writer had been pointed out as one who "knew everybody."[93] From the start, the US writer finds the boys to be extremely amusing; he takes note of Sudge's "snort and the simultaneous gruff titter of Ross which gave me a flash of knowing that between themselves the boys had much amusement at the expense of the world."[94] The worldly O'Malley recognizes that when alone Sudge and Ross engage in sessions of "snickering and chattering" about those around them.[95]

The initial evening spent with the boys is a variation of that depicted in *Memoirs of Montparnasse*. In McAlmon's novel, Sudge is miserable, suffering from venereal disease picked up from a girl he and Ross had shared. Unable to drink, he returns to the boys' flat, leaving Ross behind to continue the evening with O'Malley. The next morning, the US writer wakes to find Ross sharing his bed and wonders as to what might have transpired.

Much is drawn from Glassco's life, mannerisms, and nature. Like his model, Sudge is in line to inherit a large sum at age twenty-five. Raised in luxury and privilege, he has experienced "the drabness of a clerk's rooming-house life."[96] Sudge is "all schoolboy, nonchalant, but neatly groomed." He walks "absent-mindedly with a tip-toeish gesture of secretiveness" and becomes animated at the mere sight of Ross. Together, the two twitter "like love birds" and become "engrossed in snickers, snorts, and detailed revelations," leading O'Malley to observe:

Never in years of knowing the Quarter had I seen so fine an example of schoolboy love and accord. It brought to me memories of similar friendships of my own in the years back when I was between fourteen and eighteen, but never had my intentness on the details of the other's life been so complete as theirs.[97]

Their sexuality is curious. O'Malley describes how the boys "tittered over the possibilities of getting acquainted with various girls who 'excited' Sudge."[98] The two tend to be attracted to girls in pairs, among them characters based on Yvette Ledoux and Gwen Le Gallienne, with whom Glassco shares a *ménage a trois* in *Memoirs of Montparnasse*. Midway through *The Nightinghouls of Paris* Sudge is obliged to meet up with his family, who are on holiday in England, but will do so only after having received assurances that O'Malley will care for Ross. So used is Ross to sleeping with Sudge, that he feels the need to share O'Malley's bed. In his friend's absence, Ross confides in O'Malley his worry that Sudge is becoming increasingly "prone to being 'excited' by various girls."[99]

The $100 allowance proves too little; and when O'Malley, too, runs short of funds, the three depart for Nice, where Sudge finds two vacant rooms above a restaurant belonging to a Monsieur Poggi. Once there, all writing comes to a stop. The boys rise late and spend the balance of each day at the beach. They meet two sisters and fight when Sudge devises an elaborate plan in order to lure one of them to the apartment. Before he can bring the plan to fruition, he becomes attracted to a curvaceous Russian countess, Margot Lindstrom. Her husband, a Finnish diplomat, is in a sanatorium, and Margot's "amourous life" is "taken care of by a young Chilean, Anatolio Grijalva, who also 'excited' Sudge."[100]

The fictionalized account of the *ménage à trois* once shared by Glassco, Taylor, and Sibley begins in Nice, when the boys picked up a girl named Sanka. A woman "born to abandon," she helps Sudge and Ross run out on their landlord Monsieur Poggi and various other debtors by paying their train fare back to Paris.[101] Back in the city, Sanka moves in with the two boys, much to Ross's disgust. He complains bitterly about the situation to O'Malley: "'We did muck up a good situation in Nice taking her on. She's a slut. We told her about you, and she'll try and make you now. I found her first, but Sudge had to horn in.'"[102] However, Ross's feelings don't prevent him from sharing the girl with Sudge, nor is Sanka unaware of her effect on the boys. She confides in O'Malley: "'I feel sorta lousy horning in on them, because, I didn't see it at first, but they're in love with each other. Ross is with Sudge, anyway, and I just mess things up.'"[103]

While O'Malley views Sanka as nothing but "a loose and indiscriminate tart," his opinion of Ross is no more charitable.[104] The US writer comes to liken Sudge's companion to a frail soured old man and is not alone in expressing a growing distaste for the young Montrealer. To Hal and Kate Meng, characters based on Edwin Lanham and his wife Joan, the sister of Kay Boyle, Ross is nothing but a leech. Another character, young Frederica Groper, describes Ross as "a silly weakling … worse than a gigolo … a selfish pig."[105]

Sanka having disturbed their relationship, Ross comes to believe he can no longer rely on Sudge and his allowance. When Sudge and Sanka announce that they're getting married, Ross explodes:

> Suddenly he exclaimed, "You're a bitch. Yesterday you said you loved me, and now it's Sudge, and you try to make Kit."
>
> "Sure, I like all I can get," Sanka said gaily.
>
> Ross jumped at Sanka and caught her throat, or possibly he merely pushed her. At any rate her chair was turned over, and she slipped to the pavement. Sudge rose quickly too and struck Ross. "That's a nice way for a gentleman to act," Sanka said. Her accent and manner now was surprisingly ladylike and reserved. "I knew though you were no gentleman. You don't even make a good gigolo, so strike me if you want to. I'm not hysterical and I am sorry for you." Her well-bred boarding school manner, and her reliance on dignity at the moment was amazing, from her.
>
> Sudge and Ross stood before the café gesticulating in each other's faces. "I told you not to hit me. You said you'd never hit me," Ross wailed, tears running down his face.
>
> "You shouldn't have hit Sanka. I didn't want to hit you. You aren't hurt?" Sudge said, taking his handkerchief to wipe the blood off Ross's face below the eye. "My ring cut you," Sudge began to cry. "Ross precious, forgive me. You know I didn't want to hit you. You know I don't care for her. It's you I love, but you don't leave me alone, ever. I want to take care of you, but you don't work, and you don't let me know anybody."

"To hell with you," Ross said viciously. "I won't stay in the room with you two tonight." He swaggered towards the Dome, not so much wistful now as rather skulkingly bad-tempered.

"I have the key and he has no place to stay. I hit him," Sudge sobbed. Sanka and I exchanged glances, and she was sheepish. She patted Sudge's face and shoulders when he sobbed against her. Now she was maternal and protective, and looked ashamed. "Sudge baby, I'm not horning in on you boys. I just like fooling and having a good time."

"I hit him, I hit him," Sudge wailed. He now leaned over and put his head on my shoulder and kissed my cheek, needing to cling to somebody he knew for solace.[106]

In the wake of this storm, played out in public, Sudge opens his heart to O'Malley, revealing that the proposal to Sanka was based on the belief that she would accept the presence of Ross within a marriage: "'It would look better, and people wouldn't have rotten ideas about Ross and me.'"[107]

The relationship between Ross and Sudge never recovers from the fight over Sanka. The end comes soon after when Margot Lindstrom re-enters Sudge's life, driving a wedge between the two boys. Abruptly, an embittered Ross returns to Montreal.

The fights featured in *The Nightinghouls of Paris* and "Now That April's Here" leave the relationships shared by the Glassco and Taylor characters irreparably damaged, and both go their separate ways. Whatever effect brought by the real "quarrel" over Sibley, the fact remains that Taylor soon left Paris for Montreal. In *Memoirs of Montparnasse* Taylor returns home after receiving a telegram with the news that his father is dying. If true, the reverend made something of a recovery; he lived for six more years.

Whatever prompted Taylor's return, the fact remains that he had for months been planning to leave Paris. As early as March 1929, the beginning of his second year in France, Taylor was talking about a trip home. He wrote Edel that plans had been made to leave from Montreal right after Bastille Day, adding: "Hope not for long but I have made arrangements to be there in the middle or late summer."[108] It is probable that Taylor left Paris very close to the date he'd originally intended, but any plan of return failed to materialize. Graeme Taylor would never see the city again.

With his companion gone, the nineteen-year-old poet adopted an even more transient lifestyle. As a result, perhaps, Glassco's account of this period of his life is scattered, less detailed, and, if anything, less reliable. He claims that he moved into Gwen Le Gallienne's flat, where the two resumed their sexual relationship *sans* Yvette Ledoux or, for that matter, Sibley Dreis. However, the supposed arrangement lasts less than two weeks, broken when his bisexual lover leaves for Marseilles to meet Yvette, who is returning from Tahiti. In reality, the Canadian artist did not return until December 1929, and was then very much a couple with the surrealist painter Georges Malkine.

Glassco then has his friend McAlmon re-enter the picture. It is possible that the older writer provided some stability and, as he had in the past, cash. Late that summer McAlmon did indeed return to Paris, having spent several months in the village of Theoule on the Riviera. In the earliest known draft of *Memoirs of Montparnasse*, Glassco indicates that after Taylor left he was McAlmon's kept boy and went so far as to note in his outline: "At last he is able to sate himself sexually with me."[109] Perhaps so, but the fact remains that this arrangement could have been counted in nothing greater than days; McAlmon was soon on a liner bound for New York. He would spend the remaining months of the year in the United States and Mexico; it was not until early 1931 that he returned to Paris. Whether Robert McAlmon ever saw his young Montreal friend again is unknown, but most unlikely.

However, these fleeting sexual dalliances with McAlmon and Le Gallienne are trivialities. The focus of the period following Taylor's departure lies with a mysterious figure Glassco named Honour Quayle. He once wrote Frank and Marion Scott that she was in reality a married US socialite named Margaret Whitney. In more than one conversation, he described Mrs Quayle as a composite character, modelled on Whitney and Marguerite Lippe-Rosskam, a woman of similar background and stature.[110] Glassco told his editor William Toye, who had enquired as to Mrs Quayle's true identity, that she was an older woman named "Marguerite Whitney."

Whatever he drew from Margaret and Marguerite, Mrs Quayle is a fantasy, owing much more to Glassco's imagination than to either woman. *Memoirs of Montparnasse* includes his seduction by Mrs Quayle, a dominant figure dressed in a robe of black suede, in a bedroom "completely done in

Mrs Margaret Whitney – "taken in Montreal, 1945, on the occasion of our reunion." This photo is most probably a hoax; Glassco wrote Frank and Marion Scott that Margaret Whitney died in 1939.

leather," on a bed "covered with slippery skin of either kid or calf,"[111] in her "womb-like apartment on the rue Galilée."[112] The venereal disease she infects him with is just one manifestation of her governing, threatening presence. Mrs Quayle is a figure of insatiable sexual appetite, for whom he feels over-whelming love. And yet, within this fantasy, played through the Fatal Woman who dominated his later pornography, weighs a harsh reality that would inspire nightmares throughout the decades that followed.

In the early months of 1930, Glassco's dream of Paris came to an end. He left the city for Barcelona with Marguerite Lippe-Rosskam, and from there travelled to Majorca. The couple next set up house for themselves in a residence that Marguerite likely owned. Though the timing is vague, it can be said that all too soon for Glassco the population of the household expanded to three with the arrival of a married Englishman named Roland Lushington-Hayes.[113] "I was completely destroyed by jealousy and despair," Glassco writes in his memoirs. His next sentence is most telling: "My suffering was indescribable: I was not meant for a *ménage à trois* of this kind."[114]

Glassco spent one final month under Marguerite's roof, a period marked by jealousy, hatred, and fear, which ended in a horrifying manner when he began coughing up blood. He returned to Paris alone; not to the Falstaff or La Coupole, but to the American Hospital at Neuilly, where he was diagnosed with tuberculosis. The date of Glassco's admission is unknown, but he may have provided a clue when, in middle age, he rewrote a poem from memory, a poem to Graeme Taylor. He records the original place and date of composition as the American Hospital, September 1930.

THE BODY SAYS GOODBYE TO LOVE[115]

I
Goodnight the feasting and the fire
I pass beyond the castle door
Nor pause to speak with young desire
Who bids me drink with him once more.

II
Dear friend and you dear forms of him
You pleasures of my sinful dust
Believe me I am sick to death
I only leave because I must.

III
Here on this narrow iron bed
Watching the nurses come and go
I am still with you almost dead
You living and beloved so

IV
Your hands have other things to do
Your heart has other hearts to tease
I am no longer part of you
My body seeks another ease

V
Among the white the linen fields
The chastity of something strange
To which my tired spirit yields
And yet my heart will never change

VI
Farewell the guises of the heart
The fawning smile the tender lie
I lose my youth I miss my art
Goodnight my jolly friend goodbye.

In the postscript to *Memoirs of Montparnasse*, Glassco is examined by "the celebrated Dr Sergent," a reference to Edmond Sergent, then a leading figure in the fields of epidemiology and immunology.[116] Glassco writes: "He shook his head; but in finding I was a native of Montreal he assured me my best chance lay in putting myself in the hands of Dr Edward Archibald, the surgeon who had lost fewer patients by thoracoplasty than any other. In the spring I was strong enough to be sent back to Montreal."[117]

Family legend has it that the poet and lover, the champion of "anti-'bloody respectability,'" was retrieved by his mother, who dispatched a doctor and private nurse to bring her young son back home to Montreal.

... youth seems dead, dead, dead.[1]

Montreal may have appeared a most unlikely place in which to seek treatment for tuberculosis. In 1931, the year in which Glassco was first admitted to the Royal Victoria Hospital, nearly 3,200 Quebecers succumbed to the disease. Quebec's annual mortality rate from tuberculosis was over one in one thousand, surpassing those of all other provinces – it was twice that of Ontario. Only the territories offered a worse chance of survival. In Quebec, well over half of those diagnosed with the disease died within five years.

The province's six sanatoriums, providing bed rest, fresh air, and a healthy diet, were believed to offer the best hopes of recovery. Indeed, in 1928 the medical superintendent at the Laurentian Sanatorium in Ste-Agathe-des-Monts had reported that permanent recovery was simply not possible for any patient who resided less than a year. For treatment to be truly effective, the tubercular patient was told to expect a sanatorium stay of between two and four years. While such care was financially far beyond the reach of the average Canadian family, Buffy Glassco was a son of privilege. It was unnecessary for Doctor Sergent to make recommendations or exercise influence; there was no question that the young Glassco would become a patient of Edward Archibald.

A neurosurgeon, a clinical researcher, an educator, and the surgeon-in-chief of the Royal Victoria Hospital, Archibald was internationally a leading figure in the treatment of tuberculosis.[2] Much of the doctor's considerable reputation rested on his advancements in thoracoplasty, the procedure through which he would save Glassco's life. In 1912, Archibald had become the second surgeon in North America to carry out a thoracoplasty.[3] Although he did not invent the procedure, he had improved it significantly.

The following year, he became the first physician to publish a paper discussing the use of surgery in the treatment of tuberculosis.

The operation Archibald performed on Glassco and others involved removing portions of several ribs from one side of the upper part of the chest and collapsing the tubercular lung. In stopping respiration on the one side, it was hoped that the diseased organ might heal. Archibald's great skill, which he demonstrated during the course of each surgery, was in determining and adjusting the extent of the rib resection and the number of ribs involved. In doing so, he stopped short of inflicting irreparable stress on the heart and functioning lung.

By October 1929, two years before he first operated on Glassco, Archibald had performed 172 thoracoplasties. Nineteen of his patients had died from the operation; fourteen of the deceased had entered the operating theatre with what Archibald had considered an unfavourable state of disease. With a survival rate approaching ninety percent, the doctor was considered the foremost thoracoplasty surgeon in North America, if not the world.

In the later months of 1931, Archibald performed the first stage of thoracoplasty on Glassco. The operation was performed at the Royal Victoria Hospital, an imposing, fortresslike structure established by Donald Smith, First Baron Strathcona and Mount Royal, and George Stephen, First Baron Mount Stephen; Buffy Glassco was once again surrounded by the Montreal he'd sought to escape.

The patient's recovery was difficult, sluggish pace suggesting the gravity of his situation. It was not until December 1932 that the second stage operation could be performed. Glassco suggested that he had spent the entire period at the hospital.

Among his early doctors was Norman Bethune. Like Archibald and so many others involved in treating the disease, Bethune had himself battled tuberculosis. Diagnosed in autumn 1926, he spent the remainder of that year and nearly all of the following year in sanatoriums in Ontario and New York State. He'd expected to succumb to the disease; in "The TB's Progress" – a 1927 mural he painted as a patient at the Trudeau Sanatorium at Saranac Lake – he gives 1932 as the year of his death. Bethune saved his own life by insisting that he receive an artificial pneumothorax, an experimental treatment that involved the injection of air into the pleural cavity surrounding the affected lung. Within six weeks he was fully healed and was preparing a new mission in life: the worldwide eradication of tuberculosis.

Bethune arrived at the Royal Victoria in April 1928, after having been chosen by Archibald as his first assistant. Five years later, he crossed the island to accept a position as head of thoracic surgery at l'Hôpital du Sacré-Coeur; a move prompted, in part, by tensions between the two surgeons. Archibald would later describe his former assistant as a man who possessed a mind like a "St Catherine's wheel, always turning, always throwing off sparks, and always in a different direction."[4]

Glassco's memory suggests another side to Bethune. Late in life, he spoke of his treatment to Fraser Sutherland: "Glassco recalled Bethune would come and see him in his room in the hospital, and that he had a real healing calm. There was something much more than just the technical and medical aspects. One time he came into the room and walked past Glassco's bed and went over to the window and stood with his back to him and just left, but leaving behind a kind of healing power."[5]

Beatrice Glassco may have had her dear Buffy retrieved from his Paris hospital bed, but his years of struggle with tuberculosis caused little disruption otherwise to her finances and routine. Neither she nor her husband would pay for Archibald's services; the significant expense would be drawn from their son's inheritance at some later date. As their middle child lay deathly ill in hospital, Beatrice and A.P.S. continued to enjoy summers abroad, vacationing in the British Isles.

Glassco wrote that he spent a total of two years at the Royal Victoria. If so, it is likely that he was released and transported to his parents' dark Cedar Avenue house shortly after their return from a 1933 summer holiday spent in Bournemouth, England. He would have brought with him a sheaf of tightly written sheets, the beginnings of the aptly titled Intimate Journal, a document he maintained with varying degrees of dedication over a twenty-eight-year period. Foremost a record of his emotional condition and various literary endeavours, it features few of the key events in Glassco's life. Births and marriages are absent; only one death, that of his beloved Dalmatian bitch Lucy, would be recorded in any immediate sense. Family is mentioned, but rarely; David appears in only one entry, while sister Beatrice is entirely absent. Nor was the Intimate Journal to be anything resembling a daily account of Glassco's life; weeks, months, and seasons might pass between entries. More often than not the writing would be motivated by depression and despair, a pattern Glassco recognized in an early entry: "I think that when I am happy I never want to write about myself – in the first place I don't dare 'handle' the emotion, and in the second I still possess (probably according to the 'Doctrine of Reminiscence') the feeling that happiness is so much the natural state of man that it is quite self-supporting and a happy man needs do nothing else but be happy, while he can."[6]

The first twenty-three pages of the journal have been lost – almost certainly destroyed by Glassco himself. The earliest extant entries, written while convalescing at the Cedar Avenue house in late winter 1934, record his struggles with his parents and his health. Glassco was beset by persistent pain and fever. In early March, he was again confined to his bed, this time by the retention of pus in a pocket adjacent to his affected lung. After five horrendous days of suffering, the accumulation was released in a rush through a side wound. The despair brought by this decline in health was in no way alleviated by the family hearth; Glassco was under the very same expansive roof from which he had fled, vowing never to return, some seven years earlier. He longed for the day when he would be strong enough to leave his parents' house. Until that time, the only escape from his miserable situation was found in books and in the daily visits from Taylor.

There were attempts to write, but these too brought frustration and depression. A poem, "Dancers," had been left too long; encouraged by Taylor, he put a great deal of thought into a short story entitled "Rosa" but gave up before setting down so much as a word. He lacked confidence in his ability to write and yet was startled when *The American Mercury* rejected another story, "A Child in the House." Taylor, who was having no better luck in trying to place his own writing, sought to assure and encourage, but Glassco began to fear that his work was devoid of background and philosophy. "My poetry," he wrote in his journal, "seems very trivial, cheap stuff."[7] Despite his efforts, at the end of the winter Glassco had little more than two hundred lines of verse, most of which he dismissed simply and succinctly as "bad."[8]

It is difficult to judge the validity of Glassco's harsh self-criticism. None of the works composed during his lengthy convalescence have survived. "Dancers" and "A Child of the House," like very nearly all the early unpublished writing, were destroyed; a practice Glassco would continue well into his fifth decade.

His physical and mental health in decline, on 28 March he returned to the Intimate Journal:

I have not written anything in this journal for several weeks, because I began to see that I was writing nothing but trivialities, and perhaps getting to regard them as important. And now I hardly know why I am taking it up again, unless it be from the wish to make those little details seem important again. But tonight I am in such discouragement about my work that I feel impelled to write about it – perhaps to reason myself back into the belief that I shall really, some day, do something good.

I went out today, after more than a week spent in the house with a nasty feeling in the chest and a feeling of sickness at the stomach, and what was worse, with a horrible load of fear on my mind all the time, which has not yet quite left me. Yesterday and today I felt as if I was dragging myself up out of the morass, but I am not yet quite clear of it. The fears I am not quite certain of: they seem to rise out of my love for Graeme, and centre around my imagination of what life would be like without him – the thought is too terrible … I was struck with Thackeray's remark that it is not dying that is so bad, but the leaving loved ones behind, the pain it will cause them. I do not fear my death unduly, but I know what it would mean to Graeme. I am tormented by imaginings of him at my deathbed, where I see the pain in his dear eyes, and all the details of a protracted dying. I think it must be rather easy for a loveless man to die. But enough of this!

I have done practically no work since I last wrote in this journal [March 6], except a translation of Catullus' "Dirge for Sparrow," which cost me endless pains, and is not yet even quite finished. Also the first 4-line stanza of a poem tentatively called "March"; but this I was comparing with one of de Tabley's today and suddenly saw it was every bit as derivative and uninspired. I am beginning to believe that I may not just have it in me to write poetry. But yet I know I shall go on scribbling to the end. If I only felt that what I was doing showed even a sign of worth, with what enthusiasm I would go forward. Denied that feeling, I am in a constant state of fluctuating despair and supreme confidence – the former having far and away the best of it. The only consolation is that Graeme is a really good poet, and him I regard as part of myself.[9]

It was in Taylor that Glassco saw and trusted his future, and he looked to the day when his health would permit a final release from the "monstrous castle." As it was, the two men could do no more than plan on spending their lives together.

Two weeks later, following one of Taylor's visits, Glassco again returned to his Intimate Journal:

> This winter seems to have been made up of nothing but partings, and I sometimes grow frightened of a nameless something when I look forward to the rapidly approaching time when we will be together for always, – as if fate might be about to play us some cruel trick. It is nothing by presentiment, but what power it has![10]

Presentiment was a most appropriate word. Almost immediately, his health began to deteriorate. Within a matter of days Doctor Archibald was called to visit the Glassco residence. It was determined that another operation would be necessary. The news came as a great blow, so much so that it was only through Taylor's reassurances that Glassco was able to face the surgery.

Archibald's work, performed within a matter of days, was a success. For once, recovery was quick to come. Invigorated by his restored health, feeling "like a snake with a new skin," Glassco returned to his verse with great enthusiasm.[11] Drawing on a new enthusiasm for Gerard Manley Hopkins, his first completed work was a love poem to Taylor, of which only the first stanza survives:

> Love, for you alone,
> I have made this bosom rhyme:
> Show it to no one,
> Be you its world even as you are mine,[12]

It is clear that Glassco thought it another piece of failed verse; though it says a great deal about his new energy and outlook that he fairly shrugged off the non-success. "Strange, it looks self-conscious," Glassco wrote, "and yet it comes straight from the heart. Also, like most things that come straight from that region, it is rather common-place."[13]

Taylor, also, had been writing. In the previous two months he had completed a couple of short stories, "The Volunteer" and "An Afternoon in the

Luxemburg." Glassco considered the latter his friend's finest work to date and, comparing it favourably to Kay Boyle's "trashy bits," held out hope that it would be accepted by a magazine.[14] Having finally conquered his own health problems, Glassco became determined to dedicate himself to Taylor's wellbeing:

> I am going to try, though I don't know if it can be done, to concentrate on Graeme's happiness this summer, – so that, incidentally, he will work. Because I think he can do good, perhaps great, work, if he is happy. This sounds rather cold, but I know that a measure of fame, however small, would be good for him. And it is not surprising that, loving him so much, I should like to see him recognized.
>
> Good news! Archibald says I shall not need another operation. This is most encouraging.
>
> I only hope this feeling of *bien-être* will last![15]

It was not to be. Just two days later, as Glassco later described, he "reached the peak of well-being and sunk into a dreadful slump,"[16] which lasted several weeks. For Glassco, who would often recognize and record the precise moment of dark depression's descent, the trigger was easily identified:

> The crash came suddenly – after I had been feeling tremendously excited & enthusiastic over a story to be called "The Way Back" – the story of a masochist. It seemed that I got frightened at the depths I found in myself, depths of sexual perversion, while thinking out the story – rather like my sensations after reading Mirbeau's "Torture Garden." I wrote 500 words of a masochistic scene in great elation the night of May 31st, and then, after I had gone to bed (or rather turned out the light) the "dreadful imaginings" began. Perhaps I had strained myself mentally in writing it. At any rate, things got steadily worse for a week – two weeks – and I began to be frightened about everything. My stomach seemed to go wrong – I had the most vile feeling of nausea all day long, and couldn't smoke a cigarette without feeling worse. I am still wondering whether this was the effect of mental disturbance or something wrong with my physical condition.[17]

Glassco fails to describe the nature of these "dreadful imaginings." Might he have been influenced by Mirbeau's "*pages de Meurtre et de Sang*," with their depictions of flayings, crucifixions, and anal-sadistic desire? Perhaps they were similar to the earlier fantasies, also described as "imaginings," in which Taylor had appeared at his deathbed.[18] Whatever the horror Glassco experienced on that spring night, it most certainly would have been made worse had he known that "The Way Back" would remain with him – revisited, recast, and rewritten – over the next four decades. It would not be until the 1974 publication of a weakened version entitled "The Black Helmet" that Glassco would find himself well and truly free of this "story of a masochist."

The disturbed feeling carried by "The Way Back" lingered for weeks, and was broken only when he and Taylor rented a large red brick house on the north shore of Lake St Louis in Baie d'Urfé.[19] The move marked, at long last, Glassco's final departure from his parents' residence. Never a home, it had been the house in which Glassco had spent the bulk of his adolescence. He wrote of it as the "dreadful place," a construction that held a "ghostly atmosphere of constraint, worry, pettiness, selfishness and malice."[20] Taylor thought the imposing structure so poisoned that it forced a change in respiration to all passing over the threshold. Now living with Taylor for the first time since Montparnasse, Glassco felt liberated and confident. He was certain that the years of battle with tuberculosis had ended in victory and was determined to regain his strength. Far from his family, the destructive, consuming thoughts that had preceded his arrival in his new home quickly faded. Two days later, Glassco wrote that he was unable to recall his distress.

Taylor fashioned for his friend a crude workplace on the broad lawn, consisting of a deck chair and a card table with the legs sawn off. As the days of summer passed, Glassco, mindful of the recovery process and seeking to avoid exertion, produced very little. Yet, featured foremost among his writing projects was "The Way Back," the very same story that had given rise to his "dreadful imaginings." Revisited under the glow of the summer sun, its treacherous effect had vanished. Glassco spent four days "monkeying around" in "feverish excitement" before dismissing the once potent, damaging story as "silly."[21] "The Way Back" was destroyed, but it would arise again and again.

At Taylor's suggestion he returned briefly, and with considerable enthusiasm, to the memoirs he'd abandoned in Paris. It became just one of many projects that were picked up, monkeyed with, and dropped during what was an uneventful and relaxing summer.

Glassco and Taylor on the lawn of their rented Baie d'Urfé home, 1934.

There was, however, one blemish on the otherwise idyllic, fairly pastoral scene of two writers composing verse and prose by the shore of Lake Saint Louis: Taylor had been submitting short stories to US periodicals, receiving a steady stream of rejection letters. For a man who had placed his work with such ease in the little magazines of Paris, a writer who had been published alongside James Joyce and D.H. Lawrence, the experience was disheartening. Glassco may have wished to dedicate the season to his friend's happiness, but the sour reaction to Taylor's writing was something over which he had no control. In midsummer, after *Harper's* had rejected yet another Graeme Taylor story, "The Portrait of a Generation," Glassco wrote in his journal words that he could not share with his companion: "Of course I see why the magazines don't want his stories – they haven't enough 'punch,' being composed mostly of atmosphere with little action, – which is, after all, a fault. If only he could write one acceptable story! It would be a turning-point."[22]

Sadly, Taylor would experience no turning point, no breakthrough. It had been five years since the publication of "Dr Breakey Opposes the Union," the last of his stories to see print. Now twenty-eight, Taylor was beginning to reconsider his life in letters.

How he happened upon the idea of running a farm is something of a mystery.[23] A hint may be found in Taylor's fiction, including that written as a student and during his time in Paris, in that the settings are nearly always the old farming communities of Baie d'Urfé and Ste-Anne-de-Bellevue. It may be that as a boy he had worked summers on one or more of the farms that then covered the West Island of Montreal; an experience not at all uncommon among those of his generation. Speculation, to be sure, but what can be said with certainty is that Taylor was aware of Glassco's approaching twenty-fifth birthday, the day in mid-December when his friend would at long last receive his share of Edward Rawlings's fortune. Lacking money of his own, Taylor may have thought that by managing a working farm he would be making some sort of a contribution to their home. As it was, he'd settled back into a lifestyle similar to that enjoyed in Paris – one in which Glassco footed the bills.

Glassco's attraction to the idea is more easily explained; he was drawn to the great beauty of the countryside and saw in it the offering of sanctuary from his family in Montreal.

However, when the much-anticipated birthday arrived, it failed to bring the promised riches; Buffy Glassco's inheritance was tied up in investments. The explanation for this lapse is unknown, though the effects of the Great Depression, then in its sixth year, may provide something of an explanation. A further hint may be found through *The Nightinghouls of Paris*, in which Mr Galbraith, the A.P.S. character, profits personally by investing the capital that his son is to inherit.

Sitting in the Westmount duplex he and Taylor had rented for the winter, Glassco became burdened by depression. The mood brought by the delayed inheritance was darkened further as confidence in his poetry again vanished. While Glassco had grown increasingly confident in his abilities in Baie d'Urfé, after returning to the city he quickly fell into dismissing his verse as "derivative" and "unrepresentative of this day and age."[24] Not even the writings of others could provide relief. Reading T.S. Eliot, he felt, only demonstrated the failings of his own verse. He turned to travel literature but found that it offered no escape:

Reading Douglas' "Old Calabria" I felt that I didn't want to travel again: it is too melancholy, the idea of manufacturing memories, and resuscitating buried ones in a foreign land. I am almost frightened of reviving feelings I had five years ago – they seem strangely sad to remember now – why I can't tell: just because they are *gone*, *dead*, perhaps? The result of which has made me feel dreadfully old. Sometimes I have to push myself and remind me that I am only 25 – I can hardly believe it – youth seems dead, dead, dead.

And nothing but doubt and fear & indecision for me from now on.[25]

Yet, the summer that followed – in the midst of the country's economic crisis – was one of the most carefree and happy periods of Glassco's life. He and Taylor returned to the house on Lake St Louis, where they were cared for by a housekeeper named Madge. As the two writers pursued their craft, undisturbed by domestic affairs, she shined their shoes and proved herself an excellent cook. The housemaid was a good match in that Glassco and Taylor wanted nothing of formality and Madge had no use for uniforms. While her good looks were recognized and appreciated, Glassco's attention and intentions were focused on Adrienne Dostre de Bellot, the beautiful governess of a nearby farm. A voluptuous virgin, she fuelled his "fetishistic fantasies."[26] Though he feared straining his health and was concerned that he would be unable to achieve sexual release – "the final caress," as he put it – Glassco's pursuit bordered on the obsessive.[27] The presence of the governess lingered long after each visit had drawn to an end, exciting long and lustful passages praising her body in the Intimate Journal. His description of the "Seduction of Adrienne" – coming as autumn drew near – consumed three pages of tight script.[28]

Glassco was productive in his happiness, composing close to one thousand lines of verse, as well as new versions of "The Way Back" and "The Three Captains," an old short story that he'd hoped to make more commercial for sale to *Esquire*. However, he was considerably less optimistic about Taylor's writing, which included the beginning of a novel, *The Foundling*, and a short story, "Mr Noad." The latter Glassco considered a great advance over previous efforts but felt the chances of publication were slim. Nevertheless, he made repeated attempts to place Taylor's story, reworking and molding it until little of the original was left. "Mr Noad" finally saw publication in the March 1953 issue of *The Canadian Forum*, nearly eighteen years after the original composition. That it appeared under Glassco's name, with Taylor's knowledge, speaks to the extent of his changes; however, beneath the layers of polish, veins common to Taylor's fiction are clearly visible.

Glassco seated at the writing table that Graeme Taylor
fashioned for him, Baie d'Urfé, 1935.

The story begins in Baie d'Urfé and settles on the title character, an elderly eccentric with a fixation for heraldry; in particular, the bend sinister. The
narrator recalls a summer day when, as a boy, he and Noad had travelled by
rail to visit the country estate of Sir George Crosslands, a long-dead politician. The pair finds the property neglected and unwanted; an old real estate
sign remains attached to one of the many decrepit buildings. Overcome by
vines, desecrated by tramps, the Crosslands mansion retains little of its
grandeur. The sight of this decaying estate brings tears to Noad's eyes. As he
and the boy make to leave, they encounter a farming couple whom Noad
had known as a youth. The eccentric man's pretensions, played in full before
the farmer and his wife, prompt a confrontation during which it is revealed

that Noad is the bastard son of Crosslands. Although the narrator keeps the old man's secret, it becomes apparent that the true nature of Crosslands is known to those of a certain generation. Upon his return, the narrator's grandfather tells him: "you have the good fortune to be born in an age when public morality has made such progress that the political career of a man like George Crosslands – of the scandal of his private life I say nothing – is unthinkable, simply unthinkable."[29]

It is not difficult to see Glassco's hand at work: the image of the decaying estate and the scandalous private life of the wealthy, respectable, and powerful are common to his fiction. However, despite his rewrite, Glassco was unable to address what he considered the recurrent flaws he recognized in Taylor's stories; "not enough 'punch' or 'plot.'"[30] He would soon acknowledge his inability to produce these elements in his own fiction.

Near the close of his "most beautiful summer" came a letter from Edward Archibald indicating some knowledge of Glassco's financial situation and requesting payment for his services.[31] One of Glassco's uncles – either Henry or Walter Rawlings – later confirmed that the inheritance due on his twenty-fifth birthday could finally be issued. "It was the first time I'd heard of it; although A. [Archibald] must have heard of it from my Uncle: nice way to have your affairs conducted, – your creditors knowing your resources before you do yourself!"[32]

Glassco's prompt payment was accompanied by the realization that he must maintain tighter control on his investments. It was a fresh lesson learned when, in early September, he happened to hear an evening radio broadcast in which Prime Minister R.B. Bennett proposed a reduction in interest on the Dominion Bonds that Glassco held in his portfolio. Panicked, the next morning he and Taylor caught an early bus to Montreal:

That fearful drive in! After an almost sleepless night, to rise in the dark and catch that bus (we very nearly missed it, which didn't improve our spirits particularly), and see the the [sic] poor dumb-driven wage-slaves getting on every mile or so, their cheeks and throats raw from shaving, their neat business-suits, and that terrible patient look that goes right to the heart, and their little jokes, and all their degradation that is none the less real because only actual to someone else.[33]

That dreadful day, Friday, 13 September 1935, marked a sudden change. After nearly two years of talk, Glassco and Taylor made the first of many visits to realtors in search of a farm. They hoped to find something to their liking for $5,000 – thinking, unrealistically, that they might meet their goal within a month. Although this was not to be, they chose not to winter in the city and continued to rent the house in Baie d'Urfé. Montreal held no attraction; the few friends from their student days at McGill had scattered. Leon Edel was in New York, working as a reporter for the Agence Havas. Doug Adam remained in Scotland, also pursuing a career in journalism. A.J.M. Smith was beginning the first of two semesters as an instructor at the University of South Dakota in Vermillion. It is doubtful that they were missed; Glassco and Taylor had long since ceased corresponding with the three men. Of the remaining university acquaintances, the only one with whom they had any contact was H. Burton Bydwell, the "fat little lecher" who had made use of the Metcalfe Street apartment for his nocturnal activities some seven years earlier.[34] He was an acquaintance of various figures associated with the old *McGill Fortnightly Review* but had not been a contributor. Bydwell's reputation within the crowd had more to do with scandal than things literary, and yet with one simple act – the lending of a book – he had the most profound effect on Glassco's work.

The title in question was *Against the Grain*, an English language translation of J.-K. Huysmans's Decadent masterpiece *À rebours*.[35] Upon finishing the novel, in early October, Glassco turned to his journal, describing the work with great enthusiasm as one of the best things he'd ever read: "it even gave me a bit of a set-back – just a slight jolt – to see how thoroughly, conclusively, & beautifully the spirit of Perversity has found expression."[36]

The effect was not at all dissimilar to that experienced by the protagonist of Oscar Wilde's *The Picture of Dorian Gray*:

> It was the strangest book that he had ever read. It seemed to him that in exquisite raiment and to the delicate sound of flutes, the sins of the world were passing in dumb show before him. Things that he had dimly dreamed were suddenly made real to him. Things of which he had never dreamed were gradually revealed.[37]

Huysmans's hero is Duc Jean Floressas des Esseintes, the sole surviving scion of a once prominent, powerful, and noble family. Having immersed himself in the decadence of Paris, the young aristocrat emerges disenchanted and considerably weakened in health. Des Esseintes takes refuge in a grand house in the French countryside, where, in his seclusion, he chooses a life of intellectual and aesthetic pursuits. He surrounds himself with reproductions of the paintings of Gustav Moreau, drinks in the writings of Charles Beaudelaire and Paul Verlaine, dabbles at inventing perfumes, and creates a garden consisting exclusively of flowers he considers artificial in appearance. Ultimately, the secluded, sensual life des Esseintes creates for himself proves more harmful than the debauchery of the city and he must return to Paris for salvation, a move he likens to that of a nonbeliever attempting to embrace religion.

Glassco alludes to this first encounter with Huysmans in the preface of *The Fatal Woman*, the 1974 collection of erotic tales in which the final version of "The Way Back" appeared under the title "The Black Helmet": "Around 1934, after writing my farewell to youth, romance and action in *Memoirs of Montparnasse*, I came under the renewed influence of Huysmans, Pater, Villiers, Barbey d'Aurévilly [*sic*] and other so-called Decadents, and decided to write only books utterly divorced from reality, stories where nothing happens."[38] Though the year is off, and the conceit concerning the composition *Memoirs of Montparnasse* is maintained, Glassco is truthful when discussing the sway of the Decadents. And it is no accident that he places Huysmans before Walter Pater, the Comte de Villiers, and Jules Amédée Barbey d'Aurevilly; all were read and appreciated, but it was always to Huysmans and *À rebours* that he returned.

While Glassco's attraction to *À rebours* might easily be explained by its position as the most accomplished Decadent novel, the parallels between the character des Esseintes and the reader Glassco cannot be ignored. Both were sons of wealthy, powerful families in gentle decline. Slender, effeminate, and nervous, like des Esseintes, Glassco had drunk in the excesses of Paris. His lifestyle, decadent by the standards of the staid Montreal of his youth, had done damage to his health and he'd sought sanctuary in the countryside. Although his living arrangements in Baie d'Urfé were extremely comfortable, they were in no way comparable to those achieved by Edward Rawlings; nor had Glassco ever been surrounded by the heightened affluence in which his mother had been raised.

Most certainly some further element of Glassco's interest in Huysmans's masterwork stemmed from the great reputation it enjoyed as "a novel without a plot," Though not entirely accurate – a novel with *little* plot, perhaps – the great commercial success of *À rebours* offered promise for Taylor's stories, which Glassco recognized as being "composed mostly of atmosphere with little action."[39] Yet, what Glassco then failed to recognize was that his embrace of Decadence came at a time when the movement's writings were very much out of favour. In the 1930s, observed George Woodcock, one could purchase copies of Decadent works from the bookstalls of London for next to nothing. Suffering the devastating effects of the Great Depression, this was a decade, wrote the Canadian man of letters, "whose dominant spirit was as diametrically opposed as one could imagine to that of the Decadents."[40]

The autumn and early winter were focused with something approaching exclusivity on "The Way Back," now under the influence of Huysmans. It was very much a departure from Glassco's usual habit, which saw his attention flit from one project to another. In going through some old papers he came across thirty pages of *Philip Eugene*, an unfinished French novel he'd begun in Paris: "it was absolutely worthless stuff, – but carefully written, and I thought it sounded rather well in English translation – not that strange effect a good translation from the French gives, one that's not too free, I mean: that effect of other-worldliness, of being written in a purer language than either French or English, something between the two & straining for both, removed from speech or even thought."[41]

He was inspired to merge *Philip Eugene* with "The Way Back," affixing the title of the abandoned novel to a combined work. The result stimulated, and he set about writing charged with sexual energy:

> The only way I can work on the book is when I am sexually pretty excited, & then tone down the excitement as much as I can later, – an odd way of doing any book! I can really say that it's being written primarily for my own libidinous satisfaction: there isn't an incident in it that isn't peculiarly exciting to me and perhaps me alone: I am even going to have Miss Osborne wearing a black rubber cap that fastens under the chin in a bathing scene, & will try to arrange that Philip is whipped by her while she has it on, – details which can't interest anybody else. And yet, if the book doesn't satisfy *me*, as it sometimes doesn't, it isn't a success: I wonder if it will, when finished.[42]

This vivid scene of fetish and flagellation would not survive the numerous drafts leading to "The Back Helmet." However, the fantasy dwelled within Glassco and was adapted for use some fourteen years later in *Harriet Marwood, Governess*. Glassco recognized that his sexual fantasies were increasingly dominated by rubber and masochistic desires and sought release through *Philip Eugene*. He believed that the act of composition enabled the exploration of these fantasies, while providing relief from his desires to act on them.

Then there was the drink:

> Sometimes, at night, when I've had my second bottle of ale, I feel that it can't help but be a unique & extraordinary & really *good* book, – the kind of thing by which it seems a mediocrity like myself alone can be remembered in future years, – just by virtue of its strangeness, its limited appeal, & all the care I shall have given to it. Then, in the winter morning, I don't dare think of it at all, – for fear of pitching it in the fire.[43]

All his best writing, Glassco believed, was accomplished with bottle at the ready. He considered this dependence a weakness, but not a worry, and was convinced that alcohol provided an essential boost to his confidence as a writer. About "Day in Autumn," an unpublished poem, he wrote: "The thing has often seemed good to me, – but only when I am slightly drunk: then indeed it seems excellent, sometimes beautiful. If only it could be read by people in the same state! It would be only fair, as it was conceived, & the leading lines written, in the condition of drunkenness which began every evening after 11 o'clock this winter: sometimes I got four lines in a night, & then for weeks not a thing. I am afraid I have not gone sober to bed for a whole year."[44]

At midwinter Glassco took account of his verse, counting lines, dividing them by form and polish. He determined that there was enough worthwhile material for a collection, yet couldn't bring himself to submit a manuscript, certain that he would again meet with rejection. Turning to his journal, Glassco wrote that he had no particular desire to be read, nor did he wish to be known in what he termed the "poetry world," rather he merely wanted to see his work set in type.[45] The alternative, self-publishing, he feared would only result in unsold, useless copies.

As Glassco struggled with indecision, his old acquaintances F.R. Scott and A.J.M. Smith were preparing a long-planned anthology for publication. *New Provinces* had been conceived years earlier as a collection of the best poems from *The McGill Fortnightly Review* and *The Canadian Mercury*, but the scope had since broadened. The verse of Scott and Smith was joined by that of fellow Montrealers Leo Kennedy and A.M. Klein, along with Robert Finch and E.J. Pratt, creating what has been described as "the landmark publication that signalled the demise of the old school in Canadian poetry."[46] Through *New Provinces* and the near simultaneous celebration of Smith, Scott, Kennedy, and Klein in W.E. Collin's *The White Savannahs*, the four came to be labelled the "Montreal Group." That Taylor and Glassco were not considered, that their verse had not been included in *New Provinces*, made sense: where in 1929 the pair had been pursued by the fledgling *Mercury*, they had since become absent, forgotten figures of the past decade. Despite determination and sporadic dedication, Glassco's published poetry consisted of the snippets of humorous verse published nine years earlier by *The McGill Daily*. In this respect, he was eclipsed by even so insignificant a figure as Taylor, whose eight-line "The Unknown World" had been featured in the *Fortnightly*.

On a mild February day, as the first signs of spring broke through the winter snow, Glassco took account of his slim output, comparing the rather sedate lifestyle into which he'd fallen against the excitement and heartbreak of Paris and Barcelona:

I find myself thinking that I *must* live more intensely: I seem to have been asleep for the past four years, moving among the shadows. And with this I find I am remembering Peggy [Marguerite Lippe-Rosskam] again: will I never free myself from that woman? I think not: just to picture her in that spring coat of hers & the faun beret, tramping through the streets of Paris, or in that rough white painting smock that I used to find her in, and embrace her as soon as she opened the door, oh it's all a hundred times more real than this house, or the lunch I have just eaten, or my own face in the glass. I think I shall have to see her again ever to be free from her influence: she must be 34 now, and yet I think she will have aged well: that's it, I'm *afraid* of seeing her again, I should be wildly jealous of Roley [Roland Lushington-Hayes] if I saw him even look at her possessively, and I should be miserable. God, hasn't this woman done me enough harm already? Given me the pox, broken what heart I ever had, & almost killed me with t.b.? Well, that's rather theatrical, but literally true.[47]

Now in his twenty-seventh year, Glassco had for some time felt that youth, its splendours, and its adventures, were behind him. He'd first recorded these feelings in the unpublished "Sonnet (On My 24th Birthday)":

Then could I wish to charm the youth who lies
Within me dead, to life again and learn
From his dear lips what secrets made him wise,
What beauty wooed his inward ear, – then turn
  My face to Time's, and make a bold assay
  Of him and all the evils on his way.[48]

When he turned to his journal, attempting to give voice to his depression, Glassco would always write of his youth as a dead thing. He was haunted by images of his young body, since disfigured by surgery and the passage of time:

Last night I had another of the melancholy dreams which I have had for the past week. I dreamed that my operation & disfigurement were all a dream themselves, & that I had as unscarred and perfect a figure as I used to have. I was weeping with joy & looking at myself in the mirror: it was all as beautiful as it had ever been, the same chest & back & belly, all symmetrical & young. I felt almost like dying when I woke at last: it was cruel, after I thought I'd managed to forget all that kind of thing. – Now I know I can never even imitate the lines I had back then, even in a bathing-suit: not only is my chest shrunken & my back flattened, but I have a bit of a paunch just like an old man, which is dreadful: I have tried to get rid of it naturally, by eating lightly all winter & walking two miles a day, but it is still there, & as hideous as ever, though not increased. I suppose, after all, it is the ale that keeps it there, – for I got it in the hospital, & had it even when I was thin & underweight. My face is getting fatter, too, – and my chest sprouting hair, more & more, which is miserable to contemplate –[49]

Invariably, the growth and rebirth of the new spring failed to rejuvenate, serving only to remind Glassco of his physical deterioration. And this particular spring, that of 1936, was made worse by the recognition that the preceding months had been wasted under a cloud of doubt, indecision, stagnation, and revocation. A restless Glassco desired new faces, new countries, and new love. He desperately wanted a relationship with a woman, but considered those he encountered to be "stupid & absurd"; he wondered whether they might not be "a different kind of being" from the girls he'd known in Paris.[50] Would that he could return to that city! Glassco held that a trip abroad might provide something fresh, something of a relief, but detailed plans drawn up with Taylor were always put off or cancelled.

It was under this desire for the new that the two men resumed their search for a suitable farm. Much of the spring, summer, and autumn were spent touring available properties in the Eastern Townships. Their decision to farm in the area made little sense. The areas on which they concentrated were known for their beauty but not for land. Moreover, Glassco's only connection with the area had come during the six nightmarish months of abuse he'd suffered at Bishop's College School.

The lengthy search was an acknowledgement that Taylor's life in letters had come to an end. Glassco blamed himself for his friend's decision to give up writing: "it is my fault that he will not: my sickness, his constant worrying over me, & then taking care of me & my affairs, have all given him no time for much else. I feel guilty about this, but he is perfectly happy about this prospect of managing the farm, happier indeed than he has ever been before."[51]

By winter, they'd settled on a farm on the outskirts of Knowlton, a small village more than one hundred kilometres southeast of Montreal. Glassco was pleased with his purchase, believing Taylor's claims that the property would be a great hedge against inflation. The centrepiece, the feature in which Glassco took the most pride, was an attractive white house, which would serve as his home for the next eight years. Known in the community as Dawes House, it was rechristened "Windermere," in honour of William Wordsworth. Glassco did not exaggerate when describing Windermere – it was a mansion, of a design quite obviously intended to accommodate more than two young bachelors.

Now that he was finally settled in a place of his own and was no longer "flitting about like a moth," Glassco was convinced that he would soon be producing worthwhile work.[52] Windermere would be the place from which he would truly begin making his way as a writer. However, while Glassco may have thought his new home conducive to composition, it offered nothing of the lively literary atmosphere he'd enjoyed at McGill or had witnessed in Paris. Sitting at the wooden desk in his rural Quebec home, he was so very far away from the writers and the cafés of Montparnasse. Knowlton's sole claim in Canadian letters was that the long-dead dialect poet William Henry Drummond, creator of "Leetle Bateese," had for three years practiced medicine in the village.

He continued work on *Philip Eugene* and "The Invitations," a Wordsworthian poem he had begun two years earlier.[53] Although progress on both was slow, for the first time he was untroubled by his pace. Glassco's attentions were taken by the beauty of the Townships and an appreciation of the lifestyle it offered. He purchased a "smart-stepping little horse"[54] and spent a good deal of time exploring the countryside by buggy. The attractions of Montreal, its women, adventure, and enticements, he concluded, were more a creation of the mind. He embarked on a brief love affair with Amélie von Auchemberg, an Austrian, seven years his senior, whom he described as "divinely beautiful."[55]

As planned, Taylor looked after the livestock and oversaw the finances. Glassco stood aside as his friend grew the moneys received through the Rawlings inheritance, and was grateful when, in autumn 1937, Taylor pulled all investments out of the stock market. Glassco's father and brother hadn't shown nearly the same caution and had been "cleaned out."[56] David had lost everything. There was pleasure to be had in the fact that Taylor had demonstrated the greater talent in investing. "What a mess I would have been," wrote Glassco, "had I taken Father as my business guide, as he (F.) was always wanting me to! It's paralysing to think of: that greedy pair, timorous sheep-like & bombastic, represent the worst elements in life as they do the 'most punished' in the markets themselves. Ah well, I wonder how much longer Mother's money can hold out against the inroads of Father's silly gambling!"[57]

The Depression neither touched nor concerned him, and he paid little attention to the growing fascist din emanating from Europe. As Glassco settled into his second year at Windermere, content and comfortable in his life of leisure, he wrote little. In one journal entry, from August 1938, Glassco reports that he had nothing to show for the previous five months. The exaggeration was slight. Where his lack of achievement had once been so troubling, he'd come to consider a life in letters as something of a lark:

> Perhaps I had better give up the pretence of writing? But, I suppose
> it harms no one, & gives me a certain pleasure: whenever I fall short
> in anything, it is so pleasant to turn inwards & say to oneself: "but of
> course your ineptness in this affair doesn't matter: your calling is that
> of poet, novelist, thinker!" Nonsense, nonsense, I was an industrious,
> sensitive boy who has not developed anything but doubts so far![58]

This pleasant lifestyle, which Glassco had so fully embraced, was seldom disturbed; and the few disruptions were far from dramatic. In all the entries written in the two years since his arrival at Windermere, Glassco records just two irritants: *Esquire* rejected an essay on erotica, and his parents had proven themselves poor houseguests. Both of these events took place in August 1938, during what would turn out to be the final days of Glassco's carefree rural life.

... the pattern of paired lives ...[1]

It was while casting about for a housekeeper that Glassco encountered the person he later called the fatal woman of his life. Mary Elizabeth Wilson, whom he called Sappho, was the first applicant. He would one day describe her as a beauty queen who was seeking to escape her past. Young, tall, and energetic, Sappho soon became a third in the lengthiest of Glassco and Taylor's *ménages à trois*. This relationship was witnessed by their hired hand, and it wasn't long before the three became known to locals as "the Dirty Hermits."[2]

Although the precise date of Sappho's arrival at Windermere has been lost, the event, one of the most significant in the lives of her two employers, would have occurred in September 1938. All entries in the Intimate Journal concerning Sappho's early days at the farm were destroyed. The journal resumes partway through an undated entry, composed sometime in 1939:

> I feel I have changed a good deal since "Sappho" came. Just how I can hardly explain: but I have just read this Journal through from almost the beginning, & sense an alteration. Then, I was preoccupied with different things, moods that were trivial perhaps, but not so trivial as the things that have absorbed me since last September – day-by-day jealousies, a hand-to-mouth existence of the emotions and desires. It has been a great relief to get back to this Journal, to take up the thread of my life as it showed itself before, & to suddenly see this last experience of a third in the household as integrated in my own existence – as no more than another phase, another stage, – & to look about blithely again: "where do we go from here?"[3]

Mary Elizabeth Wilson, the woman known as "Sappho," with
Glassco and his horse Peggy, Knowlton, 1940.

Sappho exists nowhere in Glassco's writing outside his Intimate Journal. Her beauty-queen status, the *ménage à trois*, the hired hand, and the "Dirty Hermits" moniker are all elements of a 1975 interview with Kildare Dobbs. Thirty-seven years after her entry into his life, and long after her departure, Glassco had come to romanticize his former housekeeper. Sappho was no longer the disruptive figure depicted in his surviving journal entries; rather she was simply a woman of whom he "became quite fond."[4]

However, while she did share Glassco's bed, providing relief through "the final caress," Sappho's arrival brought a sudden end to the untroubled and relaxed life he'd enjoyed at Windermere Farm. Within him she provoked a bitterness and venom that he made every effort to hide within the pages of his journal. Glassco may have delighted in establishing a triangle, as Leon Edel contended, but this new arrangement was some distance from his ideal.

ROYAL SATIN
1224

Class 'A' Hackney Stallion

BLOOD BAY · BLACK POINTS · BORN 1938

Sire: SUNNY HORACE - 1071 - Reserve Grand Champion, (Best in Canada), Royal Winter Fair, Toronto, 1936. Grand Champion (Best in Province), Sherbrooke Winter Fair, 1934-1940 inclusive. Grand Champion, Ormstown Live Stock Show, 1934-1940 inclusive.

Dam: BRYNHYFRYD ROYAL PEGGY - 1446 -. Out of Brynhyfryd Sure Foot, by Montvic Flash. Royal Breeding to the year 1812, with 2 crosses of Peggy Sure.

TERMS: $5.00 at Service and $7.00 on Birth of Foal

Not responsible for Accidents during Service · Mares sold or exchanged considered as settled

*

TAYLOR & GLASSCO, Knowlton, Que. (Tel. 99)

Taylor and Glassco offering their colt Royal Satin
for stud service, c. 1940.

The situation was in no way made easier when, in late July 1940, Taylor travelled to Montreal and enlisted in the 1st Battalion, Canadian Grenadier Guards. The self-described "Typist" and "Horse Breeder" immediately began training on the city's Île Ste-Hélène for duty overseas.[5] In November, he was sent to Camp Borden, one hundred kilometres north of Toronto.

By leaving Windermere for the war, Taylor had broken his promise; Glassco was obliged to put down his fountain pen, leave his desk, and attend to the tasks once performed by his friend. For the first time, he had to manage his own farm, care for his livestock, and deal with the complexities of his finances. Glassco considered each task drudgery. The relatively slight challenges created by wartime – the refunds, the subsidies, the accompanying paperwork – taxed his abilities. In short, he was very nearly incapable of running his own farm. Added to these irritants was the simple fact that it had been a perpetual money loser, forever eating into his inheritance and restraining investments.

He took on a four-year rural mail contract, delivering letters and parcels on horse-drawn buggy or cutter along a fifteen-mile route. These twice-daily excursions through some of the most scenic parts of the province provided respite from life with Sappho. With Taylor absent, Glassco found Windermere's grand expanse too confining a space to allow escape from her presence. He became convinced that she was secretly reading his journal, and he adopted caution when writing new entries. Denied this vessel in which to discharge his embittered thoughts, Glassco began lashing out; Windermere became a house that rang "with tones of irritation."[6] As he saw it, there was but one remedy: "to become like so many married men, whose demeanour is an admission that they have made a terrible mistake."[7]

And yet, Glassco did not make the terrible mistake of marrying Sappho. Much to the surprise of his parents, who had thought their son would be the groom, it was Taylor who became the housekeeper's husband. On 18 February 1941, a few days into the private's first furlough, the threesome took the short trip into Knowlton, where, at the United Church, Taylor was wed to the twenty-seven-year-old beauty. Neither the groom nor the bride's families were in attendance; the modest ceremony was witnessed only by Glassco and the minister's wife. Glassco described the intimate celebration that followed as a quiet one but allowed that all three had consumed "the last champagne in the district."[8] He never provided so much as a hint as to the motivation behind this further skewing of the triangle; though it is certain that Taylor, who fancied himself a savvy financial manager, would have recognized the benefits to be gained in Sappho becoming the wife of a serviceman.

In later years, Glassco would ignore the fact that Taylor had married Sappho after enlisting. Instead, he told a far better story in which the clergyman's son had joined the army as a means of escaping the marriage. As described, the simple plan involved Taylor returning to France as a soldier, where he would be killed in action.[9] In at least one version of the story, Glassco added the observation that Sappho would have then become eligible for a widow's pension.

As the marriage between Taylor and Sappho was drawing near, Glassco received a letter from Robert McAlmon. Very much a surprise, it was the first contact between the two men in more than a decade. During those intervening years, McAlmon's life had descended from the fairly blessed to wholly unenviable. He had been increasingly adrift, both physically and professionally. Most of the 1930s had been consumed with travel in Europe: London, Nice, Majorca, Barcelona, Madrid, Munich, and Berlin. He'd spent two years crisscrossing the United States, visiting family and friends, half-heartedly looking for work, while zealously seeking a publisher who might be interested in any one of a number of unpublished manuscripts. By the time of his return to France in 1938, McAlmon seemed to have finally come to accept the pronouncement he'd made to Kay Boyle a decade earlier, that the "good days of the Quarter were finished."[10] He settled not in Paris but in Dampierre, a small village one hundred kilometres southeast, and chose to remain there when the Second World War began. When the Germans broke through the Maginot Line, McAlmon fled to the capital, leaving behind his books and manuscripts. Although he was not long in the city and soon returned to Dampierre, nearly everything he owned had been stolen in his absence. In summer 1940 he was interned. Only through the political and financial manoeuvrings of McAlmon's brothers and sisters was he able to return to the United States. That autumn, the figure who had been so vital to expatriate Paris arrived in Phoenix, where he was employed as a salesman of trusses, braces, and prosthetics for the Southwestern Surgical Supply Company, a concern owned by his brothers Bert and George. McAlmon had only begun the job when he was diagnosed with tuberculosis. His letter to Glassco had been written while under treatment at the St John's Sanatorium, San Angelo, Texas.

McAlmon was well along the path biographer Sanford J. Smoller describes as his "Journey to Oblivion."[11] His role as a publisher had long since come to an end, and, though he'd struggled to continue, writing as a career was all but finished. In the preceding eight years, there had been only two new McAlmon titles. The first, a 1937 collection of poems, *Not Alone Lost*, had appeared largely as a result of the urging of William Carlos Williams. Its publisher, New Directions, had been founded the previous year by James Laughlin, the twenty-two-year-old son of a wealthy Pittsburgh steel family. At first, Laughlin followed the example set by the defunct Contact Publishing Company in choosing to publish titles with limited commercial potential. In this respect, McAlmon's book was perhaps more than appropriate; it was poorly received and came to have the distinction of being "the worst selling title in New Directions history."[12]

The second title, *Being Geniuses Together*, was a memoir of his European years. Maimed by a publisher, Secker and Warburg, that was fearful of libel and obscenity suits, it too received harsh criticism. The most repeated charge was that it was a work of vengeance. Ford Madox Ford, Wyndham Lewis, and his ex-wife Bryher, were among those whom McAlmon cast in a poor light. James Joyce, to whom McAlmon had read portions of the manuscript, later dismissed the work as "the office boy's revenge."[13] Perhaps the greater issue was that the book appeared to be so very accurate. McAlmon, a man so often accused of incorporating in his fiction scenes he'd witnessed, with little in the way of embellishment or alteration, had turned to the memoir; and in doing so had produced one of the most accurate literary chronicles of the time. Again, sales were poor; thousands of unsold copies would be destroyed when a German bomb fell on the warehouse in which they were stored.

Having had no contact with others he'd known in Paris, Glassco knew nothing of McAlmon's troubles. Indeed, living a semi-reclusive life in Windermere, subscribing to no literary magazines, long divorced from those old acquaintances of the "literary and intellectual circles at McGill," his knowledge of the goings on in the world of letters was limited to what he termed the "Littery Page" of *The Gazette*.[14] In the past, Taylor's mother had posted copies of *The New York Times Book Review* from her home in West Virginia, but, with her son at Camp Borden, even this small contact with the contemporary world of letters had stopped.

McAlmon's warm letter proved a welcomed distraction. Glassco responded with enthusiasm, cheer, and camaraderie – "So you got TB too!" – betraying nothing of the tensions and struggles at Windermere Farm.[15] Rather, he painted an idyllic scene at odds with reality and in stark contrast with that of St John's Sanatorium: "I'm living with Graeme's fiancee, in a 16-room house with 5 bathrooms and acres of grounds, 70 acres of land, swimming-pool, and show-horse stable, – only the two of us to enjoy the whole place!"[16] Before signing off, Glassco asked for news of "anyone we knew" and included a special request concerning Marguerite Lippe-Rosskam: "If and when you see Peggy R. again, remember me to her, and tell her I still think about our delirious and disastrous episode! Send me more news of her, if possible, won't you?"[17]

As the newlyweds shared what remained of Taylor's two-week furlough, Glassco's thoughts were very much of Marguerite. He received a second letter from McAlmon containing her address in New York but now hesitated in contacting his former lover. Instead, Glassco turned to his old friend confiding: "If I were even half-sure she'd care to hear from me, I'd write; but I fancy she may want to forget about the whole episode. I have an irrepressible and curious hankering to see her again: just why I don't know… However, I guess there is not much likelihood of my doing so, what with being unable to get out of Canada. As I remember, she was never very keen on writing letters."[18] After some weeks of hesitation, Glassco finally wrote to Marguerite, only to find she had moved leaving no forwarding address. He soon became dogged in his pursuit and, with McAlmon's help, was finally able to get a letter through to the woman who had injured him so greatly more than a decade earlier.

Judging from the muted reaction, the response from Marguerite in no way met Glassco's modest expectations. Still, the idea of her remained in his thoughts; he wrote McAlmon that the source of his attraction "was her capacity for being a symbol of what every young man feels he should know. Yet somehow, I never managed to find out just what that is, – and now, alas, it is too late. I keep on having love-affairs (the only good thing about this war is that it has loosened morals a lot), but god help me if I can recapture the emotion I got from Peggy."[19]

He considered inviting Marguerite up from New York for a visit but was apprehensive as to how she would react to the simple lifestyle of Knowlton and the complicated relationships within his home:

> As for the sitivation [sic] here, I hardly know how or whether to explain to her. She may be adaptable, all right, and I know she's a good egg, but she might be putting her neck into something complicated. And she might prefer almost anything rather than a maison a trois, however genial its members might be: it's not much of a partnership to invite anyone into![20]

Any thoughts of meeting in Montreal were dampened by its liquor laws, tightened by the war, and Glassco worried that the city might disappoint someone accustomed to the nightlife of Manhattan and pre-war Montparnasse.

Despite his diminished capacities, McAlmon soon resumed the supportive role he'd played with Glassco and so very many others in Paris. He began sending his friend a steady stream of magazines, including multiple copies of *The New York Times Book Review*, *The New Republic*, *Vice Versa*, *Poetry*, *Diogenes*, *The Partisan Review*, and others. For Glassco, so long an exile from any new writing, who had been immersed in the work of the Decadents, all seemed revelatory. Incredibly, it wasn't until the receipt of McAlmon's first care package that he became aware of Henry Miller – and then only through reviews. He enthusiastically tracked down Miller's work and was initially much impressed by the American's verse. It appeared "so *very* brilliant and fresh, and so dismayingly more striking, more up-to-date and more technically advanced, than the stuff I have been turning out lately."[21] Yet, with further readings Glassco grew dismissive, citing what he recognized as the faults of most transitionalists: "lack of directness and simplicity, sensationalism, pretentiousness, wire-drawness and deadly sophistication."[22]

Such had been Glassco's isolation that he was unaware of *Being Geniuses Together* until the author himself happened to mention the book in a letter.[23] It wasn't until early 1942, when McAlmon lent his personal copy, that Glassco at last read the memoir. "It is really entertaining," he wrote back, "I confess my first reaction to it was to develop a tremendous thirst (there is so much drinking in it) that led me to drink considerably myself, not whisky, just Ca. Beer. So for one reader at least it may be said to be a truly 'Dionysian' (in the Nietzschean sense) work: yes, I got pleasantly boiled. I gather that the parts about Taylor and me were among those cut by the pubs.: how significant it is that the only memorable things one did were more or less unprintable!"[24]

As much as he claimed to enjoy *Being Geniuses Together*, Glassco was greatly disappointed that neither he nor Taylor figured among its grand cast of expatriates. Three years later, disappointment was replaced by irritation when fellow poet Patrick Anderson, unaware of the friendship with McAlmon, asked Glassco whether he'd ever read the book. Glassco immediately wrote his friend: "I do wish you had found space for Graeme and me in that book, now! It would have helped along my individual legend in Can. lit."[25]

While McAlmon's memoirs may not have furthered Glassco's "individual legend," he had been supporting the younger writer in other ways. This went beyond the steady flow of little magazines being mailed from Phoenix. Glassco now had someone other than Taylor with whom to discuss his work; and McAlmon proved a more encouraging judge than the "Typist" and "Horse Breeder." In Taylor's absence, without the constant criticism, Glassco grew to become prolific; this despite his rural mail route and the running of Windermere Farm. He began submitting poems and stories to *The Partisan*

Review, Esquire, The New Yorker, and other American periodicals. Writing McAlmon in March 1942, he described *Philip Eugene* as being within sixteen pages of completion and announced with enthusiasm his next project: "'The History of the Hackney Horse,' – a book for the horseman's library, elegantly bound, top edges gilt, with numerous plates and appendices giving the most famous blood-lines. For sale at $25 a copy: the standard work on the Hackney."[26] This commercial work, which Glassco described somewhat snidely as his "literary monument," would never be written.[27] McAlmon's influence on Glassco would soon be countered by Taylor's return to Windermere.

After nearly two years of regimental courses and training – on Île Ste-Hélène and at camps Borden, Valcartier, and Debert – Taylor had failed to advance in rank. Though recognized as possessing a superior intelligence, he was considered a bit peculiar: "not the usual type of Private soldier," "difficult to place," "of doubtful suitability."[28] An assessment prepared by the battalion's Intelligence Section found his "background questionable": "No mechanical interest. Has driven very little. Used to do a bit of writing; 'Played the stock market and knocked around Europe.'" It was further noted that the private appeared much older than his thirty-six years. As the 1st Battalion, the Canadian Grenadier Guards – now known as the 22nd Canadian Armoured Regiment – prepared for a September deployment to England, the chances that Taylor would be sent overseas seemed increasingly remote; it appeared likely that he would remain in Canada serving in a training capacity.[29] Bitterly disappointed, he began seeking an out.

On 22 June 1942, Taylor's medical status was reduced from "A" to "E." Three days later, he was discharged as "Medically unfit for military services under existing standards." Pleased as he was by his friend's return to Windermere, Glassco bore great resentment toward the military for what he perceived as two years of Taylor's life wasted. There was selfishness, as well. He had hard feelings about the time and energy spent in maintaining a functioning farm. Without Taylor present to oversee the investments, Glassco's wealth had diminished. It was a great relief to have Taylor resume the management of the farm and capital:

> It is really more of a feeling of security I have, being with him again, – the kind of feeling young children have when they are with their parents: I no longer have the responsibility of making decisions of a major kind. When I made such decisions, indeed, – (as I was obliged

to do when he was away), it was under the spur of unimportant things, & the decisions were mainly wrong. This relief from responsibility is one of the components of my happiness; but there are others, – & the most important seems to be the freedom I now feel I have to indulge in childish things again, – moods, sulks, & pleasures: in other words, I feel free to behave, now & then, like the spoiled child I have always been.[30]

Relieved of his adult responsibilities, Glassco allowed himself to sink back into his "moods" and his "sulks." Yet it wasn't a full return to the life he had known before Taylor's stint as a guardsman; the "pleasures" were not revisited. Less than two months after Taylor's discharge, another story having been rejected, Glassco felt "finished, completely."[31]

Over thirteen years had passed since the "Extract from an Autobiography" had appeared in *This Quarter*. His last published work, it remained the only writing for which he had ever received payment. Taylor had long since given up the notion of earning money as a writer, and Glassco now wondered whether it might not be time to similarly let go of the dream. His only champion was a sickly writer who was stuck in Arizona, selling surgical garments for his brothers. "Reinvention" is not the sort of word Glassco would have used, but in September 1942 he very much wanted to become a different person. He was determined to demonstrate *some* capacity to do *something*: "I want to dramatize myself, as if that would bring me to life again, even if only for a week, a day, an hour, as a *different* being: if I could step out of the shoes of this faineant dilettante, this failure, this fellow who is working hard, losing money, looks, appearances, aplomb & capacity for emotional experience in the most insidious way, – & become a body with a purpose."[32]

Mindful of Taylor's years of frustration in the army, he decided to join the Royal Canadian Air Force. The previous year Glassco had learned that they were looking to train radiolocators; he believed that his education and typing skills might make him an acceptable candidate for the posting. He was wrong. A trip to Montreal in early September, followed by a meeting with a lieutenant named Stevenson, only brought further rejection. The Air Force had no interest in a frail, one-lunged man with a history of tuberculosis. Glassco's spirits descended even lower but were soon lifted in an unusual manner: an overheard conversation in which two villagers admired his talent as a reins man. He took pride in the recognition:

Is this my only title to excellence? Well, perhaps it is. But I do like driving – that ecstatic feeling of one-ness with a fiery horse (I don't mind how vicious they are), the unison and mastery felt through the reins, the sense of guiding & displaying something more beautiful than I am. And old Peggy *is* beautiful – she's 22, but still like a bullet, a spring, a bow under my hands. I know her body, her nerves, as well as my own. Well, I should, after driving her for five years. And she returns no tedious female affection – she still tries to kick me every time I hitch her – does she mean it, though – she always misses by a 1/4-inch. But just to see that hind-leg lash out so fast you can't see it – a thing of beauty: perhaps I can make some kind of poetry out of that some day.[33]

In fact, this curiously named horse, which he used on his deliveries for the post office, had already played a role in the composition of verse. "The Rural Mail" was a poem of the war, in which loss and carnage join the images of rural beauty, decline, and ruin that would become so familiar in Glassco's work:

These are the green paths trodden by patience.
I hang on the valley's lip, a bird's eye viewing
All that opposes to makers and masters of nations
Only its fierce mistrust of the word, –
To the smashed records for gobbling and spewing,
Cows that exist in a slow-motion world.

For here is man on man's estate of nature,
Farmer on farm, the savage civilised
Into the image of his God the weather –
Only another anarchist, foiled highflyer
Whose years have grown as a minute in his eyes,
Whose grin reveals a vision of barbed wire:

Here birth evokes pleasure and a reflective pity,
Marriage or mating, much of the voyeur,
Sickness, an interest and some hope of booty,
And death strikes like an oddly barked command,

Confounding with its *Easy*, its *As you were*,
His stiff-kneed generation unused to bend.[34]

Giving up on the United States and their literary journals and "shiny-paper magazines," Glassco found a place for his poem in *The Canadian Forum*.[35] When it finally appeared, in the September 1943 issue, "The Rural Mail" marked his first published verse since the "Euphorian" dabblings of his student days. The poet took no delight in his accomplishment, feeling that, at age thirty-three, it was too little, too late. Still, the long silence that had followed "Extract from an Autobiography" had been broken; and within a year he would return to print with the first excerpts of *Philip Eugene*.

By March 1943, Glassco had finished the first draft of his erotic novella; but as he set about revising the manuscript interest waned and work slowed. Some impetus was drawn from a female correspondent in Montreal, likely met through a "Personals" column, who expressed interest in the project. She was, he wrote, "an odd sort of person, rather sentimental, extremely sensitive, diffident & delicate, – but very sympathetic (& wishes to become more so) & very anxious for a Platonic friendship to brighten what appears to be a rather dull life: I know nothing whatever about her, what she looks like, how old she is (except that it's about my own age) – and do not wish to. All I want for her is to exhibitionise [*sic*] in front of for about a month, until my book is done. Then we'll see about a meeting & perhaps a love-affair. My God I need a love-affair, in the worst way!"[36]

Rarely one for self-discipline, Glassco soon broke the pact he'd made with himself. Within weeks he reported that he'd travelled to Montreal, met his correspondent, and was back at Windermere reflecting on an affair he described as "one of the shortest I have ever had."[37] The relationship had ended, and with it the drive to complete the novella.

As summer 1943 drew to a close, Glassco decided to enter the manuscript in the Longmans, Green and Company Canadian Book Contest, which offered as a first prize publication accompanied by a $1,000 advance. While it might have seemed a peculiar choice of publisher, one unlikely to be interested in a short novel of masochism written under the influence of Huysmans, the idea had nothing to do with thoughts of winning; what Glassco wanted was the imposition of a deadline with which he could work.[38] And yet, as he prepared the second draft of *Philip Eugene*, he dared to consider potential sales: "... there must be many people, at least 5 or 10 thousand, who are interested, either personally-pornographically or academically, in the subject of masochism, & who, if the book were advertised in the right way, would buy it for a couple of dollars. – Oh, if only I had the incentive of some assurance that the book might pay something – even only a few hundred dollars, how I would work on it!"[39]

Support came from an unexpected source: "What has given me the greatest encouragement in the past ten years (yes, all of that), occurred yesterday, – when I discovered just how much it would mean to Graeme if a book of mine were to be successful. What a wonderful surprise this has been! and what an incentive to finish Philip, *properly & at once*! I had really never known, never imagined, that for the past seven or eight years he had been really depending on me to turn out something, after all, – but would say nothing, never urge me to work ..."[40] Within this recognition was an attempt to explain, justify, and accept the harsh judgement brought down by Taylor on past writing:

> ... the coldness & brusqueness of his criticism of what I did show him was, I see now, only the measure of his disappointment with work which he saw, at once, was feeble, trivial & unacceptable, and which was only a reminder, a confirmation of what he always suspected & yet hoped against hope was not true, – that I had no talent at all. I see also that his standards, where I am concerned, have taken the only character possible – that of the *success* of the work: they are no Philistine standards for all that: – our respective standards are such poles apart (we naturally take opposite positions in any matter of taste, – which is, as I have found out, the most stimulating situation possible!) that he could never, as he must feel, have a natural, unforced admiration for anything I wrote: the *tone* would be antipathetic. Therefore he is left with my work's acceptance by, or acceptability to, the public, as the only criterion of my success that is possible in his eyes, – and I see now just how much he is anxious that should be. So I must only *succeed*: it really doesn't matter in what way ... When people love each other, any form of success, however arrived at, or however concerned merely with temporal, transitory things, will justify their pride in the lover's qualities ... the beloved (a dreadful word!) must furnish constant proof of his lovability by the standards of the world, must justify the lover's choice endlessly, assure him he has not made a mistake as

to the particular basket into which he has put all his eggs, – merely be remaining desirable or valuable to others, either sexually, or artistically, or politically, & so forth.[41]

With Taylor's attention spurring him on, Glassco completed his revisions, including a new title, the Huysmans-inspired *En Arrière*.[42] By mid-November, a full month-an-a-half before deadline, the polished manuscript of his "everlastingly half-done" novella had been sent for consideration to the Toronto offices of Longmans, Green.[43]

Glassco should not have expected to win; it is an indication of his distance from the literary world that he came to believe it a remote possibility that a thirty-thousand-word story of sadism, masochism, and fetishism would emerge the victor of the Longmans, Green competition. The verdict – "unsuitable" – came within a month, just after the rejection of four poems submitted to *The Canadian Forum*. Again, Glassco had failed to prove himself to Taylor, and the swiftness and clarity of his failure brought him to tears. Two days after his thirty-fourth birthday, he wrote: "My whole reaction to life today is summed up in a sigh as deep as a drunkard's before he vomits. Are things going on like this forever & ever? Never a shred of success, never a pat on the back, never a kind word."[44]

He turned away from Taylor's disappointment and criticisms, hoping for guidance from his only supporter, McAlmon. Having receiving a lukewarm response to his query letter to Random House, a discouraging response from New Directions, and a blunt rejection from Longmans, Green, Glassco sought advice on submissions and agents. He began to recognize that *En Arrière* might never find a publisher and considered bringing out the book himself. McAlmon responded with characteristic generosity, offering the use of the Contact Editions imprint. It was an option Glassco took seriously. He imagined publishing the work as a paperback; a cover image done in the style of Aubrey Beardsley, the great English draughtsman, would capture something of the spirit of the book. There was no concern over recovering the costs of printing and production. "Do you know," Glassco wrote McAlmon, "the world is positively teaming with masochists, or at least Montreal is. Not that this book is smutty, far from it, but it's all about masochism (and if I do say it, it's a lot better than Masoch himself's Venus in Furs) and it shouldn't have to be 'discovered' by the addicts, who are a very timid lot anyway."[45]

It is entirely possible that Glassco would have carried through on these plans for *En Arrière*, had he not begun to make contact, however limited, with the literary community of Montreal. His entry point was *First Statement*, a little magazine begun in 1942 by poet John Sutherland. It was not the obvious choice. Montreal's other literary journal, the rival *Preview*, had F.R. Scott on its editorial board – and, so, a link with *The McGill Fortnightly Review*. Explanation may be found in Sutherland's purchase of a printing press and his ambitions to become a book publisher. Indeed, Glassco first wrote the editor asking whether *First Statement* would consider publishing *En Arrière* as a novella. The query was premature; Sutherland was not yet ready to branch out. However, he was interested in the erotic work and asked Glassco whether he might not consider submitting excerpts for publication in *First Statement* instead. Though the response was not as hoped, Glassco was eager for some validation, something to show for the years spent on *En Arrière*. All too aware of the perverse elements of the work, he sent the magazine a number of selections, described to McAlmon as the "mildest parts of the whole book."[46] Again, Sutherland's response was not as Glassco had hoped:

> This is just a hurried note to ask if you would object to our undertaking further revision of the selections from your novel. It is very good prose – as good as any writing that we have received – but Mr A.M. Klein has given us his legal opinion that it would not pass the censor. As much as we regret it therefore, we could not publish the selections in their present form and take the risk of losing the magazine.[47]

The situation was out of the ordinary, perhaps unique in Canadian letters: an instance of one Montreal poet, a lawyer, providing a legal opinion on the work of another. Whether the two had ever met is unknown, however it is almost certain that the lawyer's name meant something to Glassco. Their student days at McGill had overlapped, and both had known the names behind the *Fortnightly*. In fact, Klein had very nearly joined Glassco and Taylor as a contributor, but was rejected over his refusal to replace the word "soul" in a poetry submission. The setback had little or no effect on his progress as a poet. By the time he was asked to consider *En Arrière*, Klein had been published widely and was the only member of the *Preview* and *First Statement* groups to have his own collection of verse.

Ultimately, Sutherland chose to ignore Klein's legal counsel in the belief that a periodical with a readership of three hundred was unlikely to attract attention from the censors. The first excerpt, "Frogmore's Folly," published in the August 1944 issue, was accompanied by a deceptive, confusing note: "This is the first of several extracts from the author's own translation of the unpublished novel *Frogmore en arriere* [*sic*], which was written from 1935 to 1938."[48]

Far from titillating, "Frogmore's Folly" is little more than a dry examination of masochism in literature, written by one who assumes that the reader would be familiar with the Seigneur de Brantôme, Béroalde de Verville, and titles such *Madame Birchini's Dance*. Its six pages held no whips, no birches, no switches, and no scenes of flesh, fetish, and flagellation.

Two similar excerpts, "Frogmore and the Fatal Woman" and "Frogmore's Fancy," featured in the following issues. At the centre of each is Frogmore, the most recent incarnation of Philip Eugene, the character first formed during Glassco's years in Paris. The three excerpts published in *First Statement* featured the character's meditations, interests, and obsessions, but not his actions. Sutherland recognized as much, referencing them as "the 'intellectual' sections."[49] What was needed, he felt, was "the story itself to make them come alive."[50]

Yet, despite the limitations, Glassco had attracted some attention; if not for his work, then for his history. In summer 1944, Sutherland, his wife Audrey, and his sister Betty drove out to Windermere. Accompanying them was Irving Layton, Betty's boyfriend. To Layton, Glassco appeared as a polite, courteous gentleman from another age. He and Taylor put the four up for the evening and, as Layton recalled, "served us exquisite meals and didn't in any way let us know what intrusive bastards we were."[51]

"Ever the gentleman," "courtly," and "extremely gracious" – this was a new role for Glassco.[52] Where he'd once stood out as the youngster at any literary gathering, he found himself in the company of a more youthful crowd – Sutherland was ten years his junior; his wife and sister were younger still. Only Layton approached Glassco in age, but his health, energy, and enthusiasm, placed him firmly within the *First Statement* group, representatives of a magazine that had billed itself as "A Magazine for Young Canadian Writers." Layton saw Glassco as a link to the Paris of the 1920s, which he himself had been too young to experience: "I didn't know any of his work at the time, but someone told me he had known Gertrude Stein and Hemingway,

Fitzgerald, and Picasso. I wanted to know the man who had known them."[53] Despite Layton's intention, he never really got to know Glassco. There was little contact between the two until the early 1960s, and even then it was quite limited. When he finally read Glassco's verse, Layton was disappointed, lumping him in with Scott, A.J.M. Smith, E.J. Pratt, and P.K. Page as poets who "for all their devotion to fine writing, were as remote from what was painful and nightmarishly real in the brutal twentieth century as the planet Earth is from Saturn."[54]

The Knowlton trip very nearly coincided with Sutherland's decision that the time was right for *First Statement* to begin publishing books. While at Windermere, he suggested that the magazine, as First Statement Press, would be interested in bringing out *En Arrière*. Caution and hesitation were gone; it seemed to Glassco that the very same elements that had led the editor to seek legal opinion were now being embraced. Sutherland was "hoping for a success de scandale."[55] However, upon looking over the manuscript, he once again backed away: "after reading the whole book I am concerned about the censorship business. If we take Klein's word that the *First Statement* sections are censorable, then the actual portrayals of masochism are going to be doubly so. If we publicized the book – and it ought to be publicized if it were brought out at all – I think we would be headed for trouble. Advertisements and reviews would secure a larger audience for the novel than the extracts in *First Statement* had, and I'm afraid that it would be taking too great a risk."[56]

Coming at the end of the year, Sutherland's about-face infuriated Glassco. He felt that six months had been wasted in courting the magazine, when he could have been focusing elsewhere. His efforts had gone beyond mere hospitality; at Sutherland's request he'd solicited poems from McAlmon, but these had not been used.[57] Glassco's mood was not enlivened when the very next month First Statement Press published its first book: *Here and Now*, by Irving Layton. The poet's debut collection was soon followed by Patrick Anderson's *A Tent for April* and Miriam Waddington's *Green World*.

The rejection of *En Arrière* not only signalled the end of Sutherland and Glassco's relationship, it set in motion the latter's retreat from the small foray he had made into Montreal's literary world. He wrote only one more piece for *First Statement*; a negative review of Montrealer Gwethelyn Graham's international bestseller *Earth and High Heaven*. Included in the April-May 1945 issue, it shared space with a Ralph Gustafson essay, Irving Layton's review of A.M. Klein's *Poems*, and what was presented as a lengthy short story by Wingate Taylor entitled "The Horse-Stall." Wingate Taylor was Graeme Taylor; and the story was actually the introduction of his unfinished novel *Brazenhead*.[58] Glassco had acted as an intermediary in making the submission to the magazine. He reprised his role with a second submission, a story that had the misfortune to land in a limbo created after former rivals *First Statement* and *Preview* merged to form *Northern Review*. Months later, when Taylor's work was finally considered, the new editorial board became deadlocked. Ultimately, the story was rejected; Taylor would never again be published.

Glassco all but gave up on Sutherland and was unimpressed by the new little magazine. He wrote McAlmon that *Northern Review* was "just as deathly dull as the title suggests."[59] Five years would elapse before Glassco again submitted something to its pages. The work he chose, "The Pigtail Man," was what he considered to be his very best short story. Sutherland's rejection set off a short exchange that moved quickly from friendly and good-natured to bitter and defensive. Glassco responded with a long, combative letter in which he upheld his work while criticizing Sutherland for having published "two rubbishy stories," Edward McCourt's "The Locked Door" and Desmond Pacey's "The Picnic." Of the latter, Glassco asked the editor: "don't you think it should be printed in brochure form and distributed during next Drive-Safely week? ... Yes, I *am* sore about the Pigtail Man being rejected when you publish stories like those!"[60]

Sutherland replied the very next day, defending the decision not to publish "The Pigtail Man." "I have always admired other work of yours which I have seen," he wrote, in what would be the last piece of correspondence between the two men, "and I would be glad to see another story at any time."[61] But for Glassco, any further submissions were out of the question; he no longer had time for Sutherland and his little magazines.

No money had come from the contributions to *First Statement*; payment had consisted of three complimentary one-year subscriptions. However, in finally turning to the magazine in submitting his Frogmore pieces, Glassco had not abandoned the goal of earning a living through his writing. In 1945, he went so far as to collaborate with Taylor on a "best-seller" that they submitted to Simon and Schuster – or so he claimed in a letter to McAlmon.[62]

As he continued his pursuit of commercial success, Glassco could not help but look with envy at the career of Kay Boyle. Well over a decade had passed since they'd last seen each other and nearly every one of those years had seen the publication of at least one new Kay Boyle title. Her short stories had appeared frequently in *The Saturday Evening Post*, *Harper's Bazaar*, and other well-paying US magazines – twelve had been published in *The New Yorker* alone. She'd twice received the O. Henry Award. Glassco's praise for his old lover was tempered. "The next time you write her," he told McAlmon, "give her my congratulations. God knows she has worked hard enough for her success, and I always admired her ambition, just as one admires the sheer strength of a steam-shovel."[63]

It could in no way be considered a cruel comment; Boyle had turned increasingly toward the commercial. In March 1943, at the very time Glassco was comparing his admiration for Boyle to that felt for a crude machine, the US writer was in the process of crafting a novel with input and direction from *The Saturday Evening Post*. A story of the French resistance, *Avalanche* ran in serial form that autumn and raised Boyle's success in the marketplace to an enviable level. Early the following year, it became a bestseller when published by Simon and Schuster. The Armed Forces bought 250,000 copies, it was dramatized for the radio, and it was optioned by Hollywood. *Avalanche* was the precise measure of success to which Glassco aspired, though his envy was tempered by savage reaction by the critics. Edmund Wilson accused his old lover of having crafted a work "with an eye to the demands of Hollywood,"[64] while the reviewer for *Time* wrote, "Kay Boyle has sold the Left Bank down the river."[65]

Edwin Lanham, a far less intimate acquaintance from Glassco's Montparnassian days, had made an even more aggressive incursion into the area of commercial fiction. A Texan, the grandson of a governor, Lanham had arrived in Paris in the late 1920s, ostensibly to study art. He soon befriended McAlmon, who would claim to have given rise to the younger man's career as a writer. As Glassco and Boyle were completing *Relations and Complications* for the Dayang Muda, Lanham had been at work on a novel inspired by his experiences as a teenage runaway working on a freighter during an eight-month trip around the world. When finished, he presented McAlmon with a manuscript entitled *As We Sailed down the Bay*, which was soon rechristened *Sailors Don't Care*. Lanham and McAlmon had contradictory stories as to the origins of the title – each credited the other. It is likely that "*Sailors Don't Care*" originated with Glassco, who had picked up the line from a ribald song he'd been taught by James Miller, the captain of the *Canadian Traveller*.[66]

A decent first novel, *Sailor's Don't Care* was published in early 1929 under the Contact Editions imprint, with printing costs paid for in part by the author. Its appearance on the shelves of Shakespeare and Company marked the end of McAlmon as a publisher.[67] That same year, Lanham met and married Kay Boyle's sister, Joan, a designer for the London edition of *Vogue*. After the stock-market crash, the couple became part of the American exodus from Paris. In the early months of 1930 they arrived in New York, where Lanham began years of struggle in an attempt to make a living as a journalist and novelist.[68]

With Kay Boyle, Marguerite Lippe-Rosskam, and Hilaire Hiler, Lanham was among those after whom Glassco asked most frequently in his letters to McAlmon. One query brought an unexpected response. In relating the stumbling progress of their old friend's career, McAlmon asserted that Lanham's 1937 novel, *Banner at Daybreak*, included a character composed of himself, Glassco, Hiler, and Hart Crane.[69]

Set between 1933 and 1935, the story follows the trials of Clay Hall, an autobiographical character, the grandson of a Texas senator, who is attempting to establish himself as a painter in Montparnasse. Hall is part of a circle of American expatriates, the centre of which is held by Guy Hart, a "somewhat homosexual" poet of independent means.[70] Like McAlmon, who had once employed Guy Urquhart as a *nom de plume*, Hart is a son of Kansas and holds fond memories of time spent in Greenwich Village. By turns churlish, sneering, and petulant, like his model he is given to performing a "Chinese opera" when drunk.[71]

As the Great Depression deepens and day-to-day life in Paris becomes beyond his reach, Hall and his wife return to the United States, where they settle in New York. Hart follows some time later, by way of Barcelona, and ends up in a run-down room on Christopher Street. He attempts to get a job through the Works Progress Administration, as had McAlmon, but is unsuccessful. When they meet for the last time, Hart is in a poor state, lying in bed drinking cheap whisky. He makes a half-hearted pass at Hall, which the latter barely notices. After his friend leaves, a drunken Hart begins to dwell on a recent run-in with the police, the result from an attempt he'd made at picking up a boy in a Turkish bath. Hart turns on all the gas jets in his room, half-playing with the idea of suicide, and then falls asleep. He awakens barely able to breathe and is making his way to the stove when there is an explosion and he is killed.

McAlmon couldn't help but recognize himself in Hart and no doubt saw Hilaire Hiler in the sturdy character's pudgy face and heavy lidded eyes. While one is left to speculate as to the link McAlmon drew between Guy Hart and Hart Crane, the similarity in names cannot be ignored. It may be that McAlmon also recognized that the character shared the US poet's attraction to sailors. Certain events may have been inspired by what Lanham knew of Crane's life – his suicide, also assisted by whisky, being the most obvious. However, what McAlmon saw of Glassco in Hart is a mystery; the character shares nothing of his personality, history, and habits. Although it is likely that he read the book – he once owned a copy – any record of Glassco's thoughts on the matter is limited to a fleeting dismissal he included in a letter to McAlmon: "Apropos of Ed's composite book made up of me, you, Hiler & Hart Crane, the only end possible *was* a gas blow-up suicide. Anyone who was that kind of composite would have to blow himself up anyway: a case of spontaneous combustion. But how typical of Ed to make an explosion a solution to anything."[72]

Years after having been smarted by Morley Callaghan's use of him as a model for Johnny Hill in "Now That April's Here," Glassco was now confronted by yet another character that he'd served to inspire. A third would soon appear – from the most likely of sources.

In spring 1947, McAlmon wrote offering to send north the manuscript of his unpublished *The Nightinghouls of Paris*, the novel in which characters modelled on Glassco and Taylor figure prominently. Whether Glassco knew this when accepting the offer is unknown; any description the author might have provided, any caution he may have given, has been lost; McAlmon's letter was almost certainly destroyed by its recipient. Yet, whatever he'd been led to expect, the younger writer was particularly eager to read the novel.

Glassco received a carbon copy in June, and would have completed no more than five pages before encountering Sudge Galbraith. The familiarity of the young, weak-chinned, twittering Montrealer must have extended beyond mere self-recognition; Glassco had to have also recognized something of Callaghan's Johnny Hill, the snickering boy with the "rather chinless faun's head."[73] However, McAlmon had not been influenced by "Now That April's Here," nor was it true that he and Callaghan held contrasting views about Glassco and Taylor, an assertion put forth by the Toronto writer. The truth was that McAlmon had a superior understanding and was more familiar with his models, and so was able to better capture and mine further their persons and histories. The novel contained no insinuations and vagaries concerning the true nature of the relationship between Glassco and Taylor. In *The Nightinghouls of Paris*, the *ménage à trois* is something in which they frequently engage; in fact this triangle is shown to be essential to their relationship. As he is getting to know Kit O'Malley, the autobiographical narrator, Ross, the Taylor character, describes one such encounter:

"... I took her first, but just played around till Sudge got excited and wanted me to hurry."

It was probably always "just playing around" with girls they picked up, for Ross, I suspected. Both boys struck me as strange little animals, with few emotions or reactions generally associated with people, but Sudge was nearer that fanciful state "normal" which persists in the mind and language. Whatever they did had not marred the clear look of innocence which both possessed.[74]

The liberties McAlmon had taken in exposing the lives of his models extended to their respective families. He'd incorporated at least one Glassco family secret: that of a lengthy affair that had taken place between Beatrice and a sea captain. While Sudge's mother carries on a similar relationship, her husband, a "secretary-treasurer of a university and director of various boards," is portrayed as having extramarital relations with his secretary.[75] Ross, who dislikes Sudge's parents and considers them "so thick-witted they don't know they are alive," readily shares his contempt with O'Malley.[76] Mr Galbraith, he reveals, "gets graft money off his job and directorships" and owes his success in the stock market to his wife's family, who place him "on the inside of investments."[77] Sudge's siblings are not spared Ross's gossip. He recounts how Pinky, the eldest of the two Galbraith sons, was forced to marry after his girlfriend's parents discovered that he'd been sleeping with their daughter. Sudge's sister is described as a "nasty five-year-old" – the precise age of Glassco's sister during the time in which the novel takes place.[78] Of Sudge himself, Ross is only complimentary, though he does reveal to O'Malley that his friend suffers from *dementia praecox* – schizophrenia – a condition that is also said to be present in the Campion family.

Clearly, there was enough in *The Nightinghouls of Paris* to leave Glassco deeply disturbed. Its publication would have been embarrassing, if not disastrous, for himself and his family. He returned the carbon without comment, bringing his nineteen-year friendship with McAlmon to an abrupt end. It was a rash decision; one Glassco would come to regret. In the mid-1960s, thoughts turned to his former friend's unpublished novel and the effect it had had on their relationship. "These old things seem mistaken and rather saddening now," he would write. "But the existence of this book still troubles me."[79]

Glassco needn't have worried about the novel's appearance: in 1947, McAlmon's career as a writer was already over. He would not live to see another title published. Indeed, although he could not have known it, McAlmon had already seen his final appearance in print: a brief reminiscence of William Carlos Williams, published in the October 1946 issue of a little magazine called *The Briarcliff Quarterly*. The once-celebrated writer and publisher was forced to devote what energy he could muster to fitting trusses and prosthetics in Phoenix and El Paso. By 1951, McAlmon's health had declined to a point where he could no longer work. With the assistance of his family, he purchased a modest home in Desert Hot Springs, California. The final years were spent in a sad isolation that was alleviated only occasionally by visits from his sisters, Edward Dahlberg, and Kenneth Rexroth.

McAlmon died of pneumonia on 2 February 1956. It wasn't until 2007, a full sixty years after it had so upset Glassco, that *The Nightinghouls of Paris* finally saw print.

The friendship with McAlmon might have endured *The Nightinghouls of Paris* had the manuscript not arrived at a time when Glassco was suffering tremendous mental turmoil. He worried that he was going mad. For months there had been a recurrent "attack of the horrors":[80] "It is so hard to describe: all one can say is that what attacks one on these occasions is pure fear, – not fear of anything or anyone, just the naked primal fear that one must have been born with."[81] Glassco's attacks would manifest themselves in dizziness, nausea, spasmodic twitching, uncontrollable sobbing. He attempted to capture something of the horror in a lost poem entitled "Windmill Point" but found it impossible.

No help was sought, and, uncharacteristically, he provided no explanation as to what might be triggering his attacks in his Intimate Journal.

However, it cannot be ignored that tensions at Windermere had been building for several years, with no real relief. Glassco's *ménage à trois* with Taylor
and Sappho had long ago ended. Shut out, he could only look at their relationship as an outsider. Yet even as early as March 1943, nine months after
Taylor had returned from service, Glassco had begun to question the marriage: "… I almost think it was a mistake, – though I don't know that he does
– except at isolated, infrequent moments such as everyone has. He is not
one to do things he is likely to regret *constantly*, – and, no, it is incredible to
think his marriage was a mistake."[82]

Sappho spent a good part of 1944 working at a well-paying "fashion job"
in New York.[83] After her return, she began leaving Windermere for extended
periods and eventually took up permanent residency in Montreal. It wasn't
long before Taylor began receiving letters from a lawyer she'd hired. The two
men were distressed, fearing Sappho's intentions, until they realized that her
sole demand was a monthly allowance of $60 so that she might live in a
Montreal hostel for working women.

This insight did not prevent Glassco from destroying fifteen pages of the
Intimate Journal for fear that it might be used in blackmail or as part of
some sort of legal action. Afterward, in a very long entry, Glassco reflected
on what he feared was the end of the complicated relationship:

Why then, does that fool's paradise, the thought of it, afflict me so?
Yes, I know that although it was a fool's paradise for those 2 or 3
"good" years with Sappho, it *was* a paradise. How happy we all were
then! Yes, even she: *that* wasn't counterfeit, at least, – or at least be
happy was an integral part of the plan she formed the moment she
entered the house. There will never be springs like that one again,
never breakfasts, drives, bathes, projects & picnics, like those. And
never a woman like that again, either! After her, any others look pale
– they just haven't got that beautiful animality, that child-like perfection, that impression of a goddess – *dea certe* – come down to earth
to mix for a while with mortals. – Yes, if ever one were to meet with
that type again, it would be suspect, – and I also doubt whether one
would be able to work up the interest – the shade of Sappho would
come between.[84]

Glassco quickly came to the conclusion that he and Taylor had been played. Suspicions and snobbery tainted his view and led him to the absurd belief that since the marriage Sappho had been following an intricate, devious plan, all so that she might one day live an independent life working as a sales person in a Montreal shop. Glassco wrote as though it were he, not Taylor, who was the injured husband. It was simply beyond comprehension that Sappho would prefer "living in a Hostel for *Single* Working Girls, – when her husband has a place like this, & a life like this, to offer her?"[85] So mystified was he by her actions that Glassco became convinced Sappho's absence and threats were designed as elements of a clever effort to make herself appear more interesting and alluring.

Her departure had coincided with the sale of Windermere Farm. In addition to the house and substantial property, the purchaser bought nearly all the livestock and equipment. The sale brought some relief from the accumulating stress. Glassco was extremely pleased, convinced that he and Taylor had played the postwar boom to excellent advantage. Flush with cash, Glassco bought Jamaica Farm, eleven kilometres to the north, just outside the village in Foster. Though the new home was smaller than Windermere, its acreage was considerably larger. Together the two men set about building a half-mile racetrack and practice-ring for their horses.

With the new house came a new housekeeper. This time, however, things were less likely to become as complicated as they'd been with Sappho. "Her name is Henry," Glassco wrote, "and we think she is crazy, but a very good cook and she does all the ordering and so on. She has an illegitimate child about a year old, and there seems to be another one due in about three months. Nature is a curious thing, so persistent and successful. To look at Henry (Lon Chaney in the Hunchback of N. Dame is the closest description I can give) you'd think it was a sheer impossibility for a man to rise to the occasion; but someone must have, perhaps *two*."[86]

Jamaica Farm brought about a rejuvenation of sorts. Over the next year he placed six poems in *The Canadian Forum*, including "Brummell at Calais," ostensibly a eulogy to the long-deceased English dandy.

However, Henry was soon gone, and Glassco was unable to find a replacement. He was forced to take over the housekeeping duties while Taylor worked the farm. Once again, writing was neglected. It was a situation that Glassco found intolerable. In May 1947 he placed an advertisement for a new housekeeper in *The Montreal Star*. The only acceptable applicant, a young Montreal woman named Audrey, enclosed a photograph with her response. After meeting with her, Glassco wrote that she "quite won our hearts – being the real crazy type we like so much."[87] He was then understandably despondent when, having accepted the position, Audrey failed to show. Days were spent at the window, watching for taxis that might be carrying the new housekeeper from the train station. He imagined phone conversations and devoted the longest of all his journal entries to a detailed account of the episode. Ultimately, he came to believe that, like Sappho, the prospective housekeeper had been toying with him and Taylor, finding amusement in their reactions. Glassco considered himself a victim of "a female game which has been played to give the player a little confidence, an opportunity to dangle herself temptingly, saying 'would you like it, eh?' & then to whip off unscathed."[88] His desperation was prompted by more than a simple desire to escape housework:

> The reason for our attaching such importance to the presence of such a woman in the house is, of course, simply because we realise that without a woman beside us we are lost, the summer is lost, life is not worth living, we might just as well blow our brains out. Horses no longer matter, nor literature, nor fame, nor (really) money: the only thing that can give significance to life is a crazy woman like this, – and the desperate part of the situation is, having been brought *so close* to the solution, to the woman, to happiness, to a deferment of the collapse that man must undergo some time, and then missing it: it is simply too cruel.[89]

But many years would pass before a new woman entered the house; there would be no more complicated relationships of the type he and Taylor had shared in the past. For the next nine years the companions would live alone on their Quebec farm. In late middle age, Glassco would record an observation in his Commonplace Book: "On the *ménage à trois*. The youthful dreams of sexual paradise and the beauty of sharing. Alas, nature abhors a triangle."[90]

Last night such a sweet, sad dream …[1]

The year 1948 began very badly. Seven days into the New Year Taylor received a writ delivered on Sappho's behalf. The former housekeeper's blackmail campaign had escalated and, according to Glassco, now encompassed "vile charges, perjury, another Jewish lawyer, appearances in court. The whole bag of tricks!"[2] In response, he performed more surgery on the Intimate Journal, this time using a razor blade to excise selected passages. The destruction prompted by the writ extended to photographs and old letters that Glassco had received from Adrienne Dostre de Bellot and a woman whom he identifies only as "Amelie."[3] However, the only real sadness and regret came when disposing of the letters he and Taylor had exchanged between Montreal, Paris, and Barcelona. The correspondence had been "full of nothing but affection," wrote Glassco, "yet might be misconstrued. This wholesale destroying of records was not the result of an irrational panic: rather, Sappho's blackmail was merely the *occasion* for my doing something that should have been done long ago, & would have been done eventually. Such relics & mementoes are not things to be left behind one. And yet, it struck me to the heart to see those old letters of Graeme's writing going up in flames: the others meant nothing."[4]

Two days after Sappho's writ was served, Glassco's beloved Dalmatian, Lucy, died. It was, he wrote, the "first grievous loss by death I have ever had."[5] He set out to write a poem in memoriam but was frustrated by an inability to capture his feelings of grief and love. Glassco continued to mourn Lucy's death throughout the remainder of the winter and into the spring, the time of year that he had nearly always found so unpleasant and disturbing. Yet in citing the cause of what he described as his "wretched condition," Glassco ignored all to place blame upon Sappho and her most recent legal actions.[6]

The former housekeeper's accusations remain under seal, and Glassco revealed nothing in conversation. His only writing as to their nature is found in a handwritten note, dated October 1964, appended to the Intimate Journal. Uncharacteristic of one so meticulous, the annotation is struck out and ends in mid-sentence: "This was when I was being named in court as 'engaged in improper practices with Graeme Taylor.' Disproved &."[7] While homosexual acts were punishable under the Criminal Code, and were most certainly grounds for divorce, there may well have been more to Sappho's accusations – the lawyer hired by Glassco, future Quebec premier Jean-Jacques Bertrand, advised the two men to leave the country. In June, however, the tide took a sudden turn, so much so that Bertrand's clients were offered $500 and court costs to let the matter rest. As part of the bargain, Taylor agreed not to contest a divorce action. Within days notice was given in the *Canada Gazette* that Mary Elizabeth Wilson Taylor, "model," would be applying to the Parliament of Canada for a bill of divorce filed "on the grounds of adultery and desertion."[8] And then, silence. After nine months of waiting for Sappho to file her petition for divorce, Glassco and Taylor made plans to sue her lawyer for libel and abuse of privilege. Under threat, Sappho's lawyer moved with speed and, on 30 April 1949, the divorce was granted. "I suppose he paid for it himself," wrote Glassco. "Serve him right: he is just another person to find out that the touch of her hand is burning."[9]

When finally free of Sappho's threats and blackmail, Glassco and Taylor were entering their third year of living alone on Jamaica Farm. With no housekeeper or female presence of any sort, the two men had long fallen into what Glassco described as a "dull round of misery."[10] They slept for half the day and spent much of their waking hours in the dark of night consuming bottles of gin, rye, and ale. But now, Sappho having finally been defeated by Bertrand, her former husband drew energy to start anew. The very evening he learned that the divorce had been finalized Taylor returned to *Brazenhead*. Within two months he'd completed the final two-thirds of his once abandoned novel. Glassco then set himself on the manuscript, polishing, revising, and providing "descriptive additions."[11] Tellingly, the process took nine months, much longer than had the actual composition. At Glassco's direction, the manuscript began making the rounds of US and

"Sappho" in a rubber bathing cap. It was on this photo that Glassco described her as the "fatal woman" of his life.

Canadian publishers but was met by nothing but impersonal rejection. The reception so disappointed Taylor that he could not speak of the failure.

"After all the preachers' sons will when they begin will drink a lot and it wears them out," wrote Gertrude Stein.[12] She was referring, in part, to Robert McAlmon, but the observation was just as valid for Graeme Taylor. As the 1950s began he looked very much older than his forty-four years. His bearded face was gaunt, lined, and unsmiling. The few surviving photographs of the time capture the image of a man who appears to have experienced little happiness. As a gentleman farmer, he was a failure; as a breeder of horses, he'd only lost money. Unwanted by the military, rejected as a husband, reliant upon the generosity of another, in middle-age he'd returned to writing and the abandoned ambitions of his youth. However, *Brazenhead* was no great Canadian novel, and all evidence indicates that Taylor met increasingly with the bottle and never wrote again.

While he matched his friend drink for drink, Glassco was rallying. The period of prolonged legal process, which featured turmoil of the kind that would once have rendered him incapable of work, had been the most productive of his life. His concentration was on the risqué. "My prose muse is now entirely erotic," he confided in the journal.[13] Though work continued on his Huysmans-inspired fantasy, most of his writing was devoted to a pornographic novella entitled *The Accomplishments of Cheverel Virtue*. It was a good-natured, humorous tale of manners and sexual adventure in the eighteenth century. Glassco took great care in recreating in the literary style of the time, but abandoned the project after 36,000 words. Another project, undertaken with great skill, was the completion of Aubrey Beardsley's unfinished *Under the Hill*.

This is not to say that Glassco had abandoned verse. During the very same period he'd worked on some of his most celebrated poems, including "Gentleman's Farm" and "A Ballad on the Death of Thomas Pepys, Tailor." The former he submitted to *Canadian Poetry Magazine*, where it was rejected without delay.

Despite all his efforts, Glassco the poet remained largely unrecognized. His only published verse – seven poems in all – had been found exclusively within the pages of *The Canadian Forum*; all other periodicals had declined his submissions. Moreover, his verse had been ignored by Canadian anthologists, including his old McGill friend A.J.M. Smith. Glassco had not been considered for inclusion in Smith's 1948 revised edition of *The Book of Canadian Poetry*, a collection in which a great many of his Anglo-Quebec contemporaries – F.R. Scott, Leo Kennedy, A.M. Klein, Ralph Gustafson, Patrick Anderson, Miriam Waddington, and Louis Dudek – were well represented. His name had been similarly ignored by John Sutherland when assembling *Other Canadians: Anthology of the New Poetry in Canada, 1940–1946*, nor would there be any representation in *Canadian Poems, 1850–1952*, the Contact Press anthology co-edited by his former houseguest Irving Layton.

He'd fared no better with his prose. "Extract from an Autobiography" was a forgotten piece from a decade past; by his own admission, the *First Statement* selections from *En Arrière* had "attracted absolutely no attention" and had contributed nothing to support subsequent attempts at placing the work with a publisher.[14]

What little public notice Glassco received had come through local politics. In summer 1949 he was elected by acclamation to Foster's town council. Surprised by the respect of the community and touched by the welcome from fellow council members, he began toying with the idea of running for mayor. The repeated experience of sitting in the "shadowy council-room" served to inspire "Town Council Meeting: Undesirable."[15] A dark poem, dealing with the impoverishment and destitution of the "rural slum," it is not without humour and incorporates a parody of John McCrae's "In Flanders Fields":

> *You are the poor. Some years ago*
> *You ate and drank, put nothing by,*
> *Paid and were paid, and now you lie*
>   *In our town limits –* [16]

Glassco's profile was raised further, in both the town and the surrounding countryside, as a founder and host of the Foster Horse Show. The event, which would come to dominate his summers, was first held in September 1951 on the grounds of Jamaica Farm. The debut was unadvertised; its audience was comprised for the most part of those who happened to be passing by the property. At the end of the day, a hat was passed and the money collected was donated to the town's Anglican church. Following this success, a committee was struck. One of the original participants, Ann Johansson, remembered the second horse show as a much more elaborate event: "The next year one of the committee members was connected to a brewery – so we all got cases of beer as prizes. The ladies of the local church did not like this – so the next year we all got bone china cups & saucers!"[17]

The Foster Horse Show grew at a rapid pace and, after becoming a part of the Canadian Horse Show Association, began attracting the big stables. At its height in the mid-1960s the event drew an attendance of three thousand with nearly two hundred entries; eventually it had to be moved to the larger grounds of the Lions Community Park in Knowlton.

In summer 1951, shortly before the first Foster Horse Show, Glassco won re-election to town council, garnering 150 votes to his opponent's 30. The ease of victory encouraged him to put aside thoughts of the mayoralty and consider seeking the Liberal Party nomination for Brome in the forthcoming Quebec election.[18] Taylor counselled caution, suggesting that it would be wiser to slowly gather and then solidify support for a future run. Not swayed, Glassco allowed his name to be considered but ended up as runner-up to a novice named Raymond Lanctot, in part because the party and the local riding association insisted on running a francophone in what was a largely

English-speaking riding. Lanctot was defeated soundly when the Union Nationale incumbent received over 60 percent of the vote. Glassco felt that he'd dodged a bullet but made a commitment to run in the next provincial election, on the proviso that his candidacy for the Liberals be assured.

Certain that his party would take the next provincial election, and believing Brome to be a bellweather riding, the town councillor from Foster focused on his erotica as he awaited the next call to the polls.

He rewrote *En Arrière* twice, changing the protagonist to a woman and adapting the text to diary form. Novella-length and under a new title, "Mairobert," it continued to be rejected.

In 1952, Glassco began work on *Squire Hardman*, a pornographic poem inspired by *The Rodiad*, a flagellantine fantasy in verse often ascribed erroneously to English playwright George Colman the Younger. *Squire Hardman* marked a departure from Glassco's previous method in that it was composed quickly, without significant rewrites, and was then simply set aside. There is no evidence that he ever submitted the work for publication. Even the man who thought *En Arrière* might find a home with so conservative a house as Longmans, Green, must have recognized that a 1320-line poem told in heroic couplets, dedicated to the priestesses of the "Flagellant *regime*," and written in the manner of the late eighteenth-century would have been next to impossible to place.[19]

Another pornographic work, a novel entitled *A Firm Hand*, was written with similar speed. A simple tale of a boy's education under the authority of his beautiful, sadistic governess, it was ultimately a love story, set among wealth in nineteenth-century England. Glassco described the work as "rubbish," while defending himself with the claim that it had been "written for a *public*."[20] For the first time, he had gauged his audience correctly. A public was indeed awaiting *A Firm Hand*; it would become a bestseller.

In 1954, he submitted the novel to the Jack Woodford Press, a New York publisher specializing in hardcover risqué novels. Woodford, a prolific writer of "mildly sexy potboilers,"[21] didn't own the company, rather he was the most prominent in a stable of writers who specialized in the erotic literature of the time. Lacking four-letter words or explicit sex scenes, his stories involved "extra-marital trysts, wild parties, abortions, homosexuality and lesbianism, sexual activity, the casting couch and other 'modern' situations."[22] The press's stable was varied and included such writers as Joe Weiss, whose novels *Warped Thrills*, *Another Way of Love*, and *How Rough Can It Get?*, among others, often incorporated spanking. It's probable that Glassco came to submit *A Firm Hand* to the Jack Woodford Press because he recognized it as the publisher of Clement Wood's *Flesh and Other Stories*, a copy of which was in his personal library.[23]

The press bought the manuscript outright for $300, and it was rechristened *The Dominant One*. Plates were made and at least one galley was produced, but what was to have been Glassco's first book failed to materialize. The author's explanation, that the press got cold feet, is almost certainly correct. In early 1955, the Senate Subcommittee on Juvenile Delinquency, established to investigate the influence of violence and sex in the media on the youth of the United States, turned its attention from comic books to publications dealing with bondage, flagellation, and fetish. As their poster boy they used Kenneth Grimm, a seventeen-year-old Eagle Scout who had been found bound and dead by his father in their Coral Gables, Florida, home. Whether a suicide or victim of auto-erotic asphyxiation, blame for the boy's death was placed on work produced and sold by photographer Irving Klaw, all but ending the career of the man who had introduced Bettie Page to popular culture. Although the Jack Woodford Press was unaffected by the seizures, publishing a novel titled *The Dominant One* would almost certainly have attracted unwelcome attention; publication of Glassco's novel was postponed indefinitely. The plates had lain in storage for three years when the press at long last received the attention it had been dreading. New York City police detectives impounded dozens of its titles from bookstores throughout Manhattan, causing a fatal blow. The Jack Woodford Press ceased publishing, and Glassco bought back the rights.

For the time being, the image of the stern English governess would remain private, another player in the many pleasurable fantasies set down on paper but not shared. The turmoil brought on by Sappho had caused Glassco to turn away from women: "Oh yes, I still nurse a few daydreams, romantic & erotic, – but leave them in that condition. My satisfactions of the latter are now, I'm afraid, exclusively solitary, masturbatory: this is not good, – but better than tasting any woman again."[24]

He continued to nurse his daydreams for a time, relying on the fantasies to fuel his prose and provide sexual release. However, the desire for female companionship could in no way be satisfied by Taylor, nor would Glassco's love for Sappho ever fade to nothingness. Eventually, she reappeared in a melancholy dream, which he chose to record in the Intimate Journal:

Last night such a sweet, sad dream of S. We were walking hand in hand in summer weather up Cote des Neiges, she in her straw hat & white dress, & she was telling me once again how she seemed to be two people, two girls, one good & one evil: that she had been the evil one long enough, & she was coming back to us to be the good one again. Then we cried & kissed & walked on. But somehow I knew it was a dream, & that she would never come back. Poor S. How dreadful to think the very sight of me must now be loathsome to her, as reminding her of the failure of her foolish, wicked plan & of how she entertained it for five years.[25]

Although he would record no further dreams, his love and obsessing over Sappho continued for many years, perhaps for the remainder of his life. Nearly two decades after their final meeting, Glassco came across one of her old photographs; he turned it over and wrote on the back: "Mary Elizabeth Taylor, Knowlton 1940. The 'fatal woman' of my life ...."[26]

By 1951, Glassco was ready to pursue new affairs. He soon found a new mistress, but she only partially sated his desires: "I have only dreams of a new love: I know too well I am ripe to fall into the abyss of a great passion. Well, let it come if it will! I shall be 42 next month – the years of indiscretion are all ahead."[27]

While Taylor stayed behind at Jamaica Farm, Glassco took to the road, making frequent trips into Montreal. The drive in was made easier with a new car, a yellow Jeepster convertible he'd received as a gift from his mother. It wasn't her only gesture of generosity. At a time when the average annual income in Canada hovered just below $1,500, Beatrice had presented each of her three children with $85,000 and a promise of more to follow. For Glassco, the cash brought great relief; many years would pass before he again became concerned about his finances.

Exactly where it was that Glassco had chosen to spend his nighttime excursions he does not record, but evidence points to venues offering exotic dancers. The Bellevue Casino, Rockhead's Paradise, Café St Michel, and the Gayety – the club made famous by Lili St Cyr – are all likely destinations. As now, Montreal was a city known for its nightclubs and the beauty of the dancers featured.

A "superb experience" with one such woman brought on dreams of visiting North Africa. "While it lasted," Glassco wrote, "it was a gay affair,

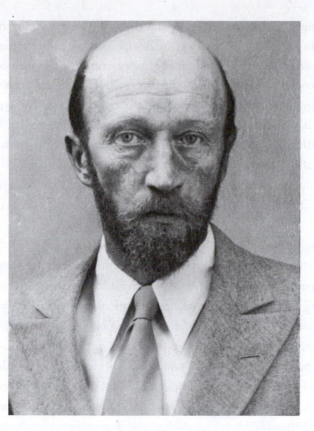

Graeme Taylor in his mid-forties.

& rather expensive. My heart was only lightly touched, but I cannot stand any attacks there any longer. I broke off when I felt myself becoming too attached to a brainless, worthless, passionless & beautiful coloured girl. Ah, but how soft her skin was, how exquisite her arms & hands. Why is it I only fall for crazy women & bitches?"[28]

In November 1954, a half-hearted attempt at rekindling the relationship ended in failure, and within three months he had moved on:

Two weeks ago I thought I had come alive again, having very nearly fallen in love with another very beautiful dancer in Montreal. Dreadful to admit – I was absolutely impotent with her: this is shocking, and only partly excusable by the fact of her own confessed frigidity with all men. – Yet for a while, with her, I was *happy* in a curiously, ridiculously youthful way, – just being with her. She is only 23. What is it I find in her? The beauty of her eyes & cheekbones, her underlying *simplicity*, her gamin intelligence – & the fact that she reminds me overpoweringly of S. Also her love of dusk, the greedy way she smokes, her nervousness & courage, the way she likes to gamble against the odds, her frustration with life, adoration of her own person, kindness to friends, animals & children. The heartbreaking sadness of her face in repose. – For a while, I was frightened of the intensity of my feelings for her, – which fear does me no credit.[29]

The new relationship caused him to reflect on that between himself and Taylor:

Ah, what is most terrible about my relationship with her is that it is the *reverse* of mine with G., – that I sense, in her, my own reactions to him – the physical rejection, the impatience, the boredom with my sentimental, senile caresses; that I feel, myself, becoming a parody of him, with this young girl. I feel I could, in time, love her as he loves me, – perhaps even that she could care for me as I care for him; and this prospect is terrifying. I have enough guilt on my conscience over the way I have treated him; I have seen how I have hurt him, & I could not bear to be so hurt myself – not again, not after Berys, Marguerite and S.[30]

Although Glassco saw no future with the unnamed dancer, and feared that she had ideas of marriage, he felt unable to break off the relationship and continued to see her for nearly a year. When the end came, it was both sudden and unexpected. In February 1956, the "poor idiotic dancer darling" received a six-month prison sentence after pleading guilty to narcotics possession.[31] She was three months pregnant. That Glassco records the fact without any concern that he might be the father may speak to the impotence suffered the previous year and most certainly reveals the relationship to be anything but monogamous.

The beginning of the dancer's incarceration coincided with the worst night in Glassco's life; an evening in which he feared that he might kill. The trigger for his "attack," as he described it in his journal, was the written confession of J. Romeo Drapeau, which had been published within the pages of the sensationalist tabloid *Montreal Midnight*. On the morning of 13 February 1956, Drapeau – a pleasant, friendly accountant – had clubbed and stabbed to death his pregnant wife and four children in their cramped Sherbrooke bungalow. The mass murder, which remains the worst in the history of the Eastern Townships, commanded the front pages of the local papers and the Montreal dailies. Drapeau's confession, which was also featured in *The Montreal Star*, is that of a man who is tortured and at a loss to explain his actions:

> My wife came downstairs to prepare breakfast and when she was seated at the table, seeing her suffer and starting a big Monday morning not having the means to have a maid, I became profoundly discouraged. Suddenly pushed by some desire I had for a week or more I took the hammer from a drawer and beat my wife and children to death, finishing my wife with a knife … I know it is difficult for those in good health to understand my point of view, nerves shot and lack of sleep, a persevering desire for a week which I fought every night. I feared for the security and happiness of my family. Evil conquered me.[32]

Glassco saw something of himself in J. Romeo Drapeau; a man who felt run down, a man who relied on pills and alcohol to fall asleep, a man whose home was suffused with unhappiness. He feared that he would follow Drapeau's lead: "I was terrified of *losing control of* myself & murdering someone – Graeme (merely as the nearest human being) – of doing something terrible – *simply* in obedience to the 'Imp of the Perverse' – simply as a release for certain not-understood impulses in myself. I had always wanted to kill my Father. (Not that it wouldn't have served him right!)."[33]

The entry's reference to A.P.S. marks the first mention of his father in nearly two decades. Unlike the Montreal newspapers, Glassco had not seen fit to record the McGill bursar's 1935 retirement. Not even his death, on 13 September 1945, following a long, painful battle with cancer, had received mention in the Intimate Journal.

As in the past, Glassco sought no help, professional or otherwise, for the attack. He suffered for hours, until it dissipated with the aid of four martinis.

The unnamed dancer's baby was born weeks after she'd been released from prison. Although there was some attempt at rekindling their relationship, Glassco found that motherhood had changed his mistress. Baby at hand, away from from the lights and sequins and coloured lights of the stage, the dancer appeared dull and spiritless. His visits to her parents' home, where the television was forever on, killed whatever passion remained.

Glassco later destroyed most of the entries dealing with the affair, and his "dancer darling" is not named in those that survive. However, it is possible that she was a beautiful, exotic, and erotic performer named Pearl Tiberi, the inspiration for "Belly Dance."[34] Originally known as "Shake Dancer," it is one of his most sexual poems:

> The corpsewhite column spiralling on slow feet
> Tracing the easel curve, the figure eight,
> Coldly unwinds the flowing ribbon
> With public motions of the private psalm
> Of supposed woman to the thought of man;[35]

This poem to his mistress culminates with an act of masturbation:

> So the man of air supplants the man of bone,
> And it is he who writhes before a glass,
> Before the figure of his only love,
> The viewless member in his nerveless hand
> Working within the adverse air.[36]

It is most clear that Taylor did not share in Glassco's Montreal adventures; indeed, one journal entry reveals that he had not so much as visited the city after his military discharge. The failed writer showed no interest in revisiting the frivolous lifestyle he'd once shared in the bars and cafés of Montparnasse – and there were to be no more attempts at *ménages à trois*. The relationship between the two men had changed in another, more important, way: whether or not he was aware, the older man was no longer the arbiter. Taylor had failed to prevent Glassco from putting forward his name as a Liberal nominee in 1951, and, as the decade progressed, his judgment and sophistication in things literary were being called increasingly into question.

Though appreciation of Glassco's work was minimal, typically consisting of one or two acceptance letters a year from little magazines, it was far greater than anything accorded by Taylor. Glassco was honoured when "Gentle-

Glassco's undated photo of Pearl Tiberi.

man's Farm," which had first appeared in *The Canadian Forum*, was selected for inclusion in *The Borestone Mountain Poetry Awards 1955*.[37] The collection marked the first time any of the now forty-five-year-old Glassco's writing had appeared in book form, and he relished the opportunity to correct the line errors that he felt had marred its magazine debut. The company in which he found himself was impressive; Robert Frost and Edna St Vincent Millay counted among the other poets featured in the anthology.

Encouraged by the recognition, Glassco's confidence grew. He began composing one of his most ambitious poems, "The Web," devoted to Ulysses's Penelope. There had been good progress when Glassco made what he knew immediately to be a mistake in showing the work to Taylor. His friend was far from encouraging and, as was his habit, suggested changes. "These were, of course, all wrong," Glassco wrote in his Intimate Journal, " – and I've had to lay it aside until I can look clearly & sensibly at it once again. *Mem: Never show anything to anybody in MS. until it's completely finished.*"[38]

Taylor, who had for so long been above all criticism, had come to be considered a bad influence. In the same journal entry, writing of his frustration with an unfinished project, a play about Byron in Italy entitled *Byron's Goose*, Glassco describes it as "*structurally unsound* – like everything in which G. has a hand."[39]

Taylor's influence over his friend's writing was further diminished by the publication of Glassco's poem "Deserted Buildings under Shefford Mountain" in the May 1956 issue of *The Canadian Forum*. A few weeks after its appearance, he was contacted by A.J.M. Smith, who sought permission to include the poem in his forthcoming anthology, *The Oxford Book of Canadian Verse*. It was an important recognition. With the 1943 publication of *The Book of Canadian Poetry*, Smith had been established as the foremost anthologist of Canadian verse. The book had found a place in the curricula of secondary schools, colleges, and universities. And yet, despite their early friendship and shared history as members of McGill's intelligentsia, Glassco had been absent from the initial anthology and the two revised, expanded editions.

The setting of the poem was the Eastern Townships – "Clark Baird's old place in Iron Hill" – an area that Smith knew well.[40] His wife's family had long owned a cottage on Drummond Point, at the northern end of Lake Memphremagog.

These native angles of decay
  In shed and barn whose broken wings
Lie here half fallen in the way

Of headstones amid uncut hay –
Why do I love you ragged things?

What grace unknown to any art,
What beauty frailer than a mood
Awaken in me their counterpart?
What correspondence of a heart
That loves the failing attitude?[41]

Late in the year, Smith read "Deserted Buildings under Shefford Mountain" on CBC Radio. The $5 Glassco received for the performing rights was the first money he had ever earned through his poetry.

Michael Gnarowski writes with accuracy in describing Graeme Taylor as "an important, if indistinct, figure who remains obscure to the present day."[42] What we know of the man is very much reliant on what Glassco chose to record – and preserve – in his Intimate Journal. Given what has been established, it seems the very safest of assumptions that Taylor viewed 1956 as the worst year of his life. At the end of the twelve months, what remained of his influence over Glassco had been brought to an end by Smith and three other influences: history, a woman, and illness.

The first, history, intruded in the form of the provincial election on 20 June. Since losing the Liberal nomination in the run-up to the previous election, Glassco had followed Taylor's advice that he build and solidify his support within the party and the riding. He'd spent five years as a member of Foster's town council, and four as an organizer and host of the Foster Horse Show. In spring 1956, with a provincial election just a few months away, Glassco's profile was such that he was offered the Liberal nomination in Brome. However, Taylor strongly urged that he not accept. Glassco declined the nomination without regret, certain that the riding could not be won by his party. He was wrong. The Liberal candidate, Glendon Brown, won the June election by a comfortable margin, ending two decades of Union Nationale victories. Brown would serve as the member from Brome, and the later riding of Brome-Missisquoi, until 1976, when he was defeated in the election that first brought the Parti Québécois to power.

Witnessing Brown's success, Glassco disregarded his prediction of a Liberal defeat and placed blame for the decision not to run on Taylor alone.

This missed opportunity, coupled with Brown's repeated electoral success, brought to an end any plans of running for provincial office.

It was that same summer that Glassco met the woman with whom he would share the longest relationship of his life: "I have a new mistress – a Russian girl who is really very fond of me and with whom I have an ideal sexual relationship. But we have not much in common to talk about! I do not love her, but admire & trust & am sorry for her: she is so completely alone in the world, is hopeless about the future, & yet remains brave & capable of gaiety."[43]

This "Russian girl," who lived in Montreal, would become his first wife and one of the great loves of Glassco's life. Elma Koolmer was a tiny woman, always impeccably dressed, but in a dated style. She would most often appear in black, a choice that, no doubt, leant support to those who thought she resembled a witch. Though a tiny woman, under five feet in height, more than one person likened her to Morticia Addams, the tall, lean, vampish creation of US cartoonist Charles Addams. Others saw her as one would a faded film star, a distressed yet glamorous remnant of the 1930s. Michael Gnarowski remembers her exotic looks as being "something almost Inuk; a beautiful round face with almond eyes."[44]

To all who encountered her, Elma would remain as she had been introduced: a figure of mystery. At social occasions – those she chose to attend – she would keep to herself, speaking only occasionally, sharing little. Her distance may have had less to do with shyness or an inability to speak English; the stance was defensive. She once told Glassco she could read others' thoughts: "so many people's thoughts … are full of fear, envy and hatred: I have to *close them off*."[45]

Glassco wrote that she had been born in Ivangorod, a fifteenth-century Russian fortress on the Narva River, twenty kilometres from the Gulf of Finland. This claim is thrown somewhat into question by her supposed date of birth, 2 April 1918, little more than five weeks after the fortress was seized by the German army. The issue is further complicated, perhaps intentionally, by Glassco's description of Ivangorod as being in the town of Narva, in present-day Estonia; when, in actuality, the fortress is located across the river in the town of Ivangorod, Russia. There is, in fact, a fortress in Narva: Narva Herman Castle, well within an arrow's flight from Ivangorod. While it is possible that Glassco was mistaken as to the name of the fortress, it is just

Elma Koolmer. Glassco would later use this image as an
author photo of Sylvia Bayer, the pseudonym he employed
for the pornographic *Fetish Girl*.

as likely that he'd invented Elma's birthplace; just as he would, on occasion,
say that he had been born in the Rawlings mansion. Certainly, the assertion
that she had come from aristocracy, the daughter of Mihail Baron von Colmar of Courland and Narva and his wife, Ann Mitri, is false. Her father,
Mihkel Koolmer, was the son of a farmer and had achieved nothing beyond
the equivalent of an elementary school education. A 1939 agricultural census
records a twenty-one-year-old Elma as living with her parents, Mihkel and
Anna, and older brother August, on a farm known as Raudmetsa no. A-28,
located in the Viru district, Narva Commune. Although a graduate of the
Narva Co-educational Gymnasium, it is almost certain that Elma was never
a *ballerina assoluta* of the Estonian National Ballet, another of Glassco's
claims. The organization holds no records in which her name features, nor

is it found in records of the Estonian National Opera or in any other listing of Estonian performers.

While it is impossible to determine whether these fantasies originated with Elma, there is certainly an option that they were of Glassco's design. It is worth noting a parallel in the history of Leopold von Sacher-Masoch, whose *Venus in Furs* Glassco admired and would one day "translate." Like Elma, Fanny Pistor, Sacher-Masoch's lover, claims a fictitious noble title, dubbing herself the Baroness Bogdanoff. What is certain is that Elma went along with the claims. Their wedding announcement, printed in *The Gazette*, identifies the bride as "Miss Elma von Colmar, daughter of the late Baron Michel von Colmar of Courland and Narva, Estonia, and of Baroness von Colmar."[46]

One most intriguing possibility is that Glassco, in writing and conversation, was simply relaying what Elma had told him of her past, that he truly believed his new love to be a member of the aristocracy, born in a massive fortress, once a ballerina on the Estonian national stage. In one letter to Elma, written before their marriage, a little over four years into their relationship, Glassco reminds her that he had once bedded the wife of the Marquis de Cardaillac, who lived in the Eastern Townships. This otherwise unidentified woman was, he claims "my only *titled* lady, except my dear tweet who is only a baroness!"[47]

Word around Foster, Knowlton, and the surrounding communities was that Elma had spent most of the Second World War interned in a concentration camp. Indeed, the German military had used Ivangorod for just such a purpose after again capturing the fortress in summer 1941. Narva, too, suffered from German occupation. In March 1944, Soviet air strikes destroyed the oldest parts of the town, while bombardment from the ground demolished much of its fortress. Apart from a single short sentence – "I and my sister were separated by severe war" – there is no account of her experiences during the conflict or in the years that followed; whatever she told Glassco he imparted to no one.[48]

In 1950, Elma entered Canada as a displaced person. Her arrival in Foster six years later prompted rumour and gossip. Desperately thin, she appeared to some a walking skeleton. There was speculation among those in the town that Elma's wartime suffering had had devastating effects on her digestive system, to the point where she was only able to eat very small portions of select foods. However, it is just as likely that her condition predated the war. Though Elma had not been with the Estonian National Ballet, it was true that she had been a ballerina; as such she was trained for an occupation in which cases of bulimia and anorexia were anything but uncommon.

Glassco's relationship with Elma was still in its early days when he wrote "A Devotion" for her. The subject isn't the romantic ideal of new love, but the act of cunnilingus. The verse combines a worship of the sexual with that of the sacrament.

> See, I'd not slip from worshipper into man
> A space yet, but remain as I began,
> Give my lips holiday from the work of words,
> A Sabbath of silence, drifting pleasurewards,
> And let my spirit, as my knees to bow
> Before this cloven idol – an altar now
> As the sweet speechless misremembered year
> Returns in noonlight – hunger and rage and fear
> Cancelled forever – and as the bloom in me,
> On the bare branches of my wintry tree,
> Like mistletoe run wild, the devotee,
> The lover and the child.[49]

By the end of the year, Elma had left her city home for Jamaica Farm, where despite her frail appearance, she adapted easily to a new role as "housekeeper," and displayed a seemingly incongruous talent in the kitchen, well-suited to Glassco's taste for fine cuisine. The introduction of this fresh female presence to the household brought no possibility of a *ménage à trois*. There would be nothing of the relationship once shared with Sappho – Taylor was dying. At the age of fifty he had been diagnosed with Buerger's Disease, a rare and incurable affliction of young, cigarette-smoking men. The initial symptoms were manifested as pain in the extremities, brought on by a clotting in the arteries and veins. Work with the horses became impossible, and his contribution to the farm's upkeep soon ended. In recording the awful news, Glassco's tone was one of irritation, rather than concern: "Graeme has developed Buerger's disease – & as this is incurable it means he will never be able to walk more than a hundred steps a day. Well, I had given up hope of ever wishing to travel."[50]

Weakened by illness, Taylor was in a most disadvantaged state. From his chair, barely able to move, he was witness to Glassco and Elma's strengthening love. As health declined, jealousy grew, and his behaviour became erratic. Stubborn, refusing all medical help, he only hastened his end. Meanwhile, Glassco, flush with the sexual excitement of a fresh love, found his old friend's expressions of self-pity tiresome.

When Taylor finally turned to medicine, it was through Glassco's insistence. Early in 1957 he was taken to Royal Victoria Hospital in Montreal, the same institution at which he'd shown such dedication through his visits to Glassco twenty-five years earlier. There was an unsuccessful surgery, which likely involved an effort to control pain by the cutting of nerves in affected areas. The alternative was amputation.

For two weeks Glassco visited, witnessing "doctors and internes [sic] coming in three times a day, waking him to prod and pull him around, auscultate [sic], finger his eyeballs, take blood tests, inject drugs. While they took their notes ...."[51]

Twelve years later, Glassco wrote Kay Boyle, who had not seen the pair since their days in Paris:

> In his last rational moment he asked me, "How could you do this to me? If you ever loved me take me home, get me out of here." And this was in a private room in the finest hospital in Montreal! When I told the head doctor I was going to take him home by private ambulance he said it was against the law, he would not allow it, and would use force to prevent it. For 48 hours before he died I sat out in the corridor listening to him moaning in his coma: I was not even allowed to enter his room. He never recovered consciousness, thank God.[52]

On the first day of February 1957, in hospital, Taylor died of peritonitis at the age of fifty-one. He was buried in an unmarked grave in Mount Royal Cemetery beside James, the older brother who had died as a baby. Glassco made no mention of the death in subsequent journal entries. It wasn't until summer 1960 that he chose to record Taylor's passing – he'd already forgotten the year of his friend's death:

As for life, Graeme died in February 1956. It seems much longer ago than that – I suppose because since then life has been unbelievably richer, fuller & freer. Here, if nowhere else, can I admit that this was a blessed thing for me (for him too, perhaps, though how should I know?), and should have happened years before it did. I have never realised before how great a clog & a drag he was on me, with that everlasting discouragement, depression, cynicism & passionate insistence on no effort or idea being worth while. Indeed, it sometimes terrifies me to think how almost entirely so much of my life was wasted with him, & how very nearly the rest of it might have been wasted too, but for the accident of his death. Good God, how lucky I was! I have no feeling of shame in saying this.[53]

To work, to work![1]

In his latter years, during the brief period in which he achieved some small degree of fame, Glassco would be something less than sympathetic when speaking of Taylor. To interviewers he described his friend as having been strange, possessive, masochistic, and a drinker; a man who "was extremely jealous of any girls I had, sometimes intolerably so."[2] The lasting message was quite unequivocal: Taylor's had been a life wasted. "Graeme had an *ambition* to be a failure, and he achieved it, too."[3]

This odd, disturbed character is markedly different from the gentle young man who appears in "Extract from an Autobiography." Understandable, perhaps, as Glassco was then writing of a twenty-two-year-old, and not the unhealthy middle-aged man he would become.

There is little to support Glassco's latter day descriptions in the Intimate Journal. Throughout the numerous detailed entries, Taylor passes as a phantom; months, seasons, and years pass without mention of his name. Yet, within these irregular, ephemeral sightings, there are indications of an artistic jealousy that tainted their relationship. Taylor is rarely a positive force, and his many criticisms are never constructive. In July 1934, Glassco writes that after showing Taylor a poem entitled "March" he came away fearing his work was "utterly worthless – so derivative: surely to God I should be able to write something original by now! But apparently not. And from being convinced of my work's futility I have passed to the author with a similar summing-up!"[4] That condemnatory influence continued well into their final years together; it was only after Taylor became weakened by disease that Glassco began to truly question his friend's judgement and challenge his authority.

Freed from Taylor's negativity, buoyed by Arthur Smith's recognition of "Deserted Buildings under Shefford Mountain," Glassco sought to re-enter Montreal's literary community. Twelve years had passed since his dalliance with *First Statement*, and he quickly discovered that much had happened since his withdrawal. John Sutherland was dead from cancer. Patrick Anderson had left the country and was teaching in England. Since his visit to Windermere, Irving Layton had published no less than ten collections of verse. *Let Us Compare Mythologies*, the first book by Leonard Cohen, had appeared to considerable critical praise the previous year.

Glassco gravitated not to the new but to the members of the McGill literary circle around which he'd skirted three decades earlier. Within months of Taylor's death, he was enjoying the first of what would be many summers spent drinking with Smith, Frank Scott, and others by the shores of lakes Memphremagog and Massawippi. At forty-seven, the balding, moustachioed Glassco was much changed from the fawnlike boy they'd known at McGill. Leon Edel, an occasional participant in these gatherings, was particularly taken aback by the transformation, finding "the young flippant, epigram-making, aesthetic Buffy" had become a quiet and meditative individual.[5] But then, three decades had passed since the days of the *Fortnightly*, "Collegiana," and "The Goose Step." The tea and coffee once sipped in the Student Union cafeteria had been replaced by potent martinis served at Scott's summer house.

On the evening of his first birthday without Taylor, Glassco sat before his typewriter and wrote of a wet, gin-soaked evening he'd spent in Montreal with Scott, Louis Dudek, Jean-Guy Pilon, and others. The company of Pilon speaks to Scott's attempts at bringing together Quebec's francophone and anglophone poets. Some years earlier, he'd begun translating French Canadian verse; an act that was both artistic and political. Translation, Scott believed, was essential in fostering understanding between the two cultures. To this end, he'd invited Louis Portugais, Micheline Sainte-Marie, and Gaston Miron to his Westmount home with the hopes of producing a bilingual anthology of contemporary French Canadian verse. The meeting led to nothing more than a page or two of rough notes, but Scott the *animateur* was not put off. He encouraged others to join him in his work, and in Glassco he found a receptive, if unlikely, talent. The younger man had never shown much interest in translation; his efforts had been limited to Catullus's

"Dirge for Sparrow," attempted while recovering from tuberculosis, and his own *Philip Eugene*, the aborted Parisian *roman* he'd adapted for use in "Mairobert." What's more, Glassco's knowledge of French Canadian verse was extremely limited; he told Scott that he knew only the work of Pilon, Claude Fournier, and Hector de Saint-Denys-Garneau. Yet, even this modest claim was an exaggeration; Glassco was far less familiar with these writers than he was letting on.

Believing that Glassco had some talent for translation, and hoping that he might participate in the bilingual anthology, Scott worked to broaden Glassco's knowledge. He provided a list of bookstores from which volumes of French Canadian poetry could be purchased, and in early November 1957 wrote a letter that Glassco credited with having initiated what would be his first major work of translation, *The Journal of Saint-Denys-Garneau*. "Since you like Garneau," Scott wrote, "may I suggest you read his *Journal*, published by Beauchemin? There is nothing like it in Canadian literature. There's a translation for you!"[6] Soon after receiving the title from a Montreal bookseller, Glassco responded with fervour: "I'm reading Garneau's Journal now. This is, as you say, a unique thing in this country. He seems to have been like one of those mediaeval prodigies who developed almost overnight: poetry, metaphysics, art, nature, music, politics – he is brilliantly at home in all of them: only his sense of guilt and forlornness, his despair, are all too modern, and give him an astonishing depth."[7]

Glassco was quick to follow Scott's suggestion, adding excerpts from the *Journal* to the list of translations already undertaken: "His prose is almost as difficult to translate as his poetry: especially as the Journal seems to have been written *straight off*, without any formal revision or polish, and with an extraordinary compression of thought and immediacy of expression. It's all so vivid, eloquent and alive that I feel this country should know about this book. But to translate the whole thing would take me about a year – and then who would publish it?"[8] As if in answer to Glassco's question, two weeks later a letter arrived from Robert Weaver. The editor of *The Tamarack Review* had learned of the *Journal* translations from Scott and was hoping to publish excerpts in the newly created little magazine. Glassco submitted an excerpt he titled "The Dimensions of Longing," which appeared six months later in the summer issue. It was preceded by his translations of five Garneau poems in the spring issue of *The Fiddlehead*.

John Glassco in middle age, c. 1957.

Through his new relationship with Scott, Glassco's contacts within the literary community continued to grow. Accompanied by Elma, he became a frequent guest at cocktail and dinner parties held at Frank and Marian Scott's home. It was there that, in spring 1958, he was introduced to Garneau's cousin Anne Hébert. Shortly afterward she sent him a copy of her second poetry collection, *Le tombeau des rois*, which Glassco began translating, sending her copies of his work for comment.

Scott was convinced that these alcohol-fuelled gatherings of Quebec's French and English-language poets were having great benefit. Two years after encouraging the *Journal* translation, he wrote Glassco: "It seems the seeds we planted in our several bilingual evenings are sprouting: whether in soil or stone we shall see later."[9] Yet while Scott, Smith, and Glassco tended the garden, their efforts were not being reciprocated by their French Canadian counterparts; interest in translating the poetry of English Canada was next to nonexistent. Glassco's concern over this inactivity was overshadowed by growing worries over the publication of his work on the *Journal*. All apprehension was more than justified: volumes of French Canadian verse in translation were notable only for their scarcity. There had been a modest 1909 collection, *Songs of French Canada*, comprising sixteen poems and seventeen folk songs, but only one book, G.R. Roy's *Twelve Modern French-Canadian Poets; Douze poètes modernes du Canada Français*, published in 1958, had been devoted exclusively to French Canadian poetry.[10] There were only a handful of slim publications devoted to a single French Canadian poet. The 1880s had seen three poems from Louis-Honoré Fréchette's work in progress *La légende d'un peuple* published as three booklets, with the originals featured next to "rather pedestrian verse by the then octogenarian law clerk of the House of Commons, Gustavus William Wicksteed."[11] These publications of no more than thirteen pages were followed seven decades later by stapled, mimeographed "pamphlets" issued under Louis Dudek and Raymond Souster's Contact Press imprint. Numbering four in total, each featured the work of a contemporary poet – Garneau, Roland Giguère, Gilles Hénault, and Paul-Marie Lapointe – accompanied by the translations of poet Gael Turnbull and Jean Beaupré, a schoolteacher in Iroquois Falls, Ontario.[12] Marked "not for public sale" and limited to editions of twenty-five copies, they demonstrated admirable dedication on behalf of the translators, who were loaned the use of the imprint for the project. However, the translations featured were flawed and the production values, quite obviously, left much to be desired.

It would seem most unusual – incredible, really – that an English-language publisher would be interested in the private papers of a poet who remained largely unknown to anglophones. That Glassco continued work on his Garneau translations speaks to his passion for the subject, to his continuing naïveté regarding the business of publishing, and of Scott's encouragement and enthusiasm. In his correspondence with Glassco, the much-published older poet gives the impression that the work would be placed with ease. Yet, despite Scott's own good efforts, a publisher was not so easily found.

Glassco's attraction toward Garneau went beyond the conviction that the French Canadian poet had been brilliant and unique; there was another reason that he chose to keep to himself. In an excised portion of a draft letter to Scott, Glassco writes: "I detect in him a curious vein of natural, delicate sadism, and I think his horrified consciousness of this was the real cause of his sense of guilt."[13] In Garneau he saw something of a kindred spirit: born less than three years apart, they were sons of privilege and were well read; they had each visited Paris, suffered serious illnesses, and retreated to lives of semi-seclusion in the Quebec countryside.

Garneau, too, had suffered severe depression and grave self-doubt. Weeks after the March 1937 publication of *Regards et jeux dans l'espace*, the only book to be published during his lifetime, he withdrew the work in the belief that it lacked authenticity. The move was followed by a nervous breakdown. By that July, Garneau had recovered sufficiently to set off across the Atlantic with his friend Jean Le Moyne for what was to have been a year-long European stay. In the end, he could bear no more than three weeks. After returning to Canada, the poet took refuge at his family's manor house in Sainte-Catherine-de Fossambault, forty kilometres northwest of Quebec City. By February 1938, Garneau had ceased writing for publication; his days were spent pursuing a wide variety of interests, including gardening, painting, and photography. Although friendships were maintained, he became increasingly withdrawn and reclusive; he was alone when felled by a heart attack while canoing on the Jacques-Cartier River.

The translator came to love this man whom he had never met and held an absurd belief that he could have saved Garneau from an early death. In Glassco's own journal he accused the deceased poet's family and friends of "a failure of human love" and blamed himself for having been "engaged in trivial psychosexual acrobatics in the very years of his torment."[14]

In the midst of this preoccupation with Garneau and growing interest in translation, Glassco's first book, a collection of verse, was published by McClelland & Stewart. Credit for the placement went to Smith and Toronto poet Jay Macpherson, who shared an appreciation of Glassco's poetry.[15] The resulting volume, *The Deficit Made Flesh*, arrived in stores in autumn 1958 as the ninth and final book in the Indian File series. Once again, Glassco found himself in impressive company; previous titles had included work by James Reaney, Patrick Anderson, P.K. Page, and Phyllis Webb.

The Deficit Made Flesh gathered twenty-eight poems, twelve of which had appeared previously in *The Canadian Forum* and *The Fiddlehead*. Among the unpublished was "A Devotion," his sexually charged celebration of Elma, and a short poem entitled "Jogging Track":

Lapping, lapping the oval,
   The timing-tower
Falling, the shaken ground,
   All day and forever[16]

"Jogging Track" was not his alone; it had begun as "a little poem of Graeme's."[17] A decade earlier Glassco had spent at least one evening "arranging & labouring" over the verse: "It has cost me infinite pains, giving it *movement*: this was difficult, as it was conceived *statically*, – & I may have spoiled it with my heavy hand."[18]

The weakest in the collection, "Jogging Track" nevertheless matched well the lengthy endorsement that Smith had provided for the dustjacket. He informs the reader that Glassco's "subject matter is the Eastern Townships of Quebec … The little pocket of country isolation, of run-down farms and stony pastures, is presented as symbolic of a kind of forlorn and heroic rejection of the mechanized and success-worship of the acquisitive society."[19] As with the accompanying claim that Glassco had contributed to "the *avante-garde* Parisian magazines, *transition* and *This Quarter*," in "the twenties and thirties," Smith was only partly correct.[20] True, *The Deficit Made Flesh* collected many of Glassco's Eastern Townships poems – "The Rural Mail," "The Entailed Farm," "Gentleman's Farm," "Deserted Buildings under Shefford Mountain," "The Burden of Junk," "Town Council Meeting," "The White Mansion," and several others – but in his description, Smith ignores the many poems without connection to the area.[21] This included some of Glassco's strongest verse, among them: "A Devotion," "The Cardinal's Dog," "Shake Dancer," "Thomas à Kempis," "Utrillo's World I," "Villanelle," and "The Whole Hog." In the words of Michael Gnarowski, a friend of both men, this selective description "helped foster the idea that Glassco's poetry was 'rural' and 'bucolic.'"[22]

The earliest review, by John Robert Colombo, was atypical in its negativity: Glassco's "theme is rural, and unfortunately, his technique is often pedestrian … It is curious to note that when Mr Glassco does treat a suburban, or even urban, subject, he does it with greater conviction than with the rustic themes of 'The Rural Mail' and 'Stud Groom.'"[23] Published in *The Tamarack Review*, the criticism stood in stark contrast with almost all that followed. In the pages of *The Fiddlehead*, J.K. Johnstone declared Glassco to be one of the country's best poets, adding that *The Deficit Made*

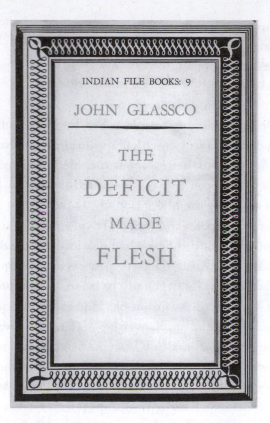

INDIAN FILE BOOKS: 9

JOHN GLASSCO

THE

DEFICIT

MADE

FLESH

Glassco's first book, *The Deficit Made Flesh*,
published in his fiftieth year.

Flesh deserved a place on "the abbreviated shelf that holds outstanding volumes of Canadian verse."[24] Closest to home, Louis Dudek described the collection as "the work of a writer who has been tagging along for some time in Canadian poetry but who now promises to occupy a role corresponding to his real merits."[25] Calling attention to "The Entailed Farm," "Gentleman's Farm," "The White Mansion," and "The Whole Hog," Milton Wilson's review in *The Canadian Forum* followed Smith's jacket blurb, describing the poems as "Canada's lyric equivalents of Wordsworth's *The Ruined Cottage*, *Michael* and *The Brothers*, poems of fallen or unfinished sheepfolds, of unnatural piety and lost covenants: arguments from the broken design."[26]

This comparison to Wordsworth marked the first mention of a name that would linger in criticism of Glassco's verse; indeed the posthumous John Glassco tribute issue of *Canadian Poetry* would lead off with a study by John Burnett entitled "John Glassco: The Canadian Wordsworth." Glassco recognized his indebtedness to Wordsworth. Nearly a quarter century earlier, Glassco had identified two of his own poems, "The Wild Canary" and "The Two Linnets," both now lost, as being derivative of the nineteenth-century English poet laureate.[27]

Glassco did nothing to combat this public perception. Indeed, he frequently expressed his deep admiration for Wordsworth. In *Memoirs of Montparnasse*, Glassco describes the man as his favourite English poet. He believed "Lines Written a Few Miles above Tintern Abbey" to be "the finest meditative poem in English" and recommended the poem in a letter to Elma, encouraging her to read it at a slow pace. "It can still raise the prickles on the hair at the back of my neck," he writes. "And yet it's *about* nothing, there are no intellectual ideas; it is just an upwelling of pure emotion, a kind of vague pantheism and affirmation of certain mysterious and undefined values. It is the *sustained* height at which he keeps for so long, the perfection of the contours: this is probably the best work of art, for feeling and *composition*, in English, for its length."[28] D.G. Jones remembers first meeting Glassco in a Toronto hotel room, on the occasion of the 1960 publication of *The Oxford Book of Canadian Verse*: "he sat on a bed, glass in one hand, and started talking to me about Wordsworth. I was so surprised. He obviously really did have a feel for Wordsworth, and he obviously had a feel for the Townships, and the two came together with an unlikely continental perspective and Eliotic note, which is part of the peculiar mix of Glassco himself, something between St Augustine and the absolute rake, between Wordsworth and the French ironists."[29]

The Deficit Made Flesh had little effect on finances at Jamaica Farm. Glassco received a $100 advance for the book and would later claim that it had sold 112 copies of its 400-copy print run before being remaindered for thirteen cents.[30] There were, thankfully, much greater benefits. The book attracted notice of other poets, including Ralph Gustafson, whose 1942 *Anthology of Canadian Poetry (English)* was second only to Smith's *The Book of Canadian Poetry* in terms of influence and prestige. Gustafson wrote expressing regret that he hadn't been aware of Glassco's verse when compiling his new *Penguin Book of Canadian Verse*.[31]

Three of the eight previous Indian File books, those by James Reaney, James Wreford, and P.K. Page, had received the Governor General's Award for poetry. Scott and Al Purdy, to cite just two names, were certain that *The*

Deficit Made Flesh would do the same. Instead, the 1958 award was received by James Reaney for *A Suit of Nettles*. To Glassco, the decision was perfectly understandable; he thought the Ontario poet's book "much more *brilliant*," adding that "the judges were understandably dazzled by the technique and virtuosity of it and also influenced by the fact that it was all of a piece." Looking back, three years after publication, he told Elma that *The Deficit Made Flesh* contained too much variety: "it is confusing, it changes in tone and background, you never know where you are with the author, every poem is a fresh start and requires a different orientation in the reader."[32]

The Deficit Made Flesh had been published between two trips to Paris. The first, in August 1958, followed decades of hesitation, postponements, and false starts made with Taylor. Elma expressed no such indecision, yet, in the early stages of Glassco's planning, she was ignored. Instead, he sought out an old flame; he wrote to Kay Boyle at her Connecticut home with the not so subtle suggestion that they meet up in Paris: "I don't want to be dead alone there – though what I want most of all is to walk the Blvd. St Michel & perhaps meet one J. Glassco (aged 18) though of course I know that is out of the question: poor boy, what in God's name happened to *him*?"[33] Boyle chose not to answer the letter, though she did mention Glassco's proposal to her friend Robert Carlton Brown, author of the Nick Carter detective novels: "Wouldn't it be a shock to him if grandma should take him at his word!"[34]

The trip did not disappoint. Elma, in particular, delighted in the city. Visiting Laurence Vail, Man Ray, Tristan Tzara, and Ossip Zadkine, Glassco was not, as he'd once feared "un étranger… lumped in with a lot of wealthy feckless trippers."[35] The welcome and acceptance extended to his completion of *Under the Hill*, Aubrey Beardsley's unfinished novel. Glassco had first attempted to place the manuscript, without success, through British novelist and critic Julian Symons the previous year. Stopping off in London before heading to Paris, he was equally frustrated when making a second attempt in person. These failed efforts can to a large extent be explained by the novel's history. The first three chapters had first appeared, heavily expurgated, in the January 1896 debut issue of pornographer Leonard Smithers's Decadent *Savoy* magazine; another chapter followed three months later. In 1904, after Beardsley's death, John Lane published *Under the Hill* in a bowdlerized version, but it wasn't until three years later that the work, as *The Story of Venus and Tannhaüser*, finally appeared in an unexpurgated edition.

Pirated by Smithers, limited to three hundred copies, it was intended "for the use of literary students who are also admirers of Beardsley's wayward genius." Lane twice reissued his *Under the Hill*, but even this censored version had been out of print for well over three decades when Glassco first presented the completion.

Coming two years before the *Lady Chatterley's Lover* trial, Glassco's attempt at an English sale was ill-timed. His manuscript was based on Beardsley's original, not the expurgated text that had been published by Lane.

In the French capital, the atmosphere was markedly different. Glassco knew that his best prospect was at Maurice Girodias's Olympia Press. Though less than seven years old, the house had already achieved considerable notoriety and distinction as the publishers of Samuel Becket, J.P. Donleavy's *The Ginger Man*, and *Lolita* by Vladimir Nabokov. As an English-language publisher located in Paris, the press enjoyed freedom from the more stringent censorship rules in force in England and the United States.

Glassco presented his completed *Under the Hill* in an afternoon meeting with Girodias at the Olympia Press offices, located in a dilapidated old house on rue de Nesle, and came away having sold the rights for $600.

When published in 1959, *Under the Hill* was unlike any other Olympia Press book. Illustrated by Beardsley, bound in green watered silk, printed on heavy paper, and issued in a limited numbered edition of three thousand copies, it was a lavish production that would never be repeated. When reprinted, *Under the Hill* would appear between the "notorious bile-green" covers, joining *The Naked Lunch* by William Burroughs, *The Black Book* by Lawrence Durrell, and titles such as *Fuzz against Junk* and *The Whip Angels* by lesser writers, in Olympia's famed Traveller's Companion Series.[36]

Glassco claimed to have first read an expurgated edition of *Under the Hill* as a boy, though it wasn't until 1948 that he first attempted completing the text. Work on the book is referred to only twice in the Intimate Journal; as something "which amuses me occasionally"[37] and, later, as "bogged down, but only dormant."[38] There is nothing of the anxious, agonizing self-doubt and torment that is so often a part of Glassco's record on other projects. It was completed without an eye on the market, rather, as he wrote, "largely as a labour of love."[39]

Glassco's interest in Beardsley's retelling of the Tannhäuser myth went beyond mere appreciation of erotica and the Decadents. As Leon Edel observed, completing the work was for Glassco "a way of proclaiming his own survival."[40] Here was one man, who at twenty-five had appeared cured of tuberculosis, going on to complete the forgotten pages of a man who had succumbed to the very same disease at the very same age. Most certainly, Glassco was thinking of his not so distant self when writing in his introduction that Beardsley's failure to complete the story is explained by "the all-too-human faults of dejection, listlessness, ennui."[41]

Glassco, who believed that Beardsley's "prose might be imitated, but never the drawings," had been meticulous.[42] He had succeeded in picking up Beardsley's thread, left in mid-paragraph, creating not so much as a seam. Yet Glassco did introduce two interests that, it would appear, were not shared by Beardsley: flagellation and the touch of governesses. In the continuation, Glassco has Tannhaüser attend a performance of *Pink Cheeks*, a celebrated pantomime-operetta that is advertised as "Two Hours of Fun & Flagellation"[43] performed by "the famous troupe of Madame Mubouleau."[44] The theatrical event, described in considerable detail, excites the chevalier for whom "make-believe had turned into reality!"[45] Later, in Rome to seek absolution, Tannhaüser sets out to transcribe his "unexamples flagitiousness, certain peccadilloes, quasi-transgressions, minor sodomies, and other things," lest he omit any sin while in the presence of the Holy Father.[46] In doing so, he casts his mind back to his nursery governess Mademoiselle Fanfreluche and "their merry games at bedtime, the caresses which like favourable breezes had urged on the forward season of his youth, all those charming things which had made him such an early impassioned connoisseur of naughtiness."[47] Ultimately, Tannhaüser's memory of the sensual caress of Mademoiselle Fanfreluche is replaced by the violent strikes of a later governess: "His recollections darted forward to his first exploit as a lover, to the act, at once result and retort, which followed on his first birching by his English governess – the summary ravishment of that spinster who, too surprised to resist or cry out, had yielded her guarded treasure with something close to complaisance."[48] This imagined English governess would soon be joined by another.

After spending the winter in Foster, the following March Glassco and Elma returned to Paris. They again visited rue de Nesle, this time with the manuscript of a work entitled *The English Governess*. The story it told was not entirely new to Girodias; he recognized the bones of *A Firm Hand*, the pornographic novel that had once been purchased by the Jack Woodford

Press. Glassco had presented the manuscript to the publisher at their meeting the previous August, but it had been rejected as too tame a work of pornography. Girodias encouraged Glassco and Elma to rewrite the book. The nature of Elma's participation in the exercise is unknown. Whether performed as a couple or by Glassco on his own, in the seven months between visits, *A Firm Hand* was cut by more than a half. To this shortened novel he added a new character, new sexual scenes, and a base language not found in the original.

Rewritten to order, the resulting manuscript was quickly accepted by Olympia. Girodias laid his terms, offering an outright royalty of 3,000 francs, with a further 3,000 francs for each printing. The publisher was quick to add: "but, as you know, we seldom reprint. You would not, however, be free to offer the manuscript to another publisher – even if we do not reprint."[49] Glassco accepted these excessive conditions but chose not to be identified as the author and selected the name Miles Underwood as a *nom de plume*. Although Girodias later claimed the pseudonym to be of his own making, it was Glassco's creation alone. He later explained that it was "dreamed up on an hour's notice to meet a printer's deadline in Paris in 1959 [*sic*]. It signifies a man who *would* be *under* by miles and miles. A 'docile' type, à la Justice Weekly."[50] In appearance *The English Governess* was a far more modest book than *Under the Hill*: a cheap-looking pocket book, it was typical of the Olympia Press format. The novel's publication, less than three months after acceptance, marked the beginning of what was to become a most peculiar and complex publishing history.

The English Governess was an immediate commercial success, a favourite in a market that relied almost exclusively on word of mouth. Contrary to Girodias's cautioning, it was mere months before Olympia published a reprint. And yet, any pride he may have felt from the success Glassco kept to himself. Only Girodias, Elma, and a friend, Milton Kastello, to whom he'd presented an inscribed copy, knew the secret. It wasn't until the latter half of 1961, when he felt obliged to seek legal advice from Frank Scott – this in response to bills of exchange having been returned by Girodias's bank for lack of funds – that Glassco began revealing himself as a pornographer. Even then, he felt obliged to explain his motivations. Moments after Scott left his company, *The English Governess* in hand, Glassco wrote his friend: "Now if you do read it, please look on this rather silly and revolting book simply as a kind of act of self-purgation of mine, a 'burning-out' (*sparked*, if you will, by the prospect of $600) of a tiresome obsession which has spoiled my prose-writing for far too long."[51]

Here he was writing to a man who five months earlier had argued in the Court of Queen's Bench against the suppression of *Lady Chatterley's Lover*, a man who was in the midst of preparing to defend the same work before the Supreme Court. Glassco need not have been concerned; Scott enjoyed *The English Governess* and returned to it more than once. In a diary entry from 1968, he writes that reading it late at night gave him "a beautiful erection and glowing thoughts."[52]

Although he gradually began to reveal his authorship to select friends, for a great many years Glassco would continue to keep it hidden from the public. Nearly a decade after publication, he responded to a query from one of Margaret Atwood's students at Sir George Williams University:

> Intelligent books on flagellation are almost non-existent. The best one I know is the masochistic novel THE ENGLISH GOVERNESS: the publisher recently sent me a few copies, and I will send you one if you like. For the flagellation of (rather than by) women, there are always GRUSHENKA, DOLLY MORTON and NELL IN BRIDEWELL, all sadistic pseudo-1st-person accounts; they were being sold a few months ago at Classic's littlebooks store. These are real Victorian "classics," which have retained their appeal: hardy perennials, as it were.[53]

In his introduction to *The Olympia Reader*, published six years after *The English Governess*, Girodias would incorrectly claim the genesis of the book for his own:

> My publishing technique was simple in the extreme, at least in the first years: when I had completely run out of money I wrote blurbs for imaginary books, invented sonorous titles and funny pen names (Marcus van Heller, Akbar del Piombo, Miles Underwood, Carmencita de las Lunas, etc.) and then printed a list which was sent out to our clientele of booklovers, tempting them with such titles as *White Thighs*, *The Chariot of Flesh*, *The Sexual Life of Robinson Crusoe*, *With Open Mouth*, etc. They immediately responded with orders and money,

thanks to which we were able to eat, drink, write, and print. I could again advance money to my authors, and they hastened to turn in manuscripts which more or less fitted the descriptions.[54]

Although Girodias's claim concerning the origins of the book are at best mistaken, his description of Olympia's publishing practices is forthright, and explains much about his difficulties in paying anything beyond an advance on royalties. For the rest of his life, Glassco would experience frequent difficulties in obtaining the monies owed by the publisher, yet the situation rarely raised anger. In the midst of his first battle with Girodias over payment, Glassco wrote some kind words to Elma: "God knows the world would be a lot duller without people like him, and books like the ones he publishes, and remarks like his calculation that '600,000 people had been corrupted by the Olympia Press.' All this is refreshing in a world that is getting too intolerably dull and stodgy and moral."[55]

In February 1965, Glassco received an unexpected letter from Moe Shapiro, a former owner and editor at the Jack Woodford Press, informing him that the assets of the defunct publisher had been purchased by a new venture, Waron Press. In going through the papers he'd acquired, Shapiro had come across a galley of *The Dominant One*, Woodford Press' title for *A Firm Hand*. It was Waron's hope that the author would again be willing to sell the novel for publication.

Glassco took heart that *A Firm Hand*, the manuscript of which he had destroyed after writing *The English Governess*, had somehow survived, and was anxious that it might still find its way into print. The obstacle, it would seem, concerned the resemblance of *The English Governess* to its original. Glassco wrote immediately to Girodias:

> The version has little similarity to TEG beyond the general plot, the sequence and some of the writing of the scenes, and the names of the two principal characters: Mr Lovell [sic] is a shadow and Kate does not exist. The book is somewhat longer than TEG, and the tone extremely tepid. It could not compete with TEG, of which, it is no more than a rough and bowdlerized draft.
>
> As there may be, however, sufficient similarity between the two books to infringe, at least technically, on your rights in the latter, I

would suggest that I pay you, as a permissions fee, 10% of whatever amount I receive from Waron Press ...[56]

While degrees can be argued, the claim that the recovered manuscript had "little similarity" to *The English Governess* is difficult to defend. Both begin with the very same words and contain many identical passages. Nor was the author being at all honest in his dismissal of *A Firm Hand* as "no more than a rough and bowdlerized draft"; the work was a more polished "clean version" of the romance between student and governess.[57]

Girodias wrote back and declined Glassco's offer, adding that he wouldn't stand in the way of publication. A few months later, Glassco received $600 for the US rights to the rediscovered work from Shapiro, who in turn resold the book to Grove Press.

In 1967, after a delay of thirteen years, Glassco's *A Firm Hand* finally appeared as *Harriet Marwood, Governess*, by Anonymous. It is unlikely that the text was much altered from that once owned by the Jack Woodford Press. In fact, it is possible that the writing of jacket copy may have consumed the greatest part of the author's attention in preparing the work for print. Lacking credit, the words bear the mark of Glassco's fancy and style:

> Although exhaustive scholarship has proven futile in unearthing the true author of *Harriet Marwood, Governess*, there is enough evidence, textual and cultural, for us to assume its composition to be autobiographical. Whether written by the female dominator or the male submissive, however, is totally unknown. Some of the delicate descriptions of furnishings and clothing have led commentators to assume a woman's hand, yet the graphic attention paid to the details of whips, harnesses, and straps lead other researchers to the conclusion that the book was written by a man, "perhaps a horseman," Dr Fritz Beobachter notes. Whatever, its author is remarkably well hidden behind a veil of crisp British prose.[58]

Any satisfaction Glassco felt in finally seeing the romance between boy and governess published as he'd originally intended was soon tempered by the appearance of a pirated edition, *The Governess*, published by Collector's Publications of Covina, California. His exasperation increased when

Girodias quickly issued a 100,000-copy abridged edition of *The English Governess*, without his consent, under the catch-all title *The Authentic Confessions of Harriet Marwood, an English Governess*. With three competing books, released within months of one another, the lucrative US pornography market now seemed glutted.

It wasn't until 1976 – by which point Glassco's authorship had become known to many in the literary community – that there would be a Canadian edition of the book. Issued by General Publishing, it afforded Glassco an opportunity to both acknowledge *Harriet Marwood, Governess* as his own and obfuscate its origins. In a preface written purposely for the new edition, he pinpoints the novel's conception to his reading of German neurologist Albert Eulenberg's nineteenth-century *Sadismus und Masochismus* some twenty-two years before. Glassco quotes a passage from this early work of sexology: "the heroine of the English masochistic 'educational' novel, those proud Victorian women who brought up the youths entrusted to them with the most humiliating service and homage in order finally to let the sun of their highest favour shine upon (or rather under) them."[59]

In fact, Glassco had not read Eulenberg's study in the original German, as he claimed, but Harold Kent's English-language 1934 translation, *Algolagnia: The Psychology, Neurology and Physiology of Sadistic Love and Masochism*. The purposeful deceit implied a familiarity with the language, thus supporting his forthcoming "translation" of Leopold von Sacher-Masoch's *Venus im Pelz*, a book that was due to be published mere months after the Canadian *Harriet Marwood, Governess*.

However, the preface contains an even greater deception, in that the words attributed to Eulenberg are Glassco's own; *Sadismus und Masochismus* makes no mention of the "English masochistic 'educational' novel," nor does the phrase feature in the Kent translation. Nevertheless, given the scarcity of *Sadismus und Masochismus* and its English-language translation, it was a clever front. Glassco builds upon the falsehood by writing that Eulenberg's description prompted a feverish, yet futile, search for the work described:

> Did these fascinating novels really exist? Or had Eulenburg only imagined them? The latter prospect was unbearable, and I decided that since there were in effect no such books I would have to write one myself.[60]

In fact, Glassco had been well aware that these books did exist. To be fair, they were not English, as he'd had Eulenburg describe them, rather these works of erotica were written in French and *set* in England. While Glassco may have been determined to write such a book himself, it was not an accomplishment he could properly claim.

Exactly when Glassco began composing the novel that would lead to *The English Governess* and *Harriet Marwood, Governess* is unknown, however the inspiration can be traced with ease back to 1938. That spring he had received from Paris a copy of *La gouvernante*, a work of erotica written under the name Aimé van Rod. To Glassco the novel was revelatory: "I was amazed and appalled to see how completely it gave expression to the same erotic situations I had already projected: everything is the same – I might have written it myself in a fit of industry."[61]

La gouvernante, by Aimé van Rod.

La gouvernante was one of a series of *livres condamnés* credited to the seemingly prolific Monsieur van Rod. His titles included *Nos belles flagellantes, Visites fantastiques au Pays du Fouet, Le Fouet au convent, Les Humiliations de Miss Madge*, and well over two dozen others. Sadly, there was no Aimé van Rod; it was a house pseudonym appended to the work of an unknown number of ghost writers employed by Librairie Artistique et Littéraire.[62] For the most part, books written under the van Rod name followed a simple formula, one best described by literary historian and antiquarian bookseller Steven J. Gertz: "the female protagonist, almost always a young, innocent girl, is violently whipped from dawn to dusk for the most picayune of transgressions, most often by some twisted schoolmistress or governess with after-hours erotic designs/actions which the girl/narrator 'cannot speak of!'"[63]

In that it presents the reader with a male protagonist, *La gouvernante* marks a departure within the van Rod *oeuvre*, taking the narrative in a direction that would have been attractive to Glassco. The tale told in *La gouvernante* centres on James Lowell, a rather effeminate adolescent boy – the product of an overly protective mother, recently deceased. The widowed Mr Lowell, "*un homme d'affaires*," is at a loss over what to do with James until a friend suggests he hire a governess for the boy. He finds one in Barbara Humphreys, "*une superbe fille qui paraissait àgée [sic] d'une vingtaine d'années*," who sets herself apart from the other applicants by appearing at the grand Lowell house in person.[64] The English governess is hired with little consideration, thus beginning James's education. Miss Humphreys adopts "*la méthode des châtiments corporels pour amener James à la perfection, – but auquel elle tendait, du moins d'après ses dires.*"[65] With the sudden, melodramatic death of Mr Lowell, the governess becomes James's guardian, and the routine of correction continues, leading to love, devotion, and, ultimately, marriage. Following the honeymoon, the newlyweds retire to a country cottage, where the bride begins an education of a different sort – James is used in demonstrating her methods of correction to a pair of female disciples.

Although Glassco claimed deceptively and with an illusion of modesty that the plot of *Harriet Marwood, Governess* had been laid out in *Sadismus und Masochismus*, it is *La gouvernante* that he follows – down to the very words. In this respect, *Harriet Marwood, Governess* marks Glassco's debut as a translator of prose.

La gouvernante begins:

James Lowell avait treize ans lorsque mourut sa mere.

C'était un petite garçon un peu insignifiant, de caractère ren-
fermé, d'humeur douce et égale.

Il avait toujours marqué une préférence pour les jeux tranquilles,
les jeux des filles, et sa mère l'avait entretenu dans ces gouts paisibles
par une sévérité distante qu'elle prétendait convenir au tempérament
des garçons.

Au collège ses camarades l'appellaient « la fille ». Il en rougissant,
mais ne faisait rien pour mériter le surnom contraire.[66]

With *Harriet Marwood, Governess*, Glassco provides the reader with
two pages of background on the Lovel family before introducing his protagonist:

Richard Belsize Lovel was fourteen years old when his mother died.
He was even then a rather insignificant boy, small for his age, shy, of
a reserved disposition and a sweet and even temper. As a child he had
always shown a preference for quiet, peaceful games, and his mother
had preserved these childish tastes in him by the exercise of an aloof
severity which she believed to be the proper treatment for boys. At
the dame's school his comrades called him *Sissy: Sissy Lovel*. He had
blushed at the nickname, but made no attempt to deserve any other.[67]

Like Aimé van Rod's Mr Lowell, Mr Lovel is a recently widowed businessman who despairs over what might be done about the rearing of his
lone child. Just as Mr Lowell's friend suggests he hire a governess, a *"filles
de pasteurs ou autres, bien pensantes, bien instruites, possédant de solides
diplômes,"*[68] the friend of Mr Lovel recommends he consider the "daughters
of clergymen and such right-minded, well-educated, certificates in order."[69]
For the first four chapters, Glassco continues the translation, rarely
departing from the text, and providing little in the way of embellishment.[70]
The weather described in the two novels is identical, the dialogue varies only
slightly, the secondary characters – Bridget, the cook who is prone to
gossip, and Molly, the caretaker's wife – retain their names, positions, and
personalities. The first significant deviation from the van Rod work occurs
in the administrations of the initial punishments. James and Richard
commit an identical transgression: failure to complete the second of two

mathematical problems. As a consequence, both boys are accused of inattention. Told to stand, van Rod's James is given a "*claque sèche sur le derrière*."[71] However, for Harriet, the more severe of the two governesses, this method of correction is not enough. Glassco skips four pages of *La gouvernante*, picking up the narrative at the start of a more severe punishment in which James – and, as a result, Richard – receives strokes with a ruler on each hand. The two students are obliged to continue their lessons in tears, each suffering under the knowledge that his punishment is not yet complete. At the stroke of eleven, each is made to kneel – James on a *fauteuil*, Richard at a black leather chair. Jackets and waistcoats are removed, the governesses draw down the boys' trousers and drawers and, each using their left arm to encircle the waist of their charge, administer the first blow with their right hands. As with the beatings Glassco and his brother received from their father, James and Richard's ordeals end with a demonstration of affection:

> "Well," said Harriet, smiling at him. "You are not so badly hurt, are you?"
>
> His tears redoubled; he felt as if he were suffocating. "N-no, Miss…"
>
> Harriet continued looking at him with a faintly mocking glance. "I have forgiven you," she said. "And you will try to behave better in the future, will you not?"
>
> "Yes, Miss."
>
> "Then come here and kiss me, Richard. We shall forget this first spanking I have had to give you. That is the way all your punishments will end, – with a kiss."[72]

It is not long before floggings are administered on a near-daily basis. The respective governesses take advantage of relative seclusion and privacy offered by the Lowell and Lovel country homes – both located near the Stour River – in order to further escalate their corrective methods.

In *Harriet Marwood, Governess*, the course toward matrimony is not as straightforward as in *La gouvernante*. Misreading the relationship between governess and employer, a jealous Richard loses his virginity to a kindly prostitute. He falls ill and, after being nursed back to health by Miss Marwood, confesses the indiscretion. The governess, in turn, must deal with the knowledge of an act that, it would seem, her punishments cannot correct. The relationship is twice jeopardized by others: Miss Alicia Barrington and Sir Robert Hartley. Urged on by her rather base, *nouveau riche* "prosperous stock-jobbing family," the former pursues Richard; while Sir Robert, whose brute masculinity stands in harsh contrast with the boy's feminine form, is drawn to Harriet.[73] The climax of *Harriet Marwood, Governess* is reached when Richard inadvertently interrupts Sir Robert's proposal of marriage. The baronet proceeds to horsewhip the boy, the first time a man administers Richard's punishment. Harriet watches the beating with growing excitement, encouraging, even begging Sir Robert further, before abruptly insisting that he cease. Helping Richard to stand, the governess announces to a surprised Sir Robert that she will be marrying her young ward. Richard is then made to undergo a vasectomy, and, after a period of convalescence, the couple are married. During the honeymoon, it is discovered that Richard's sexual appetite is nowhere near as great as that of his bride. When he falls asleep before the former governess is properly satisfied, his correction begins anew. Having succeeded in creating in Richard her model student, Harriet is now determined to bring into being the ideal husband.

Glassco's debt to *La gouvernante* was considerable, and his failure to acknowledge the dozens of translated pages left him vulnerable to a charge of plagiarism. Six years after publication, in a response to a query from his friend Geoffrey Wagner, Glassco acknowledged that the inspiration for *Harriet Marwood, Governess* was drawn from a variety of sources, including Michael Sadleir's *Fanny by Gaslight*, which had inspired "the look and smell of London in the 1880's and Harriet's costumes."[74] That Glassco made no mention of his debt to *La gouvernante*, particularly to one such as Wagner, a fellow expert in flagellant literature, may speak to his recognition of the book's scarcity. A fragile paperback, printed on cheap newsprint, it was not designed to survive into the latter half of the twentieth-century.[75]

Although it was not his intention, the ornate writing style employed by Glassco, in union with his research, would fool many into thinking that *Harriet Marwood, Governess* had actually been written in the Victorian age. Among the deceived was US critic Morse Peckham, who cited the work in his 1969 "experiment in explanation" *Art and Pornography*. In a chapter devoted to sadomasochistic literature, he compares the novel favourably to *Story of O*: "Almost as interesting is a work written, especially for its time, at an unusually high literary level, *The English Governess*, recently made available by the Grove Press as *Harriet Marwood, Governess*."[76] Peckham not only errs with his assumption that *The English Governess* and *Harriet Marwood, Governess* are exactly the same book, but he also believes that Glassco's novels – or, as he believes, novel – were written in the era of the events they describe; yet both stories are explicitly set in the narrative past: "more than sixty years ago" (in *The English Governess*, 1) and "more than fifty years ago" (in *Harriet Marwood, Governess*, 3).

Ultimately, *Harriet Marwood, Governess* was much more than a plagiarized *La gouvernante*; rather, the older novel had provided a setting and atmosphere in which his own fantasies could grow. For Glassco, literature was not static; it was open to retelling, reinterpretation, adaptation, and, of course, translation. In 1954, after completing *A Firm Hand*, Glassco had recast the story of Richard and Harriet for the theatre as *The Augean Stable*. This unproduced, unpublished drawing-room drama is not a simple adaptation, but a variation on a theme. Had Girodias not requested a reworked version of *A Firm Hand*, one would have almost certainly been written. In the resulting *The English Governess*, Glassco had done more than insert explicit sex scenes and lower the level of language, he had again reimagined the love story, drawing further from his own history. As the sounds of beatings, the slap of the strap, and the involuntary cries served to excite his mother, so, too, do the sounds of Richard's discipline provide something of an aural aphrodisiac to Mr Lovel, his mistress Kate, and the young couples "couched on beds of fern and bracken" lining the Lover's Lane adjacent to the country estate.[77]

The sale of *The English Governess* to Girodias proved to be a bright spot in what was to become an otherwise muted trip. Glassco and Elma had returned to Paris with the grand intention of settling, and as spring and summer passed, the desire to make the city their new home only strengthened. However, the months they were devoting in search of a suitable apartment to purchase were anything but fruitful. Real estate prices were high, and to Glassco it seemed that the city was becoming more expensive with each passing day. Then, in October, family matters intruded in the form of a letter from his sister Beatrice. David's failed investments had left their mother so short of capital that Glassco and his sister were forced to step in to save the house. Shortly thereafter, Glassco lost approximately $5,000 in the stock market, a jolt he blamed on the inability to properly administer finances at such a distance. Their dream of living in Paris abandoned, the once hopeful couple withdrew to Jamaica Farm.

Glassco's disappointment may have been alleviated somewhat by his proximity to so many of Canada's finest poets. While the purchase of Windermere and his retreat to the Eastern Townships had been so isolating, a quarter century later it appeared as if the other English language poets of Quebec were following his lead. Since 1941, Frank and Marion Scott had been spending summers in North Hatley, fifty kilometres from Foster. Others had settled in the town, either as permanent residents or in order to escape the oppressive humidity and brutal heat of summer in Montreal. The town's Houghton Street was home to D.G. Jones, Ralph Gustafson, and novelist Ronald Sutherland and was the location of Stone Hedge, Hugh MacLennan's summer house. Not everyone spent the season in the town Glassco jokingly referred to as the Athens of the Eastern Townships. Smith stayed at the cottage his wife had inherited at Drummond Point, while Dudek had a summer home in nearby Way's Mills.

Closer than all these people was journalist and essayist Jean Le Moyne, who had a summer place in Bondville, just a short drive from Jamaica Farm. Le Moyne had been a friend of Garneau's and had edited the poet's posthumous *Journal* and *Poésies complètes* with Robert Elie. The proximity of his Bondville home would prove to be fortunate.

Early in 1960, with growing frustration, Glassco again turned his attention to Garneau's *Journal*. The previous year, before leaving for Paris, he'd felt confident in sending a proposal and sample translations to Kildare Dobbs at Macmillan of Canada. The publisher was very much impressed with the quality of translation, but the submission was declined; the work, it was felt, would hold little interest for the general reader.

Although only Macmillan had been approached, dejection set in. Glassco wrote to his friend Scott: "If I can't find a publisher I must drop the project, though I can hardly face the prospect of this: the original book seems finer than ever to me."[78]

The manuscript was rejected again; this time by editor Ivon Owen, who didn't consider it suitable for Oxford University Press. Somewhat mixed news arrived a few months later in the form of a reader's report from McClelland & Stewart. Though largely positive, reservations were expressed as to the quality of translation. In desperation, that July, Glassco approached Le Moyne, hoping that he might act as a consultant in completing the manuscript. The two men quickly fell into a fruitful working relationship, with Le Moyne making frequent trips to Foster. By the autumn, Glassco had managed to place his translation of the *Journal* with McClelland & Stewart.

For the fourth time in three years, Glassco had managed to get a publisher behind his work, and yet he was disappointed in the progress of his career. Even the presence of Elma, whom he had come to recognize as "my only, my unique love,"[79] could not revive his spirits completely. In November 1960, not four years after Taylor's death, Glassco turned to his Intimate Journal and took account of his progress:

> Face it, dear fellow. What you want is a smashing success, recognition, your picture in the newspapers, money. In other words, I want the world to recognise me as something I suspect I am not, a man of real talent. And that will not be, if only for the reason that I am too versatile, change my spots every year or so. My ambition has always been too widely diffused: I wanted to write one book of *good* poetry, one good novel, one successful play, one good erotic book, one good work of pornography, one best-selling volume of memoirs, one fine piece of translation. Now I see that I have only done the poetry, the erotic book (*Under the Hill*) & the pornographic book (*The English Governess*) – at least these have been published; the novel (*Mairobert*) & the play (*The Liberator*) are written, but they are unacceptable to the public; the translation (Garneau's *Journal*) will probably be published in the spring.
>
> Come then, cheer up: your ambitions are almost half realised! I never realised this before.
>
> Only two more books to write – *The Monster* (this could be my one good *bad* book) and the Memoirs of a Young Man, still untitled.
>
> To work, to work! Once more I thank you, comfortable book.
>
> Let success come if it will, & if it will not then I've done *almost* my best. It can't be commanded, it's largely a matter of chance.[80]

Glassco would never return to his "comfortable book." The Intimate Journal he'd begun as a tuberculosis patient thirty years before, came to an end when, early in 1961, the disease recurred.

DUM NOCET IUVAT[1]

Bedridden at Montreal's Royal Edward Hospital, sharing a room with three sickly men, one of whom was forever coughing up phlegm, Glassco took heart. His condition was anything but dire. In the three decades that had elapsed since he'd first battled tuberculosis, Quebec's mortality rate had dropped from over 110 per hundred thousand to just seven. Advances had been made. This time there would be no need for surgery.

At the beginning of April, Glassco was transferred to the Royal Edward Laurentian Hospital in Ste-Agathe-des-Monts, 100 kilometres north of Montreal. Elma was left alone at Jamaica Farm, well over three hours away by car. They spoke often in long-distance phone calls, an expensive means of communication Glassco normally avoided, and sent each other several letters a week. "Life without you is inconceivable to me – even for a month," Glassco wrote just prior to his arrival in Ste-Agathe, yet he discouraged Elma from visiting.[2] It wasn't until mid-July, after four months apart, that the two would again see one another.

The hospital stay was begun in good spirits, in part because Glassco recognized that the routine imposed by convalescence was ideal for his work. Sending for his files and typewriter, the poet settled in for a period that he anticipated would end before autumn. The days and weeks that followed did so at a speed he found surprising: "like telegraph-poles from a railway-car."[3] Certainly, there was enough to occupy his time. From the desk in his comfortable private room, Glassco attended to Jamaica Farm, directing detailed instructions to Elma over the sale of hay, the rental of the barn, plumbing issues, bat extermination, and the tricky maintenance of his aging yellow Jeepster. He was more than content to spend his time in quiet, semi-seclusion going over finances, manuscripts, correspondence, and books. One area of concentration paid off in a surprising manner; going over old receipts, he uncovered a series of banking errors that stretched back to 1955 and managed to recover more than $1,300.

Depression visited rarely, but when it did appear it descended in dramatic fashion. At the end of the second month, shortly after sending off the completed *Journal of Saint-Denys-Garneau* to McClelland & Stewart, he experienced a sudden and extreme drop in spirit. Though he recognized his irrationality, Glassco began to fear that the hospitalization would last as long as five years. Panicked, he confronted Elma, accusing her of withholding painkillers he'd asked her to smuggle to him through the mail. "I suppose you are holding them back lest I try to kill myself," he wrote in anger, before assuring his love that the pills were not strong enough to achieve that end.[4]

As did the days and months, these periods of despair passed quickly. Glassco established himself as the "nurses' *pet*" and was allowed a great deal of latitude, which he chose not to exercise.[5] Instead, he remained a bemused bystander, watching as the other male patients snuck off into the village to drink. Even with the coming of summer weather, Glassco expressed little regret at his hospital sentence. The Foster Horse Show, held for an eleventh year on Jamaica Farm, was not missed. He wrote Elma expressing pleasure that she had taken it upon herself to present the Graeme Taylor Memorial Trophy.

Not even Arthur Smith's annual arrival in the townships broke his desire for solitude. Glassco communicated regularly through mail addressed to Drummond Point but refused to allow his friend to visit. For his part, Smith sent small gifts in the form of "Penguins" that he had thought amusing, such as Anthony Powell's black comedy *From a View to a Death*.[6] Glassco found other reading material in the hospital's large library, delighting in unlikely discoveries like August Strindberg's *The Inferno* and André Breton's Surrealist romance *Nadja*. Aleister Crowley's *Diary of a Drug Fiend* was a particular favourite; he recommended the novel to Smith as "great fun in a jolly nasty Edwardian way."[7] However, despite the library's size, and the unexpected treats it contained, Glassco was anything but impressed, describing it as "an enormous, marvellous collection of Edwardian, Georgian, and modern rubbish, made up of the kind of books people give away or leave behind in hotels and trains."[8] This sorry collection he weakened further by liberating several volumes, including M.B. Ellie's study *De Saint-Denys Gar-*

neau and *La fin des songes* by Garneau's friend Robert Elie. The pilfering weighed on Glassco's conscience not one bit. He'd long held a policy carried forward by careful inspections of library cards. If he found a volume hadn't been taken out more than twice within the past year, Glassco would simply take the book for his own collection, asserting that the cards demonstrated that his interest was greater than that of the other patrons.

Although he worked on a number of poems, including "A Point of Sky," "Luce's Natch," and "The Places Where the Dead Have Walked," much of Glassco's own writing was taken up in correspondence in which he provided amusing observations of the goings-on around him. This, in turn, prompted Robert Weaver to suggest that Glassco write a piece on his convalescence for *The Tamarack Review*. Glassco asked Elma and Smith for the letters he'd sent, and he mined the material for "The Chronicles of Ste-Misère."[9]

One of Glassco's lightest pieces, it provides a less than accurate autobiographical record of his experiences as a man caught up in a situation over which he has no control. Ultimately, it is a good-natured complaint against a system that encouraged hospitals to view each new patient as a source of further government funding. Glassco was attentive to the very real possibility that he might one day have to return for care and so decided to alter select details. Montreal's Royal Edward Hospital became the Diamond Jubilee Hospital and the Royal Edward Laurentian Hospital was transformed into the Jubilee at Ste-Misère. The names of his doctor and nurse were changed, as were those of the patients. When published as "A Season in Limbo," Glassco hid behind the near anagrammatic *nom de plume* Silas N. Gooch, a "minor poet, single, unemployed."[10] Despite the obvious parallels, he was convinced that only friends would recognize him as the author.

It was also during the convalescence that he composed another, less public piece of autobiography: his "Autobiographical Sketch." This curious confession and account of victimhood runs five full legal-sized, typewritten pages and follows a format not found in Glassco's other papers in that it ends in something of a legal format, including date – 9 June 1961 – and signature.

The "Autobiographical Sketch" is the most truthful of all Glassco's autobiographical writings, yet it begins with an act of subterfuge. In the very first sentence Glassco has struck out the true location of his birth, his parent's rented home at 49 St Luke Street, replacing it with 41 Simpson Street, the address of the Rawlings mansion.[11] What follows covers the period from birth to his first treatment for tuberculosis in the Royal Victoria Hospital. He writes openly and with little emotion of the abuse he suffered at the hands of his father, his unsettled education, and his early sexual experiences. After providing a brief account of his activities in Paris as a young man, Glassco concludes: "The remainder of my life has been happy, and after a period of quiet again became fantastic and unconventional; but this belongs to the immediate past and too many persons still living are involved for me to give any account of it."[12]

It's possible that he thought these final sentences to be truthful and accurate. Life at Windermere and in the early days at Jamaica Farm might be described as quiet but could not be considered conventional. There is no mention of Sappho, Amélie, the wife of the Marquis de Cardaillac, or the complexities of his relationship with Taylor. The unidentified "persons still living," which most certainly included Elma and Pearl Tiberi, were not limited to the "immediate past"; nor was their number set. In mid-November, as his stay at the Royal Edward Laurentian was about to enter the final month, Glassco had a sexual encounter with one of the young nurses. We know this only through a letter he wrote Elma:

Dearest tweet,

There's something that's been on my conscience for the last week. I know you won't really mind, but on the last night of the little-girl-from Ahuntsic's period of duty here or whatever they call it, she came in at 9 o'clock and bared her virgin heart. That would have been all-right, but the fact is things didn't stop there. God forgive me, she *was* a virgin, and she isn't any more. It was all so fast I really don't know how it happened: it was sort of primitive, if you know what I mean. Dearest, there's nothing to worry about: I didn't *finish*, though I pretended to, with gasps.

I don't really feel I did anything wrong. And I hope you don't feel I did either … The poor child was just all pepped up about leaving. She has gone now, and I hope she feels better – better than I do anyway. I'm really feeling wretched.

Otherwise no news.

Goodnight, my one and only love,

John[13]

The "little-girl-from Ahuntsic" was never mentioned again. The next piece of correspondence, a rather lengthy letter written two days later, begins with a long account of disappointment experienced in trying to purchase a pair of handsome handmade slippers.[14] However, the sexual encounter with the young nurse was not forgotten, and served to inspire a poem of "nightmare" and self-loathing, "For Cora Lightbody, RN":

> You are a landscape in the Tale of Terror,
>> Ca. 1910. Your bibful breasts secrete
>> Those dreamy fields, fens, fells, that sinister street
> Of the Georgian nightmare I must live forever ...[15]

Just as nothing is known about their various arrangements, agreements, and understandings, we cannot know what Elma thought of Glassco's "hospital love"; he destroyed every letter she ever wrote him. What is certain is that the sexual encounter was not the first outside of their relationship. In 1957 and 1958, during Elma's early years at Jamaica Farm, he'd had an affair with a married horsewoman, a member of a prominent Quebec newspaper family, for whom he had written the love poem "Villanelle."

A month after the confessional letter, just days before his fifty-second birthday, Glassco finally returned to Jamaica Farm. He had been instructed not to exert himself; he was content in simply wandering around his grounds. If anything, Glassco was less active than during his prolonged convalescence. The projects undertaken in winter 1962 were minor and carried out at a leisurely pace. He'd accepted a $250 CBC commission to write a radio script about Garneau's *Journal* and the forthcoming translation. Meanwhile, Frank Scott was readying for publication his own Garneau translations in *St-Denys Garneau and Anne Hébert*, a bilingual collection of eighteen poems by the two cousins. Any hopes that the Glassco and Scott translations would appear together were dashed by the rather late discovery that the Garneau family did not own the translation rights to the *Journal*. As he awaited resolution of the situation, Glassco wrote a poem for Marian Scott, the wife of the man who had inspired his translation.

> 'Airoee ...
> eh 'rhehu 'vrehu

eh villia villia 'vrehu, eh villia 'vrehu
eh velù villiu villiu villiu!
'tse dàigh dàigh dàigh
'tse-de-jay 'tse-de-jay 'tsee-'tsee 'tsìrritse-'tsìrritse
    'tsirao 'twitsee
'wìtitsee 'wètitsee 'wètitsee wit'yu woity woity woity
téeah wéeah, te-wéeah-weeàh
k'tuf à tuf à tuf à tuf à tuf à te kerry
k'rry k'rry k'rry, tu!
ka 'kea kowa, keka keka!
'tw'ait, 'tw'it. Tw'at.[16]

The most aberrant of works, "Catbird" was a reaction to the charts, typographic collages, and sound poems that were then appearing with increasing frequency in Canada's little magazines. Glassco revealed all in a lengthy letter to Smith:

> This being the lunatic season for poetry (*cf.* The ideograms, picture poems, etc. in *Alphabet* and *Delta*) I endorse this letter with my own effort, the fruits of a study of Max Müller's *Origins of Language*, are put forward: 1) language as the imitation of animal sounds (called the Bow-Wow theory), and 2) as the expression of immediate emotional reactions (the Pooh-pooh Theory). I embraced the former, and immediately sat down and wrote Catbird. Note the wonderfully sustained beauty of line 14: kooka prea, etc.[17]

Though written with tongue in cheek, of all his poems "Catbird" was to become Glassco's favourite. This affection, he wrote, was due to ease of composition: "… it gave so little trouble. I had only to listen carefully to the bird, transpose its medley of imitative phrases into writeable sounds, and then rearrange them a little. It took only fifteen minutes: never has a poem required less effort!"[18]

In November 1962, *The Journal of Saint-Denys-Garneau* was finally published with an attractive hardcover design by Frank Newfeld. It was a quiet and thankless end to a project that had consumed such energy, emotion, and dedication. The occasion, described correctly by Gilles Marcotte as, "the first time a French-Canadian work of this kind has been placed before the

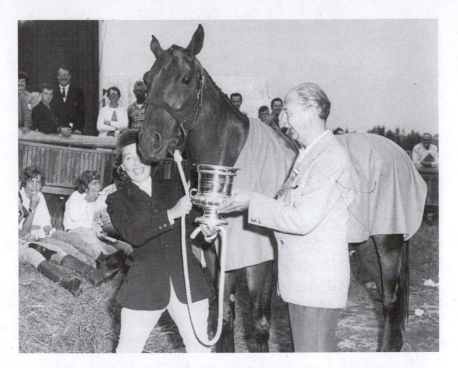

Glassco awarding Joan Southam the Graeme Taylor Memorial Trophy
at the 1962 Foster Horse Show.

English-speaking public," passed with little notice.[19] Critical attention was
limited to two reviews in the pages of *Canadian Literature* and *The Montreal
Star*. For his part, Glassco expressed neither surprise nor disappointment in
this near-silence. There was a certain satisfaction in the simple fact that what
he considered his "one fine piece of translation" had been published.[20]
Indeed, *The Journal of Saint-Denys-Garneau* joined a lengthening list of
grand projects with which he was satisfied, if only because they'd achieved
publication: *The English Governess*, his "one good work of pornography";
Under the Hill, his "one good erotic book"; and *The Deficit Made Flesh*, his
"one book of *good* poetry."[21] "Mairobert," his "one good novel" (in fact, a
novella), was complete, as was *The Liberator*, a drama about Byron, which
Glassco dreamed would be his "one successful play."[22] As 1962 drew to a
close, only his memoirs remained unrealized.

Begun with such enthusiasm in 1928, the work had lain dormant for
decades. It is probable that Glassco had done nothing with it since 1934
when, at Taylor's suggestion, he returned briefly to the project, thinking that

it might have good commercial potential. Though it appeared as another of any number of abandoned projects, he had always been determined to complete the work. In the "Autobiographical Sketch," Glassco refers to his "Memoirs of a Young Man," the longest-lasting of several working titles, as a work in progress:

> This book covers my years in Paris (where Graeme Taylor and I went in the spring of 1928) up to the period when I was completely without resources in the spring of 1929; the rest is yet unwritten. This part of the book will cover: the period when I was working as secretary and gigolo to The Princess of Sarawak (Mrs Gladys Brooke), as a guide to Montmartre nightclubs, and finally as a call-man in Martha Arlington's brothel on the rue Blanche; a succession of affairs with Robert McAlmon, Mrs Peggy Guggenheim Vail, Mrs Wm. Whitney, Lord Alfred Douglas, Kay Boyle, Jean Cocteau and the negro poet Claude McKay, none of which lasted more than a month; experiences of ecstasy, starvation and melancholia; my being with Mrs Marguerite Lippe-Rosskam and first experience of real love; our trip to Spain, where Marguerite took another lover; my suffering, and the final *revanche* of the last three years' life in the form of tuberculosis; my several months' stay in the American Hospital in Paris and eventual repatriation to Canada to undergo thoracoplasty in three stages, and my emergence from two years in hospital completely, and, I believed at the time, permanently changed.[23]

In the final entry of the Intimate Journal, written the previous year, Glassco had placed the ambition to write "one best-selling volume of memoirs" within his list of grand literary projects.[24] He never attempts to account for these decades of inactivity; to do so would counter the story he would develop that the memoirs were as he had left them in 1932, when entering the operating theatre at the Royal Victoria Hospital. The only explanation to be found in his papers is also the most likely: simple procrastination.

The spark that revived Glassco's memoirs was provided by Morley Callaghan, in particular the Toronto writer's own reminiscences of Montparnasse, *That Summer in Paris*. Although there'd been next to no contact between the two men since Callaghan's 1929 visit to the French capital, Glassco had been very aware of the older writer's career. The decade following his departure from Paris had seen Callaghan at his pinnacle; his four best books, *Such Is My Beloved, They Shall Inherit the Earth, Now That April's Here and Other Stories*, and *More Joy in Heaven,* had been published within a four-year period. However, as the Second World War drew near, Callaghan entered into what he would later describe as "a period of spiritual dryness."[25] His short stories stopped selling, his attempts at playwriting were ill-fated, and he began to suffer from writer's block. With a young family to support, he returned to journalism, writing for *Saturday Night* and *New World Illustrated,* and found further employment with the CBC as a panellist on *Of Things to Come* and host of *The Farmer's Future.* Keeping track of these changes, and perceiving a decline, in 1943 Glassco had written Robert McAlmon: "I see that Morley Callaghan (remember, the strange fugitive from Toronto?) is now an MC on one of our pinker radio programmes, and I also saw in an agricultural journal that he was recently addressing some children's farm forum down in these parts. He is going places, allright, has hitched his wagon to the people's star."[26] However, by the late 1950s, just as Glassco's career seemed to finally begin, Callaghan was enjoying something of a literary comeback. Earlier in the decade, he had received a Governor General's Award for *The Loved and the Lost,* his short novel *The Man with the Coat* had won the *Maclean's* Magazine Award, and *Morley Callaghan's Stories* had been a bestseller.

In September 1960, the two men met for the first time since summer 1929, at a carefully arranged dinner in a Toronto restaurant. Although Glassco had been anxious, he later described the evening as polite and pleasant. The following month, he wrote Callaghan to ask whether he might recommend a literary agent. "It was touching seeing you," Callaghan wrote in response, " – it brought back almost too many memories. We'll have to try again."[27] Neither man made any such attempt. Their entire correspondence, consisting of two very short letters, ended. Glassco and Callaghan would never meet again.

Published in January 1963, Callaghan's *That Summer in Paris* provided something of a description in its subtitle: "Memories of Tangled Friendships with Hemingway, Fitzgerald, and Some Others." Glassco had never been more than an acquaintance, and most certainly wouldn't have considered himself among the "Others" with whom Callaghan had had friendships. His relationship with Callaghan, however, was indeed tangled, chiefly through "Now That April's Here," the story in which he and Taylor had been portrayed as a pair of childish homosexuals. With *That Summer in Paris*, the relationship became more complicated still. Glassco would come to describe it as a long flight of the imagination containing "condescending and faintly malicious fantasies."[28]

For Callaghan, who was accustomed to being published abroad, *That Summer in Paris* proved his greatest international commercial success. Macmillan's Canadian edition was joined by others in England and the United States. Callaghan's US publisher, Coward-McCann, threw a lavish launch in New York City. In the years that followed, translations were published in Milan, Paris, and, significantly, Montreal.

Reaction to the book outside Canada tended toward the positive, if unenthusiastic. William Barrett's review in *The Atlantic Monthly* reflected the common tone: "Such is the simplicity of his art that he convinces us that the way he is telling it is exactly the way it must have been."[29] The memoir had the distinction of being reviewed by Norman Mailer in the debut issue of *The New York Review of Books*. One of the few dissenting critics, it was he who got off the best shot: "If one knows some of the people mentioned, or is obsessed with the period, then Morley Callaghan's memoir will satisfy. But it is not a good book. It is in fact a modest bad dull book which contains a superb short story about Hemingway, Fitzgerald, and Callaghan."[30]

This "superb short story," Callaghan's account of the sparring match in which he had knocked down Ernest Hemingway, ultimately destroying not only their friendship, but that which both men shared with F. Scott Fitzgerald, was the focus of William French's *Globe and Mail* review. He wrote that the memoir provided a "careful and detailed documentation of the event," perhaps leading some readers to assume that the remainder of the book was just as faithful to the past.[31] *That Summer in Paris* received not a single negative review in Canada; such high profile critics as Robert Weaver joined French in praise. Despite his limited time in Paris, no more than a matter of a few months, Callaghan was quickly embraced as the county's pre-eminent writer of the expatriate life.

To Glassco, who'd been greatly disappointed in having been left out of Robert McAlmon's *Being Geniuses Together*, and who was unaware of his fleeting appearance in Jimmie Charters's *This Must Be the Place*, the publication of Callaghan's book marked the first time he and Taylor had been included in a memoir of 1920s Paris. The author's portrayal, however, was neither gratifying nor agreeable. Identified only as Buffy and Graeme,

Glassco and his dead friend were depicted as "two 'bright boys' from Montreal,"[32] "the clever little devils,"[33] and "the two boys," the same words used for Johnny and Charles in "Now That April's Here." Indeed, the mannerisms, affectations, speech, and personalities of Buffy and Graeme were identical to those of Johnny and Charles. Nowhere is this more apparent than in Callaghan's account of the story behind "Now That April's Here." The scene opens in the Sélect, where the Toronto writer is seated with Edward Titus and Robert McAlmon, recently returned from a brief trip to the south of France:

> Along the street came those two willowy graceful young men from Montreal whom McAlmon called affectionately "the clever little devils." Sauntering into the café with their bland distinguished air, they saw us and bowed. My lighthearted wave of the hand piqued McAlmon. "Oh, you don't understand those two at all," he jeered. But I did understand that the boys shared his snickering wit. Friends of his they might be, but it didn't stop them from laughing at him. Just before his return, his Contact Press had printed one of his own poems. One boy would look at the other solemnly, quote a line from the poem, "Is this the Aztec heart that writhes upon the temple floor," then they would both kill themselves laughing.[34]

It is only here, in the sixteenth chapter, that Glassco and Taylor, previously mentioned only in passing, make their first real appearance. Effeminate and immature, Callaghan's reference to their "distinguished air" is a clever allusion to McAlmon's *Distinguished Air (Grim Fairy Tales)*, his 1925 collection of short stories united by the themes of debauchery, homosexuality, and lesbianism. It is not coincidental that the passage in which Callaghan describes Glassco and Taylor's appearance in the Sélect is followed by McAlmon's defense of homosexuals and public declaration of his own bisexuality.

Though he had known Glassco and Taylor only a matter of weeks, and had encountered them infrequently, Callaghan is so certain that his understanding of the pair is superior to that of McAlmon, a man with whom they had lived and travelled, that he accepts Titus's challenge to go head to head with the American in writing a story about the "bright boys."

The only other scene in which Glassco and Taylor feature begins, again, in the Sélect. Callaghan is sharing a table with his wife, Ernest Hemingway, and Joan Miró, when he spots "the clever little devils" entering La Coupole across the street. After drinks Miró picks up a bag containing Hemingway's boxing gloves, and the two men leave:

When Miró and Ernest had got only fifty feet beyond the café, the two boys, who had been watching carefully, came hurrying across the street.

"Wasn't that Hemingway?" Graeme asked.

"Yes, that was Hemingway."

"And the other one," Buffy said blandly, watching the two retreating figures. "His butler, I presume? Does he really bring his butler along with him now to carry his bag?"

Their little snicker, in view of the picture Hemingway and Miró made, was perfect. The remark indeed was bright. I let them enjoy their mirth for a moment. Knowing I was going to leave them feeling they had committed the most terrible of sins around the Quarter, the sin of unawareness of what was going on, I said quietly, "No, that's Miró."

"Miró! The Spanish painter?"

"Yes. Not Hemingway's butler."

"Oh," and their faces fell, and they took a couple of quick steps out to the sidewalk so they could see the hard hat and the neat square shoulders of the little man carrying the bag, in an entirely different light. Then somewhat embarrassed, they sauntered away.[35]

Exactly why Callaghan felt obligated to correct Glassco, an act he knew would bring such pain, is left unexplained, though a hint lies in the setup to the exchange in which Callaghan reflects on "the clever little devils," the two boys whom he "had got to like by this time":

Their bland superiority and their awareness of what was going on in the Quarter was often amusing. Now they sat down across the street at La Coupole. By the way they were staring over at us I knew they had recognized Hemingway, whom they had never seen at the cafés.[36]

By including the story, Callaghan again attempts to prove himself the superior observer. Just as it is he, not McAlmon, who truly understands the boys,

Callaghan writes that his knowledge of Montparnasse is greater than that of Glassco. It is he who shares a table with Hemingway, whom he says Glassco has never seen, and Miró, whom he claims Glassco does not recognize.

Glassco saw *That Summer in Paris* as a self-serving, ego-driven work; "Every Man His Own Hero" was, he suggested, an appropriate alternate title.[37] He wrote to Kay Boyle, who had been in Paris during the summer in question, asserting that a good deal of Callaghan's book was a fabrication; the anecdote about Miró included. When he came to write his own memoirs, Glassco placed his first encounter with Hemingway – while dining with Taylor and McAlmon at La Coupole – shortly after his arrival in Paris. It is a convincing scene, and perhaps as accurate a portrayal of the relationship between the two US writers as has been set down; however it is somewhat improbable that the exchange occurred when Glassco claims. The window of opportunity is a small one at best. On 17 March 1928, a few weeks after the arrival of the Canadian boys, Hemingway left Paris, setting sail via Havana for Key West, Florida. He did not return until April of the following year. It is somewhat more likely that the encounter took place later, just as it is possible that Glassco invented the entire confrontation, using his knowledge of the two men to craft an entertaining story. What is most improbable is Callaghan's claim that Glassco and Taylor had not until summer 1929 so much as seen Hemingway, a man who frequented the very same cafés, walked the same streets, moved in the same circles, and who had been a friend of their mentor McAlmon.

Leon Edel, who had first met Callaghan in Paris, later joined his friend Glassco in questioning the accuracy of the memoir. In a rather backhanded manner, he praised the memoirist's ingenuity, while drawing attention to the ways in which Callaghan had incorporated "much extensive reading he did *after* his days in Paris."[38] Edel did not believe that Callaghan could have discussed the work of Franz Kafka, who in 1929 remained largely untranslated. Nor did he think it at all likely that the Toronto writer would have discussed Proust, as he does in the memoir. Edel, the great Jamesian biographer, recalls a conversation the two had once shared in which the young Callaghan had remarked: "Why do all of you mention Henry James?"[39]

If Glassco found any consolation in the depiction of himself and Taylor within the pages of *That Summer in Paris*, it most certainly would have come from the fact that, unlike all the other figures in the book, the boys known as Buffy and Graeme lack surnames. This curious distinction may have had something to do with the pair being identified, for the first time, as the models upon whom the couple Johnny and Charles are based. In this one respect, Glassco had been spared some degree of distress; he was known as Buffy only among acquaintances and friends. Interestingly, no Canadian reviews made mention of "the clever little devils" from Montreal, one of whom had gone on to become a respected poet and translator.[40]

Within Glassco's own circle, however, the humiliation was complete. His years in Paris, an experience that had been so envied by Patrick Anderson, among others, had been exposed as a time of silliness, immaturity, and pretension. His encounters with Hemingway, which had prompted Irving Layton to visit the Windermere two decades earlier, were shown to be nothing more than a glimpse from an opposing café. Worse than all this, his relationship with Taylor, now six years dead, had now been twice depicted, in fiction and memoir, as homosexual in nature. Previous to *That Summer in Paris* the link between the characters in "Now That April's Here" and their models might have at best been a matter of speculation or rumour. Here, in his new book, Callaghan had drawn a direct link between the characters and their models.

From the age of eighteen, Glassco had dreamed of writing memoirs of his youth. Yet, for much of the thirty-five years that followed, the project had lain dormant. Callaghan's book provided the final incentive. Glassco would use his own memoirs to even the score.

That Summer in Paris became a bestseller, but no thanks to Glassco, who read it but would not buy a copy until it was issued as massmarket paperback the following year. In the meantime, he set to work on a very different sort of project, a three-day long gathering of Quebec's most important English-language poets. Held during the Thanksgiving weekend of 1963, what he called the Foster Poetry Conference, actually took place in nearby West Bolton at the Glen Mountain Ski Chalet. The event came about with a speed that belies the many complications and obstacles that plagued its organization. Glassco would modestly describe the idea as one that "had been stirring in the back of the minds of F.R. Scott and A.J.M. Smith," when in reality it was he who proposed and organized the conference.[41] He had envisioned the event as one devoted to the poetry of English-speaking Quebec, but this soon evolved with the proposed additions of Anne Hébert, Robert Choquette, Gaston Miron, and over a dozen other prominent French Canadian poets. Putting to good use his connections in the local Liberal riding association, Glassco approached Glendon Brown, the man who had been elected after he'd declined the party's nomination, and came away with verbal guarantee of a $3,000 grant.

The plan to include the "F.-C. poets," to hold a conference for all Quebecers, was one Glassco accepted but never truly embraced. This idea, which originated with Smith, was enthusiastically adopted by Scott, who saw it as yet another means to bridge the two linguistic groups. History, however, was working against him. Early the morning of 8 March, the Front de Libération du Québec hit three Montreal armories with Molotov cocktails, marking the beginning of a campaign of violence that would reach its climax with the October Crisis seven years later. In April, the group began using bombs, and by Victoria Day had set off a dozen explosions throughout Montreal and Westmount. The events rattled the government of Jean Lesage, resulting in a disorder that reached into all ministries. In June, Glassco received a phone call from Brown informing him that the events of the past few months had made the government wary of financing any gathering of intellectuals. The apprehension had little or nothing to do with poets such as Scott, Smith, and Layton and everything to do with the participation of the francophone poets. During the conversation, Glassco reverted to the original plan, that of holding a unilingual conference. The funding, it seemed, was secure, provided he take the extraordinary step of drafting a letter outlining the conference program and listing the poets who would be in attendance. But even this intrusive measure proved not enough. Several weeks later, he and Brown shared a second phone call in which the politician relayed that Georges-Émile Lapalme, Lesage's vice-premier, had taken an interest in the matter and had decided that it would be best if the conference was put off until the following year. Glassco's notes as to Lapalme's concerns provide an indication of the confusion within the government: "Reason for his demur is his fear that if C. [the conference] is bilingual the French might either not show up at all – which would look bad – or if they did they would take over the show & issue nationalist press-releases etc., and if it was unilingual it would look as if the French were being haughtily excluded."[42] This time Glassco stood his ground and told Brown that the conference would go ahead as a privately financed event, if necessary. By the end of the conversation, the proposed conference was again a bilingual event, with twenty poets representing each linguistic group. In chasing the funds, Glassco had made a promise with which he was uncomfortable: "Lapalme would prefer if we could make 5 or 6 of these French ones of whom we were sure (was that right of me?), that is, who were personal friends."[43]

In the end, Glassco received only a third of the three thousand that had been promised. The reduced funding came with conditions that were in keeping with the absurd negotiations that had consumed much of his summer: the Foster Poetry Conference was to be unilingual, it was not to be publicized, and Brown's name was not to be mentioned.

Within days of settling the matter, on 27 August 1963, Glassco's mother died in her Westmount apartment at age seventy-nine. The final years had been lived modestly, her great inheritance having been diminished through generosity to her children, losses in the stock market, and David's poor fiscal management. The loss of their mother did nothing to calm the troubled relationship between the two brothers. Michael Gnarowski recalls an incident that took place roughly seven years later:

> I'd had lunch with Buffy at a little place on Bishop Street, I think. We were passing in front of the Ritz when I noticed that he was staring at a man walking in the other direction. After he'd passed I asked Buffy whether he knew the man.
>
> He replied, "That was my brother."
>
> "Oh, well, why didn't you introduce me?" I said.
>
> Then Buffy said, "We don't speak. He lost all of my mother's money."[44]

The funeral for Kathleen Mabel Beatrice Rawlings Glassco took place at St James the Apostle, the church where she had been married nearly six decades earlier. She was buried next to A.P.S. at Mount Royal Cemetery, beneath a gravestone bearing only her husband's name. Two weeks later, Glassco returned to St James the Apostle, and married Elma.

By provincial order, no francophone poets were invited to attend the Foster Poetry Conference, neither as delegates nor as members of the audience. It remains, however, the greatest gathering to have ever taken place of Quebec's English-language poets. Scott, Layton, Dudek, and Milton Wilson each gave seminars, Glassco joined Scott in leading a discussion on the translation of French Canadian poetry, and Smith delivered a public lecture entitled "The Poet and the Nuclear Crisis." The afternoon of the second day was dedicated to a three-hour reading, featuring among others, Scott, Smith, Layton, Dudek, Ralph Gustafson, Eldon Grier, Eli Mandel, D.G. Jones, Leonard Cohen, and Seymour Mayne. Glassco, always reluctant to take the stage, chose to recite just one poem, "Lines Addressed to a Dozen Young Canadian Poets, after Unwisely Devouring Five Little Magazines at a Sitting":

> Enough, enough. Gentlemen, I protest
> Over and over and over
> These mementos of your fornications
> Vignettes of your sensitive childhood
> Kicks from jazz,
> And all these poetics about poetics about poetics
> And the fearsome insults and fulsome accolades
> AND your girl-friend's vulva
> AND your trip to Mexico
>
> Please, gentlemen, please.[45]

The selection was playful, directed, one suspects, as much at the fifty-one-year-old Layton, as it was at Cohen, Mayne, and the rest of the younger poets. For Mayne, then nineteen years-old, and easily the youngest of the delegates, the conference held great influence: "I remember one night in Eli Mandel's room Leonard Cohen read us the first of his poems from *Flowers for Hitler*. I just sat there on the edge of the bed and watched Irving and Leonard and Eli talk. Milton Wilson and I, we just listened. There was nothing we had to say, we just sat there. I knew I was privileged to be there at that moment."[46]

Scott considered the Foster Poetry Conference to be the greatest of successes, an important event in the history of Canadian poetry, and encouraged Glassco to edit an anthology of the proceedings. Within six weeks of the event, McGill University Press had signed the book, and the province had agreed to provide funding. However, compiling the material proved to be a much slower task. Glassco came to resent the work. He felt overwhelmed by the seemingly endless stream of correspondence and factchecking and would resent the frequent encounters with "petty literary jealousies."[47] The simple title, *English Poetry in Quebec*, seemed to him not

Irving Layton, Milton Wilson, Leonard Cohen, Eli Mandel,
and Aviva Layton at the Foster Poetry Conference.

bland, but pretentious. Most of all, Glassco recognized that the contents of
the book, which amounted to nothing more than a gathering of the papers
delivered, complemented by a selection of the poetry from the afternoon
reading, failed to capture anything of the exuberant nature of the conference.
Only three of the discussions that followed the seminars were included, and
these amounted to little more than brief reactions of selected poets. The
late-night conversations, the raw exchanges, the fellowship, the drinking –
almost all that had been informal, spontaneous, and dynamic had been left
unrecorded. In his introduction, Glassco acknowledged the book's failing,
and attempted to pass on some essence of the event:

> There was a constant sense of clash and conflict, not only between
> the arrière-guard and avant-garde, between the forces of tradition and
> revolution, between the elders still presumably stumbling around in
> post-war academic darkness and the clear-sighted children of a puta-
> tive post-nuclear dawn, but between sharply differing conceptions of
> the role of the poet in society and even the nature of poetry itself.

There was indeed no one who did not contribute – either as one who spoke *in foro*, who murmured in the background, or who argued in the bar – to the nipping and eager air which was blowing during those three days.[48]

He could not wait to rid himself of *English Poetry in Quebec* and was discouraged when the galleys arrived from the press. The quality was of such a poor state that the November 1964 publication date had to be scratched. For months, the anthology hung over his head as he awaited, with dread, the reset galleys. What arrived was much improved, and he moved quickly to clear the sheets from his desk. Then, just when his work appeared to be finished, Glassco discovered that he had been saddled with the task of distributing payments to the twenty contributors. The irritation was only compounded by the small sums. Smith received $20 for his address and a further $3 for each of the three poems that had been selected for inclusion. Leonard Cohen received $3 in total, barely enough to purchase a copy of the book.

When finally published in April 1965, *English Poetry in Quebec* was a mere 142 pages in length. Though modest in length and scope, editing and production had taken so long that the editor had already successfully organized a second conference, held the previous May at Stanley House, the former vice-regal fishing lodge on the Baie des Chaleurs in the Gaspé.[49] Glassco entertained no thoughts of a subsequent anthology.

At the Foster Poetry Conference, Glassco had included himself within the ranks of the "arrière-guard," yet his bibliography looked much like that of a much younger man. *The Deficit Made Flesh*, published five years earlier, remained his only book of verse, translated or otherwise. Although other titles had followed, the two Olympia Press books and his translation of Garneau's *Journal*, it wasn't until October 1964 that Glassco's second poetry collection, *A Point of Sky*, was published. The first of four titles published with Oxford University Press, it was part of a relationship that began when Smith personally placed the manuscript in the hands of editor Ivon Owen. Glassco had considerable confidence in the collection; as with *The Deficit Made Flesh*, he had deferred to Smith's judgement when making his selection, writing his friend: "There is no one who has given me more than you have."[50]

A Point of Sky was a much newer collection; of the twenty-seven poems, only nine had been published previously. This freshness made the critical reception hard to take and left Glassco with a disappointment greater than he would experience with any other book. Eight months after publication he had detected little more than silence: "No reviews *at all*, – except Louis Dudek's very laudatory one in the *Star*, which has a faintly cloying odour of friendship: he seemed a little tired, too!"[51]

In fact, Dudek's was the second review, the first being an unenthusiastic piece by John Robert Colombo in *The Globe and Mail Magazine*. However, Glassco was correct that there had been little attention paid to the book. More than a year passed before critical comment began appearing in the country's little magazines – and then they fell in line with Colombo, not Dudek. Critics tended to pick apart the collection, focusing on poems they liked a great deal ("Quebec Farmhouse," "Luce's Notch") or those that were considered failures ("Ode: The Autumn Resurrection"). If there was one consolation to be had, it may have been that only one reviewer, bill bissett, dismissed the book outright. "They all look like bad trips to me," he wrote in *Alphabet*, advising Glassco to "get th air thru yur windew no English literature its du yu/ feel good."[52]

As *A Point of Sky* and *English Poetry in Quebec* were being prepared for publication, Glassco had at long last returned to his Parisian memoirs. Beginning in February 1964, he proceeded with workmanlike discipline, assisted by a great many tumblers of gin. He revised his word count on a daily basis and compared the slowly growing total with that he'd estimated for *That Summer in Paris*. In early May, Glassco reported to Jean Le Moyne: "My memoirs (no title yet) now amount to 75,000 words, with only 20,000 left to write."[53] That autumn, he borrowed Michael Gnarowski's abandoned flat at the corner of Derocher and Sherbrooke, using it as a base while doing research at McGill. It was easy work, performed with a sense of exuberance. "Every night now I enact the first scene of *Faust*," he wrote Le Moyne. "I shed my robe and my false beard, the wrinkles disappear, I have a new head of hair, and I sport for about 1,000 words in the green meadows of a well misspent youth."[54]

By mid-December, he'd completed the book, recording a count of 99,500 words. The manuscript was mailed off to Willis Wing, the New York agent Callaghan had recommended during their brief correspondence four years earlier. It was soon returned as "not likely to be of interest to a publisher."[55]

Rejection was not new to Glassco – most of his poems, short stories, novellas, and essays had been turned down at one time or another – yet the return of the memoir was an experience he could not help but take personally:

> The force of this rejection was multiplied beyond endurance by the fact that the book was a reflection of myself, my whole youth, the Paris I had loved & the period when I had been happy. I could hardly believe it: for three days I was numbed. I kept torturing myself by recalling the parts of it I had thought were so good, & putting them in apposition to the cruellest phrases of Wing's letter (no, it was not even Wing himself, it was a junior partner in the firm!), that it seemed "non-persuasive" (i.e. unconvincing, i.e. mendacious), and that the "exposé element was unaffecting." So much for telling the truth! Then, I did not even dare look at the returned manuscript: it had been termed a lying chronicle, and with my own wretched suggestibility I would soon have believed the term was correct and that people and things did not happen as I know they did. – No, not altogether as they did: I have *re-arranged* many events, telescoped still more, & invented much of the dialogue – but the facts are all true, & the tenor of the life in those days, and the behaviour of everybody, faithfully reproduced.[56]

The dreams of youth, now so fully expressed, and the pursuit of best-sellerdom were again set aside. He made no attempt to interest other agents, nor did he submit the manuscript to publishers.

Late that summer, while working on his memoirs, Glassco was informed by Maurice Girodias that one of his books had been seized by the French authorities. The title wasn't *The English Governess*, but the more subdued and cultivated *Under the Hill*. The unsold stock, amounting to more than half of the three-thousand-copy print run, was threatened with destruction. In order to defend the book, Girodias was placed in the absurd position of having to prove Aubrey Beardsley's status as a well-known and respected artist in a French court of law.

Five years earlier, while convalescing at the Royal Edward Laurentian, Glassco's peace had been broken by C.H. Rolph's account of the *Lady Chatterley's Lover* trial. Though Glassco disliked the D.H. Lawrence novel, which his friend Scott had defended in Canada, he became enraged by the actions of those who had aligned and allied against it: "all those married spinsters of both sexes, those oily clerics and that dreadful old ghoul Rebecca West."[57] Censorship was not something Glassco would tolerate, yet he had always done his best to avoid the censors. His personal library consisted of several works of erotica received through mailed packages addressed to "Rev. John Glassco"; a simple tactic that, it would seem, fooled simple people.

Under the Hill forced Glassco to deal with the censors head on, and he moved quickly, with a certain passion in defending the work. After sending Girodias his valuable 1908 Floury edition of the French *Sous la colline et d'autres essays en prose et en vers*, he approached Scott's wife, Marian, an accomplished painter who had studied at Montreal's École des beaux-arts and the Slade School of Art in London, for an opinion that might be presented in court as to the famous Decadent's standing as an artist.

The seizure of *Under the Hill* was not Girodias's first encounter with the French censors. The publisher's travails began in summer 1956, when the minister of the Interior banned twenty-five Olympia Press titles. Girodias sued, and in January 1958 the sanction was reversed. However, with the fall of the Fourth Republic five months later, and the rise of Charles de Gaulle – and, not inconsequently, Mme de Gaulle – Girodias found himself under a barrage of lawsuits and countersuits. At its worst point, he received a six-year jail sentence, the equivalent of $80,000 in fines, and was prohibited from publishing activities for eighty years.

The case against what Girodias described as "Aubrey Beardsley's sweetly decadent (but, alas, devastatingly innocent) Victorian tale" was as weak as it was ridiculous.[58] With the fate of the book still before the court, the publisher dared to write publicly of the trial:

> My edition of the book, which is limited, numbered, and expensive, contains illustrations by Beardsley himself, and I cannot resist the pleasure of calling back to memory the recent vision of the magistrate (who, do I have to labor the point again, does not read English) poring over those images in furious, vein-bulging concentration, in the hope of discovering some half-hidden improper detail on which to rest his case. Alas, no peg for his hat was found, there was not an inch of obscene flesh to be clawed at in the Beardsleyan oceans of lace and frills; and yet the good man obviously suspected the existence of some esoteric meaning attached to those innocent illustrations; and he sus-

pected that only I could have explained it to him. But he dared not ask; he just sat there and hated me for my unshared knowledge.[59]

The charges brought by *Under the Hill* attracted interest from other quarters, including an offer from the New English Library in London. Through Girodias, Glassco agreed to a £500 advance on royalties of five percent, a far better return on his work than the flat $600 he had received from Olympia Press seven years earlier. The purchase of the English rights was a timely one, coinciding with the start of what would be an immensely popular retrospective exhibition of Beardsley's work mounted by the Victoria and Albert Museum. Yet, in the midst of all this excitement and interest in things Beardsley, Girodias lost his case. All copies of the beautiful, silk-bound Olympia Press edition seized eleven months earlier were destroyed by the French authorities.[60]

Glassco was heartbroken and could not understand the defeat, in that he'd never considered *Under the Hill* to be at all pornographic. In an unsent letter to Scott, he defended the work: "It is romantic, rococo, *faisandé*, Huysmanesque, playful, madly affected, solidly in the tradition of dandyism; it's even got a highly moral ending, with Tannhäuser officially damned & trapped for ever under the hill. I wouldn't be in his elegant slippers for anything."[61]

Despite all his pains to save *Under the Hill*, Glassco was never once considered for prosecution by the French authorities. The only possible explanation for this oversight was provided by Girodias: "The irony in all this, naturally, is that according to French law, you, as co-author, should have been prosecuted also, as your name appears in the book, the copyright is in your name, etc. Curiously, and strangely, the prosecuting magistrate preferred to consider that you did not exist, and that you were a figment of my imagination, if you pardon the expression. I did not oppose that view naturally."[62]

Girodias's good-natured letter reflects nothing of the pressure that the courts had brought to bear. Having lost the case, he was facing three months of incarceration and a fine of 5,000 francs. Again, Glassco did what he could to support the embattled publisher. He set about collecting signatures from some of the country's leading writers, among them Scott, Layton, Robertson Davies, and Hugh MacLennan, petitioning for the publisher's release. It was in the midst of this effort that Glassco made a disconcerting discovery: Olympia had the previous year reissued *The English Governess* as *Under the Birch*. Girodias had pulled a fast one. The target of his deception, however, hadn't been the author, but the French constabulary. On 10 January 1961, some six months after its initial publication, *The English Governess* had been suppressed under a decades-old decree targeting "*périodiques et ouvrages de provenance étrangère*."[63] The reissue under change of title was in keeping with Olympia's usual practice, having been employed on a number of banned bestsellers. Armed with an alphabetical list, members of *La Brigade mondaine* were unable to make the connection between *Helen and Desire* and *Desire and Helen*, or *The Organization* and *The New Organization*. While the new title applied to *The English Governess* was less transparent, the cover and title page of *Under the Birch* bore the Miles Underwood name and the subtitle "The Story of an English Governess."

Knowing nothing of the book's suppression, Glassco had Scott quickly draft a letter demanding $1,000 for copyright – which, it needs be pointed out, the publisher already owned – on the proviso that he receive a 10 percent royalty for each copy sold. Despite the great distance, it took Girodias just three days to respond with an offer of a further 3,000 francs and a piece of advice: "we live in a rather precarious world, and it is a good policy not to pick quarrels with one's natural allies."[64] Glassco later apologized for his letter, the tone of which Girodias had deplored, explaining that it had been "composed by a lawyer (a signatory of your petition)."[65]

Under the Hill and *The English Governess* were more than mere reflections of Glassco's interest in the erotic, the Decadent, and the Victorian; both captured traces of what he describes in his "Autobiographical Sketch" as the "two features of my psychosexuality, the fetichistic and masochistic."[66] Writing with characteristic self-criticism, Glassco recognized what he termed "the fatal effect" they had had on his literary development.[67] These obsessions with the "fetichistic and masochistic" had, he wrote, "held it back, made my work abortive and futile. The indulgence of these tastes has brought me incalculable pleasure; but where any genuine accomplishment is concerned, they have been an unmixed evil. Only in my poetry have I kept clear of them."[68]

This bold assertion aside, it wasn't at all true that poetry had been spared the rod. In the early 1950s he had written *Squire Hardman*, a work mischievously ascribed to George Colman the Younger, a once popular, now forgotten literary figure of the eighteenth and nineteenth centuries. In doing so, Glassco perpetuated a hoax dating back to 1871, when John Camden Hotten, a successful publisher of flagellant literature, first issued *The Rodiad* by "George Coleman." Published as part of a fictitious "Library Illustrative of Social Progress," fraudulently dated 1810, the long poem had nothing to do with the true George Colman. The identity of the author remains a matter of speculation, though credit has come to be given most frequently to Richard Mockton Milnes, Lord Houghton, a friend of Victorian poet Algernon Charles Swinburne.[69]

Whether Glassco knew of the attribution is unknown. What is certain is his knowledge that *The Rodiad* was a hoax; he was equally aware that others familiar with the poem knew that it had not been composed by Colman. In private, Glassco speculated that the author may have been Swinburne, who, like Milnes, had been a frequent patron of flagellators. If true, *The Rodiad* would not be the poet's first work of masochistic pornography; Swinburne is known to be the author of "A Boy's First Flogging at Birchmaster," "Reinald's Flogging," *The Flogging Block: An Heroic Poem*, and other flagellantine verse. His unfinished novel, *Lesbia Brandon*, was one of Glassco's favourite books.

A long poem, covering sixty-two pages in its first edition, *The Rodiad* is a satirical ode to the joys taken by teachers in flogging schoolboys:

> … A nice look out in truth,
> For us, the Teachers of ingenuous youth:
> Who, when we must not mark our discipline
> In bright red letters on their hinder skin,
> And once have lost command of their posteriors,
> Will soon be taught who are the true superiors.[70]

This brief passage points to the primary difference between *The Rodiad* and *Squire Hardman*. In Glassco's work it is a woman who is the flagellator. The plot, as he described it to a friend, is simple: "the good squire marries a flogging governess, and then they undertake the education of three foundling boys …. He tells the story of their wedded bliss with great *brio* and a kind of rollicking coarseness …. The flagellation of the three lads is quite frankly recognised as an aphrodisiac, and forms the ground-bass of life in the Hardman ménage."[71]

Squire Hardman had been lying dormant for well over a decade. Only six lines had seen print – as an epigraph in *The English Governess* and *Under the Birch*:

Indeed it seems to want no demonstration
The best thing for a boy is flagellation:
The doctrine need not exercise our wit,
'Tis shown by Reason, and by Holy Writ.
All Education is summed up in this: –
A good sound whipping never comes amiss.[72]

In late 1965, Glassco decided to publish the poem himself and contracted a French Canadian printer in Waterloo, not far from Foster, to print an edition of fifty. He took possession of the copies the following April, along with a handbill that announced the book could be had for $10, postage paid. Featuring a whip-wielding cherub above the words "*DUM NOCET IUVAT*" (UNTIL INJURY DELIGHTS), the advertisement, which he had written himself, trumpeted *Squire Hardman* as "unquestionably the most brilliant flagellantine poem ever written."[73]

"Printed on heavy deckled paper, sewn, in stiff wrappers," it was an attractive, though modest-looking little book.[74] Glassco was most concerned with the appearance and had gone to great lengths to imitate the early nineteenth-century style employed on the title page of *The Rodiad*. He was justifiably proud; he wrote to the young Canadian poet Daryl Hine: "The introduction is in my best dated and documented style of Hoaxery; the nice title-page, decorations, layout are all mine too; I even stuck the labels on the covers."[75]

Central to the hoax was a five-page introduction, written by Glassco, in which he discusses Colman while comparing and contrasting *The Rodiad* and *Squire Hardman*. Why, he wonders, has the former been "reprinted many times," while the latter has been all but ignored?[76] Acknowledging that there is some question as to Colman's authorship, he writes:

The truth is that the two poems can be ascribed to Colman on the basis of internal evidence alone; and strong as this is, it is not really conclusive. All that can be affirmed with certainty is that both poems are by the same hand, and that their brilliance cannot lower the reputation of a writer who usually compounded coarseness with the graver faults of hypocrisy and dullness – from both of which these two poems are at any rate free.[77]

Glassco filled the orders himself, recording each transaction with meticulous care in a receipt book devoted specifically to the project. Most of the cheques received were issued by university libraries in Canada and the United States, though there were a few private orders. Not everyone was fooled. One purchaser, British Columbia naturalist Roderick Haig-Brown, wrote to thank Glassco for filling his order: "it impresses me as strongly and seriously satirical and obviously written by someone who knew THE RODIAD; but I'm not too sure it is by the same hand."[78]

Another admirer of the work was Iris Murdoch, to whom Glassco had sent a copy at the urging of a mutual friend. The amused English author reported: "It was opened by the censor, but when he saw that it was just a dull learned eighteenth century poem he closed it up again!"[79]

In the meantime, the Beardsley and Glassco version of *Under the Hill* returned to print; not in Paris, where sale was still prohibited, but in the suddenly more enlightened, swinging city of London. Where Girodias's ornate edition had received no critical notice, the New English Library edition was widely reviewed – and widely panned. The British critics were the harshest of a brutal lot. For the most part, their negative reaction stemmed from a dismissal of Beardsley's original work, which William Cooper described in his review as "a sort of fingering giggle for the Flagellant Brigade, as arch as it's wet."[80] Writing in *The New Statesman*, Ian Hamilton concluded: "Beardsley's strenuously titillating, smirkingly elaborate fragment was maybe short enough to be worth glancing at. It's now, thanks to Glassco, long enough to deserve neglect."[81] These criticisms were fresh in mind when Glassco, interviewed by *The Montreal Star*, dismissed "the view of all those people who are so much against eroticism in literature as against an airy refusal to take sex seriously."[82]

One piece of criticism, that of Geoffrey Wagner, stood out as both the most considered and the most positive. Writing in *The Kenyon Review*, he praised the completion of Beardsley's unfinished novel as a "literary rescue operation" and "a perfectly valid piece of art."[83] Shortly afterward, Wagner addressed a highly complimentary letter to Glassco, which marked the beginning of a warm and steady correspondence. In Wagner, Glassco found a person who could advise him in the business aspect of pornography and would serve as an adviser and contact through who he approached a number of important publishers of quality erotica. Moreover, Wagner acted as something of a watchdog, informing Glassco of the pirated edition of *The English Governess* and Girodias's *Under the Birch* reissue.

Under the Hill occasioned a second series of correspondence, beginning with a gushing four-page letter, ornate in both design and prose, from a sixteen-year-old student and Beardsley enthusiast who signed himself Féllippé Core. In flowing script, Féllippé wrote of the influence that the Victorian artist had had on his own work and offered to send one of his own drawings in appreciation of Glassco's "brilliant completion":

> Please do not think that this is any sort of commercial gesture; it is only that in the somewhat stifling atmosphere of Middlesex School (in Concord, Massachusetts) which I attend, I find little chance to discuss my interests in the '90's – so, by letter, I oft attempt to introduce myself to persons of a similar interest, and in such a manner I have corressponded [*sic*] with R.A. Harari (of whose collection of Beardsley's drawings little but "magnificent" may be said) in London, and Vyvyan Holland (Oscar Wilde's aging but intriguing son), and I should be indeed more than grateful to write to you as well.[84]

Handwritten on stationary that featured the whip-wielding cherub and motto, "*DUM NOCET IUVAT,*" used in the *Squire Hardman* handbill, Glassco's answer was nothing more than a brief note acknowledging Féllippé's words. It was not the response from a man intent on entering into an exchange with an adolescent schoolboy. Indeed, the correspondence might have soon ended had Féllippé not sent Glassco a copy of *Palm Fronde Alphabet*, a seventeen-page booklet he'd written, illustrated, and self-published two years before. Glassco was so impressed by the title that he ventured to send a copy of *Squire Hardman* to the young respondent's Middlesex School address. In the accompanying letter he asked whether the precocious artist might be hired to illustrate the work for a "new and larger edition."[85] Glassco, who had earlier warned Féllippé that he was "no critic of art," had the eye to recognize the young student's talent.[86]

Born in Dallas in 1951, the self-styled Féllippé was in actuality a well-to-do American named Philip MacCammon Core. Most of his privileged young life had been spent in New Orleans, where at the age of seven he had won the City of New Orleans Vieux Carré Artists Open Competition. Even before he'd entered his teens, Core had discovered Beardsley and had begun cultivating an interest in *fin de siècle* art and writing. He was intent on becoming an artist himself and set about creating pen and ink illustrations for the Marquis de Sade's *La philosophie dans le boudoir*, as well as imaginings of events in the lives of Arthur Rimbaud and Paul Verlaine. Yet, it was Beardsley who remained at the centre of Core's interest, and to whom he owed the greatest debt of influence.

Glassco certainly saw something of his younger self in this private-school boy, and in employing the artist he recognized that Core's youth and fawning admiration would make him particularly receptive to direction. After Core submitted the first two commissioned drawings for *Squire Hardman*, Glassco wrote in response:

The two drawings are delightful. Not at all too free for the text. The style will do beautifully – turgescences and all.

But my dear boy, the first one gives us Squire Hardman in the active role – and not his good lady as it is in the text!

This, I am afraid, rules it out as an illustration of the scene, in spite of the beauty of the youth's figure and stance.

I am holding both drawings until I hear whether you are willing to replace the Squire with Mrs H.!

While many of Beardsley's illustrations of *Salome* had no relation to Wilde's text, I'm afraid we must not take his inspired irrelevance as a model. Not just yet![87]

Despite Core's considerable skill as an illustrator, he was very much the amateur in the relationship. Indeed, it wasn't until several completed drawings had been provided that the artist suggested a fee, accepted at $15 per drawing; and it was only upon completion of the project that he thought to enquire about royalties.

For a period lasting several months, there was a regular exchange of letters sent from the author's home in Foster to the artist at Middlesex School. Under Glassco's direction, Core, now signing himself Féllippé Fecit, produced six full-page scenes of flagellation and sexual enchantment, a title page, and a *cul-de-lampe*.

One of the six unused illustrations for *Squire Hardman*
drawn by sixteen-year-old Philip Core.

There can be no argument that Glassco took great delight in the *Squire Hardman* illustrations; however, what exactly he'd intended in commissioning the work is left to speculation. Plans for a "new and larger edition," if any, did not exist. It may have been that Glassco found the costs involved in creating an illustrated book prohibitive. Perhaps he worried that he might not be able to find a printer willing to reproduce the images. He may have come to the conclusion that including the illustrations would compromise the effectiveness of his hoax — accomplished though they were, Core's sketches quite obviously weren't of the time. He told Core that a manuscript deadline for another project was forcing a delay in his search for a publisher. The date he provided was a fiction.[88]

Elma had arrived at Jamaica Farm under the guise of a housekeeper. The position was a cover through which some semblance of propriety had been sought. Few were deceived by the arrangement, and there had been no surprise when, seven years after her appearance, the housekeeper had married her employer. The tiny, thin, elegantly dressed woman had never seemed suited to the role; her contributions in maintaining the large farmhouse rarely extended beyond the preparation of meals.

Elma had never been strong. Living alone at Jamaica Farm during Glassco's nine-month convalescence at the Royal Edward Hospital in Montreal and the Royal Edward Laurentian Hospital in Ste-Agathe, she had suffered a number of mysterious ailments. At one point, her weight had slipped below eighty pounds. During the cold month of March 1965, Elma began to complain with increasing frequency about her health. Although there appeared to be nothing physically wrong, this figure, whom Kim Ondaatje remembers as "the thinnest woman I ever saw," again began to lose weight.[89]

Jamaica Farm was becoming too much for the slight ballerina and her one-lunged husband, now well into their middle years. Moreover, Elma had never liked the old, wood-frame farmhouse, which she found drafty and cold. A dreadful fear of fire stopped her from using the fireplaces, and she spent much of each autumn, winter, and spring seated in the kitchen, wrapped in a blanket, with her feet in the electric oven. After eight years on the farm, she wanted a change. Glassco suggested that they sell the property and move to Knowlton or North Hatley, but Elma's idea was far more adventurous. She proposed that they travel the world – convinced that through a combination of luck, intuition, and simple gut feelings they would stumble over a place where they both wanted to live. Glassco could bear neither the prospect of seemingly endless travel nor the idea of leaving such an important decision to chance. In the end, he sold off most of the property but retained a number of acres on which he would build a new house of their own design.

It was on 10 June 1965, during the couple's final month on Jamaica Farm, that Elma suffered her first known breakdown. Seymour Mayne, then twenty-one, was witness to the beginning. That day, at Glassco's invitation, Mayne and his girlfriend, Viviane, visited from Montreal. After disembarking the bus at Knowlton, they were met by their host and transported by yellow Jeepster to Foster. Elma, Mayne recalls, looked particularly frail and small. Highly nervous, she reacted with degrees of alarm to every motion, no matter how slight, and after having been introduced, seemed to vanish. Ever the gracious host, Glassco gave the young couple a brief tour of the farm, after which the trio got back in the Jeepster for a drive through the Knowlton hills and a small picnic, before returning to the property. "The understanding was that we would stay overnight in his barn," Mayne recalls. "For a young couple a barn looked like an interesting place to spend the night. We settled down and he went to talk to Elma as we wandered around the property. He came to us and he apologized profusely in a breathless way. He said: 'I … I don't think you can stay tonight. I … I'm sorry, something's come up. You must go back to Montreal.'"[90]

Glassco drove the pair back to Knowlton, where they caught the last bus bound for the city. Mayne later received a brief note from his host apologizing for the abrupt cancellation, accompanied by a promise that he would one day explain. Six years later, the explanation came in the form of another letter. Remembering the "memorable visit," Glassco wrote:

I had a whole load of fresh hay delivered, and spread it with my own pitchfork in a corner of the barn, twirling each truss lovingly. But that night Elma's psychosis broke: she thought you were agents of the NKVD and stormed and wept and pleaded with me not to let you stay. So I had to give you that excuse of insurance. You ask, *how could I?* Well, it was all I could do. The real schizophrenia set in soon after, with all the classic hallucinations and paranoiac symptoms. I've never had anyone here since then, by the way. So now you know … It's all too sad even to talk about. – But I still recall spreading that odorous upland hay, thinking how you would enjoy it.[91]

Weeks after the initial breakdown, Glassco and Elma moved out of their home into a small house, at a very cheap rent, in Knowlton. Construction on the new house was delayed due to trouble in finding a reliable contractor. It wasn't until September that the foundation was laid; still the couple hoped to move in at first snow. It was an unrealistic goal. The Glasscos weren't able to move into their new home until the beginning of the New Year.

A wood-framed house with a stone facade, it was much more modest than any of Glassco's previous homes. There were five rooms to Windermere's sixteen, and nothing of the opulence and splendour of the Rawlings mansion. Glassco told visitors that the interior had been modelled, in part, after the house in which Flaubert had written *Madam Bovary*. True or not, one eighteenth-century element the new house lacked was a fireplace. It was a construction that reflected Elma's desires and fears.

The new house solved nothing. Glassco, who had believed it would serve to invigorate his wife, sunk into depression as he witnessed Elma's growing discontentment. Her health continued to deteriorate, and in November she was admitted to the Royal Edward Hospital in Montreal with a fingernail-size cavity in her lung. Due in part to her unhappiness with the hospital, she was released to recover at home. Once back home, Elma began hallucinating, hearing voices, and, according to Glassco "getting warnings."[92] He tried to cope but was soon overwhelmed by waves of terror, obsession, and abuse. Eventually, he was forced to listen to medical advice and, on 16 December, the day after his fifty-seventh birthday, had Elma committed to the Douglas Hospital, formerly the Protestant Hospital for the Insane, in the Montreal suburb of Verdun.

Early the next morning, after downing twelve ounces of gin, he wrote a poem to his wife:

FOR ELMA (MY DARLING WIFE WHO WENT MAD)[93]

Is this the end of love?
Am I forgetting you already

You
Now worse than dead
And far away?

You and
I:
What did it mean
What did it ever mean
But this final desolation
This heartbreak
Where I go sobbing through an empty house
Calling your name?

What is your name?
What is mine?
We are both trapped in your madness
Are these the plots of God?

Is this the end of love?
Am I forgetting you already
My heart's darling
Now worse than dead?

Yes, I shall forget your name
Even your face, your words
In time
As you have already forgotten mine
In the night that has already fallen
Tonight
Let your awful night take us both in its arms.

"For Elma (My Darling Wife Who Went Mad)" was not his best work, indeed he considered it proof that "drunkenness and emotion make the worst possible poetry."[94] It would never be published. Though Glassco wrote himself a reminder to destroy the poem, he could never bring himself to do so.

EIGHT | 1967–1969

Love can give so little, it seems.[1]

Glassco rarely visited Elma. Her doctor, Heinz Lehmann cautioned that each appearance encouraged the belief that her husband had arrived to take her home. If there was any comfort to be taken, it lay in Lehmann's reputation as a psychiatrist at the forefront of advancements in the treatment for mental illness. The clinical director of the Douglas Hospital, in 1954 he had been the first in North America to prescribe the antipsychotic drug chlorpromazine. Glassco respected and admired Lehmann from the start, considering the psychiatrist a brilliant and compassionate man.

During the few trips Glassco made into the city, he received support and comfort from Frank and Marian Scott. With Ralph Gustafson and his wife, Betty, they eased the passage through the holiday season that Glassco had, even in the best of times, found so trying. He'd been told that Elma could expect an extensive stay, yet six days into the New Year, just three weeks after her admission, she was considered healthy enough to return home. Glassco was overjoyed. Writing Arthur Smith just after she'd arrived back in Foster, he attributed Elma's recovery to "one of those new marvel drugs."[2] He felt her progress was beyond belief and shared the experience with fellow poet Ron Everson, whose wife had also been treated by Lehmann: "It was his prescription of largactil that pulled Elma out of her psychosis with such miraculous speed."[3]

His outlook high, his confidence in modern medicine strong, Glassco began planning a winter trip for two to Haiti. Then, just ten days after Elma's return to the little Foster house, he was shaken when she suffered a relapse.

What Glassco hadn't anticipated was that placing his wife in the Douglas had put a further strain on their relationship. She felt stigmatized by the experience and would never forgive her husband for having placed her in a mental health institution. As Valentine's Day approached, Elma attempted suicide through overdosing on pills. It was some time before Glassco noticed; he had thought she'd been sleeping and had failed to take in her true state until it was almost too late. She was just barely alive when rushed twenty kilometres to Sweetsburg Hospital in Cowansville. Elma remained unconscious for three days. Though he'd saved his wife from death, Glassco felt enormous guilt, blaming himself for not having been more attentive.

Elma hated all hospitals but felt no comfort at home. She likened the new house Glassco had built for her to a prison. Yet, it was to the house that she returned following the suicide attempt; and as the winter drew to an end and the spring began, she remained indoors, listless, overcome by melancholia, refusing to venture out. Glassco lived trapped under her cloud: "Yes. All day long now, and for the rest of my life, I must face the fact that I have wrecked hers. And it is so inescapable! I cannot go away, even for a night, without putting her in misery; she will not go away, even for a night, by herself."[4]

Seeking some sort of escape from the cramped Foster house, he hastily arranged an April trip to Paris. Glassco was certain that the visit would have a restorative effect on Elma and, as their departure approached, became convinced that the mere anticipation of Paris was aiding a full recovery. And yet, the trip was delayed in March when she again entered the hospital. This time Elma was not released for six weeks. Although the stay was twice as long as any of her previous treatments, on 15 May, mere days after her release, the couple were on a flight for a three-week stay in Paris. There was none of the sociability they'd enjoyed on their previous visits; Elma was simply too fragile, while Glassco was fearful of another breakdown. He returned certain that the trip, which he referred to as their "legal honeymoon," had done some good, but he could not fool himself into believing that the effect had been permanent.[5]

The couple landed at Montreal's Dorval Airport on 5 June, just as Canada's centennial celebration was approaching its climax. Glassco and his fragile wife were forced to deal with the crowds of tourists flying in to visit Expo 67, the Universal and International Exhibition being held on Île Ste-Hélène, where Taylor had once trained, and the manmade Île Notre-Dame. Glassco hated everything about the exhibition. Its theme "*Terre des hommes*" he considered a "title fitly taken from/ That crypto-fascist phoney De Saint-Exupéry."[6] Worst of all was the individual who had first envisioned this futuristic landscape, Jean Drapeau, then in the fourth of his eight terms as mayor of Montreal. This little man with "the lipless grin/ Under the little merciless moustache" and his "concentration on the cash" had made the city "Not beautiful/ But only big, and rich, and dull."[7]

Expo 67, its omnipresence and its effects on the city, was just one of many elements contributing to what was becoming the most trying period in Glassco's life. Six months earlier, he and Elma had ushered in the centennial year in a manner that would have once seemed inconceivable. His wife had lain heavily medicated in a public hospital bed, while Glassco had been one hundred kilometres away in Foster, listening over the radio to words he had written being read by Governor General Georges Vanier.

Seven months earlier Glassco had received an unexpected offer from the poet and diplomat Robert Choquette. The two had been in contact for some years through Glassco's persistent efforts to pull together an anthology of French Canadian verse in translation. Glassco himself had translated an excerpt of Choquette's long poem, *Suite Marine*, which had appeared in *The Literary Review*. From his post as Canadian consul general in Bordeaux, Choquette wrote that he had accepted an invitation from the Canadian Interfaith Conference to write both French and English lyrics to a hymn of the Confederation. Now, months later, he was beginning to doubt his abilities in producing an English version. "What I am coming to is this:" he wrote, "should I fail miserably in the English version, would you consider lending me a hand or two? Would you even consider undertaking a full-fledged translation or adaptation of my text?"[8]

Glassco was flattered by the request and offered his assistance in what he anticipated would be a trouble-free project. The following month, the two poets shared a pleasant evening in Montreal discussing the hymn. Looking over Choquette's words, Glassco quickly realized that a dedicated translation of the lines would not work. His challenge was compounded by the music composed by Healey Willan. Glassco, who had never before translated lyrics, considered abandoning the project. Nevertheless, in early August he travelled to meet with Willan at his Toronto home. It became obvious to both composer and poet that the English translation fit poorly with the hymn and would have to be discarded entirely. With the deadline less than a month in the future, Glassco set to work on fresh lines. "It is now admittedly more an adaptation than a translation," he wrote Choquette. "This has been forced on me, first by those feminine endings, and then by the absolutely unforeseen need for *stressed first syllables* in *every* line of the English. Dr Willan especially asked me for the latter when I saw him in Toronto on August 3 …. The resulting metre (which, when unrhymed, made me think of a man trying to start a motorcycle) called for rhymes and half-rhymes to give the lines at least some verbal music."[9]

The adaptation was submitted on time, and Glassco was relieved to be rid of a problematic project, one that had taken considerable time and energy. He was therefore furious when, after weeks of silence, he received a phone call saying that his words were unacceptable. The Interfaith Council Board had wanted lyrics suitable for congregational singing but had not shared this information; both Choquette and Glassco had understood that the hymn was intended for trained choirs.

What bothered Glassco all the more was that the first of the two adaptations appeared to meet the requirements of the board. As he wrote Choquette:

> It was Dr Willan's increasingly difficult technical requirements – subsequently imposed, as you will remember, on my smooth and simple first version – which "floored" me in the end! Since a simple and moving hymn like the original was impossible to produce in this really fantastic metre, I came up, *faute de mieux*, with a tour de force which, as the Directors found, was a "poetical anthem" and not a "hymn" at all. (Perhaps the original difficulty lies in the fact that "*hymne*" is not properly or primarily "hymn" at all; it is "anthem"; "hymn" in the English Low Church sense, is "*cantique*.")[10]

Less than three months before the work was scheduled to debut, Glassco submitted a third adaptation of Choquette's *Hymne*, along with a letter informing that he would regretfully withdraw from the project if the new lines were not accepted. Despite months of steady work, Glassco saw his contribution to the "Anthem for the Centennial of Canadian Confederation" as negligible. Upon viewing the sheet-music proofs, he instructed the publisher, BMI Canada, to delete the ascription to himself from the covering page, asking that it be run in small type after the composition's ending. Willan, too, took little pride in the piece. Though offered a place of honour at the first performance on Parliament Hill as the centennial year began, he chose to remain at home in Toronto, listening on radio.

Glassco visited Expo only once, to attend the World Poetry Conference, a four-day event held in early September. Among some of the Montreal poets, expectations were high. In the pages of *The Gazette*, Louis Dudek made a rather bold prediction: "of all the memorable events taking place at Expo this year, none will be more significant in the long run."[11] The poet was, perhaps, less than forthcoming, neglecting to mention his role as a member of the organizing committee.

While Dudek's considerable efforts to bring in Ezra Pound were met with a last-minute cancellation, the conference attracted many prominent international poets, including Robert Lowell, Robert Creeley, Denise Levertov, Czesław Miłosz, George Barker, and Judith Wright. Of the Canadian poets, Scott was perhaps the most notable and noticeable, attending in a handsome tuxedo. What Irving Layton lacked in style of dress, he attempted to make up with a bravado that made Glassco cringe. This performance was a memorable moment in what Glassco saw as an otherwise entirely forgettable summit. Even Dudek had to admit that the conference "was perhaps to some extent a bore."[12]

The grand "flop" inspired such glee in Glassco, and he readily shared his own opinion of the conference with several correspondents.[13] "It was," he wrote Leon Edel, "simply too big, too inchoate, and somehow taken over by a group of the most longwinded bores imaginable."[14] He took to comparing the World Poetry Conference to the Foster Poetry Conference, noting that the latter had gone from conception to birth in just seven months and had received only $1,000 in grant money.

He found pleasant distraction from the dying days of Expo and his troubles at home through Margaret Atwood, who, having accepted a teaching position at Sir George Williams University, was newly arrived in Montreal. "He had a little moustache and blinky eyes," she recalls, "so he looked a lot like the walrus in *Alice in Wonderland*'s 'The Walrus and the Carpenter.' He would always greet you at the door in some flamboyant red silk embroidered dressing gown, or something like that. He just loved playing the decadent aesthete."[15] Atwood recognized performance behind the "decadent aesthete." Though she was certain that Glassco had experienced some of the things he claimed, it was, she thought, primarily a role: "He enjoyed being that person."[16]

Glassco was then fifty-eight, but to Atwood and other younger poets like George Fetherling he appeared as a very old man. Perhaps his embrace of things Edwardian contributed to this perception; certainly the two struggles with tuberculosis were a factor. Glassco had long recognized the discrepancy between his appearance and his age; since his mid-twenties he'd feared he was growing old prematurely.[17] Now, before stepping out in public, he would fuss over his physical appearance. "I am vainer than ever," he admitted in one journal entry. "I look at myself in the mirror more and more, pay more attention to my dress, my hair which I still set in silly little negligent curls above the ears. Ridiculous old man!"[18] He despaired at the way in which the young people of the late 1960s dressed, complaining not of exposed flesh but of ill fitting, ragged, and unattractive clothing. Yet Glassco took advantage of the times and showed up at several *vernisages* and *lancements* in leather pants. On select afternoons, he would meet Atwood and Angela Bowering, wife of George Bowering, sharing long lunches. Poetry was not on the menu. "What he liked to do was go out and flirt and make naughty jokes and tell scandalous stories," Atwood recalls. In the company of the two young women, Glassco was in his element, taking delight in teasing and trying to shock. "It was not a deeply intellectual relationship."[19]

When Expo finally ended late that October, Glassco was not among what the Canadian Press described as the sad crowds who bid adieu. His backwards look was markedly different from those whom journalist Joseph MacSween likened to "children departing some long-loved fairyland."[20] In *Montreal*, the long poem Glassco completed after the world exhibition ended, the spectacle is remembered with a mixture of distaste and relief:

> (Thank Heaven! the crisis
>   The fever is past,
> The frightful pavilions
>   Demolished at last –
> And the horror of Expo
>   Is over at last!)[21]

For Glassco, Montreal's "crisis" did not revolve around the events of October 1970, which had also passed by the time of the poem's publication, but the fever and destruction brought by Drapeau's futuristic visions.[22]

The centennial year most certainly counted as one of the most troubled of the poet's life. The effects of the spring trip to Paris were, as he'd predicted, temporary; still Glassco was taken aback by the rapidity and extent of Elma's decline. Throughout the Expo summer, his wife had become increasingly unstable, spending each day staring trancelike out their living room window, smoking in silence. More often than not, Glassco would have to speak her name several times before getting anything in the way of a response. He could find no way around her refusal to take the largactil that she'd been prescribed. Wracked with guilt, tormenting himself unfairly with charges of selfishness, he could not stop comparing Elma's situation with the suffering of Taylor's dying months. "It all comes back to me now –" he wrote in his journal, "my weak clinging to those I love, my absurd hopes that they will not die: they *must* not die! And so I do the very thing I execrate: I make them suffer, I will not let them go in peace."[23]

If Glassco recognized any bright spot in the dismal year, it would have been the arrival of a letter from Kay Boyle in San Francisco. It was the first contact that he'd had with the US writer since his days in Montparnasse – Glassco's letters to Boyle in the 1940s had gone unanswered, and the attempt made in 1958, in which he'd proposed that they meet up in Paris, had similarly been met with silence. Now, however, Boyle required a favour. In what Glassco identified as the very first letter he'd ever received from his one-time lover, Boyle announced that she was revising Robert McAlmon's *Being Geniuses Together* to incorporate her own memories of expatriate Paris. She added that he and Taylor would be appearing in the revised text. Glassco, who had so regretted being left out of the original, reacted with great enthusiasm, including a veiled offer of notes concerning McAlmon's thoughts on writing "taken down verbatim."[24] In subsequent letters, he provided the notes, along with several faded images of himself, Taylor, and McAlmon, taken in a photographer's studio and on the beach in Nice. Other requests from Boyle were frustrated by failures of memory. He had no recollection of having stolen phonograph records from the Dayang Muda. When asked whether he could remember any of the "fantastic quotes" he and Boyle had "put in the mouths of the great" in *Relations and Complications*, none came to mind.[25]

Graeme Taylor, Glassco, and Robert McAlmon, Nice, 1929. One of the photos Glassco offered Kay Boyle for her reworking of *Being Geniuses Together*.

While the passage of time, very nearly four decades, may provide an explanation, these lapses in memory might also be explained by the severe stress and depression caused by his wife's declining health. As her illness progressed, Glassco found himself unable to work. For the first time in his writing career he was turning down offers, including several from Maurice Girodias, who asked whether Glassco might work on cleaning up the manuscript of his autobiography and oversee the republication of Austryn Wainhouse's translations of Sade.

Although he had been told otherwise, he held out hope that Elma's psychosis had been made worse by menopause and had faith that it would subside once the change of life was complete. Any and all small signs of improvement sparked hope. When she kissed him on the cheek, one cold day in early November, he recorded the act in his journal. It was a gentle moment in a time of increasing tension. Glassco began to fear for his health, a concern that was shared by Elma's doctor. He urged the poet to readmit his wife, lest the stress cause him to suffer a nervous breakdown. Yet Glassco refused to subject his wife to what he considered the desolation and ignominy of a hospital. When, in January 1968, Lehmann determined that

Elma was incurable, Glassco remained determined to keep her at home in Foster. Her newfound conviction that she was a daughter of Tsar Nicholas II, somehow conceived after his death, did nothing to change his mind regarding hospital care. It wasn't long before Elma's claim to the Russian throne was joined by a new belief: that she was the reincarnation of Queen Nefertiti. "We have some interesting conversations," Glassco wrote Smith.[26]

In March, Elma became violent to a point at which Glassco could no longer handle her. She was returned to the Douglas Hospital for what would amount to a six-week stay. In order to be closer to his wife, Glassco took an apartment on Bishop Street in downtown Montreal. From San Francisco, Boyle tried to provide some encouragement, writing him: "I know somewhat the pain and despair you are suffering, for two of my five daughters *were* schizophrenic. There were years of the deepest anguish for them and with them, and they have come safely through and have happy family lives."[27]

Meanwhile, Boyle was experiencing hardships of her own. One daughter, Faith, was living on a commune complete with guns, drugs, and a portrait of Charles Manson under which fresh flowers were placed daily. At sixty-five, her finances were thoroughly stretched through generosity to her adult children, so much so that she in turn was forced to rely on the goodwill of others. Professionally, Boyle was struggling to fulfil a three-book contract with Doubleday while teaching at San Francisco State College. Of her many troubles, she shared only two with Glassco. The first involved a forty-five-day prison sentence she'd incurred by blocking the Oakland Induction Center during a demonstration against the war in Vietnam. The second began when Boyle, only days into her sentence, discovered a small lump on her breast. She was released and operated upon in mid-April, a week after the death from cancer of her ex-husband, Laurence Vail.

Two months later, the reworked version of *Being Geniuses Together*, newly touted as a "binocular view of Paris in the '20s," was published.[28] As Boyle had promised, this time Glassco and Taylor featured in the book, not only in her own chapters but also in rescued bits from McAlmon's manuscript.[29] The misspelling of his surname – "Glasco" – did nothing to temper her old lover's enthusiasm. He wrote Boyle a letter overflowing with praise:

> What a wonderful book *Being Geniuses* is! It holds the essence of those days as no other book of the period does. But surely Bob never wrote as well as this! You must have done some very judicious revising to

make him articulate without losing his own particular "quality" (that favourite word of his!)

You have been kinder to Graeme and me than either of us deserved: and such lovely photographs … My reaction of a personal sadness – it seems so long ago, almost like something I am *re*-reading – is overbalanced by a wonderful feeling that the whole period has really been pinned down for the first time. Your idea of alternating your own work with Bob's was brilliant; it gives both variety and a kind of double vision trained on the scene. Your own part strikes me as better than his: Bob never gave himself, the way you do.[30]

This over-the-top reaction was perhaps not what Boyle had desired. In crafting a new version of *Being Geniuses Together*, she'd hoped to improve both McAlmon's profile as well as his reputation. However, the method of interleaving her chapters with his only served to encourage comparisons in which, almost without exception, Boyle was judged the superior writer. Jean Stafford, writing in *The New York Review of Books*, praised Boyle's chapters, dismissed McAlmon's writing as "repetitious and boring."[31] The reviewer for *Newsweek* summed up this common opinion with the succinct, if inelegant and uninspired: "She writes rings around him."[32] Nor did everyone share Glassco's opinion that the method of alternating chapters was "brilliant." Reviewing the book for *The London Daily Telegraph*, Anthony Powell was particularly critical: "One absolutely gasps at Boyle's including her own life. That she was there surely does not include the right to chop up his book and superimpose her own."[33]

What's more, in pairing herself with McAlmon, Boyle had altered the very title of the memoir. Gone was the clever flippancy; the geniuses had become McAlmon and Boyle, whose portraits were featured on the dust-jacket cover. Indeed, while McAlmon appeared only once, Boyle's image appeared twice.

Of the many reviews garnered by Boyle's reworking, none was more prominent than that of Malcolm Cowley, which appeared on the front page of *The New York Times Book Review*. Cowley had an advantage not shared with the other critics in that not only had he lived in Paris but he had known McAlmon, if only briefly. In fact, the reviewer was among the many who had benefited from the writer's generosity.[34]

Whatever gratitude Cowley once felt toward McAlmon may have been tempered by the opinion of his own work contained in the memoir. "In any case," McAlmon wrote, "Cowley soon went back to America and joined the staff of the *New Republic*, where he could be duly ponderous, the young intellectual fairly slow on the uptake."[35] While the review was complimentary of Boyle, Cowley dismissed her deceased co-author as a writer who "never in his life wrote so much as a memorable sentence."[36]

Boyle was livid. Convinced that Cowley had been motivated by "personal spite,"[37] she turned to Glassco and enlisted his help in defending their old friend. With no recognition of the irony, Boyle asked for help in her search for memorable McAlmon lines to use in her rebuttal. Glassco, who had never been much impressed by McAlmon's writing, had no real quarrel with Cowley's judgement; still he sent Boyle a cheap collection of McAlmon short stories, *There Was a Rustle of Black Silk Stockings*, in which he'd marked a few passages from "Miss Knight."[38] Yet, Glassco could never praise McAlmon without the suggestion of criticism. "I think they demonstrate Bob could write brilliantly in prose when he took the trouble," he wrote Boyle; then proceeded to detail the story's weaknesses and those of "The Lodging House," another piece in the collection.[39] Glassco expanded on what he saw as McAlmon's failings in a further letter, written after Boyle had sent him the Cowley review: "I do think C. has a point about 90% of Bob's writing: it *is* pretty slapdash. Not always: the parody of Gertrude Stein is both funny and perceptive, and goes with a fine swing. It shows, I think what Bob might have done if only he'd taken more *care* with his writing."[40] Boyle, who had fallen into the habit of writing Glassco on average twice a month, followed his comments with four months of silence.

Ultimately, Boyle's goal to rescue McAlmon from near oblivion had failed. His books remained out of print. Five years previous, in *That Summer in Paris*, Morley Callaghan had written: "Of all the Americans who had been in Paris – those who appear in memoirs and movies – McAlmon is the overlooked man."[41] Boyle's bastardization of *Being Geniuses Together* had changed nothing.[42]

In the months before the book went out of print, it was read by several members of Glassco's circle, including Leon Edel, who was prompted to write his old McGill friend about their Paris years. *Being Geniuses Together* revived memories for Glassco, as well: "Yes, there was a time I shunned the past. Now, however, I look back on these days, with which I broke so entirely aetat. 21, as if they were something I read about, and that *jeune* was someone I knew – oh, quite well, but lost track of somehow! And here he is again, that susceptible teen-ager who could never say no to anyone. Redivivus, as they say …"[43]

During the months leading to the publication of *Being Geniuses Together*, Boyle had encouraged Glassco to submit his own expatriate memoirs to Doubleday. "The 'twenties are fascinating to the public at this time," she'd reported in one letter.[44] Now, with the critical success of Boyle's chapters in *Being Geniuses Together*, Glassco was prompted to again revisit the memoirs that had lain dormant since the terse rejection by literary agent Willis Wing's underling. Six excerpts were sent to *The Tamarack Review*, a submission that prompted founding editor William Toye, the editorial director of Oxford University Press Canada, to request the complete manuscript. Keen on taking up Boyle's old offer, hoping to draw on her connections at Doubleday, Glassco held back. In early December, he sent her three of the excerpts, titled "Morley in Paris," "The Clutch of Circumstances," and "Two Old Ladies":

> Do they amuse you? But most importantly, do you object to my fabrication of your part in "Two Old Ladies," which *Tamarack* also wanted but which I held back since I didn't have your permission. Worse than this, however, is that I have practically created a character modelled after you (beautiful, brilliant, sensitive, witty, charming and footloose) whom I've given another name but who is probably recognizable by anyone still surviving from those days. In short, our friendship has been blown up, glamourized and made intensely significant in the framework of the story itself. (The events of the whole book have been re-arranged, telescoped, speeded up and dramatized in the same way.) You see, we have long invented dialogues, do things we never did, go places we never went, etc. It's really fiction: I was trying to re-create the atmosphere and spirit of the Paris of those days as it was for *me*. The way George Moore and Casanova did for the world of *their* youth.[45]

In his pursuit of Boyle's publisher, he included a false claim that McClelland & Stewart were all set to publish the memoir. He told Boyle:

I would much rather have it done by Doubleday. On the strength of these 3 extracts, do you think you could recommend it to them? If so, I'll send you the whole manuscript on the understanding that if you wish I will give "Kay Boyle" another name and disguise her beyond recognition. And I would never publish it anywhere without your permission. By the way, in the version McC. & S's editor has seen your name was changed. But I would like to restore it, not only for its legendary value but as furnishing a romantic record of what might very well have been. What actually happened between us was after all so insufficient, and now it's not.[46]

Boyle's response was delayed by her departure for a month-long stay in Europe. It eventually came in February, accompanied by a request for donations to the striking professors of San Francisco State College:

On principle, I don't mind at all your inventing a romantic sequence for me in your book, but I do mind this sort of distortion which you have of me in this part. I don't mind your using my name, provided that I *talk* like me. But I don't believe I could ever have said "cushy" or said that the Dayang Muda "spent money like a drunken sailor." Nor could I have said I was "fed to the teeth" – and numerous other remarks. Even if you have not used my name, the character would be recognized as me now that *Being Geniuses* establishes that I wrote the Dayang Muda's memoirs. And in your description in these pages, it is really not me. Also the description of Lucien Daudet is very far from my memory of him. He did not have a moustache, either dyed or otherwise, when I met him at the Princess's. I wonder why you felt it was necessary to have you move into her apartment? This seems a bit weak as statement, or is it because I know it was false?[47]

Whether distorted or not, in making her many criticisms, Boyle chose to ignore the great many liberties she herself had taken in reworking *Being Geniuses Together*. McAlmon's memoirs of the years 1931 to 1934 had been excised, and with them the cautionary account of his 1932 trip to Germany, during which he witnessed Adolf Hitler and his Brown Shirts parading through the streets of Munich. She had further excised several sections of the original in which McAlmon had cast himself poorly. In doing so, Boyle had refashioned the memoir to better resemble her idealized image of the deceased writer, a man for whom she had felt an unreciprocated romantic love. In her own chapters, which comprised over half of the book, Boyle fabricated for herself a richer history. She claimed to have studied architecture, when she did nothing more than take a few courses in mechanical drawing; her attempt to get a job at *New Masses* occurs five years before the magazine came into existence; and she moves up her marriage to Laurence Vail by a year. In short, Boyle had "re-arranged, telescoped, speeded up and dramatized" events, just as Glassco had told her that he had done with his own memoirs.

Taken aback by Boyle's comments, Glassco was uncharacteristically slow to respond. He sent a cheque for $50 made out to Boyle's union, accompanied by a letter that was full of apologies and explanations:

Of course you're right about the dialogue I've given you in the extract from MEMOIRS OF MONTPARNASSE. It's not the way you speak, and never was. But how could I remember after 40 years?

I think the best solution to the whole problem of your appearance in the book is to *dis-identify* you yourself entirely with the character I created so long ago in your image, and, by changing your name, nationality, appearance, profession and background, turn this character into an imaginary *persona* whom no one could possibly connect with you. This has already been done in the extract dealing with the Princess: you are now only mentioned, in the most passing and complimentary way, as the author of her Memoirs.

By the way, I *did* live in the Boulevard Beauséjour apartment for a few weeks! It was intolerably dull …

I'm sorry if I have offended you, as I seem to have done. Rest assured that all the pages of this extract in which you are named – and all those in the rest of the manuscript in which you have been named – have now been destroyed, and no one saw them but ourselves.[48]

In his confused fusion of excuse and explanation, Glassco employed the fiction of early composition in an attempt to distance himself from a younger self, the one who had so long ago "created" a Kay Boyle "character," yet he pleaded to be excused for his failure to remember the way she spoke. He attempted further explanation in a follow-up letter:

You see, I look on the real value of "memoirs" as being not so much a record of "what happened" as a re-creation of the spirit of a period in time. The first approach is so often simply tedious, faded literary gossip, name-dropping, disconnected anecdotes, etc., like 50% of Bob's book; your own record, on the other hand, has the ring of genuine experience and feeling, and above all a good story-line: everyone here says so! The second approach is that of Rousseau, Casanova and George Moore. None of them felt tied to historical truth; they were all liars and produced works of art by *invention*. Who cares about their lies now? Who knows, for instance, whether Casanova's "Henriette" even existed? Yet she lives. I don't compare myself to them, naturally, but my book is in their style. And Casanova is the greatest writer of Memoirs the world has ever seen: *this* is the 18th century, and the portrait of a man as well. He's better than Pepys, even.[49]

That Glassco dwelt on the matter to such an extent is a reflection of his caution in his depiction of living people – even in episodes that contain little or no scandal. The title page of the manuscript bears the standard note of caution common to works of fiction, particularly *romans à clef*: "All the characters in this book, except the author, are fictitious, and any resemblance to actual persons, living or dead, is purely coincidental."[50]

No doubt Boyle would have agreed that this statement, which did not make its way into the published memoirs, is the flimsiest and most transparent of claims. Only someone wholly unfamiliar with expatriate Paris would have been unable to identify the "May Fry" of the manuscript as US author Kay Boyle.

Smarting from the response Boyle gave to her portrayal in "Two Old Women," Glassco split the Kay Boyle character in two: Kay Boyle, the Dayang Muda's ghostwriter, and a "famous British novelist" named Diana Tree.[51] Though this second personality and model are similar, he distanced them somewhat by providing different publishing histories: in the 1928 of the memoirs, Tree has written at least four novels, while in truth Boyle's first book, a collection of short stories, hadn't yet been published.[52]

Glassco must have known from Boyle's reaction that she would be unlikely to champion *Memoirs of Montparnasse* at Doubleday. Instead, he submitted the manuscript to Oxford as Toye had requested, sending the Boyle and McAlmon memoir under separate cover. In the accompanying letter, Glassco was much more honest about this new *Being Geniuses Together* than he had been with Boyle, referring to the text as "disingenuous, 'genteel' and lacking in frankness. This was *not* the twenties!"[53]

Impressed by Glassco's manuscript, Toye decided to accept the memoirs, despite the fact that it was outside the press' usual areas of publication. Within two weeks of submission, Glassco had a contract in hand.

Toye, a careful editor known for meticulous and extensive revisions, thought the manuscript would require little work. Publication was set for early 1970, the same year in which he hoped Glassco's anthology, *The Poetry of French Canada in Translation*, would also appear. The collection had been accepted by Oxford in 1965, originally under the condition that the press would obtain a $2,500 grant from the Centennial Commission with which to pay the poets and translators involved. Although the application was turned down, the publisher remained committed. In 1967, the project received a $2,000 grant by Quebec's Department of Cultural Affairs to cover permission fees for all the French texts. However, it wasn't until two years later, when the Canada Council awarded $4,000, dedicated to paying the translators, that the project was finally scheduled for publication.

The anthology had not been lying dormant. Glassco had turned to it frequently – dropping, adding, and substituting – often after consulting with Smith. Translation in Canada had greatly changed since 1957, the year in which Scott had first suggested the anthology. The number of French Canadian books published each year in English translation had grown sixfold. So, too, had French Canada changed. Quebec had experienced the Quiet Revolution, the formation of the Rassemblement pour l'Indépendance Nationale, the Front de libération du Québec, and the Parti Québécois. The politics of the younger poets appeared quite different than those of Canadian Consul General Robert Choquette and future Liberal senator Jean Le Moyne. In 1968, Glassco looked on these upheavals in Quebec's political landscape with amusement and had great faith in the new prime minister whom he thought was the most promising the country had ever had. "Pierre Trudeau is almost too good to be true," he wrote Boyle.[54] "One of *us*, you could say. *Not* a politician, or a wheeler-dealer, or a deadbeat. A real humanist, and a man of extraordinary sincerity and courage."[55]

Despite his past aspirations and his involvement with the Liberal Party, Glassco tended to avoid discussing politics, something not always possible when dining with the Scotts. He limited his writing on the subject to just a few correspondents, including Boyle, who was then immersed in 1960s radicalism:

> We have this problem in Quebec, where the French are fighting a 200-year-old neurosis. A *conquered* people who can't forget the defeat of Montcalm and their desertion by France. They never stop to think that if Montcalm had beaten Wolfe the whole of French Canada would have been sold by Napoleon to the U.S., like Louisiana. And now they're hankering after de Gaulle, that old poop. So we have the *séparatistes*, the FLQ, who go around putting bombs in mailboxes and killing harmless old ladies by accident. Also writing bad poetry.
>
> This poor Quebec. Their church and their leaders have always sold them out, and they're still seeking a mother-image. De Gaulle, Castro, Mao: any womb in a storm. O this idiotic nationalism.[56]

For the most part, Glassco's contacts with what he called "French Canadian poets" came through his requests to translate their work and related correspondence. Even so, he could not have been entirely surprised by the unpleasantness he witnessed at an August 1968 poetry reading in North Hatley. The event was organized by Sheila Fischman, newly married to D.G. Jones, and featured anglophone and francophone poets, including Jones, Scott, Smith, Roland Giguère, and Gérard Godin, the future Parti Québécois cabinet minister. "I'd only just arrived in the village – which I didn't know at all," Fischman remembers. "I'd never lived in Quebec before. I couldn't stand the fact that there were English and French living side by side who didn't even know each other's names."[57]

Averse to reciting his work, much less reading from it, Glassco's contribution to the evening was of a different kind. "There was a liquor strike on … everyone was dry. But Buffy knew a bootlegger who, I think, had a day job as a postman. Coincidentally, there was a mail strike at the same time, so his bootlegger was able to come up with a few bottles of really good wine."[58] As the evening progressed, the liquor contributed to mischievousness, misunderstanding, and ill temper, leading ultimately to tears for the organizer. "When someone would get up to read in English, Pauline Julien would say, *'En français, en français!'* The tone rose and the insults flew. Some people walked out."[59]

The evening was one of the factors that contributed to the founding of

Ellipse, a new little magazine dedicated "to generating a more intimate commerce between the two languages,"[60] which was started by Jones, Fischman, Giguère, and critic Joseph Bonenfant. Glassco was flattered when offered the position of consulting editor, the only editorial position he would ever hold.

Those who had attended the doomed poetry reading had little idea of the challenges Glassco faced daily in Foster. By autumn 1968, Elma had taken to spending all but two hours a day in bed. Whether awake or preparing for sleep, this once stylish, impeccably dressed woman refused to change her clothes. She had worn the same dress for a month and had taken to defecating on the bathroom floor. Adding to the horror, Elma was displaying obvious symptoms of bulimia. "Although she eats enough for 3 people (every day a pound of butter which she eats with a spoon, a whole loaf of bread, 6 eggs, a bottle of milk, two tins of vegetables, a pound of cooked ham, a pork chop, crackers, pickles, mayonnaise, 10 ounces of gin, and many other things), she is losing weight and strength steadily: she vomits about 4 to 5 times a day, by that curious compulsion which seems to be part of her *mental* illness."[61] As witness to these disturbing episodes, Glassco was at an extreme disadvantage; it would be another decade before bulimia would begin to be recognized as an autonomous psychological condition.[62]

Within months, Elma had moved from bingeing and purging and had begun refusing food altogether. Glassco was convinced that his wife was committing suicide through starvation, but he saw no point in again taking her to the hospital. Intravenous feedings, drugs, and vitamin injections would, he believed, do little more than prolong her life by a few weeks. Moreover, in healthier times, they had each made a pact not to let the other die in hospital. Every day was spent by Elma's side, encouraging her to eat, but she would accept nothing more than a daily menu of a few grapes or strawberries, an occasional teaspoon of caviar, and a glass of champagne. Her skin began to flake from dehydration, spots of scurvy began to show, and, unbeknownst to Glassco, her tuberculosis had returned. Within a month he felt she had ventured past all mental suffering. Indeed, as he reported to Boyle, she seemed comfortable and happy. With seemingly clear mind, this reincarnation of Queen Nefertiti announced that she would soon again be reincarnated on the surface of the moon.

In late March 1969, at her own request, Elma was placed in an ambulance and once again returned to hospital, this time to the Royal Edward Lau-

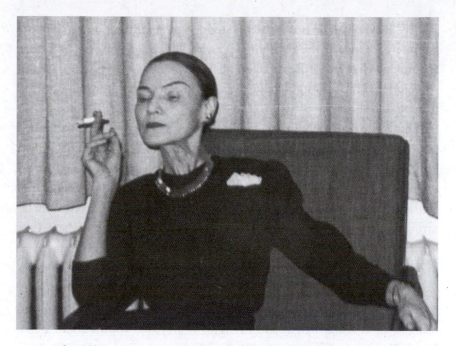

Elma Glassco in 1969 at Frank and Marion Scott's Westmount home.
The photograph was taken by the poet Micheline Ste-Marie.

rentian Hospital in Ste-Agathe. She was determined to die, to move on to her next life, and to do so in the comfort provided by nurses and doctors. Her weight had dropped to fifty-five pounds. As death approached, she told Glassco that her love for him was strong but that her desire for death was stronger. He reported what he'd expected to be one of their final conversations to Boyle: "'You will adjust,' she says. 'You loved me more than I loved you, though I loved you more than any man I knew. Perhaps I am incapable of love. My bridegroom was always Death.'"[63]

Reconciled with his wife's seeming fate, Glassco made preparations. He brought Elma's white satin wedding nightgown from Foster, readying it for use in her burial, and consulted the head nurse about local undertakers. He took a hotel room in Ste-Agathe to be near his wife when the end came. Then, just as approaching death seemed imminent, Glassco was gripped by a sudden fear of being alone. He dreaded the emptiness of the new house. Living by himself was something he'd never truly experienced. Even the two difficult wartime years with Sappho at Windermere had been better than living alone. Glassco felt entirely unloved and took only small comfort in reassurances from Elma's psychiatrist that her hatred and distrust – she had come to believe that Glassco was conspiring to murder her – were, in fact, the polar opposites of her true feelings.

Enduring these trials, Glassco settled on a course of action: after Elma was dead, he would put his affairs in order, see the memoirs and the French Canadian poetry anthology through to press, and would then commit suicide.

Elma did not die. Her doctor at the Royal Edward Laurentian was confident that she could be saved. Through largactil, tubular feeding, and artificial evacuations, Elma was pulled back from what Glassco described as "the very edge of the grave."[64] In May she was taken to Montreal for a series of tests and treatments, and by the following month had gained five pounds. Elma's slow progress continued through the summer as her psychosis diminished. To her eyes Glassco was no longer her murderer, rather he was now seen as "a person whom she just happened to marry in a fit of absent-mindedness some time ago, and who brings her fancy things to eat."[65] By November, her weight had increased to sixty-nine pounds, the tuberculosis had been cured, and she was able to spend two days and nights away from hospital. Glassco took her to Montreal, where they spent two days and nights at his Bishop Street *pied-à-terre*, not half a block from St James the Apostle, the church in which they'd been married. Although her balance had not returned, Elma managed to steady herself and walk by pushing her wheelchair. Together the couple strolled along St Catherine Street, taking in the stylish women of Montreal in their maxiskirts. Elma shared the memories of what she'd experienced in drawing closer to death – serene images that Glassco later related to Boyle: "it seemed to her to comprise and prefigure an eternity of beautiful dreams – all light, greenery, birdsong and repose – perceived with a great but tranquil intensity. This is good news indeed. I only hope it's the same for everyone else!"[66]

The days spent together in Montreal were like a new beginning. Back in Ste-Agathe, Elma's remarkable recovery continued. In early December, the couple learned that she would be permitted to return to Foster for the holiday season. "I can hardly wait for this happiness," wrote Glassco, "of having my own darling with me again. Face it, man, you have never been so deeply, ecstatically, hopelessly in love in your whole life!"[67]

Knowing I am nothing, I have always tried to persuade
the world to the contrary.[1]

The year in which Glassco had intended to kill himself – 1970 – was a time of projects completed and dreams realized. By any measure, it was the most active twelve-month period of his life in letters. It was the year in which his long-planned anthology *The Poetry of French Canada in Translation*, first suggested in 1957 by Frank Scott, finally saw print. The publication coincided with another work of pornography; an elaborate hoax, through which Glassco would introduce a new and original literary technique to an unsuspecting readership. However, both accomplishments, though significant, were overshadowed by the arrival of his *Memoirs of Montparnasse*. Its release, on St Valentine's Day, brought critical praise of a level he hadn't enjoyed, public notice of a sort he had never experienced, and achieved the bestseller status he had for so long craved.

When the first copies of *Memoirs of Montparnasse* appeared in bookstores, his two slim collections of verse were out of print, as were *The Journal of Saint-Denys-Garneau* and *English Poetry in Quebec*. Whether pseudonymous, anonymous, or otherwise, the pornography published in Foster, Paris, London, and New York, was largely unrecognized, unread, and unobtainable in his native land. Aged sixty-one, he had been the subject of only one article, written by Michael Gnarowski in 1966 for a special John Glassco issue of the little magazine *Yes*. In the main, this bald, moustachioed man in smoking jacket and ascot had been known only to readers of Canada's little magazines. The brief biographies that had appeared on their contributors pages invariably included mention of the years Glassco had spent in Paris but didn't so much as hint at the sort of life he'd led in the city of lights. Taken by surprise, the Canadian reading public embraced the memoirs of an unconventional young man, one of their own, who had encountered and conversed with so very many of the famous and infamous of 1920s Paris.

An introduction by Leon Edel, solicited and molded slightly by the memoirist, served to lend considerable weight to this chronicle of youth. The Pulitzer Prize-winning biographer recalled Glassco's "willowy silhouette as he sauntered on the boulevard du Montparnasse" and his "slouched world weary" bearing at the Sélect.[2] Edel had visited Glassco, Taylor, and their girl from "the Canadian West" at their Italian *pension* in Nice.[3] To these fleeting reminiscences of "the golden time of youth,"[4] Edel added praise: "If his book is more modest than most of the Montparnasse memoirs," he wrote, "it is more immediate – possessing almost the effect of 'instant' memory, total recall. The other memoirs (I have read I believe most of them) look back from middle life. Buffy couldn't wait that long. He wasn't sure, when he wrote them, that he would have his middle age."[5] Other writers and critics accepted Glassco's account of the composition and long dormancy of the memoirs. In one of the first reviews, published in *The Globe and Mail Magazine*, William French reported that the author had "resisted the temptation to rewrite or edit the memoirs."[6] Writing in *The Tamarack Review* Margaret Laurence praised Glassco's "celebration of life, partly written out of a knowledge of death."[7] Further enthusiastic notice appeared in *Canadian Literature, Le Devoir, The New York Times Book Review, Saturday Night*, and *The Sunday Star* out of Washington, DC. *The Financial Post* declared the memoirs "a masterpiece."[8] Though the praise of the venerable business paper was high, it could not match the influence of the book's greatest champion, Malcolm Cowley, the very same critic who had so offended Kay Boyle with his dismissal of Robert McAlmon's writing. To the US critic and chronicler of the lost generation, Glassco's reminiscences were "fresher and truer to the moment" than those of Boyle, Ernest Hemingway, Henry Miller, and Gertrude Stein.[9] It was the work of "a precocious Canadian boy with a sharp eye and an accurate ear."[10] Glassco, Cowley wrote, had captured "the tenor of the life in those days, and the behaviour of everybody, faithfully reproduced."[11]

The memoirist was vindicated; the dark doubts and torment brought by Willis Wing's rejection five years earlier were assuaged. Within weeks of its publication, *Memoirs of Montparnasse* was, as Glassco himself noted, selling copies by the thousands. He delighted in the reception:

Glassco in front of le Mas des Oliviers restaurant, a few doors down from his Bishop Street pied-à-terre, three days after the release of *Memoirs of Montparnasse*.

My pleasure in its success stems from something much more discreditable. From the envy it arouses – the envy of my own pseudo-life. How basely I depend on others' views of me! *I desire & court envy: I would rather be thought happy than be so.* This is my hideous ambition – now realized. So, I am a public figure – though in a small way – and am enjoying it. My own real unhappiness I will conceal from everyone.[12]

Glassco told several intriguing stories about the composition of *Memoirs of Montparnasse*. In the prefatory note, he claimed that the book had been written in two stages: chapters 1 through 3 as an eighteen-year-old living in Paris, and the rest four years later as he lay close to death in the Royal Victoria Hospital. In interviews, Glassco provided supplementary fictions, implying that the book had failed to attract the interest of publishers during the Great Depression. He told one journalist that the manuscript had remained untouched for nearly four decades, stuffed into a suitcase in an unidentified attic. Finally, ultimately, there was the story of his having felt torn between the desire to rewrite and his sense of history that prevented tampering with the work. In the end, it was history that had won out; so the memoirist claimed.

However, some of Glassco's friends knew otherwise. Michael Gnarowski, Eldon Grier, Frank Scott, and Arthur Smith were among the correspondents to whom Glassco had written about the progress of the memoirs in the early 1960s. In fact, during those same years Smith had encouraged and supported his friend's pursuit of the project.[13] Yet, Glassco's work on the memoirs was anything but common knowledge within the community of Montreal's anglophone poets. Irving Layton, who had not been among those in whom Glassco had confided, included an impossible story concerning *Memoirs of Montparnasse* in his autobiography, *Waiting for the Messiah*:

In his Prefatory Note, Glassco states, "I did not look at the manuscript again for thirty-five years." It was during one of my visits with him that I got him to take the mildewed notebooks out of a drawer where they'd been kept for over three decades, and read large sections to me. My exclamations of surprise and delight visibly moved him. He told me he hadn't looked at those pages for so long he'd almost forgotten he had ever written them. I like to think that it was my frank enthusiasm that encouraged him to complete the work by the addition of several more chapters.[14]

It was left to Layton's friend and foe Louis Dudek to first raise the possibility that events in *Memoirs of Montparnasse* might not be as Glassco had recorded. In writing his enthusiastic review – "A Decadent in Canada in the 1970s? Yes!" – for *The Gazette*, Dudek performed the simple check that other reviewers had neglected. Comparing the memoirs' first chapter with "Extract from an Autobiography," published forty-one years earlier, he reported: "not a single sentence in the two texts is identical, unless it be a few spoken words attributed to others and even these are somewhat miscast."[15] The discovery of what the reviewer referred to as "high-level literary tactics" did not dissuade Dudek from praising *Memoirs of Montparnasse*.[16] Indeed, he described the book as "the best book of prose by a Canadian that I have ever read."[17] Dudek ended the review, "I would warn the reader not to underestimate this book, or its author. He does enough of that himself. His real value time alone will tell, and I think the verdict may well surprise us all."[18]

In the years that followed Glassco's death, after the truth about the composition became evident, Dudek reconsidered his appraisal of the book. No longer was he so amused by "high-level literary tactics"; Dudek came to accuse Glassco of making "irresponsible claims" and implied that in doing so Edel's critical reputation had been compromised.[19] Nearly a quarter century after Dudek had praised *Memoirs of Montparnasse*, he wrote in his notebook a short piece under the title "Tainted Meat":

> For some years now I have noticed that I cannot read any of the autobiographical writings of Ford Maddox Ford; that is, ever since I realized he was a habitual fabricator, utterly unreliable in his account of things. For the same reason I have been unable to reread any part of John Glassco's *Memoirs of Montparnasse*, although I once praised it as "the best book of prose written by a Canadian."[20]

Dudek's reappraisal had everything to do with content rather than composition. When penning his 1970 review, he recognized *Memoirs of Montparnasse* as the work of an older man but added with certainty that the book had followed the notes of a decades-old draft: "They report actual doings, and meetings with famous men."[21] After Glassco's death he knew this not to

For Frank & Marian
with love from
Bulls

and Numerous footnotes in Holograph,
forming a Key to the disguised
Characters in the Work —

Jan. 6, 1970

The inscription in Frank
and Marion Scott's copy of
Memoirs of Montparnasse.

be true. The issue that most drew his ire concerned the distortion of literary history. Dudek's caution to readers "not to underestimate this book" had been replaced by a very different warning: "Memoirs of Montparnasse is a great little book, but only if you remember that it is not a memoir, it is not a history, it is a work of imagination and fantasy."[22] Edel would also come to reconsider the memoirs. Writing a decade after publication, he would describe *Memoirs of Montparnasse* as a book "filled with imaginary touches and hardly a verbatim record."[23]

Dudek's concern for literary history proved to be well founded, as passages from *Memoirs of Montparnasse* came to be included without question, comment, or caution in biographies of Gertrude Stein, James Joyce, Djuna Barnes, Man Ray, Harry Crosby, Peggy Guggenheim, and others.[24] The respected English biographer and critic Humphrey Carpenter would come to quote from *Memoirs of Montparnasse* frequently and at length in *Geniuses Together*, his 1987 volume on US writers in 1920s Paris.

Glassco chose to leave brightly lit signposts pointing to the truth, many of which are found in his Personal Journal, 1965–1969. Here we have a man who had on several occasions removed and destroyed segments of his Intimate Journal, choosing to leave behind admissions of deceit:

And now it is time to state, in this privacy of myself, that one-quarter of this book *was* lies. This is what I have been trying to avoid saying, even to myself. I never met Frank Harris (it was Graeme who did, & told me about it later); Man Ray never discussed Jane Austen with me; Joyce held no conversation with me about *Ulysses* or "Gob" (he did attack Richardson); Ford's conversation is more than half fabricated … Ah, confession is good for the soul. Already I feel better.[25]

Of the widely varied and dispersed documents Glassco left in his wake, perhaps the most revealing is found in Boyle's copy of *Memoirs of Montparnasse*, which he inscribed the month before its publication date:

Dear Kay, this loose and lying chronicle
You'll understand, and all its young intention
To dress the naked facts and brightly tell
A young man's story and what him befell
In love — and other sports I will not mention —

For you, the finest writer of our age
Who knows what best to exclude, what to invent,
And how the falsehoods of the printed page
Are the true image of our vocal rage —
Will find the inward sense of what he meant

In these too-frothy pages. Take a little
Away, and give a little again: then see
(Since truth is all too dull, too noncommittal)
The form and feature of a youth too brittle
Ever to be described, never to be

Grasped save by an open heart like yours,
Heart always warm, certain to comprehend,
To accept and pardon all the painted lures
Of fiction, for the sake of Art — yet end
As you began, I hope, his dearest friend.
6/1/70 — Buffy[26]

"This little poem in my book came straight from the heart," he wrote in an accompanying letter, "and was not revised or polished. Hope you like the book itself, though I doubt you will. Once again, the rue fable D. Tree is *not* you, and could never be."[27]

Although Boyle thanked Glassco for sending the book, her praise was limited to the inscription. She never did record her reaction, though it would appear Boyle wasn't happy. As a woman who had in recent years endeavoured to elevate Robert McAlmon, she would without question have been irritated by Glassco's depiction of their mutual friend as a drunk who expressed negative and confused ideas "with such petulant incoherence they could hardly be taken seriously."[28] Glassco, to whom she had turned for assistance in defending McAlmon's reputation against attack by Cowley, had written in his memoirs that McAlmon's "style and syntax revealed the genuine illiterate."[29]

With Boyle's receipt of *Memoirs of Montparnasse*, the steady stream of correspondence between the two writers all but ended. Five months passed before Glassco again heard from his former lover; Boyle provided no indication that she had read the memoirs. There would be only two more letters, both written in January 1972, in which she encouraged Glassco to help the elderly expatriate nightclub owner Bricktop in writing her autobiography.[30] In her correspondence, Boyle mentioned *Memoirs of Montparnasse* just once – and then only in the context of Cowley's laudatory review: "I was very much annoyed over Malcolm Cowley's reference to McAlmon (in his review of your book in *The New Republic*) as 'the bitter homosexual novelist.' I wrote him that if he identified McAlmon in that way he should refer to Gertrude Stein as 'the Lesbian innovator' or to Henry Miller as 'the sexually promiscuous novelist.'"[31] Glassco never heard from Boyle again, nor did he ever accept the invitation to visit her San Francisco home. Perhaps the best indication of her feelings toward *Memoirs of Montparnasse* lies in the fact that Boyle shortly thereafter sold her inscribed copy to a California book dealer.

Two months after the publication of *Memoirs of Montparnasse*, the Canadian branch of Oxford University Press issued its second Glassco title of the year. *The Poetry of French Canada in Translation* was a modest-looking book, barely larger than a massmarket paperback; Glassco was troubled by the relatively expensive $4 cover price. The small format and modest appearance were anything but reflections of the contents: 195 translations by 22 translators of 47 poets. Glassco himself had contributed 75 of the translations.[32]

The breadth was equally impressive, ranging from Scott's translation of a 1606 poetic address by the Parisian lawyer Marc Lescarbot at Port Royal to three contemporary poems by twenty-eight-year-old André Major.

The critical notices in English Canada were admiring. Poet and translator Philip Stratford considered the introduction "as interesting for its insights into the nature of French-Canadian verse as for its seasoned reflections on the art of translation" and praised Glassco's ability "to be able to change into half-a-dozen poetic idioms as gracefully as a well-dressed man casually displaying his wardrobe."[33] Only one reviewer, Fred Cogswell, whose translations of Rina Lasnier, Gaston Miron, and Sylvain Garneau had been included, considered the anthology a failure. Cogswell likened the collection to "a cigar, bulging with quantity and no quality in the middle." Glassco's own translation of Louis Riel's "A Sir John A. Macdonald" excepted, Cogswell considered the inclusion of any work predating Émile Nelligan to be "a dreary waste."[34]

Cogswell was less than open in his criticism; in reviewing the book he neglected to mention the nearly simultaneous appearance of his own collection of French Canadian verse in translation. Published by Fiddlehead Poetry Books, *One Hundred Poems of Modern Quebec* featured thirty-seven of the province's French-language poets, the earliest being Alain Grandbois, born in 1900. Although the translations were Cogswell's own, several people, Glassco among them, had provided advice. The anthology would be followed the next year by *A Second Hundred Poems of Modern Quebec*, and then, in 1976, by a third anthology of French Canadian verse in translation, *The Poetry of Modern Quebec*. Not a one would have the impact of Glassco's little book.

The reception of *The Poetry of French Canada in Translation* was quite different among the francophone poets, many of whom took issue with the introduction that had so impressed Stratford. Exception was taken with Glassco's statement that the eloquent and impassioned poets who had followed Hector de Saint-Denys-Garneau appeared "too often preoccupied by political and national ideas, by the one incandescent ideal of a beleaguered Quebec." This assertion, coupled with Glassco's stated belief that "it is a truism that politics and nationalism have never managed to make really good poetry" caused tension between the anthologist and several of the younger poets.[35] Glassco could have avoided conflict; he was all too aware of the changes brought on by the Quiet Revolution. No longer was it the poetry of French Canada, but that of the Québécois. In March, the month before publication, he'd watched with disdain as verse was used for political purposes at the *Nuit de la poésie*, organized by Gaston Miron and Claude Haeffely.[36] This and similar events, most notably *Poèmes et chants de la résistance*, a show organized to raise money for those described as political prisoners, served to inspire a poem:

TO CERTAIN QUEBECOIS POETS

I salute you, traitors of the word,
Exploiters of hatred in the name of poetry,
Intolerable tub-thumpers when you are not
Crybabies seeking a breast
To replace the bosom of *bondieuserie*,
Always barking about the tongue, the roots, the blood, the soil
(Where have we heard those words before?)
Giving us words to flesh out a want of thought,
A vacuum of ideas,
Words like wind from an empty intestinal tract,
Reverberant, redolent, inane.
    Ah, we the quiet ones,
Custodians of the word, what can we do
But hold our noses, and sigh
Before your eructations
So surprisingly set as verse?
 We know you now indeed,
Wicked shepherds, misleaders of the flock,
Stranglers with chains of words,
Killers and closers of the door,
We know you by your words
(O braggarts and bullies *en herbe*)
The words you feed to the people with open mouths,
The mouths of hunger you fill with words which are
Non-words,
Words not to be understood but only to be spat or bellowed

And which are – O you traitors using poetry for a crutch and
a bandwagon –
Becoming extremely tiresome.[37]

He dedicated this bitter verse to Michèle Lalonde, who had recited her
poem "Speak White" at *Poèmes et chants de la résistance* and *Nuit de la poésie*.
These events sparked conflicting emotions concerning the woman he called
"la belle Lalonde."[38] Four of her poems were featured in *The Poetry of French
Canada in Translation*. In fact, he'd hoped that the anthology would bring
attention to Lalonde within English-speaking Canada and had been determined to include at least sixty lines of her poetry. Glassco had himself
translated "Nous avons dormi" and had helped Smith craft several drafts of
"Le jour halluciné." Ultimately, personal affection and admiration for her
talent trumped "To Certain Quebecois Poets"; he shared the poem only with
Smith. To Glassco, Lalonde's gift set her apart from the other poets involved
in *Nuit de la poésie* and similar events; his issue was not so much her work,
but the use of her verse to achieve political goals. Indeed, despite his con-
tention that "politics and nationalism have never managed to make really
good poetry," Glassco admired "Speak White," describing it as an "eloquent
and impassioned plea for French culture against an invading and inevitably
English-speaking North American culture."[39] Lalonde, Glassco thought, was
a unique talent; his criticisms of André Brochu, whose poetry had also been
included in the anthology, was more typical of his stance on verse inspired
by nationalism and politics: "His poetry is fluent, felicitous and polished
especially in his light, satiric, and erotic vein; his more serious poems,
imbued with the most fervent Québec nationalism, are more in the nature
of rhetorical exercises and political effusions."[40]

The animosity demonstrated toward *The Poetry of French Canada in
Translation* reached its peak that autumn during the October Crisis. As
Glassco made the rounds of *lancements* in the company of his friend John
Richmond, the literary editor of *The Montreal Star*, he discovered that the
anthology was "intensely disliked, and that the Introduction found intoler-
ably patronising."[41] In letters sent to Smith in far removed East Lansing,
Michigan, Glassco shared the experience of venturing into evenings dark-
ened by the crisis:

The remark that "nationalism has never made really good poetry" seems to have maddened all of them, critics and poets alike. Gaston Miron will not speak to me now. No wonder: I have attacked his one and only Muse, a dear old Québec whom he seems to visualise as a kind of Marquis de Montcalm in drag, living in St Henri. Pauline Julien says that Frank and I will be hanged on the same gibbet, come the Revolution. Well, as Richmond says, we are "showing the flag." And we talk endlessly with them. At times I feel like a psychiatrist.[42]

He endured accusations that many of the younger poets had been excluded for political reasons. Given Glassco's introductory comments, it was an easy, if unjust, accusation. The anthology, which spanned 364 years of French Canadian verse, featured work by fourteen poets who had not yet celebrated their fortieth birthdays. Moreover, *The Poetry of French Canada in Translation* included a great many poets whose views on Quebec sovereignty were diametrically opposed to those of Glassco. Any perceived weakness concerning the younger poets might be better explained by the anthologist's taste and comprehension. Five years earlier, Glassco had written Scott about problems he was experiencing with the "*jeune poésie*" and their work: "there is just so much of it that I hardly know what to choose, much less how to translate it (it's so often so personal and hermetic)."[43]

Through that troubled autumn he continued to socialize with "pequiste [*sic*] poets"; those who would have him.[44] On 12 November, he was very nearly arrested at Jilly's, a Crescent Street bar, two blocks from his Montreal flat. The three *péquiste* poets with whom he'd been sharing drinks were taken into custody fifteen minutes after his departure. Nevertheless, Glassco stood with his friend Scott in supporting the imposition of the War Measures Act. He considered himself a "Trudeauiste among the pequistes [*sic*]"[45] and held no sympathy for the aspirations of the Front de libération du Québec. In December, when brothers Paul and Jacques Rose were captured and charged in the kidnapping and murder of Pierre Laporte, Glassco dismissed them as being little better than members of the Manson family.

Writing to Smith, he complained that Sheila Fischman, D.G. Jones, Ronald Sutherland, and others in the province's anglophone literary community were "over-truckling" to their francophone counterparts.[46] Worse still, Glassco believed that names like Miron and Jean-Guy Pilon, poets who had ten years earlier been guests at Frank Scott's home, had become radicalized and as a result had betrayed their respective talents. There had been a great shift since the meetings of the late 1950s, when Scott had worked to bring Quebec's anglophone and francophone poets together. As Miron and Pilon turned their backs on his old friend, Glassco responded in kind.

From 1958 through 1972, Glassco had forty translations of French Canadian poetry published in little magazines. There would be only one more: a translation of a poem by Yves Préfontaine, carried out at the request of Sheila Fischman, with the condition that his name not appear. Credit for the translation was given to a fictitious retired beekeeper on the Isle of Wight. The long exhaustive struggle to get *The Poetry of French Canada in Translation* into print, the hostile reception, the accusations of exclusion, and the "québecisme"[47] may have contributed to a lessening in interest on Glassco's part. It could not have escaped Glassco's notice that his dedication and promotion of the poets of French Canada had rarely been reciprocated. Only a handful of his poems were ever published in French translation. Even his erotica, the work that had the greatest commercial potential, failed to attract interest. Increasingly, his work was being made available in German and Dutch, but not in the language of Hector de Saint-Denys-Garneau.[48] However, Sheila Fischman sees a much more simple reason for the decline in his interest: "He had had very strict standards. He was adorably inflexible. I suspect that he had run out of poems that he'd wanted to translate or that he thought he should translate."[49]

Responding to a request from poet Ken Norris made five years after the publication of *The Poetry of French Canada in Translation*, Glassco found he could recommend not a single contemporary French Canadian poet, adding "I've rather lost interest in contemporary F.-C. poetry. Which strikes me as too thin, derivative and gimmicky at the moment."[50] The last poetry Glassco translated was not of a work from French Canada, but one by Surrealist poet Robert Desnos. Given that Glassco had long ago dismissed Surrealism, the choice of "Les quatre sans cou" was an odd one. It might best be explained by Glassco's claim that Desnos had translated Glassco's own "Conan's Fig." For more than two decades, Glassco was consistent in his description of the Denos translation – a pamphlet titled *Figue de Conan*, published by Kra in

1930; it doesn't exist, and sadly never did. Yet, in publishing his translation of "Les quatre sans cou," Glassco appeared to reciprocate; an imagined circle had been closed.

The publication of *The Poetry of French Canada in Translation* coincided with that of another Glassco work: a slim massmarket work of pornography. The publisher, Hanover House of North Hollywood, California, had neither the cachet nor the history of Oxford University Press. It was part of American Art Enterprises, a confusing conglomerate consisting of a distribution company, magazines like *Black Silk Stockings*, *Torrid Teens*, and *The Bitch Goddesses*, and a couple of book imprints. Essex House published original erotica written by Charles Bukowski, Kirby Doyle, and Philip José Farmer, while Brandon House Library Editions was dedicated primarily to quality erotica of centuries past. Both were creations of Brian Kirby, a young rare-book dealer and jazz drummer from Detroit who also served as sole editor.

Though an admirer of both imprints, Glassco had never thought to send any work to Kirby. He did so only at the suggestion of his New York friend Geoffrey Wagner, who was himself an Essex House author.[51] What Glassco had in mind to submit was *The Temple of Pederasty*, a curious work of pornography rooted in both 1920s Paris and seventeenth-century Japan. In his query letter to Kirby, Glassco described the manuscript as "nine pornographic *collages*":

> The text, including a 1,200-word Introduction by Dr S. Colson-Haig, runs to 20,000 words, is my unrestricted property. I enclose a sample of the manuscript, which appeared in Prof. George Henderson's recent essay *The Art of Pornography*.[52]

In fact, Glassco was the true author of "The Art of Pornography," in which *The Temple of Pederasty* had been discussed. The essay, Professor George Henderson, and Doctor S. Colson-Haig were all Glassco's own creations. Much of what he told Kirby were fantasies and half-truths, including the claim that the manuscript was a translation performed by the late Doctor Hideki Okada of work largely based on that of Ihara Saikaku. Like Henderson and Colson-Haig, Okada was a figment of Glassco's imagination, but not so Ihara Saikaku, a Japanese poet of the seventeenth-century.

While it isn't possible to know precisely when Glassco began work on *The Temple of Pederasty*, we can say with certainty that the seed from which this peculiar book grew was shed by another collection of tales, Ken Sato's *Quaint Stories of the Samurais*, which had been published in 1928 by Robert McAlmon. Sato was a Japanese national who had received some education in the United States. He'd lived in Paris for several years during the 1920s and, though a minor figure in Montparnassian culture, had been friendly with McAlmon and James Joyce. In *Quaint Stories of the Samurais*, Sato presented several tales by Ihara Saikaku; in the main, those found in *Nanshoku ōkagami*, a title Sato translated as "The Glorious Stories of Homosexuality."[53] First published in 1687, *Nanshoku ōkagami* consisted of forty stories centred on the themes of love and sodomy, chiefly among the Edo warrior class and their pages. The second half of *Nanshoku ōkagami*, set mainly in the Osaka area, concerns homosexual love among the boy actors of the kabuki theatre. In broken English, Sato described the work to McAlmon: "There is not a single obscene language or indecent passage in the stories. In old Japan, the knight encouraged to have man lovers instead woman, as they thought woman makes man weak, coward and effeminate. Pederasty lovers devoted to each other, sacrificing their own life many times. These stories are very interesting in both points, one as an old Japanese classic and as a study of the old feudal Japan."[54]

Quaint Stories of the Samurais wasn't a translation of Ihara Saikaku, as Sato claimed, but a retelling of nine tales from the first half of the work. His "quaint stories" were shorter, simpler; they were also very badly written.[55]

McAlmon wrote mutual friend Sylvia Beach that he'd intended to couple the supposed translations of Ihara Saikaku with Sato's own tales, but that the latter had been lost in the mail. There is, however, no evidence to support the publisher's claims. It's possible that McAlmon was attempting to make allowances for what Beach considered a substandard book. Sato's weak writing was mirrored by McAlmon's editing; indeed he printed the manuscript as received. The publisher explained the decision in a brief, anonymous note written for the book's title page:

These stories, translated by Ken Sato, who was born in Japan and lived for some years in America, have been printed as translated. Mr

Sate's [*sic*] foreign use of the language was thought te [*sic*] have particularly retained the primitive and quaint quality of the tales.[56]

He wrote Sylvia Beach that there was real value in Sato's "primitive" language, which he felt had a "'No don't kill you; let me kill me or I kill the third man' sort of quality."[57] While published in an edition of only 510, the title failed to sell through. Even Ethel Moorhead, one of McAlmon's greatest defenders, could raise no enthusiasm, and dismissed the book as a "bore."[58]

That *Quaint Stories of the Samurais* was published in autumn 1928 raises something of a mystery. Glassco's unbound copy, now housed at Queen's University, is inscribed:

> For John Glassco, my friend
> R. Ken Sato
> Paris, 1928

Sato left Paris for Japan in December 1926, fifteen months prior to Glassco's arrival. The two men never met, and it is unlikely they knew one another through correspondence. Moreover, the inscription and signature are not in Sato's hand. As the penmanship is similar to Glassco's own, we may speculate that he had at one point attempted to increase the value of the unbound pages with a forged inscription.[59]

Glassco had long been attracted to *Quaint Stories of the Samurais* and in June 1947 had written McAlmon, complimenting his old friend for publishing a "first-class little book":

> I was leafing through a copy of Quaint Tales [*sic*] of the Samurais a little while ago and found it just as good as it seemed originally: the pathos and simplicity of the original seem somehow to gain from awkward translation. Passages like this have a very distinctive charm: "One summer evening I stood in a beautiful garden, enjoying a nice cool breeze after a very hot sweating day. A tiny artificial streamlet crept on between fancy stones and imitated turfed hills. The scene looked like a mountain dwelling of some hermits, who indulge only in spiritual beauties and clean mental pleasures ...." I've been trying to think of what this kind of writing reminds me: now I see that it is more like

Aubrey Beardsley's Under the Hill than anything else, – the same effect of *contrived elegance*, where the words are used with certain startling naivete, just a little out of their proper meaning.[60]

In correspondence dating from the 1940s, Glassco twice asked McAlmon what he knew of Sato's whereabouts. It is a curious query; while Glassco often inquired after mutual friends, he'd never so much as met the Japanese author. In all likelihood, Glassco was testing the water. McAlmon could provide no information, having had no contact with Sato since their last exchange of letters in 1930.[61]

At some unknown point Glassco decided not only to perform the editorial work McAlmon had neglected but to enhance, creating a bawdy version of the tales Sato had written. He called this technique the "erotic *collage*," an "interpolation of libertine phrases, dialogue and incident in the body of classical texts" and claimed that it had long been practiced in Japan, "where, far from being regarded as a desecration of the original, it is applauded as an elegant embellishment which calls for the exercise of the greatest taste, humour, delicacy and restraint."[62] In fact, the erotic *collage* was Glassco's invention. A decade earlier, during his second Paris trip with Elma, he'd shared the "recipe" with Daryl Hine: "take one straight, simple, rather wishy-washy and sentimental story with a good story line, and *write in* pornographic scenes. I suggested he [Hine] try something like *Jane Eyre* (not Jane herself, of course, though she has distinct possibilities); but he went one better by picking Ballantyne's *Coral Island*, and was in the course of turning it into a pornographic homosexual tale."[63]

With *Quaint Stories of the Samurais*, Glassco used the technique to good effect; something typified in the alterations to the second tale, which Sato had titled "The Final Reward for His Long Cherished Love." The original begins:

When Hideyoshi governed all over the Japan after the Ashigaka Shyogun family was expired, he resided in Fushimi. And all the lords of every provinces of Japan had to live in there.

At that time, the lord of Izumi province had a page named Muroda. He was very beautiful yet very brave. His outside appearance was fragile as a delicate cherry blossom, while his spirit was daring like a War-God. At the first glance, he could be mistaken as a pretty maiden of some royal palaces. His lord loved him more than any of his other pages.[64]

In *The Temple of Pederasty*, Glassco refines Sato's words and adds his own, rewriting the tale as "The Reward of True Love":

When the Emperor Hideyoshi ruled the whole of Japan after the Ashigaka Shogun family was extinct, he took up his residence in the city of Fushimi. And all the lords of every province of Japan had to live there too, with their retainers and troupes of page-boys.

At that time, the lord of the province of Izumi had a page-boy named Muroda. He was very beautiful yet very brave. His appearance was fragile as a delicate cherry blossom, but his spirit was daring as a War God. At first glance, he could have been mistaken for a pretty maiden of some royal palace with his beautiful complexion and his swaying hips. His lord loved him to madness, and sodomized him more than any of his other pages.[65]

Before submitting *The Temple of Pederasty* to Kirby, Glassco had twice been unsuccessful, in 1963 and 1968, in offering his tales of "sentiment, sodomy and cherry-blossoms" to Maurice Girodias.[66] By October 1968, a month after the second rejection by the Olympia Press, the *collagiste* had begun to despair. He turned to Philip Core, then in his final year at Middlesex School, and commissioned ten illustrations at $20 apiece for "a collection of nine 17th-century Japanese tales with a strong homosexual motif."[67]

Glassco sent the schoolboy a copy of his introduction and of "Love and Friendship," a story of love between Nagatonokami Kimura, a sixteen-year-old lord, and a young samurai named Ichizaimon Sugiyama. He directed Core to provide illustrations of a type that would be captioned "I Know the Art of Sucking a Boy's Penis" and "The Three Youths Spent the Night in Love-Play," both lines from the story. The pen and ink drawings Glassco received in return demonstrated not only Core's progress as an artist but his understanding of Japanese erotic art; about which he'd previously been unfamiliar. The work was the artist's own and owed nothing to his idol Aubrey Beardsley.

Glassco and Core resumed the working relationship they'd once shared. As before, the pair collaborated through the post. Over the course of four months correspondence moved between the small house in Foster and the conservative private boys' school in Concord, Massachusetts. Though he certainly recognized the risk he was taking, Glassco assumed only the slightest of precautions in writing to the teenage boy: all letters, whether sent to Middlesex School or Core's parents' New Orleans home, were registered.

Glassco was much more particular than he'd been with the illustrations for *Squire Hardman*. Several drawings were returned to Core for further work; one was rejected outright. In a letter written prior to Christmas 1968, Glassco writes:

> By the way, if you have not yet done The Punishment of Kenpachi (p. 13), the chambermaids should be represented with *Japanese-style* whips of the period, either in their hands or tucked under their arms while they are urinating on him. These whips are about 2 feet long, made of leather and shaped like this:
>
> [Glassco provides a rough illustration]
>
> They should not be the long, elaborate kind in your *Squire Hardman* illustrations.
>
> With all the compliments of the season.
>
> P.S. Only one other thing. So many of these characters are *ejaculating* that the message seems to me to tend to become "typed." The drawings are much too fine for this kind of uniformity of message, I do think ...[68]

A few weeks after he'd received the last of Core's drawings, done to his satisfaction, Glassco succeeded in placing the book with Brian Kirby. The *collagiste* was certain that the sale was largely due to Core's illustrations. In actuality, the drawings had been an impediment; Kirby had had to make a case for their inclusion in the book. After the publisher's attorney had advised against the use of illustrations being associated with either Essex House or Brandon House, Kirby created the Hanover House imprint specifically in order to publish the book. Glassco was obliged to commission four more drawings from Core, bringing the total to eighteen, including a title page. Each of the interior images incorporated titles, such as "He Often Watched the Boy Brandling Himself" and "The Three Played with Each Other's Genitals."

In drawing up the contract for *The Temple of Pederasty*, Kirby assumed that either S. Colson-Haig or Hideki Okada were pseudonyms and wrote wondering whether it might be possible to substitute Glassco's own name. In his reply, Glassco revealed the former as a *nom de plume*, adding: "Dr Okada, unknown outside Japan, died many years ago, but his name should appear on the title-page as translator even though his text is my own unrestricted property."[69]

A further problem arose in the months leading to publication when the Copyright Office in the United States made inquiries about the translator. Glassco tried to clarify things by offering an explanation that came closer to the truth:

> As stated on page 9 of my introduction, this translation was collated by me with the earlier translation of Ken Sato, but only as a check on the accuracy of incident and detail.
>
> The text you now have is an entirely new translation of the stories, not only incorporating much additional material but differing widely from Sato's in style and literacy.[70]

Glassco had succeeded in avoiding problems with US authorities but was wholly unsuccessful in dealings with Canada. In April 1970, while expecting the twelve author's copies of his newest book, he received instead a letter from Léonard Trudel of the Customs and Excise office in Granby. *The Temple of Pederasty* had been intercepted at the border and, after having been examined in Ottawa, had been classified as "immoral or indecent."[71] Glassco's grand hoax, his little joke, would not be allowed in the country.

He had the publisher send six copies care of General Delivery in East Richford, Vermont, fifty minutes south of Foster, then smuggled them across the border in the large American car he called his "Mafiamobile." The banning of *The Temple of Pederasty* became a point of pride. Whereas ten years before he'd hidden his authorship of *The English Governess*, Glassco was pleased to share his latest work of pornography with others. George Fetherling, then known as Douglas, recalls accompanying Margaret Atwood on a morning visit to Glassco's Montreal *pied-à-terre*:

When we arrived, he affected not to be expecting us, but he was wearing a silk smoking jacket and a cravat and he was having his breakfast champagne. Perhaps because he had heard that I took a liking to them (chameleons are the most polite of creatures), he made a point of playing up the colonial aristo, posing, with perhaps a bit more enthusiasm than strict accuracy allowed, as a sort of dissolute and bohemian Vincent Massey …

… Later, when we had joined him in champagne and strawberries, he took an ornate little key from the pocket of his smoking-jacket and opened the front of an antique *cloisonné* secretary to retrieve a book.

"Douglas, perhaps you might be interested in seeing my latest work."

It was called *The Temple of Pederasty* and purported to be the translation, by a modern Japanese, of an ancient Japanese text by one Ihara Saikaku.[72]

Many hours later the trio was joined by George and Angela Bowering for an evening dinner at a Chinese restaurant. The newly published work of pornography was still very much a topic of conversation:

Buffy fantasized that public demand would soon make a second printing of *The Temple* necessary and that, to satisfy this eventuality, we should all compose jacket blurbs. He passed a pen and blank sheet of paper round the table. George wrote in praise of the subject matter, saying that if his mother had taken him to a pederast when he was a boy he wouldn't have bad feet today. When the paper came to me I wrote, "John Glassco's *The Temple of Pederasty* is a book that leaves nothing to be desired." But Peggy produced a splendidly subtle squib, a thing so expert that only physical examination could have detected the tip of her tongue in her cheek.[73]

There would be no second printing. Between production and distribution, Kirby was suddenly dismissed. His sole contact gone, Glassco was left to chase after royalties through the labyrinths of American Art Enterprises. One year after publication, he heard from a Robert Reitman, who on behalf of the publisher reported that nearly five thousand copies of the 18,258-copy printrun remained in the warehouse. If true, sales of *The Temple of Pederasty* would have disappointed when compared to Essex House and Brandon House titles. Misreading the letter, Glassco believed that only five thousand had been sold. He feared the remainder would be pulped and wrote Daryl Hine: "Sad to think of 13,000 copies of this little book being converted into grocery-bags and toilet-paper."[74]

While *The Temple of Pederasty* was nowhere near as accomplished a work as *Squire Hardman*, as a hoax it had even greater complexity. Perhaps as a result, Glassco was much more open and took more pride in the prank. The few copies he managed to bring into the country were distributed to friends like Frank Scott, Arthur Smith, and William Toye. In Michael Gnarowski's copy Glassco included an inscription in which he identified himself as "the anonymous collagiste."[75]

As a prankster himself, Glassco had admiration for those who carried out literary deceptions. He'd recognized and appreciated John Sutherland's "harmless little hoax,"[76] in publishing "The Mysterious Question," by the fictitious John Goodwin, "a high school student in North Vancouver," which was, in fact, plagiarized from Petrus Borel's nineteenth-century short story "Gottfried Wolfgang." Its appearance in *The Northern Review* had taken in a great many people, including novelist Ethel Wilson, who had been so impressed by the work that thirteen years after publication, in a 1964 issue of *The Tamarack Review*, she had wondered as to the whereabouts of its author. Arthur Smith, who was well aware of the truth, perpetuated the ruse by including "The Mysterious Question" in his 1973 anthology of post-Confederation prose, *The Canadian Century*.

Glassco took even greater delight when the truth about Frederick Philip Grove began to surface in the late 1960s. Two decades after his death, the Swedish immigrant writer, winner of a Governor General's Award for his all too appropriately titled autobiography, *In Search of Myself*, was found to be Felix Paul Greve, a minor German writer and translator who had staged a suicide as a means of escaping debt. After learning of Grove's hidden life, Glassco remarked to critic Ronald Sutherland:

I did hear about the Grove hoax. Lots of fun. I was particularly glad about it, as I had always sensed something phoney about the early parts of IN SEARCH OF MYSELF. (I am here going on record that I feel just the same way about Boswell's LONDON JOURNAL, without

The Temple of Pederasty, Glassco's banned book.

knowing much about its provenance! I mean, I think it's as much of
a fake as those MEMOIRS OF A YOUNG LADY OF FASHION about a
dozen years back). The truth just might make him a bit more interesting, though it's too much to hope he might have been a self-exposer
or child-molester.[77]

Elma's condition had remained relatively stable during Glassco's year of critical applause, conflict, and censorship. There had been no need to turn to
the hospitals; she'd remained in Foster, a diminished figure, saying nothing
and eating little. Glassco's faith in modern medical treatment, like his belief
in the miracle of largactil, had exhausted itself.

In winter 1971 she managed to accompany her husband to a poetry reading given by W.H. Auden at McGill. Three decades earlier, Glassco had
expressed his dislike of Auden and his poetry, writing Robert McAlmon:

"We would loathe each other if we ever met, instantly and irrevocably, I know. He may be good, but not for me."[78]

The older Glassco thought and felt differently:

Auden reads beautifully, no declamation or ham tricks or rhetoric. And at a small dinner party at the Ritz later he was simply charming. His face is incredibly seamed & wrinkled, like an old alligator handbag, but he projects an extraordinary sexual attraction. He seems to have read everything ever written. He had even read my Memoirs, and said they were "jolly good, and much better than Hemingway on the same period!" What a compliment from the greatest living English poet! I had to pinch myself.[79]

Before the evening was out, Glassco presented Auden with a copy of *The Deficit Made Flesh*, which he inscribed: "with deepest admiration."[80]

That reading at McGill, followed by a dinner at the Ritz-Carlton Hotel may have been Elma's last appearance in public. She weakened through the spring, due in part to two cavities discovered in her lungs. Convinced that her doctors were impostors, she fought against treatment. Glassco knew that there would be no true recovery; Elma would remain a ghostly reminder of the woman he had loved. Increasingly, he sought sexual release through others. He hired a dominatrix, who would strap him to a wooden horse and administer beatings. Another relationship, that with a twenty-one-year-old "boy," "a wealthy child" identified in his journal only as "A.," involved no exchange of money.[81] In their afternoon encounters at his Bishop Street flat, Glassco would dispense beatings with a horsewhip, playing the "Fatal Man."[82] Over a nine-day period he composed five erotic sonnets for the young man, words of praise for "… the game that gives Love back his eyes, / And puts the whole mad world back into joint."[83] Yet, even when writing these words, Glassco knew them to be untrue. The afternoon adventures were not putting his "mad world back into joint," and he had long grown weary of the relationship. "No, it is not me he loves," the poet wrote in his journal, "it is the stern father-figure he has made of me. I have never been loved for myself – except perhaps long ago by Elma, but that is all gone now."[84] Glassco was determined to conceal the loneliness caused by his wife's illness and in interviews turned to drink as a means of raising cheeriness and charm. He was pleased with the effect and came to enjoy the attention.

Among those who met with Glassco in 1970 was Marion McCormick, a journalist known as one of the finest interviewers in the country. By the following March, Glassco expressed surprise in his journal: "My God, I have fallen in love again."[85]

Born Marion Whitehouse on 3 February 1924, at Ludlow, Massachusetts, she was more than fourteen years his junior. She'd arrived in Montreal as a young woman, initially to study at McGill, where she began writing for *The McGill Daily*. Her career in journalism began in the entertainment department of *The Gazette*, followed by work as a reporter and movie critic for *The Montreal Herald*. There she married the tabloid's managing editor, Ted McCormick, with whom she had two sons, Christy and Joel, who became journalists themselves. William Weintraub remembered the McCormicks from the 1940s, describing the couple as "the height of sophistication. She was so attractive, so intelligent, I used to gaze at her across the table. They reminded me of Scott and Zelda Fitzgerald."[86] In 1958, the union ended in divorce. Marion moved to freelance work at the CBC. "She was an excellent journalist because she could get herself anywhere," her son Christy remembers. "She swept Mayor Drapeau away from a press conference I attended for *The Gazette* with all the journalists blaming me for what my mother had done to them. She interviewed Elvis Presley the day before he enlisted in the Army. Quite a trick for a CBC freelance radio journalist."[87]

For a time, she lived with *Gazette* medical journalist Brian Cahill. No one, not even her sons, was ever certain whether they'd married. Joel McCormick recalls that the couple had planned to marry in Mexico: "They made the trip alright but I was never sure what actually happened. M later told me the marriage never occurred; at another point, she asserted Mexican marriages had no legal standing in Quebec, so for all intents and purposes the marriage never happened."[88]

Novelist Edward O. Phillips, who as a young man had had an affair with Marion, once thought of her as "the most beautiful woman in Montreal."[89] However, by the 1970s her looks had been lost to the decades of drink, smoking, late nights, and overwork.

To some, including Phillips and his partner Ken Woodman, Glassco and Marion seemed the most unlikely of couples. Marion was in so many ways the opposite of Elma. An outspoken, large woman, she cared little for clothes and outward appearance. Phillips, who had maintained a friendship with the journalist, was perhaps more surprised than most; many years before

Marion McCormick in 1972, two years after she met Glassco.

Marion introduced him to her new love, he had encountered Glassco at a *vernissage* for the sculptor H.W. Jones. "I had to spend the evening dodging him," he recalls. "Even though I am a gay man, he just wasn't my cup of tea."[90] Phillips never mentioned the previous encounter to Glassco and often wondered whether the poet had any recollection of the incident.

What Marion knew of Glassco's past sexual and romantic adventures is unknown. She had, of course, read *Memoirs of Montparnasse*, but even those distant escapades were not open for discussion. "She was surprisingly puritanical about such things," says Phillips. "His past was a closed book."[91] When, in conversation with Kildare Dobbs, Glassco spoke of the *ménage a trois* he had shared with Taylor and Sappho, Marion had commented dismissively, "I find it hard to believe in all those orgies."[92]

They were both fired by new love. Though Marion was forty-seven, the couple spoke of having a baby, an idea Joel McCormick dismisses as "complete nonsense, at most something that came after draining a 40 of gin."[93] Yet, Glassco fretted over the idea for several weeks: he didn't think it fair to ask Marion to devote two of the latter decades of life toward raising a child; he worried that the possibility of an early death might mean that the child would grow up fatherless; he grew concerned that the child would have to endure the stigma of being illegitimate. Most of all, Glassco feared that he would be supplanted when it came to Marion's love and attention. He finally admitted, "I am not fond of children, *I would not make a good father:* children need love."[94]

In July 1971, Elma returned to the Royal Edward Laurentian Hospital for treatment of her tuberculosis. While she was being under care, Glassco travelled with Marion for a two-week tour of the Gaspé. He considered this trip, full of fun and laughter, a "honeymoon"[95] and described one sexual encounter in a Tadoussac motel as "Sheer, ineffable, ecstasy: a rebirth, an epiphany, a kind of sacred action binding us together for all time."[96] More than a consummation of their relationship, Glassco saw in his rebirth a cleansing, what he considered a "farewell to all my sexual aberrations, my boys, my masturbatory fantasies, my explorations in the underworld of sex with dancers and professionals and the lost souls who haunt the 'personal' columns of underground newspapers."[97]

He was determined that they would live together, yet Glassco could not abandon his wife. In mid-October, after Elma had returned home, he made a confession in the pages of his journal:

I see I am already counting on Elma's death. Are my thoughts wicked? No, she *wishes* to die. She has told me so. But I will never connive at her death, even by inaction. What a curious compassion! To wish for her death as a grand release, and still to love her even as the nonperson she has become. This tears me to pieces: all that saves me for life is my love of another living, vivid woman; my love of Elma has the smell of death, like her poor dear wasted body, her lipless smile, her fainting voice. Dear God, all I know is that I must cling to my living love, and cherish my dying one.[98]

Five days later, when Elma demanded that she be returned to the Royal Edward Laurentian, he put up no argument. She left their home by ambulance, accompanied only by the attendants. Several days passed before Glassco made the two-hour drive north to visit. He arrived to find that hospital care had done nothing to improve her condition: "She was finally & definitively *mad*. I seemed to upset her. She said she never wanted to see me again as long as she lived. – A terrible confession: *this gave me a tremendous feeling of release*. I suddenly realized I don't want to see her again ever, either! One can only stand so much pain."[99] He resolved to never see her again.

Days later, Glassco gave up the Bishop Street flat and had moved into Marion's two-storey rented apartment on rue Jeanne-Mance, the very same street on which he'd lost his virginity. Situated on the eastern fringe of the McGill ghetto, the place was typical of an older Montreal. One had to mount an iron staircase outside, followed by another steeper staircase inside, before gaining entry. It was a large place, made to seem smaller through decades of accumulated furnishings, to which the couple added a brass double-bed, creating a cluttered nest in which they would "twitter and coo all day long, like elderly pigeons."[100]

This flurry of activity coincided with the autumn publication of Glassco's *Selected Poems*, his fourth and final book with Oxford. A slim volume containing just eighty-seven pages of verse, it was nevertheless his largest collection. The cover copy stated that the poems had been chosen by Glassco but credit properly belonged to Smith; the senior poet had not only made the selection but had arranged their order, altered titles, and made several editorial changes.[101] One thing Smith didn't provide, however, was a title with which Glassco felt comfortable. *Selected Poems* he thought pretentious and considered "*Nothing Doing, A Waste of Time* and anything incorporating the word 'minor'" but was concerned that he might appear depreciatory and frivolous.[102]

Ultimately, Glassco deferred to Smith's judgement and was particularly pleased by his friend's decision to close the collection with "One Last Word," which was dedicated to Marion. Glassco described the poem as a "kind of spell, a charm, almost a prayer that our love would not end the way the poem ended, like the flight or death of a bird."[103] However, if the poem had been written for anyone, it was most certainly not Marion. It had been composed before Glassco had met his new love, and under the titles "Your Hand" and "May I Have Your Hand" had appeared several years earlier in *Saturday Night* and *Adam International Review*.

Of all the poems Smith had decided to leave out of *Selected Poems*, Glassco argued for the inclusion of just one: "The Places Where the Dead Have Walked." "The only poem whose loss I rather regret is 'The Places Where the Dead, etc.,'" he wrote his friend.[104] "It was written when I thought Elma was dying, and everywhere she had walked was very precious and in fact almost sacred."[105] Again, Glassco was weaving a story. "The Places Where the Dead Have Walked" had been composed during his 1961 convalescence in Ste-Agathe, many years before Elma's psychosis had broken. In fact, it had been featured in the 1966 John Glassco issue of *Yes*. Still, he maintained this richer, more romantic history of the poem, and, as the end of his own life approached, Glassco wrote Smith that it had been begun "two years before Elma died, but when I knew she was going to die and realized those 'places' which she wouldn't see again really held more of her, then, than did her poor deranged self in the hospital in Ste-Agathe (the same one in which I wrote *A Season in Limbo* at your suggestion.)"[106]

Whatever his inspiration, a decade later, to Glassco the words were now for Elma:

The places where the dead have walked
   Possesses them wholly: the true tomb
Of love is in the circle chalked
By fancy where the dead have walked
As in a visitable room,

An immense grave. What piece of ground
   Impressed by a beloved foot
But has not gathered up the sound
To keep it captive underground
   And store its music underfoot?[107]

On the first day of December Elma lapsed into a coma and died early the following morning. Four hours passed before Glassco was informed of his wife's death:[108]

Did she call for me? I will never know. O God, the pathos of the deaths of those we used to love. My poor mad darling, going into the dark alone, and I not there to take her hand. – But no, she *hated* me, might have died cursing me, me the man whom she believed had ruined her life. Better that I was not there. But oh how I have deserted all those who once loved me – so many.[109]

The pretence of Elma's noble heritage was carried beyond her death. Glassco composed a brief notice that ran in *The Gazette* the next morning:

Glassco, Elma, at Ste-Agathe December 2, 1971, after a long illness, Elma Rosalba von Colmar, beloved wife of John Glassco of Foster, Quebec, daughter of the late Baron Mihail von Colmar of Narva, Estonia. Funeral private.[110]

Elma's small body was transported to Mount Royal Cemetery, the resting place of her husband's parents and of Graeme Taylor, where it was placed in Canada's oldest crematorium. Glassco carried the urn back to Foster and to the little brook that ran through their property. He broke a hole through the ice, scattering her ashes in the water before the spot Elma had often sat to enjoy the songs of birds. Later that day her few possessions were burned, just as she had requested. The only items to escape were her ballet slippers, which Glassco could not bring himself to throw in the pyre. He had spent many years grieving over Elma, watching, unable to help as she'd wasted physically and mentally. It was only with her death that grief came to an end – it was replaced by intense feelings of guilt. Glassco feared that he would be punished for having abandoned her, just as he had Taylor nearly a quarter century earlier. In both instances, he'd replaced an old love with one that was fresh and healthy.

The guilt never left him, and was still strong when in March he learned that he would receive a Governor General's Award for his *Selected Poems*. There was surprise that the modest little paperback had been chosen over

The Collected Poems of Irving Layton, the expected winner, a 605-page hard-cover collection that had been published to mark the twenty-fifth anniversary of Layton's first book, *Here and Now*. The Canadian edition of *Time* reported on the upset: "In his courtly way, Glassco pointed out that Layton will have other chances. 'I have stopped writing poetry,' he said. 'And Layton hasn't.'"[111] In May 1972, Glassco travelled to Ottawa to accept the award and the accompanying cheque for $2,500. The next morning's edition of *The Ottawa Citizen* published a photograph of Glassco standing with Governor General Roland Michener, Mrs Michener, and Pierre Berton, who had received the nonfiction award for *The Last Spike*. The poet was identified in the accompanying text as "Paul Glassco."[112]

The unexpected honour may very well have been a case of what Eleanor Wachtel once wrote of as "the Academy Award syndrome: slighting a significant book and then trying to remedy things by rewarding the next, often inferior title."[113] Many had expected Glassco to receive the nonfiction award for *Memoirs of Montparnasse* the previous year, among them his friend Ralph Gustafson. Shortly after publication, the poet had written Glassco predicting a win, adding: "If the book's grace is not enough, no jury can pass over the book of a Canadian who has spit in the eye of Gertrude Stein. One lone Canadian was not mesmerized by the black silk ribbon attached to Charles God Damn Robert's pince-nez. Incredible."[114] In the end, the jury had found no book it considered worthy; there was no 1970 Governor General's Award for English Language Non-Fiction.[115]

The following year, Gustafson found himself involved in the Governor General's awards, serving with Al Purdy and foreman Wilfred Watson as a member of the poetry and drama subcommittee. Though the three men were divided initially, they determined that the award should go to Layton; a decision that was overruled by a vote of the committee overseeing the awards. Purdy believed that Watson, who had always argued for Glassco's *Selected Poems*, had reversed himself. Annoyed by the whole process, he presented his interpretation of what had taken place to *Globe and Mail* columnist William French: "One of the most obvious faults of the awards is that when a writer should have received the award one year and does not, then he is liable to be given it in a later year for a book that doesn't deserve the prize. And there is also some evidence on the basis of past selections that judges wish to spread around, and make sure all writers of a sufficient level of excellence shall sooner or later receive an award."[116] Glassco assumed that Purdy, a frequent correspondent, had supported *Selected Poems*, and, oblivious as to the true course, wrote him in gratitude.

The award had engendered considerable envy and resentment within Montreal's literary circles – or so Glassco believed – and he decided to spend the spring lying low in the Jeanne-Mance apartment, delighting in the joy and pride Marion took in his win. It is possible that some minor tension and unpleasantness was avoided during this late hibernation, but ultimately the isolation encouraged anxious thoughts. A contributing factor was the imminent publication of *Fetish Girl*, a new pornographic novel he had written under the female pseudonym Sylvia Bayer.

Glassco's fetish girl is Ursula, "a pretty long-legged bitch of wide and varied experience."[117] At twenty-seven years old, she is frustrated in sex and romance, as she's been unable to find a man who shares or appreciates her sexual fixation on things rubber. Ursula is on vacation at an "out-of-the-way motel" when she spies Adrian, a slightly effeminate man, her physical ideal, in gleaming black latex bathing trunks.[118] After he dons a close fitting rubber diving hood, she pursues Adrian, only to discover that he is gay. Nevertheless, she manages to bed this otherwise ideal man and his lover Tony, forming a *ménage à trois* through which she enjoys a series of sexual adventures. Glassco supplies a happy ending: Ursula marries Adrian, and the *ménage à trois* continues.

He placed the new novel with *Harriet Marwood, Governess*, describing the pair as his two favourite books. As with "Catbird," the poem written in fifteen minutes, much of Glassco's affection for the work was derived from the ease with which it had been composed. Both were appreciated as works that had caused few problems.

The bulk of *Fetish Girl* had been written in the first year of his relationship with Marion. During its composition, he had placed an anonymous personal ad in the 22 April 1971 edition of *The New York Review of Books*:

SUCCESSFUL WRITER IN LATE FIFTIES, tall, attractive, amusing, seeks quasi-Platonic relationship with mature, sensitive woman interested in wearing rubber. Montreal area. NYR, Box 3500

One of the respondents was US freelance journalist Philip Nobile, then researching a book on rubber fetishism. Not knowing to whom he was writing, Nobile asked what sort of response the advertisement had elicited. Glassco was evasive, writing: "This ad was inserted in the hope of contacting women interested in the subject of rubber fetishism, who might help me to discover its popularity and thus contribute to the verisimilitude of the novel I was writing at the time."[119] When Nobile wrote a second time, asking whether he could include Glassco's response in his book, the request was denied.[120]

That Glassco placed the ad for research purposes is debatable. Certainly he had a greater knowledge of the fetish and its culture than he let on in his correspondence with Nobile. In a letter to Margaret Atwood, written only three months after the personal ad was placed, Glassco writes:

> Thank you for THE UNDERGROWTH OF LITERATURE. I was specially struck by the chapter on rubber fetishism, which I see as Rampant over there. As a latex fan since the age of 4 (my true Venus has always worn a frogman's suit), I enjoyed it enormously. Also, I had just finished a short novel whose characters wallow delicately in this fetish, and it is encouraging to read about its popularity in the U.K. – how revolting about the editor of *Rubber News* being muzzled and fined! But I believe he has now started up a new mag. called *Impermeable Delectable.*[121]

Glassco considered Ursula "the sweetest character" he had ever created, declaring to his friend Milton Kastello: "I'm madly in love with her!"[122] This fantastic creation was the embodiment of so many of the author's fantasies, the most obvious being his growing fetish. He confided in his journal that he dreamed of finding a woman with whom he could dress in rubber and engage in mutual masturbation.

Eager to see visual depiction of the fantasies laid out in *Fetish Girl*, he again turned to Philip Core. Two years had elapsed since their last collaboration, a fairly brief period during which both men had experienced very significant events. Glassco had suffered through Elma's final decline and death, new love had come with Marion, and he'd seen the publications of *Memoirs of Montparnasse*, *The Poetry of French Canada in Translation*, *The Temple of Pederasty*, and his *Selected Poems*. During this same period, Core had graduated from Middlesex School, attended Harvard, and had spent a year in Paris studying with Philippe Julien, biographer and illustrator of

Proust. Through Julien, he encountered many surviving figures of Glassco's Montparnasse. Now, having returned to Harvard and short of money, he was pleased to be contacted with offers of more work.[123]

As they had before, the pair collaborated through the mail. Their method, unchanged, began with Glassco's ever precise instructions: "The only thing to remember is to stress the skintightness and above all the *sheen* of costumes (as in the attached yellow pages, which are sent only to show the desired *highlight* effect), since this is very important to our audience. And, of course any or all of the figures must be physically attractive in a ripe decadent way, as well as wearing the costumes in the text."[124]

Core often found Glassco's instructions curious, and would question his client concerning the desired effect: "One thing: *what* in Heaven's name is so important about the bathing-cap ridges? They utterly mystify me, unless they are supposed to look reptilian?"[125] The artist's queries would go unanswered.

In commissioning Core's illustrations, Glassco must have realized it unlikely that they would be of interest to a publisher. Very few publishers of paperback pornographic literature included images in their novels. New York's Venus Library, the Grove imprint that had also published *Harriet Marwood, Governess*, was no exception. They accepted Glassco's novel but turned down the Core illustrations. Ultimately, the draughtsman's work would end up among Glassco's papers at Library and Archives Canada.

Glassco had wished to dedicate the novel to Marion and even went so far as to draft the dedication:

> For Marion McCormick, who didn't like it –
> with love – John Glassco[126]
> 20/vi/71

He was, however, all too aware that the gesture would not be appreciated and had the imaginary Miss Bayer not only dedicate the novel to John Glassco but inscribe a presentation copy: "And once again to Buffy from Sylvia."[127] Glassco justified the tribute in a letter to Leon Edel: "since I am getting on in years and no one ever dedicated a book to me, I decided in an inspired moment to dedicate this one to myself."[128]

Though fiction catering to rubber fetishists had existed for some time, the genre had been for the most part limited to short works, either published in periodicals such as *Gaytime Mackintoshes Magazine and Review* and *Continental Bizarre*, or as staple-bound booklets usually numbering no more than forty-eight pages. Glassco described *Fetish Girl* as the first rubber fetish novel, a claim he repeated often, ignorant that a lesser pornographer properly owned the achievement. Five years earlier, as Lana Preston, Paul Hugo Little had penned *Rubber Goddess*, described fittingly by Stephen J. Gertz as "the tender tale of a lesbian dominatrix fetish fashion designer."[129]

Glassco had completed *Fetish Girl* the previous summer, just prior to the Gaspé trip with Marion. In doing so, he'd held out an unrealistic hope that, through writing the novel, his uncommon sexual obsession might somehow be exhausted. He wanted *Fetish Girl* to be his "farewell to perversion."[130] Yet the pleasurable act of composition had in no way exorcised the fetish. As the spring of his hibernation turned to summer, Glassco became ever more disturbed that the fixation remained. Where he'd been untroubled by his bisexuality, never seeking explanation in theory and never once contemplating treatment, Glassco became consumed by his quest for an explanation of his "stupid contemptible fetish."[131] Though more intense, it was nowhere near the first time he had made such an exploration; the first surviving account is contained in his "Autobiographical Sketch":

I was precociously sensual. My first orgasm occurred when I was seven, while swimming in the MAAA [Montreal Amateur Athletic Association] pool. Even before this I had developed a curious fetichism for *rubber*. Starting with a fondness for wearing rubber gloves, it soon became focussed in the wearing of a bathing-cap. At that time I was aware of no connection between this taste and sexual feelings. I only knew that while wearing a cap I felt happy, and that after swimming quite hard I could experience an orgasm, which at that time was merely felt as a sharp pleasure in the genital area; I did not know what was happening.[132]

Glassco wrote several accounts of what he became convinced was the source of his fetish: the sight of his mother in her bathing cap, showering in the Rawlings mansion, when he was five. Yet, in his longest and earliest version it is his father whom he had glimpsed:

> How in Heaven's name did this *thing*, this image, this article of swimwear, ever come to govern my whole erotic universe? It must have been that bathing-cap my father wore in the shower-bath way back on Simpson Street, when I was 5 years old. I remember seeing him wear it once when I went into the bathroom & saw him, hairy & naked, wearing it, and averting my eyes from the sight of his huge penis. How strange, that such a momentary vision should have had such a tremendous, lasting effect on my whole life! After forty years of quite normal sexuality, the effect has re-asserted its power and cannot be suppressed. Well, it has given me extraordinary pleasure, has involved me in many ridiculous & disappointing situations, and has had a very bad influence on my literary work. But the fetish itself has remained to me as a kind of absolute, something that has supplanted all my *religious* feelings, has been almost a substitute for deity. Well, I will never be free from it, thank God. I embrace it, love it to distraction with a desire surpassing anything I can now feel for woman [*sic*]. Absurd, yes. But what a never-failing comfort & resource![133]

This switch between his father and mother might be explained by Glassco's familiarity with Sigmund Freud's "Fetischismus." In this 1927 essay, the psychiatrist theorizes that fetishism is the result of psychological trauma. According to Freud, a boy, longing to see his mother's penis, averts his eyes in horror when he discovers that she has none. The object upon which his eyes settle is clung to as a substitute for the absent sex organ. It is possible that in his knowledge of the theory, Glassco came to believe that it was not his father whom he had seen in the shower in the Rawlings mansion but his mother and that, in averting his eyes, he'd settled on her rubber bathing cap.

Now that he was with Marion, the fetish was no longer a "never-failing comfort & resource," but a barrier. Glassco was certain she would not participate in his fantasies. Still, he held out hope that she would at least accept the fetish. To this end he composed a tortured letter, a plea of sorts, in which he attempted to explain his attraction. It is doubtful that he ever presented this letter to Marion. No reaction is mentioned anywhere in the open and obsessive personal writings about his fetish. Still, that August Glassco did gather the courage to tell Marion about his fetish. The result did not meet his wish: "She was repelled. And so my dream of ecstasy is finished: I could weep – and was very close to doing so all today."[134]

Marion returned to Montreal, leaving Glassco alone in Foster. He had shared something of himself that his love could not accept, and so had provided evidence to support the conviction that she would end things once his true sexual nature began to show. For days Glassco believed that they were through. Though she did return, much to his surprise, he saw the relationship as doomed, and in recognition composed an epitaph on their love: "Here lie M. and B.: *their fantasies could not coalesce*."[135] And so, when Marion suggested that they marry, he was dumbstruck.

Glassco's struggle with the idea of marriage continued well into the New Year and was demonstrating no sign of resolution when he received an unexpected reminder of his past marriage in the form of a letter sent from the Estonian SSR. The correspondent was a stranger, Alma Koolmer Baltser, his sister-in-law. Eighteen months after Elma's ashes had been scattered, she had finally learned of the death. In polite, broken English, Baltser asked whether the widower might be so kind to send some of her younger sister's personal effects. The request brought about an exchange of letters that was as comic as it was sad. Having burned Elma's belongings, Glassco had only her ballet slippers to offer, which he intended to send. Would she also, he wondered, accept a copy of *The Deficit Made Flesh*, the volume of poetry he had dedicated to her sister?[136] Before receiving a reply, Glassco wrote again after discovering that used footwear was prohibited from entering the Soviet Union. He had considered declaring Elma's slippers as new but was afraid her sister would be obliged to pay duty. Baltser responded with the request that he send on the shoes, the book, and, if possible, some boxes of cigarettes for her son. It was the last he ever heard from his sister-in-law.

Fetish Girl was the most contemporary of all Glassco's pornographic works. Unlike *Under the Hill*, *The English Governess*, *Harriet Marwood, Governess*, and *Squire Hardman*, it had not been set in the past; there had been no attempt at recreating writing styles from previous centuries. The language Glassco used in the book had been dictated by the marketplace. Bold, brash, and crude, it stands apart from his other works of prose. However, while he'd adapted readily and easily, mimicking the style of contemporary pornography,

Glassco was both unable and unwilling to make any changes to his verse. He recognized without regret that many considered his poetry dated:

> As a writer, I'm superannuated. And I won't try to keep up, technically, with the young ones – like dear old Earle Birney with his "modern" gimmicks, excised punctuation, small "i"s, blanks, and all – no, it's too undignified: all my "dignity" is saved for my work: personally, I have none nor wish to have, yes, even though I may sound and behave like an old fool.[137]

In autumn 1973, Glassco published *Montreal*, his final book of verse, an "epic-macaronic history" of the city of his birth.[138] Work on the 698-line poem had begun in the mid-1960s. Initial inspiration had been drawn, in part, from Expo 67; indeed, the original intention had been to finish the poem with a barrage against the world exposition. However, he'd come to recognize Expo 67 as another assault, another insult among many visited upon what had once been the most beautiful city in North America. His poem referenced history and prehistory, but most of all it commemorated a Montreal that the poet had known and lost:

> City, city of my childhood
> I know you only by the names of streets
> Gone from me now like old mistresses…[139]

Little remained of the splendour of the Golden Square Mile, into which he had been born. Half a century had passed since the Rawlings mansion had been razed, supplanted by Chelsea Place, a large cooperative apartment complex. A lone chestnut tree just outside the fence of the development was all that remained of Edward Rawlings's luxuriant home and grounds.[140] Glassco's view of the city's decline never wavered. Two years after publication, he wrote Ken Norris about *Montreal*: "The poem itself was completed in 1968, just after Expo. Since then the process of the city's ruin has been speeded up considerably, and only awaits the Olympics next year to be complete."[141]

For five years, excerpts of the work in progress had been appearing in little magazines – *Yes, Poetry Australia, Neueve,* and *Alphabet* – and it was Glassco's hope that the poem would find a home with Delta Canada, the small press run by Louis Dudek, Michael Gnarowski, and Glen Siebrasse. However, by the time he finally submitted the work, the publisher had begun to pull apart. *Montreal* only added to the disunity. As Gnarowski recalls, "Glen Siebrasse and I argued against publishing the book. We thought it not up to par. Louis disagreed." Months later, the press dissolved. Dudek held on to *Montreal* for over a year, eventually accepting it for his new DC Books imprint, on the condition that he receive the $200 cost for printing from the Canada Council. In response, Glassco wrote, "I've never liked those apologetic little notes recording 'the assistance of the Can. C.'!"; he suggested they simply split the costs.[142]

In publishing with Dudek, Glassco had to tone down his expectations. He'd wanted the cover to feature an early engraving of the city, from the vantage point of Chambly Road, but settled instead on a rough profile of Mount Royal drawn by Marion's son Joel, printed on bright orange card stock. The resulting book, a mere thirty pages in length, sold for $2. From the start, Glassco was dissatisfied with what he perceived as Dudek's inaction in promotion and sales. This book, written by a poet who had received the Governor General's Award less than two years earlier, received little notice. "Louis is not interested in selling the books he brings out," Glassco complained to Daryl Hine. "The trouble is, the Canada Council covers all his printing costs, so he has no inducement to get the books out of his basement and into bookstores. He waits for them to come to *him*. Which is ridiculous. My dear Marion, for instance, sold 200 copies of *Montreal* to Classic Books (25 stores all across Canada) inside of fifteen minutes. Just by going to see Brian Melzach the Paperback King in his store on St Catherine St. I think Louis looks on all salesmanship as somehow undignified."[143]

Months earlier, as *Montreal* had inched its way toward publication, Glassco had fussed over the poem, tinkering with the structure. His belief in *Montreal* began to weaken. He began to question his decision to publish but was reassured by Arthur Smith, who was enthusiastic about the poem and reported from Michigan that he had taken to "reading it aloud all over the place to great applause."[144]

The reception in Canada was more muted and considerably less passionate. Writing in *The Dalhousie Review*, Douglas Barbour described *Montreal* as "a fine poem";[145] while in the pages of *CrossCountry* Joanne Harris Burgess acknowledged that it wasn't "a great poem" but was nevertheless "an amusing and sophisticated pleasure."[146] Other reviews sided toward the negative;

writing in *The Globe and Mail* Miriam Waddington was painfully direct: "surely it isn't too much to ask, that he treat a serious subject seriously instead of intellectually, and that he come out from behind the worn shabby skirts of irony and speak with his own true voice."[147] She took particular issue with the final line of the poem – "Not for me this shroud of ashes"[148] – believing that it had been intended to indicate the promise of a new beginning. In this, Waddington writes, Glassco fails: "the image of death and ashes contradicts all sense of life – unless we believe in phoenixes or enjoy the wit of double negatives."[149] However, the reviewer was wrong, Glassco held no belief in a rebirth for Montreal. Although this is apparent in *Montreal*, nowhere is it more obvious than in the addendum, which was inexplicably dropped from the published poem.

The City is a creature man has made
Not from his love of beauty, but afraid
Of night and noises in the night; it has
No other provenance; what of old it was,
Was all by sport and chance, Oh, therefore sing
The beauty of aged cities as a thing
Of purest accident, beside the point
With man's most genuine ambition, which
Is simply to be powerful and rich.
Montreal's now no place for beauty, so
Let it accede to ugliness, and go;
Let it live in my memory
That contradicts all that I breathe and see –
Those quiet, green and shady colonnades
Of streets all slowly murdered, the dear shades
Of Guy and Sherbrooke, Bishop and Mackay,
All as they were under a sparkling sky
Of vanished seasons and a vanished town
Now beaten to death ...[150]

Now in his sixty-fourth year, a time when most looked toward retirement, death was very much on Glassco's mind. In the cooling autumn of 1973, he made this observation:

My three lifelong terrors:
    Of poverty
    Of women
    Of death.
Now only the last remains, and the older I get the less it becomes, thank heaven.[51]

... the final sigh ...[1]

Beginning in 1958, the year after Graeme Taylor's death, there had been very nearly one new John Glassco title each year. *Memoirs of Montparnasse* had sold out its hardcover edition and had been reissued as a trade paperback in both the Canadian and US markets. On the strength of the Governor General's Award, *Selected Poems* had received a total of three printings. Impressive though they were, these sales paled when compared to *The English Governess*, *Harriet Marwood, Governess*, *Fetish Girl*, and his accomplished completion of Aubrey Beardsley's *Under the Hill*. It was the pornography that had had the greatest commercial impact, and yet, aside from his own Pastime Press edition of *Squire Hardman*, not one of Glassco's erotic works had been published in his native country. This would change with the publication, at long last, of "Mairobert," the work begun in summer 1934 as "The Way Back."

In 1962, he'd written Arthur Smith that "Mairobert" had been rejected thirty-two times. It's a claim that sounds inflated, but may very well be true; Alfred A. Knopf, First Statement Press, André Deutsch, Peter Martin Associates, Klanak, Oberon, Random House, Oxford University Press, and Longmans, Green, were just some of the varied publishers who had turned down the novella. Whether in ignorance or desperation, Glassco had even attempted to interest Ryerson Press, the publishing house owned by the United Church of Canada. Ryerson turned down the masochistic fantasy, as had McClelland & Stewart, which in 1959 returned the manuscript along with an anonymous reader's report that dismissed the novel as a work of a "diseased imagination," a "stifling concentration of the stale breath of

Romance and Decadence."[2] Even Maurice Girodias, who'd shown such enthusiasm for *Under the Hill* and had experienced one of his greatest commercial successes with *The English Governess*, told Glassco that he had no faith in the manuscript.

In April 1969, Glassco had sent "Mairobert" to Louis Dudek at Delta Canada, convinced that it would find a home with the small press. However, after six months of silence, the manuscript was returned, this time with a note that encouraged the author to self-publish. For Glassco, this particular rejection came as a shock – the submission had been accompanied by an offer to offset all costs. Added to this, the rebuff had come from a man who'd invariably championed his work; Dudek had praised Glassco's translations in the pages of *The Gazette* and *The Montreal Star* and had written strong, positive reviews of *The Deficit Made Flesh*, *A Point of Sky*, *Under the Hill*, and *Memoirs of Montparnasse*.

More in simple desperation than out of respect for Dudek's suggestion, Glassco again considered publishing the novella himself. He managed to contact Philip Core, now a freshman at Harvard, and commissioned cover art for which he paid $30. As with his previous assignments, Glassco provided a series of detailed directions. For the first time in their relationship, Core disappointed. The images he provided in no way met those of Glassco's fantasies. Wholly dissatisfied with all attempts, the author and fetishist eventually gave up not only on Core but on the whole idea of self-publishing the work.

The path that led to the publication of "Mairobert" began with a 1973 query letter in which House of Anansi editor James Polk asked whether there might not be any material that the author would care to submit. What Glassco sent in response was "The Finger in the Dyke," a dystopian satire that he'd once tried placing with New York publisher Abelard-Schuman, owned by his old McGill friend Lew Schwartz. Although Polk was interested, at eighteen thousand words, the work was simply too short to be published by itself. A few months later, Glassco added "Mairobert" and another work, "The Monster," which together proved enough to flesh out a collection called *Mistresses – Three Tales by John Glassco*. Of the trio, only "The Monster" needed any real attention, containing, in Polk's opinion, "much repetitive reverie that was dragging the narrative down."[3] Much of Glassco's work on the project dealt not so much with rewriting but with presentation. The order of the three tales was set, then reconsidered, and all were given new titles. In fact, the collection as a whole would be rechristened *The Fatal Woman*.

At Polk's suggestion, a preface was added. Modest in tone, but not panache, Glassco used the opportunity to serve something of an apology: "These three novellas, written over a period of no less than thirty years, ought at least to show some aesthetic or intellectual development. Re-reading them now, I am afraid they do not. Neither the tone nor obsessive pattern seems to have changed since my twenty-fourth year: the preoccupations remain the same, though the style becomes a little less lush."[4]

"Mairobert," retitled "The Black Helmet," is the first and the strongest of the collection's three tales. The hero, Philip Mairobert, is his own version of Jean Des Esseintes, the hero of J.-K. Huysmans's *À rebours*. Like Des Esseintes, indeed like Hector de Saint-Denys Garneau, Mairobert suffers from a spiritual fatigue and retreats to his ancestral home – in this case, his great-grandfather's manor. Though located in the Quebec countryside, as opposed to urban Montreal, the slowly decaying structure is inspired by the old Rawlings mansion on Simpson Street. Indeed, there is something of Edward Rawlings himself in Mairobert's great-grandfather, a bewhiskered man of business and industry "who built that early skyscraper, shaped like a portable gallon can."[5]

Mairobert lives alone, haunted by a love for his old governess, Miss Marwood. As did Sappho in Glassco's life, the fatal woman enters the tale in the form of a beautiful housekeeper, Adrienne Delarchet, who with her brother, conspires to destroy Mairobert.

Glassco assigns the dates 1936–44 at the end of the novella when, in fact, "The Black Helmet" was the culmination of four decades of work. This deceit concerning dates is reflected in the preface, where Glassco describes "The Fulfilled Destiny of Electra," the new title given to "The Monster," to be the oldest of the three tales. Though he claims to have begun the novella in 1934, after coming under "the renewed influence" of the Decadents, it was actually written much later.[6] Charles, the protagonist, lives on a rural estate with his mistress, Inger, and Sophie, her daughter. Sophie has been groomed to replace her aging mother as a sexual partner, yet when the time comes, Charles finds himself impotent.

Glassco describes his final tale, "Lust in Action," formerly "The Finger in the Dyke," as being "satirical and ribald."[7] Here he replaces the ever-present mansion of his imagination with a Gothic prison. The setting is a gynaecocracy in which only lesbian relationships are recognized and males are castrated at the age of twenty. The male sexual appetite is more than merely anarchic; it is considered a danger to the state. The tale's two boy heroes, Thurlow Smart and Arthur Dumont, are able to create havoc by playing on their captors' unfamiliarity with the male sex organ. They threaten to display obscene illustrations, to expose themselves, and to make hetero-sexual advances. The pair are eventually brought under control and sent for early castration, but not before one has ravished an elderly guard.

As *The Fatal Woman* went to press, and with it the long obsessed-over story of Philip Mairobert, Glassco's contentment was tempered by his forced involvement in a sorry episode that he would refer to as "an erection in a teapot."[8] The actual vessel was *Northern Journey*, a lively little magazine being published on an irregular basis by Fraser Sutherland and Terrance MacCor-mack. Glassco's connection with the periodical stretched back to June 1971, when Sutherland wrote requesting that he contribute. As he recalls: "My co-editor and I were scouting around for likely prospects and actively solic-iting people, so to speak. Glassco just seemed like – in today's parlance – such a cool guy."[9]

In Glassco, the editors received more than they'd anticipated; he was a keen supporter from the start. On the cover of the premiere issue, Glassco's name appeared first, heading a list that featured, among others, Al Purdy, Earle Birney, George Johnston, Raymond Souster, Patrick Lane, Henry Beis-sel, and John Metcalf. While *Northern Journey* no. 1 credited Glassco with two pieces – "Euterpe's Honeymoon (Notes on the Poetic Process)" and "Onan; or Little by Little," a cautionary found poem on the topic of mas-turbation – within the list of contributors was a single female name: that of Sylvia Bayer.[10] Glassco had not only contributed the first chapter of the forthcoming *Fetish Girl* to the little magazine, he'd had "Miss Bayer" submit an introduction, along with a brief biography:

I have been writing since I was eight; but my poetry was all birds and flowers, and my stories all waltzes, heartbreak and moonlight. After doing stints as an interior decorator, swimming instructress and inter-preter … I started writing this kind of thing six years ago, and my first book *Eros, my Angel* (Gargoyle, 1965) had just enough success to keep me at it. I am a native Montrealer, a fourth-generation Canadian of

U.E.L. (German-American) stock, and proud of it ... My favourite poet is Margaret Atwood, and I still hope to meet her some day.[11]

This brief sketch had been accompanied by a photograph of the authoress, dressed and photographed in a manner reminiscent of the late 1940s. To those who recognized the woman captured, the use of the image was in very poor taste. The picture Glassco had supplied was, in fact, one of his wife, Elma, who'd then been lying close to death in the Royal Edward Laurentian Hospital.[12]

While Glassco submitted no further work to *Northern Journey*, his name had nevertheless again appeared in its pages. In October 1973, the little magazine's third issue included a work of fiction, "Slow Burn," by a young journalist named Wil Wigle. The short story features a character named Margaret Atwood, "the reigning queen of Canadian literature," who after a reading and the reception that followed is taken by car to her hotel: "Ms Atwood sat up front. She said she was satisfied with the reading but not as pleased as she was in Montreal where John Glassco had paid her a grand compliment. After her performance there, 'Buffy' had come up to tell her that she had given him 'a great big erection.'"[13]

Glassco had not read the story – nor, it would appear, had any of his friends and acquaintances, including Ralph Gustafson, who had a poem in the very same issue. George Woodcock reported that he'd been unaware of the Atwood character and her anecdote concerning Glassco because it was the one piece in the issue that he had found "too tedious to finish reading."[14] Indeed, in the three months that followed its publication, "Slow Burn" had received no public notice and would likely have been forgotten had it not been for a letter addressed to Sutherland from lawyer Rosalie Abella, who was acting on Atwood's behalf. Referencing "libellous material" in the story, the future Supreme Court justice demanded that *Northern Journey* undertake impossible task of recalling "all issues [*sic*] of the October journal in which this material is contained from any and all libraries, bookstores, individuals or agencies who have this volume in their possession."[15] In addition, Abella sought adequate proof that the recall had taken place and that the next issue would include an apology from Wigle "for any embarrassment caused to the parties concerned."[16]

Sutherland remembers Wigle as being shaken and quite prepared to apologize. However, the editor and contributor were at odds as to what course to take. "I was pretty hard-nosed about it," he says, "we weren't about to back down one little bit."[17] In fact, Wigle was more than willing to express regret; faced with the possibility of a lawsuit he was eager to have the issue recalled and had been prepared to borrow as much as $2,000 to devote to the hopeless project. After a week had passed, the author of "Slow Burn" wrote Atwood a letter in which he attempted to explain the story.

Meanwhile, the magazine responded to Abella with a letter asking that she define the libellous material featured in the story. The request was accompanied by an offer of space in the upcoming issue so that Atwood could address her complaint. Both query and offer were met with silence.

Wintering with Marion in Guantajuato, Mexico, Glassco knew nothing of Wigle's story or the growing controversy until contacted by Sutherland. By the time he'd returned to Foster, the Writers' Union of Canada had become involved in the dispute. The chair, Marian Engel, wrote Sutherland a bizarre letter in which he and Wigle were accused of breaching a seemingly agreed upon practice:

> What causes us distress is the attitude you and Mr Wigle take, that people whose names are public property may have any words, however embarrassing, put into their mouths. If this policy continues in direct opposition to understood fictional conventions, no one will be safe.
>
> The convention of changing names is a safe one and all writers and editors should obviously respect it. To violate it shows an insensitivity to the nature and power of fiction unworthy of your previous good work in this area.
>
> We gather you have offered Ms Atwood space to defend herself. It is not Atwood, but the whole concept of fiction that needs defending.[18]

In the March 1974 edition of the Writers' Union newsletter, the executive, composed of Engel, Rudy Weibe, and Harold Horwood, recommended that members not contribute to *Northern Journey*. The issue attracted the attention of Margaret Laurence, who after reading the Wigle story turned down the magazine's invitation to review Wiebe's *The Temptations of Big Bear*.

Glassco was greatly irritated by the threatened lawsuit and took offense in what he perceived as Abella's assertion that she was acting on his behalf. In mid-March, he wrote Sutherland urging him not to issue an apology: "I think these girls are being very silly and altogether self-reverent."[19] The next day, he sent off a letter to Abella, disassociating himself from the quarrel:

> In declining to be a party of this dispute, I would like to point out:
> 1) that the story is too slight a literary effort to be taken seriously;
> 2) that one of the main functions of little magazines like *Northern Journey* is to allow young writers like Mr Wigle to "do their thing" in public, however feeble and tasteless it may appear to the not-so-young; and, more importantly,
> 3) that there is nothing libellous in the legal sense, either of Margaret Atwood or myself, in the story."[20]

It was, if anything, a restrained piece of correspondence. Acting under Marion's advice, Glassco kept his anger in check. In a second letter, which remained unsent, he slammed Atwood's lawyer for her use of his name in addressing Sutherland, an editor for whom he had "nothing but friendship and admiration," and further for having involved him publicly in "an illiberal and policemanlike attitude in literary matters."[21]

Glassco received no response from Abella, and it wasn't until well into April before he at last heard from Atwood concerning what she termed "the curious Wigle Affair."[22] The issue Atwood had with Wigle's story wasn't limited to what the young writer had had her say, she also objected to being used as a character in a piece of fiction. Atwood wrote, "the fact is that by US law anyway – this comes through my agent [Phoebe Larmore] – once you've allowed yourself to be used as a fictional character under your own name and image *without objecting*, the road is clear for anyone to use you in a similar way in other pieces of fiction."[23]

Glassco, who considered himself a friend of both Atwood and Sutherland, was greatly relieved to learn that there would be no court case. After the letter in which Glassco had disassociated himself from any possible legal action, *Northern Journey* heard no more from Atwood's lawyer. Nevertheless, the controversy continued to be fought among members of the Writers' Union and in the pages of *Quill and Quire*. Eventually Woodcock was asked by Engel to perform the role of mediator between the two sides. However, before he could begin, the National Council of the Writers' Union issued a policy statement in support of Atwood. Woodcock resigned from the organization in protest. Glassco's message to the union was much less dramatic; he simply allowed his membership to lapse.

To those not personally involved in the controversy, the magazine's stance seemed to be a mystery; *Quill and Quire* asked: "Why did Northern Journey refuse to apologise publicly to Margaret Atwood?"[24] The answer was quite simple: the editors were certain that, contrary to Engel's assertion, Wigle hadn't put a single word into Atwood's mouth. The automobile ride described in the story was based on one that had taken place two years earlier, during which Atwood had related the anecdote about Glassco in the presence of Wigle, Terrance MacCormack, and a third journalist. "Wigle made public an occasion which was obviously private," wrote Woodcock in *Quill and Quire*, "when a writer was relaxing among other writers *after* a public appearance; it was a situation whose confidentiality should have been taken for granted, and the editors of *Northern Journey* have compounded his lapse of literary-journalistic ethics by printing his wretched little piece of taxi gossip."[25] The editors of *Northern Journey* were not swayed by Woodcock's argument. The very next issue featured a statement of principle: "Whatever the artistic merit of 'Slow Burn,' we find no need to apologize for liberty of expression when it is, in this case, further safeguarded by accuracy. We cannot apologize for, but rather affirm, the right of an author to use actual incidents in his work."[26]

On the first anniversary of the publication of "Slow Burn," the magazine placed an advertisement in *The Globe and Mail* touting the number in which "Slow Burn" appeared as "the offending issue."[27] It was, obviously, an attempt to capitalize on the controversy, but the tension had already subsided. The erection in the teapot would subside, without satisfactory conclusion.[28]

On 5 June 1974, in the midst of the controversy over "Slow Burn," Glassco and Marion were wed in a simple, private service held at St James the Apostle, before no more than a dozen guests, including Joel McCormick: "I well remember the struggle Buffy had trying to fit the wedding band on her finger; it was too small but he wouldn't give up until my mother brought her right hand down sharply on his hand ending a scene that threatened to dissolve into an Ealing comedy. A reception followed at the Ritz Carlton where we dined on bouillabaise."[29]

Slap aside, the event proved a moment of calm in an otherwise stressful summer. As publication of *The Fatal Woman* drew near, Glassco became worried that he was committing something so very revealing of his person to print. While *The English Governess, Squire Hardman, Harriet Marwood, Governess, The Temple of Pederasty,* and *Fetish Girl* had been published anonymously or under pseudonyms, the collection of three novellas would mark the first time he'd be revealed as the author of a work that was, in his own opinion, pornographic. Moreover, Glassco was fully expecting reviews to be condemnatory or, at best, dismissive. He was surprised when the initial reviews, those by Roy MacSkimming, Kildare Dobbs, and Peter Buitenhuis, were positive.[30] Among those who complimented him on the book was Louis Dudek, who quite obviously didn't recognize "The Black Helmet" as a reworking of "Mairobert," the novella Delta Canada had rejected five years earlier.[31] And yet, the overwhelmingly positive reception quickly wore thin. Rereading *The Fatal Woman,* Glassco thought it awful. His opinion was supported by Marion, who "out and out disapproved."[32] He enlisted his bride's help in fending off media requests, determined to hide himself from the public eye. "The only image of myself I ever consciously created was that of the young man of the *Memoirs,*" Glassco wrote in his journal. "Everything else has been made by others."[33] No longer would he afford these "others" – the media and his fellow writers – this opportunity. He would emulate Hector de Saint-Denys-Garneau, "a model of public modesty," and avoid the spectacle created by poets like Earle Birney, whom he considered base publicity-seekers.[34]

Though he'd attended many readings, and had himself recited ten short lines of verse back in 1963 at the Foster Poetry Conference, Glassco had never much liked the idea of poets taking the stage, any stage. He believed that the writer should communicate with his reader through text; public events, like the 1975 International Poetry Festival held at the University of Toronto, maintained "the naive listener's belief that he is getting 'closer' to a poem by hearing it from the poet himself."[35] While there was no denying the pleasure to be had in well-recited verse – the CBC broadcast of *Montreal* read by John Bishopric had been a particular pleasure – he knew that very few poets were so gifted. Glassco was well aware that his hesitant, stammering speech did his verse a disservice, just as he recognized that others more sure of voice were playing to the crowd by presenting poems that they knew would provoke laughter, gasps, and the greatest applause. These concerns were addressed in "The Poet as Performer Debases His Art. You Hear

Him, Not His Poetry," a commentary published with prominence on the editorial page of *The Globe and Mail*. In the piece, Glassco set his sights not so much on poets like bpNichol – though Nichol was singled out – but on the League of Canadian Poets, which years earlier had instigated a program designed "to bring together Canadian poets and their audiences." Glassco had been a member since the League's inception in 1966 but had never been much of a supporter. He thought the name silly and had from the start fought on the side of exclusivity. The battle had been lost. In the first decade of its existence, the League of Canadian Poets had grown more than tenfold to 160 members. It had, Glassco believed, been inundated with "sensitive housewives from the Maritimes and the Prairies, all awful, all published at public expense in hideous little chapbooks."[36] By rights, these individuals should not have belonged to the same League that included Frank Scott and Ralph Gustafson. He placed blame on Fred Cogswell and others who had pushed for a more inclusive organization. "If I understand Dr Cogswell correctly," Glassco wrote Henry Beissel, "his position is that everybody can and should write poetry, not so much in the pursuit of excellence or as a demanding vocation, but as a hobby or even a kind of therapy. This acknowledgement of the plight of the Sunday poet struck me as deeply humanitarian: we all know there is no one so pitiable as the person without talent who aspires to be a poet, and I can think of no one better qualified to represent her or him than Dr Cogswell, as his own work and his many sponsorings [*sic*] have shown over the years. He deserves the support he receives from these unhappy men and women. But I am troubled to see the league being taken over by them ...."[37]

Certainly one of the most accomplished of its number, Glassco held his upturned nose and maintained his membership. "My present situation vis-à-vis the League of Canadian Poets is frankly selfish," he admitted, "I look on its annual meetings as no more than an opportunity for a free trip to somewhere or other in our broad land. Poets, I think, give so much to the world, and for so little, that they're entitled to this annual junket at the Canada Council's expense."[38] The League's *Catalogue of Members*, published a few months before his death, records his entry in big bold type as "John Glasgow."

It took little effort from Marion to keep the media at bay. In a season dominated by *Peter Gzowski's Book about This Country in the Morning* and *Colombo's Canadian Quotations*, a collection of tales written in the Decadent tradition garnered little media attention and modest sales. Any failings Glassco identified within *The Fatal Woman* he blamed on himself. He'd enjoyed working with Polk – a feeling that was mutual – and a year after publication submitted an unsolicited work entitled *The Collected Short Stories*. It was a mess of a manuscript, nothing more than a haphazard gathering of eight odds and ends, both published and unpublished. Within this lot was "Deaf-Mute," the Graeme Taylor story that had been published in the summer 1928 issue of *transition*. Indeed, in preparing the manuscript, Glassco had photocopied the *transition* appearance, carefully pasting his name over that of Taylor. In the preface to his collection, Glassco describes the genesis of the story, never once mentioning his deceased friend: "'Deaf Mute' [*sic*] was written in 1927 when I was still a student at McGill University. It was sparked by the sight of an adulterous francophone couple on the Montreal lakeshore, merrily playing cards under a roadside street-lamp and the surveillance of a gibbering grey-bearded idiot."[39]

Similarly, Glassco claims the second story in the collection, "Dr Breakey Opposes Union," as his own, ignoring the fact that it had appeared under Taylor's name in a 1929 issue of *This Quarter*: "'Dr Breakey Opposes Union' dates from Paris in the summer of 1928. It was founded on an anecdote, and I can now only recollect that Dr Breakey's first name was that of the then Dean of Arts at McGill University (an absurd person) and his last was that of a horrible boy at Bishop's College School in Lennoxville, Que. where I passed the most miserable year of my life."[40]

Glassco acknowledges one theft: the title of a third story, "The Portrait of a Generation," taken "from a long unreadable novel by Robert McAlmon."[41] What he doesn't acknowledge is that "The Portrait of a Generation" was also the title of a lost Taylor short story, which in 1934 was rejected by *Harper's*. What Glassco presents is the tale of a Canadian painter who visits Paris where he had lived as a young man. In his preface, he claims to have written the story in 1938, yet it features the airport now named after Pierre Elliott Trudeau, which was at the time the site of a race track surrounded by farmland in the town of Dorval.

In laying claim to stories originally published under Taylor's name, Glassco may very well have revealed something of the collaborative process he'd once shared with his deceased friend. It was one aspect of their curious relationship that McAlmon saw first hand; indeed the elder writer's vantage appears to have inspired a passage in *Nightinghouls of Paris* that takes place after the boys move into Kit O'Malley's spacious studio apartment. There, Sudge, inspired by *Confessions of a Young Man*, works on his memoirs, writing of all the Montparnassian personages he encounters, while Ross works on his "family novel":

> They would each do a page and show the other the result whereupon they emitted a series of snorts and snickers. Ross gave Sudge no suggestions, but Sudge actually told Ross what to write. Still they agreed that Ross was the great man who would be known to the world as such someday. Sudge was sure of Ross's delicacy of perception; Ross assured me that Sudge was a common little bourgeois who'd be hopeless if he hadn't been rescued from that boob family of his.[42]

Michael Gnarowski recalls a curious exchange that likely took place in 1970, when he was teaching at Sir George Williams University, little more than one block north of Glassco's Bishop Street apartment: "He would come up and we'd go and have lunch together at one of the little French bistros on Crescent or one of those streets. One day – and I don't know why, it was not very kind of me – I said to him jokingly, 'I bet those poems that you published were all written by Graeme Taylor.' And I guess I wounded him, because the next day he came back with a sheaf of poems. He said, 'These are Graeme Taylor's poems. You see I didn't use them.'"[43]

The sheaf consisted of ten poems in total, held in an old *New York Times Review of Books* envelope on which Glassco had written "Graeme Taylor's poems, fair copies & original MSS. (none written after 1936)." They were unaccomplished, demonstrating no progression beyond Taylor's 1927 *Fortnightly* poem "The Unknown World."

Polk recognized "Deaf-Mute" and "Dr Breakey Opposes Union" as Graeme Taylor stories – Glassco himself had described them as such in *Memoirs of Montparnasse* – yet he never pursued the issue of authorship. The collection was, he recalls, "of an uneven quality with too much of the writing not at the level of his best."[44] *The Fatal Woman* would be the House of Anansi's only John Glassco title.

The Collected Short Stories was both symbolic and symptomatic of a decline in creativity. While the 1970s had seen the publication of many titles – *Memoirs of Montparnasse*, *The Poetry of French Canada in Translation*, *The Temple of Pederasty*, *Selected Poems*, *Montreal*, and *The Fatal Woman* – each had been all but completed several, and in some cases, dozens of years earlier. By the decade's mid-point, he had produced only one truly new work: *Fetish Girl.*

"I've stopped writing poetry (why did I ever start?) and pornography (why did I start so late?): one demands too much of the spirit, the other of the flesh," he wrote Milton Kastello.[45] Glassco was determined to follow up *Fetish Girl* with a novella that would be his masterwork. Titled *The Father,* it would be "the great porno book"[46] and would have as its theme:

> the beauty & fulfilment of the partnership of absolute power and absolute submission, my vision of psychosexual paradise .... It's homosexual, as it must be. The interpretation of the two characters requires this, limits the frame of reference, *focuses* the philosophic concept on the masculine consciousness, the only one I understand. Man and boy, each changing roles in their own imagination, putting themselves in each other's place, achieving maturity & recapturing youth at the same time. The idea of mastery and service, age & adolescence, coming together, coalescing & gaining a kind of temporal immortality, an annihilation of time itself, a defiance and defeat of death. And a happy ending – All my novels have happy endings! I am the supreme romantic.[47]

The pornographer could see it all before him, knew how the plot would progress and, most importantly, how the romantic happy ending would be achieved, yet he wrote nothing. He blamed laziness, eating, drinking, reading, his social life, and the distractions of couplehood. Life, as he described it, was "so pleasant, so amusing."[48]

A good part of his day was now devoted to attempts at clearing out old, sometimes stale, projects. The abandoned, the frustrating, and the all-but-forgotten were submitted to magazines and publishers in Canada, Great Britain, and the United States. "The Pigtail Man," the short story that had been rejected in 1950 by *The Northern Review,* was accepted by Joe Rosenblatt for *Jewish Dialog,* as was "Countess Isabel and the Torturer," a medieval romance he'd written in his forties. Far greater success was had with Oberon Press, where Glassco finally found a home for his *Complete Poems of Saint-Denys-Garneau.*

Nearly all of the eighty-four translations dated from the late 1950s and early 1960s. It had begun under the influence of Frank Scott, who had, at the time, been working on his own translations of Garneau. Scott explained his approach in his 1962 *St-Denys Garneau and Anne Hébert*: "My principal aim in translating is to alter the poem as little as possible, and to let it speak for itself in the other tongue. This means a preference for literalness rather than for alternate renderings; for one poem in two languages, instead of two similar poems."[49]

On this matter, Glassco, the pupil, had long ago parted with his mentor Scott. In his introduction to *Complete Poems of Saint-Denys-Garneau*, Glassco writes: "In translating these poems I have followed a course that was bound to result in the intrusion of my own personality. Such personal colouring, however unwelcome and however resisted, is inevitable ... These renderings are faithful but not literal."[50]

Where the *Journal* had received little attention thirteen years earlier, Glassco's second volume of Garneau translations drew significant notice and praise. Among the more considered and positive was Eli Mandel's lengthy *Globe and Mail* review, in which he compares both Scott and Glassco's approaches to translation and finds both valid. However, the younger poet has an advantage not shared by Scott: "the appeal of Saint Denys Garneau to Glassco, the reason for the translation, may very well be the attraction, the fateful attraction of a like personality, a double. John Glassco knows a great deal about early death and rebirth, about exclusiveness, fastidiousness, about the vulgarity of what he calls 'emotional depaysement.'"[51] Further praise followed in *Quarry*, *Queen's Quarterly*, *Canadian Literature*, *The Canadian Forum*, and *The Times Literary Supplement*; the sole dissenting voice, that of Grazia Merler, writing in the *West Coast Review*, arrived many months after *Complete Poems of Saint-Denys-Garneau* received the Canada Council Translation Prize.

In an interview with *The Ottawa Citizen*, Glassco said that the publication of the Garneau poems left him with a feeling of accomplishment, such that he no longer felt a need to continue translating French Canadian literature. In fact, that particular passion had died within Glassco many years before, killed in part by Quebec nationalism and the harsh reaction to *The Poetry of French Canada in Translation*. There were, however, several translations to come: *La femme de Loth*, by Monique Bosco; *Un dieu chasseur*, by

Glassco in 1976, a few weeks after his sixty-sixth birthday.

Jean-Yves Soucy; thirty songs of Gilles Vigneault for Victoria's Belfry Theatre; and several scenes for an aborted television production of *Les Plouffe*.
Of all these works, he cared only for *La femme de Loth*. He considered Bosco
"one of the most accomplished novelists of French Canada"[52] and saw something of himself in the suicidal heroine, a writer who laments: "Alas, I'll
never write anything but stupid stories without beginning or end, full of
strange characters gnawed by obscure sufferings."[53] Glassco's motivation was
money – $5,000 for the Soucy translation – though he did demonstrate dis-

crimination, turning down requests for translations of works he thought untranslatable, like Anne Hébert's *Poèmes*.

In the midst of all these projects, one stands out: Austrian, not Canadian; written in German, not French; Glassco's supposed translation of Leopold von Sacher-Masoch's *Venus in Furs* was yet another work from a previous decade. As *Venus im Pelz*, he'd first encountered the classic erotic novel during summer 1934, while living with Graeme Taylor in their rented Baie d'Urfe home. He'd found delight in the masochistic fantasy, and with it the inspiration to continue "The Way Back." However, the German had been a struggle and he looked forward to a privately printed English-language edition ordered from New York. When it arrived, dodging customs, Glassco was disappointed; he considered it a "vile bit of work" and was certain that he could do better.[54] Dating from the late 1950s, the version Glassco sent around relied greatly on the weak translation and had almost certainly benefited from Elma's input. He had next to no knowledge of German, his only real exposure to the language having come through a lone course he'd had as a boy at Selwyn House. It was rejected by the Bodley Head, McGill University Press, and the House of Anansi before being accepted by Blackfish, a small press run by Brian Brett and Alan Safarik in the Vancouver suburb of Burnaby.

Even then, Brett was skeptical that the translation was as Glassco had presented. "You could never get the provenance of anything out of Buffy," he recalls. "I thought he basically just stole it. What he did was he looked at the translations and wrote his own. I don't know if he ever actually looked at any German."[55]

For his part, Glassco let nothing slip. Despite his limitations, he maintained that his was the finest translation of the Sacher-Masoch classic and took pride in his introduction, which listed *La maîtresse et l'esclave*, *Lesbia Brandon*, *Aux pieds d'Omphale*, and *The English Governess* "by Miles Underwood" as the only four serious masochistic novels to have appeared since Sacher-Masoch's classic. He admired the Blackfish design, which included the original illustrations by Franz Buchholz. Designed by Brett, published in an edition of 1,500 copies, with 26 hardbound in marbled boards, slipcased, lettered from A to Z, and signed by the translator, it was the most elegant production of a Glassco work since Olympia Press's silken edition of *Under the Hill*.

Brett and Safarik's shared goal, to produce a finished book that looked as though it belonged to the previous century, brought with it many problems. Because their printing press was unable to produce uncut pages, the pair first turned to Trinity Western College, an arm of the Evangelical Free Churches of Canada and America, but the school reneged on the arrangement after developing the negatives featuring the Buchholz illustrations. The book ended up being printed in the gym of former Olympic weightlifter Doug Hepburn, once considered the strongest man in the world, on a press he'd bought to print labels for his vitamin-pill business.

Demand for *Venus in Furs* wasn't great, but it was steady. Brett recalls that it sold very well in one particular gay bookshop in San Francisco.

Sacher-Masoch's *Venus in Furs* contains vague, distorted similarities with Glassco's own life. It takes the form of the journal entitled "Confessions of a Supersensual Man," kept by Severin Kusiemski, a Galician aristocrat, which begins with his stay at a "little Carpathian resort." There he falls in love with a stone sculpture of Venus and – observed by Wanda von Dunaiev, a beautiful, rich young widow – spends his evenings draped over the pedestal. Severin begins a relationship that relies on Wanda's lash and comes to think of her as a goddess. They travel, and in doing so Severin is stripped of his name and rides in the third-class compartment as keeper of the furs. In Florence, he is unsuccessful in taking his life and is whipped by another man. The reader later learns that the origins of Severin's desires trace back to childhood when his aunt, the cook, the kitchen maid, and the chambermaid bound and whipped him. When the punishment is complete, he is untied, forced to his knees, and must express gratitude and kiss his aunt's hand.

George Woodcock praised the translator, writing that Sacher-Masoch suffered in comparison to the flagellentine fantasies manifest in *Harriet Marwood, Governess* and *The Fatal Woman*. This was an anomaly; though received with enthusiasm in certain circles, the reviews were in general quite harsh. The most unforgiving came from Chris Scott, who in *Books in Canada* dismissed "Glassco von Sacher-Masoch's" prose, Buchholz's illustrations, and Blackfish's production as valueless.[56] In *The Globe and Mail*, Brian Vintcent complimented the translation and Glassco's introduction, but not the original Sacher-Masoch work, speculating: "we may be so unredeemably jaded in these days of glossy aberrations that such an innocent and discrete tale as Venus in Furs read for its pornographic content is nothing but ennui and yawns."[57]

The review was very much in mind when Glassco wrote Brett:

> The reviews of VIF did not surprise me either. We must remember that the reviewer's standard reaction to this kind of thing is "I was *bored.*" Wild horses could not evoke anything else. If they did, he could never again hold up his head among his fellows; a horrible fate … I'm glad to hear that the public are sensibly buying the book all the same, in droves. There are of course more "closet" masochists than the world dreams of – literally hundreds of thousands all over the world – and I like to think this revival of Leopold's novel may persuade them, in Canada at least, that they are neither degenerate or criminal or mad. In fact, M.'s come from all walks of life – all the way from truck-drivers and construction-workers to Crown Prosecutors and judges. The whole S.M. thing is more prevalent than most people imagine … And all those I know are such nice, quiet people – both men and women – but so sadly frightened and ashamed of their predilection. The way homosexuals used to be.[58]

The following summer, over dinner at Frank Scott's summer house in North Hatley, Safarik proposed that the press reprint some of Glassco's pseudonymous erotica. Fuelled by martinis, Glassco suggested a new edition of *Squire Hardman* in which he'd own up to his hoax, followed by his translation of the memoirs of seventeenth-century transvestite François Timoléon, the Abbé de Choisy. Before these, he submitted the manuscript for an anthology featuring works by the Abbé de Choisy, the Chevalier André Andrea de Nerciat, Ihara Saikaku, John Cleland, Algernon Charles Swinburne, Harriet Daimler, and Edith Wharton. The collection was to be titled *The Art of Pornography*, after the introductory essay, with selections intended to support his view of the genre as art in that its proper intent "like that of all literature, is simply to please."[59] It is unlike "the ribald or the bawdy, whose aim is to evoke laughter; nor the erotic, whose tone is mainly sentimental or lyrical; nor the obscene, with its appeal to impulses of brutality, desecration and revolt"; rather pornography is a "deliberate attempt, by all the resources of the written word, to stimulate the sexual appetite."[60] Begun as "Nasties," the essay rejected by *Esquire* in 1938, "The Art of Pornography" was the culmination of nearly four decades of thought. It had finally seen print in the summer 1969 number of *Edge*, and the pornographer was eager that it appear in a book.

Glassco might have been cheered by the thought that he had found an enthusiastic publisher for his many works of pornography, but Brett, for one, wasn't terribly interested. "*Venus in Furs* was fun, but I wasn't really into that stuff. We did it as a bit of a lark."[61] The relationship fell apart months later when Scott expressed growing anger in not having received royalties for his *Poems of French Canada*, a collection of translations that Blackfish had published the previous year. Poisoned, the relationship between Glassco and the press drew to an unpleasant conclusion. He wrote Safarik asking for the return of *The Art of Pornography*: "*Please*, no more delays, excuses, promises, chitchat, etc.! Just send the AOP and we'll forget all about VIF"[62] By January, he had seen neither royalties, nor the manuscript, and made a long distance phone call to Safarik in which he threatened legal action. A cheque for the royalties arrived the following month, but Glassco never again saw *The Art of Pornography*. Brett thinks it likely that the work got mixed in with the materials of a rather chaotic little room at the back of their printing shop.

Glassco's disappointment with Blackfish as an outlet for his pornography speaks to a great incongruity: he revelled in playing the gracious, dirty sophisticate, and enjoyed teasing the ladies with talk of rubber, ropes, whips, and dog collars, yet feared exposing his exceedingly obvious fetishes, indulgences, and peculiarities. After a drunken interview for the Saturday newspaper supplement *The Canadian*, he'd turned to his journal, fearing that he'd said too much: "I have now come out of 'the closet' of sadomasochism, displaying my most personal failing to the world."[63] This from the man who had added elements of flagellation to *Under the Hill*, published *Squire Hardman*, claimed the introduction to *The Temple of Pederasty*, revealed himself as the author of *Harriet Marwood, Governess* and *The English Governess*, and had achieved a certain degree of critical acclaim with *The Fatal Woman*.

In his mind, all would be revealed with "the great porno novel" he'd come to call *Guilt and Mourning*. Having rid himself of "Mairobert" with the publication of *The Fatal Woman*, this new work had come to dominate his fantasies. Progress, however, was slow; it was several years before he set down the first word. "Instead of working on it," he complained in his journal, "I masturbate while thinking of its conception."[64]

By spring 1977, when *Venus in Furs* was beginning to arrive in select bookstores, he'd mustered up enough self-discipline to write something approaching 10,000 words. Glassco was composing at an ever-diminishing rate, unable to manage no more than a few minutes of work each day. Several efforts had been made to ignite creativity by copying other works: lengthy passages that had been cut from "Mairobert" and a paragraph from a newspaper account of Albert Einstein's death in which his protagonist's name was substituted for that of the great physicist. There were also descriptive passages, plagiarized from several Iris Murdoch novels, which he'd hoped would assist in setting the tone. Glassco's only source of encouragement lay in the conviction that he had at last settled on a title: *Those Endearing Young Charms*. This new title,[65] the final of fifteen, he took from verse by Thomas Moore.[66] Glassco thought the new name "catchy" and hoped that it would somehow enable him to brighten the mood of the novel. He found the work emotionally taxing and came to place blame for his growing depression on the composition. He wrote in his journal: "Why do I keep on writing this absurd book? Only the vision of its theme & thesis – the reconciliation of my own guilt & my mourning for all I have done and lost – keeps me going. And the feeling, the next day, of not having wasted the time God still gives me to create something, however faulty."[67]

He was anxious that death would take him before the novel could be completed. It was a justified fear. David, nineteen months his elder, had died in 1974. Their father had barely made it to the age of sixty-five.

Since his sixtieth birthday, he'd been suffering twice-yearly infections. In September 1975, he'd contracted a virus leading to a week-long stay at the Montreal General Hospital. Ignoring his fondness for drink, his smoking, and his erratic sleeping patterns, he wondered that a "clean, country-living person" like himself could be so vulnerable.[68] He cited inability to create, loss of appetite, insomnia, and nightmares as symptoms and a deepening of his depression.

He was buoyed by his wife's energy and initiative. Marion had driven the Mafiamobile to New York so that he could finally meet with Geoffrey Wagner. The couple had spent a number of winters in Guanajunto, had stayed with Leon Edel at his home in Honolulu, and in 1978 had visited Portugal,

Italy, Spain, Greece, and Yugoslavia by freighter. Glassco took to this relatively unconventional, stripped-down mode of travel, with its echoes of the *Canadian Traveller*. Free of distractions, with the advantage of duty-free liquor, it appealed. He calculated the cost at $14 per day. He enjoyed visiting ports and cities that were well off the normal tourist itinerary. Upon their return he encouraged Marion to make plans to take the same ship the following spring.

On 26 March 1979, two days before they were due to board a freighter for Yugoslavia, Glassco suffered a heart attack. He was taken to the Montreal Chest Institute and, after some consultation, was transferred to the Royal Victoria Hospital. The trip was off. With Edward Phillips's help, Marion made haste to the freighter, rescuing a considerable amount of alcohol that had been squirreled away for the voyage. Disappointment over the cancelled trip was compounded when the Jeanne-Mance flat was burglarized. The brightest of spots during this rather bleak time could be found in the fact that Glassco's prognosis was good. Two weeks after the heart attack, he was discharged from hospital and returned home to the Jeanne-Mance flat. It was there that he was prescribed Inderal for his heart and told to limit his salt intake, but he believed he'd been told he could continue to drink as much as he wanted. He again sank into a depression for which he could not account. Curiously, incongruously, he considered himself to be in good health, while he considered the heart attack a signal that he did not have much more than ten more years of life.

In August, he and Marion travelled to Ireland with Kildare Dobbs and Colleen Dimson. Upon his return he discovered that a translation of the Abbé de Choisy's memoirs had been published only six years earlier. The bad news was offset to some extent by a letter from Éditions Hurtubise bringing news that Jean-Yves Soucy had proposed a French-language translation of *Memoirs of Montparnasse*.[69]

He consulted a psychiatrist, who assured him that depression among men at his stage in life was quite common. Drugs were prescribed. He once again considered suicide and sought the newly published guide *How to Die with Dignity* from Scottish Exit.[70]

Whenever his thoughts turned to suicide, he would think of Marion. While he couldn't bear the thought of leaving her, he was aware of the effect his depression was having on the relationship. With this in mind, he wrote in his journal that it would be better to be dead than mad.

In October he returned to his doctor and was told that his lingering depression was a side effect of the Inderal. As he decreased his dosage, ending it one week later, Glassco began to feel chest pains. He felt Inderal was a poison that lingered in his system. His depression had lessened somewhat but continued to be unbearable.

In early November, he returned to his journal, writing in a shaky hand:

I have already resolved to give myself until the spring. If this depression continues, life will simply not be worth living, and I will commit suicide. Get stupidly drunk, close up the garage, start the car & let the monoxide do its work.

If I weren't feeling a little better I would not have the courage even to record this resolve.

I will not go mad & be put in the Douglas Hospital.[71]

His health and spirits in decline, Glassco returned to *Those Endearing Young Charms*; not to work on the book, but to append a note expressing doubts that the novel would ever be completed. It was something of a defense, in which he writes of the intention to perform a major revision of the work. In his journal he described depression as "the worst, deepest & most continuous" of his life.[72]

Four months later, five days after his seventieth birthday, he appended a second note: "This novel, begun in 1972, has now been finally & definitely abandoned by me. – It is worthless."[73] The next day, the depression became intolerable; he made a point of recording it in his agenda as the worst day of his life.

Glassco never returned to the novel. Left behind were several notebooks filled with cramped, often shaky, script, along with numerous typescripts and dozens of small scraps of paper with handwritten notes. The final draft Glassco produced was just thirty thousand words in length, a novella.

Those Endearing Young Charms is in many ways set in the Montreal predating Glassco's birth; the lost city that the author never knew but for which he'd often longed. It's a metropolis in which citizens walk on slate sidewalks lit by gaslamps; a Montreal that is "British and blessedly colonial."[74] And yet the year is 1972, the result of an "amusing Wellsian quirk that moved the world into another and parallel dimension of history where the course of time had veered off and slowed to an earlier pace and an earlier moral climate."[75] The explanation is as jarring as it is fleeting; but it does serve to allow the author to carry forward select elements of the past, bastardize the present, and, as in "Lust in Action," insert a state correction system of his own devising.

Glassco carries this notion of a parallel dimension through to his protagonist, Ainger; a judge, he holds the occupation A.P.S. had chosen for his second son. The novel opens with "the Judge" descending Mount Royal by Panhard, and then through the confusion of congested city streets toward his mistress Cicely, an illiterate black woman. Her fifteen-year-old daughter, variously named Cissy and Cissie, the "girl of the flashing smile and slender ankles," loves Ainger, whom she considers her father.[76] However, the Judge has come to believe otherwise, thus allowing him to fantasize of the day, not too far hence, in which she will take her mother's place in his bed. Ainger's dream turns nightmare when he arrives to find the girl has been raped. The attack brings on "a kind of dementia praecox," and Cissy is hospitalized.[77]

When it becomes apparent that Cissy will not recover, the Judge has mother and daughter brought to his country estate. Cecily is no longer desirable and is reduced to the role of housekeeper. Ainger spends his days caring for his horses, following a carefully drawn regime that is intended to allow little time for contemplation or mourning. However, the plan is not wholly effective. Reflecting on his past, the Judge descends into self-loathing; he considers himself unloved, unlovable, and incapable of loving. Cissy's illness seemingly incurable, he is resigned to living a life without purpose.

Ainger presides over the trial of her rapist, Dilly Green, a fifteen-year-old boy who lives with his mother and grandmother in that most familiar of Glassco settings, a dilapidated family mansion. The harsh term, twenty years, is handed down for no other reason than it is the number of years the Judge believes he himself has left to live.

Dilly is sent to a penal institution known as the Farm, where he is strapped to a canvas-covered vaulting horse and flogged daily by Colonel Mildmay, a grotesque figure in Victorian bathing costume and rubber woman's bathing cap. The boy accepts his punishments; indeed, he soon recognizes that he would have gone mad for lack of them. Mildmay teaches the boy that through beatings he might be healed, assuaged of grief, and absolved of guilt. The act performed by means of horse and strap is seen as necessary for restoring Dilly's dignity. A mutual affection and understanding quickly develops between the two.

While the other boys talk of escape to the United States, Dilly takes no part in their discussions; nor does he participate in their homosexual activities. Masturbating in his cell, the boy's desire is increasingly taken up with the image of an anonymous elderly man.

His world is again shaken when Mildmay attempts to kiss him, and he realizes that Mildmay is not the older male he seeks. Dilly escapes and – by "a strange stroke of fortune," "the kind of symbolic coincidence engineered in a novel by Victor Hugo" – finds sanctuary at Ainger's country estate.[78] The boy remains with Ainger, whom he recognizes as the judge who sentenced him to the Farm. Together the man and boy share the routine of the stable.

Dilly soon comes to view the Judge with desire and, sensing Ainger's attraction to the strap, sets out a course of seduction. The novel ends with Dilly fellating the Judge, while Cicely watches from a balcony.

After seven years, Glassco had so very little to show for his efforts; he left behind a remarkably slight work that could not be legally published. During the final months of struggle with *Those Endearing Young Charms*, he recorded the message of the novella: "sadist-masochistic relationships are doomed."[79] Yet, the final draft belies this claim. Ainger and Dilly are set upon what appears to be a longlasting relationship. The only failed relationships in the novel, sexual or otherwise, lack sadomasochistic elements: Dilly's father abandons the family because his wife is unfaithful; Cicely's sexual relationship with the Judge ends as her looks begin to fade.

Where in these works Glassco's interests in flagellation and rubber fetishism dominate, in *Those Endearing Young Charms* he draws on events and relationships from his own life. Judge Ainger is an "equestrian dandy" given to dressing in the manner of an English country squire.[80] Cicely, Ainger's mistress, is black and a dancer, recalling the woman with whom Glassco had an affair in 1954. During her brief hospitalization, Cissy is treated by Doctor Lehmann – after Heinz Lehmann, the man who had so impressed Glassco when treating Elma at the Douglas Hospital. Indeed, Cissy's symptoms are drawn, with no embellishment, from those of Elma: her emotions swing wildly between joy and extreme despair; she defecates on the floor; she eats a pound of butter with a spoon one day and announces the intention to starve herself to death the next. Ainger's journal entries are near transcriptions of entries made by Glassco during Elma's illness:

Her mind has gone; her beautiful smile has turned to a grimace of hatred. Stammering, she told me that I had ruined her life, that she could not bear the sight of me. Dr Lehmann has informed me – oh so kindly! – that due to some strange transvaluation of feeling that is common in such cases, that this hatred is the measure of her underlying love. I suppose I should take comfort in this.[81]

Like Algernon Charles Swinburne's struggles with *Lesbian Brabdon*, Glassco was too close to his subject; he was groping in vain for the right technical stance, the proper balance between his sexual obsession and his art, and finally put it aside in despair. But more than all this, he was an artist who had been left by his creativity. He'd known this for years and in 1976 had written:

Shall I ever write poetry again? I doubt it. Dear Arthur Smith complained to me only last summer that he could no longer write poetry. Well, our occupation's gone. A pity, since we all have the *technique*, the mastery of line, cadence, perfection of ear, all the skill – all that is lacking is the vital spark; the Muse, the *mania*, has left us, us the old men. We are the tired generation, the finished men.[82]

Glassco had always found the end of each year a trial; indeed the month of December was a time in which he often felt as if he were dead. It was "that morte saison," "a season of feasts and hallow frightfulness, with all its anniversaries both public and private."[83] His birthday, Christmas and New Year's Eve, three events he dreaded, falling within sixteen days of one another. After inclement weather had all but ruined one birthday celebration, Marion moved the celebration to 15 June, six months after his true birthday. The parties were attended by the Scotts, the Smiths, the Gustafsons, Edward Phillips, Ken Woodman, and John Bishopric and his wife. Glassco once wrote Smith: "I believe, anyway, that birthdays should be dated from the moment of conception or fertilization, because that was undoubtedly a pleasanter occasion for everyone concerned."[84]

The depression, ever present, had a horrible effect on his marriage. He began fighting with Marion. They discussed cancelling their trip to visit Edel in Honolulu but ultimately decided to go ahead. The morning of 30 December, they boarded a Canadian Pacific flight at Dorval. It was a mistake.

He spent much of the Hawaiian trip in tears. Five days into the trip, he sought help at a local clinic and was prescribed Elaril. The depression lifted but was replaced by apathy. He felt weak.

In April 1980, Edel sent Glassco a copy of a paper he would be presenting at the upcoming Callaghan Symposium being held at the University of Ottawa. The mention of Morley Callaghan, as it always had, opened the old wound: "I feel most flattered to find myself so amply quoted, and am only concerned about Morley's possible painful reaction. I imagine he's pretty well fed up by now with hearing about the Memoirs; but after all, he started the whole thing with that rather nasty story in *This Quarter*, which was really what H.J. [Henry James] would call an 'unconscious intrusion on privacy.' And he kept right on in *That Summer in Paris* ..."[85]

Although it is not known whether Callaghan reacted in pain to the quotes from *Memoirs of Montparnasse*, in July Callaghan and Edel shared a lunch during which they discussed the summer that had taken place in Paris over one-half century earlier. Edel took little time in reporting the conversation to Glassco:

> We talked from noon to 5 p.m. and you will be interested to know that his version (perhaps you have heard this) of why he wrote the story about you and Graeme was that he had been ruffled because you were hard on Bob McAlmon in your talk when he wasn't around and in the strange Camelot world of Morley this was a kind of disloyalty – I thought this one of the strangest explanations to date offered to me, gratuitously, especially since I know how light McA made of all that was said about him etc. M. has no sense of humor. I pass this gossip of ancient things along to you for what it suggests about the high moral tone Morley can't forego.[86]

Glassco wrote back:

> Interesting to hear Morley's reason for that story about Graeme and me. Of *course* it had nothing to do with our making cracks about McAlmon! It was simply a safety-valve for his moral pique – and published in *This Quarter* so we'd be sure not to miss it. Not that it isn't a very readable story, and in fact pretty good: it has a nice balance, brevity and *swing*. As for Morley himself, you can't help liking him,

though his 'moral stance' has always puzzled me because it's so hyper-latitudinarian. He's not a spoiled priest, just a confused altarboy."[87]

In the spring he was approached by Michael Gnarowski to provide a new translation of the Jean-Charles Harvey novel *Les démi-civilisés* for Carleton University Press. Although Glassco was not familiar with the book, he was attracted by the compensation and the scent of scandal. Originally published in 1934, when Harvey was editor-in-chief of *Le Soleil*, Quebec City's leading daily, its irreverence and anticlerical message brought swift denouncement from J.-M. Rodrigue, Cardinal Villeneuve, who placed *Les démi-civilisés* on the index of forbidden books. Harvey was pressured to make a public apology and had the novel withdrawn from sale. However, the move did nothing to save his position: he was promptly fired from *Le Soleil*.

Les démi-civilisés had suffered an earlier translation by Lukin Barette and, as *Sackcloth for Banner*, been published in 1938 by Macmillan. The first translator had taken a great many liberties, which included various inventions, omissions, and alterations. Under Glassco, it became one of a very few French Canadian novels to receive a second translation.[88] It took a little over a month to complete the work and submit the final draft. Glassco worried over his tentative title, *The Backward People*; though accurate, he feared it might be misconstrued. He explained the title to Gnarowski: "The words 'half-civilized,' or 'semi-civilized,' or 'demi-civilized' never occur in either Barette's translation or mine, but 'backward' recurs again and again, referring to the academic, religious and cultural 'élites' of the early 30's in Quebec, never to the farmers or working-class."[89]

His work on translation complete, he cast about for other projects but found himself lacking in motivation and enthusiasm. William Toye attempted to interest him in writing a screenplay for *Memoirs of Montparnasse*. It was a troubled project, one that had endured four years of failed scripts while under option with a Westmount production company. Toye suggested that the two might collaborate on a screenplay and presented Glassco with several pages of notes. Glassco's attempt, begun in August, amounted to a couple of incomplete scenes and less than a dozen pages of rough notes, most concerning, in some detail, the *ménage à trois* he'd enjoyed as an eighteen-year-old with Yvette Ledoux and Gwen Le Gallienne.

As the summer passed and the days grew shorter, the depression deepened. For the first time, Glassco left letters from regular correspondents unanswered. Visiting Arthur Smith at his Drummond Point summer home, he became extremely distressed, reporting later to Edel that their old friend "looked like death."[90]

On 21 November, the forty-fifth anniversary of the debut of *The McGill Fortnightly Review*, Smith died. Following a lengthy illness, the death did not come as a surprise; still the loss was greatly felt. It was three weeks before Glassco could write Edel: "we both were 16 or 17 when we met him, and his disappearance is as if we had lost some beloved and lively and somehow invariably witty and challenging elder brother or intimate. I think many of us learned from Art: and then behind that curious bourgeois exterior he countenanced no sham and his feelings for poetry and the irony and wit of things was invariably true."[91]

After the loss of his mentor and friend, all entries in Glassco's daybook ceased; the record of dosages of various medications ceased. The remaining pages were left blank, unused.

Then, as the year was drawing to a close, there came a poem. Its appearance was a surprise, even to Glassco's intimates. For so long, he'd claimed to be through with poetry. Published in the December issue of *Saturday Night*, "The Heavenly Boy" was the first Glassco verse published in three years. It was a love poem he'd written to Marion some months earlier:

THE HEAVENLY BOY[92]

Lovers are always children. We return
To the absolute and else impossible page
Of the double image where the master passion,
Written in milk and water long ago,
Revives under the breath of autumn.
This is the way the alphabet's re-spelled, the primer
Given again into our liver-spotted fingers
By the heavenly boy, his arrow stuck
In the obsolete heart. And so we read
His contract over.
                        Kiss me, we say,
As the old script obliges us to do,
And seal the partnership that is as close
As lip to lip or bicycle to bum.

And this is all our happiness today:
This autumn love that rages like a ram
Coos also like a pigeon in the eaves.
But that contract was the stroke of doom:
Dearest, we have no end at all
More lasting than this skeleton of desire
That holds our marriage in its arms. And so
Kiss me again, and let us share
The common night of falling stars and apples,
Trapped animals, broken hearts and the final sigh
That children heave when the long daylight goes.

Praise was quick in coming. Ralph Gustafson was particularly enthusiastic and wrote his old friend a letter:

Dear Buffy,

What a pleasure it is to come on poetry that is! My reaction to your poems is nothing new – but again I take faire reading that last page in the *Saturday Review* [sic]. You do with such apparent ease that difficulty – the stance of perspective and yet the intimate involvement – the paradox that makes poetry. "The Heavenly Boy" is great pleasure.

Alas, that Arthur is gone, I had been away somewhere and only inadvertently learned. I had said good-bye to Arthur that afternoon I had with him last August at Drummond Point. He knew and I knew …

My mind goes back to the afternoon when he drove me (recklessly) to Cowansville and we stopped off at your farmhouse and I first met you who wrote poetry.

All good remembrances.

Ralph[93]

In the final weeks of 1980, Glassco endured his seventy-first birthday, Christmas, and New Year's Eve. New Year's Day brought no resolutions, no hopes of a fresh start. Sheila Fischman remembers seeing him a few days later: "Marion had some people over and he had come down a little on the late side. He was unshaven – which I had never seen before – and just sat in his chair. He didn't speak to anyone. He was the very image of sadness and depression."[94]

In the middle of the month he had lunch with Gnarowski. "I took him out to lunch at an Italian restaurant on Prince Arthur Street. He was very frail, and I had to help him with his coat. He said to me during lunch, very seriously, 'You started out in university intending to become a chemist. As a chemist, Michael, would you know how many Dalmanes it would take to end one's life?' I was struck by that at the time, and remember it quite vividly."[95]

Early in the day, on 29 January 1981, Glassco received poet Stephen Scobie at the Jeanne-Mance apartment. The host was a frail figure; a mere vestige of the playful, aristocratic-mannered man who once treated his morning guests to Champagne and orange juice.

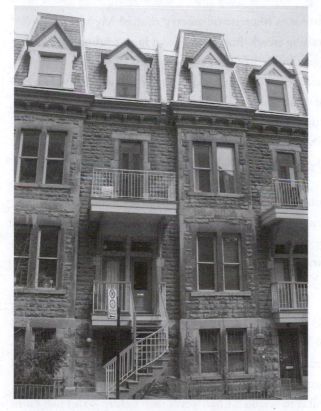

3663 rue Jeanne-Mance (right door, two uppermost floors), Glassco's final Montreal address.

Scobie had come to present Glassco with his most recent book, *McAlmon's Chinese Opera*, which would win a Governor General's Award. A long poem, imagining Robert McAlmon's reflections on his life, the title had been inspired by the drunken evening at Bricktop's that had featured so vividly in *Memoirs of Montparnasse*. Indeed, it was through Glassco's writing that Scobie had been introduced to his subject. He'd not only dedicated the book to Glassco but had included a depiction of the memoirist's younger self as "… open, / naive as a child, susceptible, spending his body like a man / might spend his money who felt ill at ease / at being rich when all his friends were poor."[96]

After Scobie had left, Glassco negotiated the steep, slippery flight of stairs outside his apartment, descending to the snow-covered Montreal street. He ate a sandwich alone at a local café and returned to find that the mail had brought an issue of *Poetry* edited by his friend Daryl Hine. Glassco took the little magazine upstairs to his workroom next to their bedroom. It was small, with a desk and old bed upon which he would often relax, reading after lunch. A few minutes later he called to Marion and asked that she bring something for indigestion. She prepared a bicarbonate of soda and went upstairs to find her husband half on and half off the bed, lying still, not breathing.

Sheila Fischman, who lived just around the corner, was the first person Marion called. "I've never forgotten Marion's words," says Fischman, "because they were so at once literary and touching. She said, 'Oh, Sheila, Buffy has died.' So, I went racing over. It was the one time in our lives that we ever embraced; she was not like that."[97]

The last words written by John Glassco take the form of an inscription in Stephen Scobie's copy of *Memoirs of Montparnasse*. Even then, ever the perfectionist, he composed a rough draft on a small scrap of paper:

For Stephen Scobie, with affection and kindest regards from one of the minor – and only surviving! – characters in his poem –
    Buffy Glassco
    February 2 '81[98]

The date, 2 February 1981 – the twenty-fifth anniversary of Robert McAlmon's death – was incorrect. Four days in the future, it was a sad anniversary that Glassco did not live to see.

Coda

"I remember him saying to me, 'I'm not afraid of death itself; it is the dying, not the death that disturbs me,'" Fraser Sutherland recalls. "'All that fussing about' – he somehow assumed he might be attended to by people."[1] Half a century earlier, as a young man struggling for life in the Royal Victoria Hospital, Glassco had experienced that fussing about; mercifully, he avoided it when his end came.

News of Glassco's death far exceeded the extensive coverage accorded that of his wealthy and powerful grandfather. Across the country there were obituaries and affectionate tributes. "The rare things about John Glassco, the writer, and John Glassco, the man," wrote M.T. Kelly in the *Globe and Mail*, "was how similar they were. Glassco's seemingly effortless prose was matched in life by a graciousness, the kind of good manners that seemed as great a gift as his talent. He had the ability to fill all that he wrote, and much of what he said, with grace." Quoting the passage from *Memoirs of Montparnasse* in which Glassco describes his arrival in Paris, Kelly concluded: "Anyone who can create such a mood, who can feel the ecstacy in this world has given us far more than a place or even a dream of excellence and beauty. John Glassco has left us with a sense of joy that he existed. He has left us with, above all else, a sense of possibilities."

The funeral took place four days after his death, at noon on the second of February, the date he'd mistakenly recorded in his last piece of writing. The setting, for the last time, was St James the Apostle, the church associated with key events in his story: his parents' lavish wedding and his marriages to Elma and Marion.

All took place according to his wishes. Glassco's body, wrapped in a plain shroud and placed in a cheap casket covered by a plain black pall, was not embalmed. The service was as brief as the Book of Common Prayer would permit; there was no eulogy and no personal reminiscences. It was the most simple of funerals, attended by a small gathering of friends and acquaintances: Michael Gnarowski, Louis Dudek, Mordecai Richler, and William Weintraub, among them. A young woman, whom no one appeared to know, wept loudly at the back of the church.

There was no mourners' limousine, the result of an unfortunate error made by the funeral director. Joel McCormick's bright orange Lada was pressed into service as lead escort, following the hearse as it wound its way through city streets to Mount Royal Cemetery. The body was cremated that same afternoon.

A widow at age fifty-six, Marion never remarried. In 1994, she suffered the first of a series of strokes that left her unable to work and robbed her of her sharp mind. She died in January 2004, one month short of her eightieth birthday.

For a short time she'd held onto the small house in Foster. Her last social occasion there came in June 1981, five months after Glassco's funeral, when she played hostess at the final gathering in celebration of Buffy's false birthday. The next morning, she set out with William Toye, looking for a suitable place in which to scatter her husband's ashes. It was Toye who first noticed the spot, what he describes as "a pretty scene."[2] Together editor and widow made their way toward a gentle stream, carrying two small plastic bags of ashes. Toye remembers being slightly surprised. "I don't know what I expected," he recalls. "Mixed in with the ash was something like bone, small pieces of bone."[3] Yet, when Marion poured out the contents of each bag, the bone and ash disappeared, vanishing on contact with the water. Just as he had wished, the physical being that had been John Glassco left no trace.

Appendix:
"Extract from an Autobiography

The only extant Glassco work from the time covered in Memoirs of Montparnasse, *"Extract from an Autobiography" was published in the spring 1929 number of* This Quarter. *It is reprinted here for the first time. Typographical errors and misspellings from the original have been retained.*

In the winter of 1928, George Graham and I were living in an apartment on Metcalfe Street in Montreal. We were working in the Sun Life Assurance Company of Canada, and we have many times since then agreed that that month and a half was the most wretched period of our lives. To get up at eight o'clock of a Canadian winter morning, to bathe insufficiently in a small bathtub which neither of us ever had the courage to clean, to dress without attention to an individual appearance, and to stumble down the street with our cheekbones nipped by the frosty wind, all these things might have been endured more easily had there not been the prospect of a day's work before us.

I had entered the employment of the Company for reasons which, at the time, seemed to justify my doing anything. The stupidity and pettiness of McGill University disgusted me greatly, and my father and mother could not understand why I was unable to ignore it all and merely bend to my books. One episode in my dealings with the teaching staff at McGill comes to mind, when an instructor with whom I was taking a course in writing, passed criticism on a short story of mine with the words: "After all, it is only the work of a night." I did not ask him if he had considered himself any less because he owed his being to activities of an even shorter duration, but begged him to give me a fuller appreciation of the story. He then showed me that his understanding of it extended to the name and sex of the principal character.

On my telling my father that I refused to go to college an longer (I was seventeen yerads old, and starting my third year), and would he allow me to write, I was told I was a great disappointment to him and to my mother, that I was ungrateful and lacking in manliness, and that I could go to work; I would be allowed to remain at home. Thus it was that at this period of my relations with my family that I decided to leave the house and live with my dearest friend. It was a fine gesture and took them quite by surprise.

In return for his services at the Sun Life Assurance Company George received ninety dollars a month, and I eighty. Neither he nor I had ever worked in an office before, but the difference of ten dollars in our monthly cheques was due to George's having attended that same university of McGill for two years longer than I had. These were miserable enough sums to live on, but our condition was bettered considerably through the financial help of two acquaintances, who when they heard that we were taking an apartment, put on their dark overcoats and bowler hats and visited us with a proposal – that they should each of them pay ten dollars of our rent every month for the privilege of using the room on certain nights. Their manner of making this proposal was dark and strange, as if they were plotting to overthrow the Dominion, and they rigorously avoided any vulgarity in speech. George and I were more than glad to take their money, although we found it hard to repress our smiles as these gay rounders gazed craftily around the room, surveying the shutters, curtains, locks and bolts. Indeed, in a moment of merriment I leapt upon the bed, bouncing up and down several times, and crying, "You see, it is solid and sound!" They were greatly upset, and left as soon as possible after the business had been transacted.

We found the extra twenty dollars a fine addition to our monthly income, and we were hardly discommoded by having to remain away from our apartment until late on certain nights of the week – less so than we had at first thought, when it transpired that one of the men was never at the place, undoubtedly owing to the fact that he could obtain no one who would accompany him thither. This, however, he would not admit, continuing to pay us his money in an embarrassed silence when pressed for it. I remembered him in preparatory school many years ago, when he had won a medal for being the best boy in the school, and it amused me to reflect that in spite of all his evil intentions he was still fulfilling the role.

After a month or so I patched up a peace with my father, with whom I pleaded that I be given an allowance which he could afford, and be left to my own devices.

"But I am not going to have you do nothing," he said to me, "because I don't believe that idleness makes for happiness. Why don't you study English Literature, or some foreign language?

After a great deal of hypocrisy on my part, and of generosity o his, he consented to give me a hundred dollars a month for seven years. I was greatly touched by this, and overcome with delight, although I do not believe that I would have been so fortunate had I not said things about myself, my ambitions and literature that make me blush when I recall them. I left the presence of my father with a mixture of joy and shame.

"It is awfully difficult to know what to do; I've never had any experience of bringing up boys with literary aspirations – there's never been one in the family," said my father.

After a great deal of argument and pleading I persuaded George to leave the hated offices of the Sun Life, and agree to come with me to Paris, where we could both live more cheaply than anywhere else. Before he had finally agreed, we had sat many evenings in the Traymore Cafeteria, I urging, he remaining silent and thinking of my financial good.

"But George, you know that I cannot go to Paris without you. I can go nowhere without you. To think of you living alone here, without me whom you love so much, sweating in the policy vaults of that organization down the next street, and coming in here by yourself in the evening, looking around – do you think I could enjoy myself in Paris, had I ten women in my bed every night?" I delivered this earnestly.

George sunk himself a little further in his chair, his mouth puffing out, and his eyebrows drew together with concern for my physical well-being abroad.

"But this is so ridiculous. Where will we get to eventually by doing this? You know I would love it, but remember that you have a future ahead of you – there is no reason why you should not succeed in writing something good, and you can certainly do that without me along, to persuade you that your work is better than it is." He beamed at me, adding, "And you confess that you would like to be a celebrated 'man of letters.'"

It was a long time before he came around, and I had to make out little plans and charts at the table, showing how we could both live on the money. When he finally consented I immediately fetched a newspaper and turned to the shipping page in great excitement.

"If we could only get over on a freight boat, George, run by the Canadian Government Merchant Marine – they're awfully cheap, but one has to have a lot of influence higher up to wrangle a passage on them."

I was interrupted by George, who remembered that his cousin's husband, was legal advisor to the Canadian National Railways, and that it was more than probable that he could get us a cheap passage in some clever and unethical way.

O the bustle and confusion, the waiting in offices downtown, the anxiety and dread we had while strings were being pulled – I remember all these very clearly now. And I remember the note George's brother, pushed under the door of our apartment, telling us that at last our passage had been arranged, and that we were to sail on the *Canadian Traveller*, leaving St John, New Brunswick, on the fourth of February, and carrying us as far as London. George received a free passage, and I was to pay a half-fare of fifty dollars.

The news so excited us that George went out and bought a black felt hat, sriding out of the shop with it on his head. He hated Montreal more than even I did, I think.

We were both in the mood for fine celebration, and it happened fortunately that that night we were both taking a beautiful girl, Mona McMaster, out to a show, and afterwards to the night-club on St. Catherine Street which is called "the Venetian Gardens." As the evening was to be our last in Montreal (we were leaving the next day) we decided to do everything as nicely as possible.

In front of the glittering Mount Royal Hotel we hired an open sleigh, smothered in buffalo robes, with a strong white horse between the shafts. We were bundled into it by the aged French-Canadian driver, who adjusted the fur robes over our knees and stomachs and tucked them in our sides. We gave him Mona's address in Westmount to drive to, a mile and a half away through the city, and we slid away.

The white horse trotted along the bright street, the bells on his neck jingling pleasantly, while the cold night wind made me nestle comfortably in the collar of my fur coat. The sky was full of stars, and I thought that we could not have chosen a finer night on which to call for a woman in a sleigh. Automobiles whizzed past us, many of them taxis. Had it been an ordinary night, we would have called for Mona in a taxi. In the rear window of one that passed I saw two heads, one leaning uncomfortably against the other, and I chuckled to think of this depressing country I was leaving. This common picture of two heads, in the rear window of an automobile, seemed to me the epitome of well-bred youth in Canada. Still smiling, I remembered how I had been one of them myself for a few months, some years ago when my social ambitions made me a well-known figure at coming-out dances.

The wind blew more strongly against my face, as we came into the wider streets of Westmount.

My recollections took another turn, farther back, when driving in a sleigh as a child of eight or nine I had been flushed and happy. Those drives on Sunday afternoons with my mother and my elder brother David came back to me with a fine clarity – we had driven on the mountain in the sunshine, among the crowds of people out walking, and with the ski-ers shooting down the steep snow-covered hills, and my brother and I had been pointed out as handsome children.

As I write at this moment, the memory of that night in very strong, as strong as was the memory of my childhood. I sit at this table in the apartment George and I have taken in Paris, and it is late in the evening. George, in a pair of blue pajamas, lies all humped up in bed, his face stares at me, crushed up sideways in pillow. He is sleepy, and has been waiting for a long time for me to stop writing and go to bed. As I bend again to write, his voice startles me suddenly in the silence that has not been interrupted in the last half hour.

"I saw you as an old man with whiskers, writing."

When Mona saw the sleigh in which we called for her she did not outwardly evince the delight which most women might have, but all the way from Westmount to the theatre her face bore the expression which I am sure my own did when I was a happy child. I myself felt that it was all very pretty. George was in high spirits, having succeeded in sitting with his left side-face towards Mona. He had carefully planned this beforehand because he thinks his profile is much better when seen that way. I sat opposite to them both, my knees pressed against hers, feeling now and then a pleasant twinge of desire. She and George had known each other since their childhood, and I envied each of them for those years. George was in love with her in a fantastic way, and had written a poem the day after we had taken her to the Mount Royal Hotel to dance. I remember this much:

> *"Now that the cabaret was in candlelight I forgot your virginal heaviness for some one said your clothes were only a week after the latest style. You might as well have worn a party dress and several starched petticoats, fluffed them out to sit on the floor where you ate pistachio ice-cream at twilight ..."*

George had wanted to read the poem to her, but had thought the words 'virginal heaviness' might hurt her feelings. So he could only tell her he had written a poem.

The fare for the cab-drive came to two dollars, and when I paid it we went into the dark theatre. The show proved rather poor, but it did not bore us as much as it might have. As for Mona I believe she was rather disappointed in the performance that had been greatly advertised in Montreal, but she kept turning from one of us to the other, smiling very charmingly. Her large dark eyes looking into mine excited me immoderately. George told me afterwards that it was an unconscious habit of hers to stare straight into the eyes of whomever she was addressing.

After the show was over we wakled along St. Catherine Street for the few blocks that separated us from the 'Venetian Gardens,' enjoying the cool air after the warmth of the theatre. Outside, on the sidewalk before the night-club, the taxi-drivers were lounging and smoking.

"The Venetian Gardens" was a place that had been in existence for a number of years, and at the present time was being patronised by the younger set of Montreal, together with a large sprinkling of Jews. Nevertheless it was the most beautiful room in the city for cabaret – very large and with a low ceiling, the tables being set around the dance floor; along one entire side of the room were french windows, letting in the night sky. That night we ordered red wine and I danced the first dance with Mona.

As the evening wore on I found that the Italian wine I was drinking made me feel very well, and very charitably disposed towards those people of Montreal who for the last three years had offended my adolescent mind. At one time I walked across the floor to speak to Dodo Dawson an occasional song-and-dance man in vaudeville and at times a trader in pelts in the far

North-West. His elder brother, Morris Dawson, was a devout Catholic and played the piano. Morris was often bothered by the thought that he might be taken for a Jew on account of his name and musicianship but nothing bothered Dodo when he had someone to talk to. I told Dodo I was leaving, saying good-bye to him, and he, not to be outdone, said he was thinking of going to Paris, to work as a gigolo. He was a beautiful dancer, and good-looking, but he has a very serious impediment of speech.

"If you work as a gigolo," I smiled, "you might capture an American heiress. That is the conventional fairy-tale."

He puffed out his chest like a pigeon, but then turned tenderly to his companion, a girl in a red dress who looked like a spaniel. He took her hand and looked at me.

"H-h- here's my only l-little hei-hei-hei-heiress," he said. I remembered someone telling me he had been trying to seduce this girl for three weeks.

George, who very seldom dances, was on this occasion stepping around the floor very nimbly. I sat and watched the dancers, and listened to the conversation going on at the tables around me. Nothing of moment occurred, except that I drank a great deal more Chianti than was good for my stomach.

In the vestibule of Mona's home in Westmount George took his final leave of her, as he told me later. I remained in the taxi, envying them their sentimental parting; I myself had no one to sentimentalise over, because the only person I loved was coming with me. These reflections were disturbed by the gradual suspicion that I was going to be sick, and I recalled the red wine with a quiver of displeasure.

George rejoined me and we drove home through the empty, well-lit streets. Later I lay in bed, not daring to close my eyes lest things should start whirling around, as they did as soon as I tried to sleep. George was sleeping soundly, apparently with no thought of his supplemental examination in a few hours, the passing of which would determine whether or not he was to become a Bachelor of Arts. This examination he had failed to pass twice beore, yet had this time paid the ten dollar fee out of his small resources for another try. He had carried with him for a week a large book on the subject, written by the best authority, but had never had the time to study it. He slept, smiling slightly and I left the room, proceeding down the hall to the w.c., which we shared with other tenants on the ground floor.

Returning down the hall I was astonished to hear a violent knocking and banging on the street door, which caused me no little displeasure. I felt disinclined to open, wishing to seek my bed immediately, but the noise increased and I heard my name being hallooed nervously, but strenuously, from the outside.

I opened the door, and a fat little lecher whom I knew very well, entered, with a woman in a red hat at his heels. I drew my dressing-gown about me as a cold blast of wind blew in with them, and closed the door. Bertie was buttoned up in his coon-skin coat and his serious, circular face, above the outstanding fur collar, resembled a hen sitting on its nest. He had pushed the woman in the red hat behind him, and was explaining, in a hoarse whisper, his reason for calling in at five o'clock in the morning.

"You can get into bed with George for a bit, can't you?" he asked, "I won't be long – don't turn me down for God's sake because I haven't got the price of a room. Just for old times' sake …?"

"Why, certainly, if you wish," I replied, striving hard not to laugh frantically. I was half asleep and barely master of my limbs, but opened the door for him and his companion to enter the pitch-black room. He bundled the woman in ahead of him.

"In the same room?" I asked rather stupidly feeling that the whole business was rather bizarre, but he replied that the lights would be out.

I climbed into George's bed, lying like a log. For a long time they seemed to be muttering away by the other bed, and kept wishing that they would hurry up before I fell asleep. Then I heard Bertie cursing softly with rage, and the bed creaked as they stood up.

Before I fell quite asleep I remember Bertie saying something to me about his companion being an honest woman, and she didn't like the fact that two other men were in the room as well, and so they had to go, although he didn't want to. Then they went out, and I fell asleep.

I woke late next morning, and shaved and dressed with care, for it was my last day in Montreal. While I was at my toilet, our landlady, a woman called Mrs Casey, who looked like a witch, knocked sharply at my door and entered. I hated her very much, but bowed good morning.

"I was thinkin' Mr. Stinson," she said in her polite, but barbed, manner, her eyes shooting around the room and occasionally resting on me, "that I should receive something for the state you've got this room in. I've never had a tenant who done like you and the other gentleman does. So if you could give me something for the cleanin' up it'll require …"

"Yes, yes, Mrs. Casey," I said reassuringly, wishing to get her out the room on such a beautiful morning. "I will fix that up. Of course I can understand the way you feel about it, but do not bother about my settling everything in full."

After smirking ghoulishly and thanking me in the profuse and apologetic way that made her so odious, she left, making vain hints that I should pay her then.

I resolved that Mrs. Casey should not receive a cent from me that was not stipulated in the lease. She was a horrid creature, and could often be heard beating her children in the stuffy basement that she inhabited. "Get into bed now, you little bugger!" she would cry, after whipping her young son.

The loveliness of the bright morning exhilarated me. The snow, the air, the creaking underfoot on the hard-packed side-walk, and one's breath making a fine, white cloud – all is so hard and gem-like in Canada at eleven in the morning. Three blocks away, I thought, the morning is curling its edges around the thick walls of the Sun Life Assurance Company, while inside the men and women are all busy denying their dark gods. Their prospectus says that their head office staff numbers "fourteen hundred workers, beside many others in the branch offices, and those carrying the banner in the field."

I was going to wait for George at the McGill Union, and hear how he had fared as a prospective Bachelor of Arts. Of course, he had no illusions about the distinction of a degree from McGill University, and placed no value on its bearer in the world of commerce. The fact was that George had spent four years at college, and in his dogged way was determined to have what others would consider the great reward. In addition, he had been disgustingly treated by many of the teaching staff, particularly by the head of the English Department, to whom George had imprudently revealed a taste in letters which went beyond an appreciation of Byron Burns, Bliss Carman, Joe Howe, Stevenson and Sir James Barrie. George's relations with this back-woodsman make amusing reading, and the chapter in his book *Shadow Play*, entitled *Si tu es pot de chamber tant pis pour toi*, is a delightful treatment of the whole affair.

I strode along St. Catherine Street on my way to the Union, with groups of shop-girls, on the early lunch-hour, passing by in their closely-wrapped coats, and the young men slouching along, with varnished hair and wide-bottomed trousers. When I arrived in the union George was not yet come from his examination, so I sat in the lobby. Many acquaintances, and people I had been pleasant to in my charitable moments at college, came around. On hearing that I was going away they immediately inquired, practically, what I was 'going to do,' and when Paris was mentioned they made appropriately stupid and disgusting remarks. I remember a swarthy well-bred Jew who might have sat for the portrait of "Brennbaum," by Ezra Pound, saying: "Well, goodbye, and don't do anything I wouldn't do." I had once been slightly interested in him on account of his musical ability, but since then he had come to believe that the company of Christian louts and football players was more compelling a statement of his social standing than any other. I am sure that he derived great comfort from Blake's pathetic poem beginning,

My mother bore me in the Southern-wild,
And I am black, but O, my soul is white!
White as an angel is the English child,
But I am black, as if bereaved of light.'

I rose from my seat in the lobby, deciding to wait for George on the steps of the building. Lounging there, an amusing spectacle was afforded me, when the Dean of the Faculty of arts, because he is a Canadian, passed on the opposite side of the street, looking like a green-grocer, with his cane, gloves, and morning trousers. Unaware that anyone was watching him, he turned his head and shoulders completely round to gape lecherously at the calves of a trim co-ed who had just passed him. When he saw me, motionless on the steps, watching him, he buried his face in his collar and scurried for cover around the corner.

A little later saw George trudging down the campus, and in front, almost obscuring him, the immense figure of Sir Arthur Currie, Principal of University and ex-War Lord of the Canadian Expeditionary Force. I could not help but observe what a poor figure George cut behind this white-spatted symbol of the Army, attired like the editor of *Vanity Fair*. George might have a BA, but Currie had a dozen honorary degrees and a good high-school education.

George did not know whether he had passed his examination or not, as he had twice before been sure of success and then found he had failed. But we did not bother long about the matter, as we had to pack and do many things before we caught the train to St. John at seven o'clock that evening.

As I was midway in my packing, hurrying in a frantic haste to get everything ready before half-past six, George suddenly stopped throwing what clothes he had into an old canvas-backed trunk and turned to me.

"Hurry." I cried, "we've got loads to do, and if we miss this train we may never get out of Canada," I confess that I was at that time quite sick with nervousness, imagining that fate was preparing some awful blow for us, to keep us in Canada.

"You know." George said with determination. "I left my fountain-pen by mistake, with a stenographer in the Sun Life. I have had that pen for five years, and no sentimental stenographer is going to get it. It's an expensive pen, too. So I'll just run down to the office and get it from her now – we've got lot's of time, it's only a quarter to six, and I'll be right back to help you finish packing your books."

In vain I protested. He bundled into his coat and his black hat and disappeared through the door.

I continued to pack, cramming all my clothes into the trunk indiscriminately, a thing I hate doing, and crushing my suits in a disgraceful manner. I kept thinking of George and his pen, and the black-haired sensual creature who had it. George, I knew, was a queer enigma in the office he had worked in, and the women had vainly tried to rouse him to speak to them on terms of serious equality. At first his cold, Danish stare had made them giggle, and later his candid remarks, with their revelation of an antique world, set them wondering if he was not a sort of Pan. They found only momentary refuge in the word "conceited," and became weirdly attracted. Then there was a conversation with a pretty Irish typist who had learnt he was going away.

"I'd love to go wit you," she said, smiling slightly.

Wishing to make the situation less enviable, he replied that we would be very poor in Paris, and be in rags and tags.

"That wouldn't matter. I'd go with you, any way at all."

George burst into the room in high spirits. He had succeeded in recovering his pen from the reluctant stenographer and in addition he had met those two rogues who had used our room with the former's woman, all chatting on the steps of the Sun Life Building; in the background a stuttering fool, C.H., was capering, trying to say goodbye before George should hurry away. The former two had been a little flustered at seeing him, just when they thought they had seen the last of both of us. We, who knew their secret, were going away – although their gladness on this account was tempered, I am sure, by a feeling of loss: they had no homelike, sung apartment now, and the woman, R— W—, had looked a little sad, so George said. Then he set to work to help me pack.

All our things were finally stowed, making a great deal of luggage, and we realized that we would have to have three taxis to take us to the station. Soon the room was filled with burly taxi-drivers who fought among themselves as to who should carry the lighter articles. The smallest of the men, who was eventually left with my immense trunk to carry out, was rewarded with my over-shoes, which I would need no longer, and the keys to the apartment.

"Give the keys to the landlady, won't you?" I asked, for conscience's sake, knowing full well that he probably would not. I was surprised that Mrs. Casey had not appeared before this, to demand something for the state of the room. Only when everything was loaded into the taxis did I see her. She came out on the steps, jumping up and down with rage and trying to make herself heard above the roar of the taxis. So George gave orders to proceed swiftly to the station, and we moved off. There being no room inside, George and I were forced to hang on the side of one of the cars; thus we had a fine view of St. Catherine Street, all lighted up, as our fleet of taxis skidded and bumped over the street-car tracks in the direction of Bonaventure Station. It was a pleasant thing to be seeing the last of Montreal in this fashion.

Almost until the very moment of boarding the train I had been sick with reasonless anxiety, but when all the business of baggage was complete, and George and I were striding along the station platform behind a porter, our arms full of overcoats, then I relaxed. Under the great roof which covered the lines of the tracks, with the engines shooting off steam all around, I felt my great moment of exaltation as we walked alongside the train bound for the Port of St. John.

Acknowledgments

My first debt is to William Toye, John Glassco's literary executor, for his support and kind permission to quote from Glassco's published and unpublished writing. Bill welcomed me into his home, and has provided invaluable feedback and advice during the past six years.

This biography benefits greatly from the good work of Michael Gnarowski, whose introduction and annotations to the 1995 second edition of *Memoirs of Montparnasse* have shaped my approach to the work.

Through Glassco's friendship with Robert McAlmon I entered a lively correspondence with McAlmon biographer Sanford J. Smoller. It was Sanford who alerted me to the existence of *The Nightinghouls of Paris* – then unpublished.

I am grateful to the following people for sharing their memories of Glassco: Margaret Atwood, George Bowering, Brian Brett, Greta Chambers, Kildare Dobbs, George Fetherling, Sheila Fischman, Diana Gnarowski, Daryl Hine, Ann Johansson, D.G. Jones, Marcy Kahan, M.T. Kelly, Seymour Mayne, Christy McCormick, Joel McCormick, Stephen Morrissey, Kim Ondaatje, P.K. Page, Edward O. Phillips, Jim Polk, Gilbert Rhicard, Debbie Rotherman, Peter G.M. Smith, Marna Tucker, and Ken Woodman. In particular, I wish to thank Fraser Sutherland, whose *John Glassco: An Essay and Bibliography* also proved an invaluable aid in my research.

William Weintraub was generous in sharing his memories of Glassco – "the great Miles Underwood" – and helped guide me through a Montreal nightlife that is now five decades gone.

Pennie Redmile and Patrick Wholer assisted in my research into the Rawlings and Glassco families. Stanley Whyte was kind enough to visit and confirm or correct my memories of several Montreal addresses at which Glassco had lived.

Late in this process, Jim Dooley generously visited Library and Archives Canada on my behalf, checking into various questions that had eluded me on previous visits. Amy Creighton performed a similar function in going through Glassco's childhood writings at the McGill Libraries, Rare Books and Special Collections Division and, with Cathy Blundell, assisted in my efforts to track down information on the Foster Horse Show.

Many people were kind enough to answer my queries: Nelson Ball, Heidi Bauer, Monique Bosco, Bob and Raye Briscoe, Susan Briscoe, Barry Callaghan, Irwin Cohen, Wayne Cooper, Patrick Crean, Kathy D'Alesio, Sandra Djwa, Hugh Doherty, Janine Fuller, Gary Geddes, Stephen J. Gertz, Jay A. Gertzman, Anton Gill, Alwynn Gillett, Briony Glassco, Alex Goss, Michael Hadley, David Helwig, Kevin Holland, Peter Howard, Bob Huggins, Donald Jay, Patrick J. Kearney, Earl Kemp, Brian Kirby, James King, Eric Koch, Dennis Lee, Jeremy Lewis, Aron Malkine, Ginny McCormick, Peter F. McNally, Joan Mellen, Peter Morris, John Morrissey, Desmond Morton, Philip Nobile, Michael Ondaatje, Florence Richler, Linda Rogers, J.B. Rund, Peter Dale Scott, Jenaterina Shirai, Marlene Simmons, Lee Skallerup, Joseph W. Slade, Sandra Spanier, Nicolas Steinmetz, Scott Taylor, Tyrone Tillery, and Bruce Whiteman.

Fern Malkine-Falvey, daughter of Georges Malkine, provided information on her father's first wife, Yvette Ledoux. With her help, I was able to correct some false assumptions in the story of this sadly forgotten Canadian expatriate. My research into the writings of Ken Sato, another overlooked figure in the writings on Montparnasse, benefited by correspondence with Professor Eishiro Ito of Iwate Prefectural University.

Professor Bruce Ryder of Osgoode Hall Law School, York University, answered my questions concerning the banning of *The Temple of Pederasty*.

Assistance in my research into the background of Elma Koolmer was provided by Harry Jaako, Honorary Consul, Republic of Estonia, and Peeter Kekmann of the State Archives of Estonia.

Doctor James Martin of the McGill University Health Centre was kind enough to answer my questions concerning tuberculosis and the treatment described by Glassco in his Intimate Journal. My limited knowledge and understanding of the issues of mental health was broadened through conversations with Doctor William Davies and Doctor Peter Uhlmann.

Ataraxia of the International Association of Rubberists was kind enough to permit me to post queries concerning early rubber fetish literature on the association's website.

I have also benefited from discussions and correspondence with Marc Côté, Adrian King-Edwards, Diane Martin, Brian Trehearne, and my much missed friend Sonja Skarstedt.

I am fortunate in having been assisted by a great many librarians and archivists: Anne Goddard, Catherine Hobbs, Sophie Lacasse, Daniel Somers, and Alfred Deschênes at Library and Archives Canada; Doctor Richard Virr of the McGill Libraries, Rare Books and Special Collections Division; Mary House of the McGill University Archives; François Cartier at the McCord Museum; Mary Glezos of the Friends of Mount Royal Cemetery; Sharon Cozens at Selwyn House School; Pat Hitchcock at Queen's University; Jennifer Toews of the Thomas Fischer Rare Book Library at the University of Toronto; Kim Arnold of the Presbyterian Church of Canada, Archives and Records Office; Professor Michael Peterman at Trent University; Janice Millard at the Trent University Archives; Barbara Edwards at the Vancouver

Public Library; John Monahan and Anne Marie Menta of the Beinecke Rare Book and Manuscript Library at Yale University; Scott Krafft of the McCormick Library of Special Collections, Northwestern University Library; and John Dobbins and Jean Paule of Occidental College.

Diana and Michael Gnarowski, Karl and Linda Feige, Patrick J. Kearney, and Sanford Smoller read various drafts of this biography, providing much appreciated feedback.

Katheryn Mulders and Samantha Haywood provided considerable support for a project that took a great deal longer and was considerably more complicated than originally anticipated.

I am grateful to the British Columbia Arts Council, whose support aided the completion of this biography.

I am indebted to family and friends who provided food, drink, shelter, transportation, and encouragement: Pauline Busby, Karl and Linda Feige, Mark Gundel, Stéphanie Lemyre, Melissa Pitts, Nicole Freeman, and Stanley Whyte. Michael Bartsch proved an insightful travelling companion with a talent for navigation.

This book owes its existence in no small measure to Mark Abley, whose enthusiasm, encouragement, and editorial guidance helped usher it into print. The biography was further improved by the editorial work of Claude Lalumière; his sharp eyes and patience are much appreciated.

And finally my greatest debt is to my wife Anyès Kadowaki, and to our daughter Astrid, with whom begins each new day.

Notes

The following abbreviations are used throughout the notes:

AJMSP	The Arthur James Marshall Smith Papers
J.G.	John Glassco
JGf	The John Glassco fonds
JGp	The John Glassco papers
LEp	The Leon Edel papers
RMA	The Robert McAlmon Archive

Unless otherwise indicated, all citations are to the first edition.

INTRODUCTION

1 J.G., *Memoirs of Montparnasse*, 38.
2 Malcolm Cowley, "We Had Such Good Times," 28.
3 George Woodcock, "Literary Worlds and Their Denizens," 67.
4 Ibid.
5 Leon Edel, "Introduction," J.G., *Memoirs of Montparnasse*, x.
6 Louis Dudek, "Look on the Book as Fantasy."
7 Ibid.
8 J.G., as quoted in Stephen Scobie, "The Mirror on the Brothel Wall: John Glassco, *Memoirs of Montparnasse*."
9 Michael Gnarowski, letter to the author, 14 September 2008.
10 Louis Dudek, *In Defence of Art*, 164.
11 J.G., "Journal, Feb. 25, 1970 to July 5, '75," 26 October 1973, JGf.
12 J.G., Intimate Journal, 29 July 1934, JGp.
13 Louis Dudek, Notebooks: 1960–1994, 231.

CHAPTER ONE

1 J.G., "Search."
2 W.H. Glassco, Sons & Co. Advertisement, *The Globe & Mail.* 6 December 1871, 3.

3 John Girdlestone "Jack" Glassco, brother of A.P.S., also remained in Montreal after his graduation from McGill. He first found work in the meter department at the Royal Electric Company, then as a lecturer at his alma mater. He later worked in Los Angeles and based his decision to return to Canada on the toss of a coin. In 1909, Jack Glassco settled in Winnipeg, where for thirty-two years he headed Winnipeg City Hydro. Described as "the father of cheap electricity in Western Canada," he was likened to Sir Adam Beck. News of his retirement in 1944 received national attention.

4 At the time of his death, it was claimed that Edward Rawlings's maternal grandfather, the Reverend Dr Millar, rector of Killalce, served as chaplain to Edward, Duke of Kent, the father of Queen Victoria.

5 Later board members of the Canadian branch included François LeClaire, William Workman, and Robert Cassels. Sir Hugh Allan was serving on the board at the time of the society's collapse. Allan's position almost certainly contributed to the transfer of clients to his Citizens' Insurance Company of North America.

6 Until 1881, the business was known as the Canada Guarantee Company.

7 "Death Claims Prominent Man in Business Life," *The Montreal Daily Herald*, 13 December 1911, 2.

8 Personals, *The Montreal Daily Star*, 19 September 1905, 13.

9 Ibid.

10 Births, *The Montreal Daily Star*, 15 December 1909, 19.

11 In a 1975 interview with David Cobb, Glassco claimed that there had, in fact, been only three governesses, the last of whom, Hester Marryat, A.P.S. had dismissed for failing to administer the corporal punishment that he himself wished to provide. I have been unable to confirm the existence of the beloved Hester Marryat; she does not appear in the 1901 and 1911 censuses, nor does her name feature in baptism and burial listings for the Province of Quebec. Glassco dedicated the 1976 General Publishing edition of *Harriet Marwood, Governess*, the only to appear under his name:

> *To the Memory of*
> HESTER MARRYAT
> *(1885–1925)*

As far as I'm aware, this is the only mention of Miss Marryat's name in Glassco's writing, published or otherwise.

12 J.G., "Autobiographical Sketch," JGf.

13 Ten storeys in height, the new head office was hardly a skyscraper. The building was completed in 1913 at a cost of $200,000. It has since been demolished; the 500 René-Lévesque Ouest now sits on its site.

14 J.G., quoted in Flavia Morrison, "The Writer Obsessed."

15 Glassco's future sister-in-law, Cecily Hallowell Glassco, would take the same

title in 1935. The Hallowells and Glasscos had been summertime neighbours on Pointe Claire's Golf Avenue during John Glassco's youth.

16 J.G., "Autobiographical Sketch," JGF. There is some evidence that Edward Rawlings was something of a minor inventor. In 1874, as "Co-inventor with and Assignee of A.M. Neave," he registered an "advertising medium containing the advertisement in combination with a match scratch" with the Canadian Patent Office (*The Canadian Patent Office Record*, vol. 4, no. 1, January 1876).

17 Born in November 1909, Lorraine Morgan was the daughter of Frederick Cleveland Morgan (1881-1962), a member of the family that owned the department store Henry Morgan & Co. The manager of the department store's decorative arts department, he was a passionate collector. In 1917, he helped to establish the Montreal Museum of Fine Arts' department of decorative arts and served as voluntary keeper until his death forty-five years later.

18 The extent of Sir Herbert Holt's influence and reputation is perhaps best reflected in the cheering elicited by the announcement of his death during a 1941 Montreal Royals baseball game.

19 J.G., "Autobiographical Sketch," JGF.

20 Edgar C. Moody and Robert A. Spiers, *Veritas*, 9.

21 J.G., letter to Geoffrey Wagner, 24 April 1970, JGF.

22 Ibid. The President of the Treasury Board at the time of Glassco's writing was Charles Mills "Bud" Drury (1912–1991). A member of Parliament from 1962 to 1978, representing Saint-Antoine-Westmount (later Westmount), Drury held a number of portfolios in the cabinets of Lester Pearson and Pierre Elliott Trudeau. During the time at which Glassco claimed Drury played on the Selwyn House "Senior hockey team," the politician would have been eight years old.

23 J.G., "Most of You Was a Great Smoky Mystery," The Gazette [Montreal], 1. The Beaux-Arts Linton Apartments were constructed in 1905 at the corner of Sherbrooke and Simpson Streets. Both this building and the Linton Mansion (constructed 1868) were across the street from Edward Rawlings's property.

24 J.G., "Autobiographical Sketch," JGF.

25 Ibid.

26 Late in life, Cecily Hallowell Glassco would confirm Glassco's account of the beatings. See Patricia M. Whitney, "Darkness and Delight: A Portrait of the Life and Work of John Glassco," 44.

27 J.G., "Autobiographical Sketch," JGF.

28 J.G., *The Deficit Made Flesh*, 59.

29 J.G., "It's Harder Now to Walk These Streets."

30 J.G., "Autobiographical Sketch," JGF. In the sketch, Glassco writes that in 1958 the Cedar Avenue house was torn down and replaced with an apartment building.

31 J.G., Intimate Journal, 23 August 1935, JGP.

32 J.G., "Autobiographical Sketch," JGF.

33 Ibid.

34 Leon Edel, "The Young Warrior in the Twenties," 8.

35 J.G., "Autobiographical Sketch," JGF.

36 "Death Claims Prominent Man in Business Life." *The Montreal Daily Herald*, 13 December 1911, 2.

37 Henry J. Morgan, *The Canadian Men and Women of the Time*, 846.

38 Walter Vaughan and A.P.S. Glassco, *McGill University Centennial Endowment*, 16. Walter Vaughan and his son aside, the only literary figure of any note that A.P.S. had any contact with was Stephen Leacock. On 12 June 1935, the bursar sent a letter informing the humourist of his forced retirement from McGill.

39 J.G., "Extract from an Autobiography," 200.

40 J.G., "Autobiographical Sketch," JGF. An Edward Rawlings is included in William Carew Hazlitt's *A Roll of Honour: A Calendar of the Names of over 17,000 Men and Women Who throughout the British Isles and in Our Early Colonies Have Collected Mss. and Printed Books from the XIVth to the XIXth Century.*

41 This undated article was published in *The Montreal Standard*. In *John Glassco: A Personal and Working Library*, Fraser Sutherland records the date of publication as circa 1930.

42 Beatrice Glassco, letter to J.G., 24 October 1962, JGF.

43 J.G., Selwyn House notebook, JGP.

44 J.G., *Memoirs of Montparnasse*, 56.

45 A Scot, Douglas C. Adam was a rector's son who took pleasure in quoting the "mild and now-dated sexual innuendoes" of James Branch Cabell. According to Leon Edel, Adam "cultivated urbanity and aphorism; he was more relaxed than Buffy and Graeme" (*Memories of the Montreal Group*, 11). After graduation, he returned to Scotland, where he embarked on a career in journalism. He worked in Glasgow for *The Sunday Mail* and *The Daily Record*. Edel writes that Adam died in "mid-century." The last piece of correspondence from Adam to Edel is dated 12 August 1959.

46 Leon Edel, *Memories of the Montreal Group*, 9.

47 Leon Edel, "Literary Revolution: The 'Montreal Group,'" 117.

48 Ibid.

49 Leon Edel, *Memories of the Montreal Group*, 10.

50 Ibid.

51 *The McGill Fortnightly Review*, 1:1, 21 November 1925, 2.

52 J.G., *The McGill Fortnightly Review*, 1:9–10, 22 March 1926, 73.

53 J.G., letter to Michael Darling, 17 June 1978, JGF.

54 J.G., "Autobiographical Sketch," JGF.

55 The *Alaunia* left the port of Montreal twice in the period during which Glassco claimed to have been a passenger. The first sailing, on 8 May, was perhaps too early for a student attending McGill. If Glassco did sail on the

Alaunia, it likely he was onboard for the ship's 14 June departure.

The second Cunard vessel to bear the name, in 1926 the *Alaunia* was a new ship. It was launched the previous year, making its maiden voyage was between Liverpool and Montreal. The ship was scrapped in 1957. The original *Alaunia* was launched in 1913 and sank three years later, after having struck a German mine off Sussex.

56 J.G., "Autobiographical Sketch," JGf.

57 Ibid. Hoddom Castle was built in the sixteenth century by Sir John Maxwell of Terregles. At the time of Glassco's supposed visit it was owned by the Brooks, a philanthropic family that had made its fortune in silk. In the early twentieth century the Brooks took up residence in nearby Kinmount. During the summers of 1926 and 1927, Hoddom Castle was rented out. Though there exists no evidence to suggest that Glassco did not visit the castle, there is a possibility that he is having a bit of fun in making the claim: Hoddom being a rhyme for Sodom. I am indebted to Mark Gundel for this observation.

58 Ibid.

59 Ibid. Glassco may have been mistaken as to the particular summer in which he first visited Paris. In a letter to A.J.M. Smith (AJMsp), Leon Edel writes: "Buffy Glassco returned from Paris which in no way improved his previous tendencies." The letter is dated 24 October but lacks a year. Content indicates 1927 to be the year of composition: Edel describes *The McGill Fortnightly Review* as "defunct" and relays news that Smith's poem "Varia" appeared in the previous month's *Canadian Forum*. The final issue of *The McGill Fortnightly Review* was published on 27 April 1927. "Varia" appeared in the September 1927 issue of the *Forum*.

60 Leon Edel, "John Glassco (1909-1981) and His Erotic Muse," 109.

61 Ibid.

62 Ibid., 110.

63 J.G. [Euphorian, pseud.], "Collegiana," *The McGill Daily*, 8 December 1926.

64 Louis Schwartz [as L.S.] and J.G. [as J.S.G.], "Collegiana," *The McGill Daily*, 20 October 1926, 2.

65 Ibid.

66 Ibid.

67 "The youth of a country": J.G. [as J.S.G.], "Collegiana," *The McGill Daily*, 27 October 1926.

68 Quoted in J.G. [John of Anjou, pseud.], "Collegiana," *The McGill Daily*, 10 November 1926. In his journal, F.R. Scott dismissed Houdini's appearance as "a ranting vaudevillian turn – it could not be dignified with the name lecture" (Diary, 1926–28, 19 October 1926, F.R. Scott fonds, Library and Archives Canada). With Schwartz, Glassco had taken a swipe at Houdini's visit in a previous column (*The McGill Daily*, 20 October 1926, 2): "They turn out in the largest crowd of many a year to hear a vaudeville lecture on spiritualism – O God!"

The queen consort of Ferdinand I of Romania, Marie was English-born, a granddaughter of Queen Victoria. She is famously mentioned in another poem, Dorothy Parker's "Comment":

Oh, life is a glorious cycle of song,
A medley of extemporanea;
And love is a thing that can never go wrong,
And I am Marie of Roumania.

69 Ibid.

70 Bruga and J.G. [Euphorian, pseud.], "Collegiana," *The McGill Daily*, 24 November 1926, 2.

71 Louis Schwartz [as L.S.] and J.G. [Euphorian, pseud.], "Collegiana," *The McGill Daily*, 12 January 1927, 2.

72 J.G. [Euphorian, pseud.], "Collegiana," *The McGill Daily*, 17 November 1926.

73 "The Goose Step," *The McGill Daily*, 26 January 1927, 2.

74 Louis Schwartz [as L.S.] and J.G. [Euphorian, pseud.], "Collegiana," *The McGill Daily*, 12 January 1927, 2.

75 "The Goose Step," *The McGill Daily*, 16 February 1927, 2.

76 "The Goose Step," *The McGill Daily*, 9 February 1927, 2.

77 PEW, letter, *The McGill Daily*, 18 February 1927, 2.

78 The concerns of Harkness in this regard are not without foundation. Several pieces published in "The Goose Step" amount to injokes. One example is "Externals," a poem featured in the column of 9 February 1927:

Belloc
Looks like a Banker
And
Fat, hairy Chesterton
And Bennett, and Wells
Greengrocers,
And Dean Inge
A Fishmonger,
And A.J.M. Smith

79 "The Goose Step," *The McGill Daily*, 16 February 1927, 2.

80 "The Goose Step," *The McGill Daily*, 23 February 1927, 2.

81 J.G. [anonymous], "Moscow Gold." Allan Latham had expressed similar criticisms of a real book, *Bolshevism in American Labor Unions*, by John A. Dyche (New York: Boni & Liveright, 1926), in the 3 November 1926 edition.

Glassco's fake review of *Moscow Gold* and his prose meditation "Search," published the previous year, were, he maintained, his only contributions to *The McGill Fortnightly Review*. Half a century later, Leon Edel recalled another piece, "Jazz: A Plea for Tolerance," as having been penned by Glassco and Taylor under the name "Carroll Davis." Glassco insisted that he'd had nothing to do with the piece and expressed disbelief that Taylor had been the author (J.G., letter to Michael Darling, 17 June 1978, JGf).

82 Sandra Djwa, *The Politics of the Imagination*, 84. Within Djwa's thorough biography is an interesting account of the efforts taken by Currie, Bovey, the Board of Governors, and the RCMP to investigate communism at McGill.

83 Walter Vaughan and A.P.S. Glassco, *McGill University Centennial Endowment*, 16.

84 Latham's influence on his students and the literary circles of McGill has been overlooked and is only now beginning to emerge. Described by sociologist Helen MacGill Hughes as a man "who knows not Ring Lardner less for knowing Chaucer more," the professor was viewed with great respect and affection. This is reflected in the dedication found in the first and all subsequent editions of A.J.M. Smith's *The Book of Canadian Poetry*: "To the Memory of My Friend and Teacher." Latham's influence is perhaps most evident in the life of Leon Edel. In his book *The Visitable Past*, the acclaimed biographer credits Latham, whom he describes as his favourite professor, as the first to suggest that he write about Henry James.

85 Taylor's title is drawn from "As I Ebb'd with the Ocean of Life," by Walt Whitman:

Ebb, ocean of life, (the flow will return,)
Cease not your moaning you fierce old mother,
Endlessly cry for your castaways, but fear not, deny not me,
Rustle not up so hoarse and angry against my feet as I touch you
or gather from you.

86 Graeme Taylor [Jon Grahame, pseud.], "The Unknown World."

87 J.G., "Autobiographical Sketch," JGf.

88 Ibid.

89 Clive Harcourt Carruthers was the author of *Studies in Greek Noun Formation* (Chicago: University of Chicago, 1926). He is perhaps best remembered for his Latin translation of Lewis Carroll's *Alice's Adventures in Wonderland, Alicia in Terra Mirabilis* (London: Macmillan, 1964), an inscribed copy of which Glassco had in his personal library.

90 J.G., letter to Clive Harcourt Carruthers. Fraser Sutherland, *John Glassco: A Personal and Working Library*. 31.

91 J.G., "Autobiographical Sketch," JGf. Glassco adds that he never lived with a prostitute "as has been alleged." The source of this allegation is unidentified and is likely a figment of his imagination.

92 Ibid.

93 In the "Autobiographical Sketch," Glassco writes that he was convinced to return home "in the fall," but that "inside of two months" he had again left the Cedar Avenue house. By the end of December he was working for Sun Life.

94 Glassco's McGill transcript records: "Left Dec. 10th 1927." Another hand has added "To study in Paris, France." Although the transcript clearly indicates that he completed only two of the four years required to earn his BA, Glassco is included 1929 edition of *Old McGill* as a member of Arts '29.

95 J.G., "Extract from an Autobiography," 198.

96 J.G., *Memoirs of Montparnasse*, 3.

97 In *Memoirs of Montparnasse*, Glassco identifies "Birdlime" as belonging to "McGill's Department of Extramural affairs" (3), a body that did not exist. An educator and lawyer, Bovey (1882–1956) was the author of *Canadien: A Study of French Canadians* (1933) and *The French Canadians Today* (1944).

98 Sandra Djwa, *The Politics of the Imagination*, 133.

99 It is likely that Mona McMaster is a false name. Several other figures featured in "Extract from an Autobiography" appear under pseudonyms.

100 J.G., "Extract from an Autobiography," 203.

101 Ibid., 204.

102 J.G., *Memoirs of Montparnasse*, 8. The *Canadian Traveller* was built in 1921 by the Harbour Marine Company in Victoria for the Merchant Marine. In 1932, it was renamed *Procida* after being purchased by Achille Lauro and Company of Naples. During the Second World War the ship was captured by the British and renamed, with no small amount of irony, the *Empire Volunteer*. It was torpedoed and sunk sixty-five miles west of Rockall by a German U-boat on 15 September 1940.

CHAPTER TWO

1 J.G., *Memoirs of Montparnasse*, 1.

2 Ibid., 9.

3 This observation was first made by Thomas E. Tausky in "*Memoirs of Montparnasse*: 'A Reflection of Myself.'"

4 Leon Edel, *Memories of the Montreal Group*, 10.

5 J.G., *Memoirs of Montparnasse*, 10.

6 Ibid., 1.

7 This observation is made in Anthony Sutcliffe's essay "Montréal, une métropole," in Isabelle Gournay and France Vanlaethem, eds, *Montréal métropole, 1880–1930*.

8 *Memoirs of Montparnasse* contains an imagined conversation between Glassco and the surrealist poet Georges Pol in which the former implies familiarity with the works of Paul Morin, Robert Choquette, and Émile Nelligan. However, in 1957, Glassco told F.R. Scott that he had read only three French Canadian poets: Saint-Denys-Garneau, Jean-Guy Pilon, and Claude Fournier (the latter two were born after Glassco's imagined conversation). No mention of any French Canadian poets is found in Glassco's writings prior to this year.

9 F.R. Scott, *The Collected Poems of F.R. Scott*, 284.

10 It should be noted that A.J.M. Smith had once considered Carman alone

among the Confederation Poets as being worthy of praise. In fact, the first issue of *The McGill Fortnightly Review* features an unsigned editorial penned by Smith, in which the university is commended for having invited "as distinguished a poet as Bliss Carman" [*The McGill Fortnightly Review* 1:1 (21 November 1925): 2.]. Smith would later write of Carman as "a *fin-de-siècle* aesthete turned out of the overstuffed boudoir into the almost equally stuffed out doors" (A.J.M. Smith, ed., *The Book of Canadian Poetry*, 25).

11 Gertrude Stein, *Paris France*, 11.

12 Bertram Brooke (1876–1965) was a member of a peculiar dynasty begun in 1841 when Englishman James Brooke wrestled approximately 125,000 square kilometres of land from the Sultan of Brunei, thus becoming the first White Rajah of Sarawak. As eldest brother of Vyner, the third White Rajah, Bertram was considered heir apparent. In 1946, the Brooke family ceded the territory to the United Kingdom.

13 Robert McAlmon and Kay Boyle, *Being Geniuses Together*, 289.

14 Ibid., 332–3. Boyle adds that they at times incorporated suggestions made by Robert McAlmon. For his part, McAlmon appears to have considered Glassco's contributions of greater value than his own or those of Boyle. In *The Nightinghouls of Paris*, he depicts Sudge, the Glassco character, as someone who worked with diligence and professionalism:

The new script of the memoirs was beautiful, for Sudge typed well and got the manuscript up with professional competence. Later, when the book appeared it had a slight success, but anybody knowing the Princess knew that all the dainty wit and bright malice in the book were Sudge's. Dale had furnished Irish gaiety and wit here and there, but she admitted that Sudge slipped in the best cracks. He had a talent for drawing old dames and gents with cruel caricature, and while his contributions to the book were trivial, the memoirs were so trivial that Sudge's contribution took on profundity. (64)

15 Ibid., 333. According to Boyle, the limerick in question was:

There was an old lady of Sheen
Whose hearing was not very keen.
She said, "It is odd
But I cannot tell God
Save the Weasel from Pop Goes the Queen.

16 Ibid. In *The Nightinghouls of Paris*, Sudge employs the very same method when stealing gramophone records from the Princess of Faraway.

17 J.G., *Memoirs of Montparnasse*, 190.

18 Sylvia Beach, *Shakespeare and Company*, 25.

19 McAlmon also shared his story about Canadian service with William Carlos

Williams, who included the claim in *The Autobiography of William Carlos Williams* (172). In his 1959 monograph, *Robert McAlmon: Expatriate Publisher and Writer*, Robert E. Knoll reported that he could find no evidence of McAlmon having served in the Canadian military. The assumption that McAlmon had fabricated this part of his war record stood until corrected in Sanford J. Smoller's very thorough 2007 introduction to *The Nightinghouls of Paris*.

20 McAlmon later served several weeks with the Second Field troop Canadian Engineers.

21 Ezra Pound, "Paris Letter," *The Dial* (February 1922): 192.

22 When McAlmon wrote, it was at a rapid pace with little regard for grammar; the very notion of rewriting was an anathema. Joyce had suggested *A Hasty Bunch* as the title of McAlmon's first collection of short stories because he found the "American use of language racy," but he might just as well have been describing the author's rate of composition.

23 J.G., letter to Kay Boyle, 28 June 1968, JGf.

24 J.G., letter to Hugh Ford, 20 June 1972, JGf.

25 J.G., *Memoirs of Montparnasse*, 53.

26 Although McKay was in Paris during this period of time, Glassco's account of their meeting appears questionable at best. He depicts the Jamaican-born and -raised author as speaking in an American manner; indeed, in Glassco's account, McAlmon seems to assume that McKay is American based on accent alone. In fact, McKay first came to the United States as a student in his early twenties. Although he spent a good portion of his life in the country, and was a key figure in the Harlem Renaissance, McKay never lost his Jamaican accent.

27 J.G., *Memoirs of Montparnasse*, 59.

28 Ibid., 60–1.

29 J.G., manuscript of *Memoirs of Montparnasse*, second scribbler, 80.

30 J.G., *Memoirs of Montparnasse*, 94.

31 Ibid., 96–7.

32 In his memoirs, Glassco calls the actress Caridad de Plumas, describing her as "an attractive big-nosed Spanish girl with violently hennaed hair" (J.G., *Memoirs of Montparnasse*, 16). A dancer, Laberdesque was Georges Malkine's lover and muse during the years immediately preceding Glassco and Taylor's arrival. Of her, Malkine writes in one of his notebooks: "*Aimant, Follement, Passionnément, depuis le 7 Avril 1926, depuis bien plus longtemps, La Femme Rousse. Paris le 10-12-26.*" My thanks to Malkine's daughter, Fern Malkine-Falvey, for sharing this quote with me.

33 Named Sidney Schooner in *Memoirs of Montparnasse*, Hiler (1898–1966) was a Minnesotan who received at least part of his art education in Canada. The Jockey Club, which was located at the corner of the rue Campaigne-Première,

was covered by his murals of cowboys, Indians, and other images of the US southwest. It was a favourite drinking spot of McAlmon.

34 Daphne Berners in *Memoirs of Montparnasse*, Le Gallienne was a sculptress and painter. Le Gallienne's considerable talent is all too often overshadowed by her profile within lesbian circles of expatriate Paris. The stepdaughter of *fin-de-siècle* writer Richard Le Gallienne, film actress Eva Le Gallienne was her half-sister.

In *Memoirs of Montparnasse*, Glassco claimed that he was called upon to transcribe Richard Le Gallienne's historical novel *There Was a Ship*. Although there is evidence that this is true, the extract quoted in the memoirs is a fabrication, created when he was unable to find a copy of the book in Montreal.

35 Angela Martin in Glassco's memoirs, Yvette Ledoux (1898–1945) was born in Trois-Rivières, Quebec. Her father, Urbain J. Ledoux, was a successful businessman and accomplished United States diplomat who achieved his greatest fame as "Mister Zero," working among the poor in New York's Bowery. Yvette served as a nurse in Europe during the First World War, danced in the Ziegfield Follies, and for a time resided in an artists' colony in Woodstock, New York. In 1928, she was living in Paris, a neighbour of Robert McAlmon. The following April, she left for Tahiti aboard the ship *Antinous*. It was during the voyage that she fell in love with surrealist painter Georges Malkine, whom she married on 27 February 1930, two months after their return to Paris. After the outbreak of the Second World War, Yvette moved to be with her father in New York and was there for his death in April 1941. She spent much of the conflict in a failed effort to have her husband join her. Ledoux died on 9 November 1945, a victim of tuberculosis, at a sanatorium in Castle Point, New York.

Curiously, the name Yvette Ledoux, "an unhappy girl," is among a list of working-class women mentioned in Morley Callaghan's 1951 novel *The Loved and the Lost* (80).

36 Jimmie Charters, *This Must Be the Place*, 211. One presumes that the book's US editor, Clifton Fadiman, did not believe the "fine Canadian chaps" worthy of mention. The brief mention, which initially appeared in the 1934 the English house Herbert Joseph edition, was excised when reissued by New York publisher Lee Furman in 1937.

37 This was the subtitle of the English edition, published in 1934 by Herbert Joseph. The first US edition (New York: Lee Furman, 1937) carries the subtitle *Memoirs of Jimmie the Barman*. I have found no evidence that Glassco was aware of either edition or the previous use of *Memoirs of Montparnasse* as a subtitle.

38 Leon Edel, "Book Chat from Paris; News of New Books And Gossip of Litteration," *The Montreal Daily Star*, 24 November 1928, 15.

39 Ibid.

40 A.J.M. Smith, letter to Raymond Knister, 8 February 1928, AJMSP.

41 So certain was Adam of his prediction that while stationed in India during the Second World War he would write Leon Edel: "Has the great novel of Montreal been written yet?" (5 February 1945, LEP.)

42 Leon Edel, letter to A.J.M. Smith, 5 April 1928, AJMSP. In *The Visitable Past*, Edel writes: "I did try my hand at short stories, and dreamed about a novel set in Montreal. Others would write such novels later on. I was 'literary' in my readings, but too young to understand that serious writing was a lifelong task. I had enough imagination, without the aptitudes" (225–6). Neither Edel nor Kennedy published novels; no such works are found among their respective papers.

43 J.G., *Memoirs of Montparnasse*, 170.

44 Ibid., 1.

45 Leon Edel, "Book Chat from Paris; News of New Books And Gossip of Litteration," *The Montreal Daily Star*, 24 November 1928, 15.

46 Robert McAlmon and Kay Boyle, *Being Geniuses Together*, 307. In *Memoirs of Montparnasse* Alberto Poggi is named "Amédéo Dongibène."

47 Graeme Taylor, letter to Leon Edel, 31 October 1928, LEP.

48 J.G., *Memoirs of Montparnasse*, 72.

49 There is some evidence that "Conan's Fig" did exist; the 30 July 1936 entry in his Intimate Journal features the notation "*Conan's Fig* – what tripe!" Glassco maintained that *transition* printed the poem as a pamphlet in 1928, and he often included it when asked for his bibliography. However, there are no known copies, and the little magazine did not publish pamphlets. Glassco told Fraser Sutherland, his bibliographer, that the printing had been destroyed, adding that a small portion survived in manuscript form. No trace of the poem is found in Glassco's papers.

   A related claim, that the poem was subsequently translated by Robert Desnos and brought out by Kra, fails for similar reasons: no copies exist and Kra did not publish pamphlets. It is perhaps unnecessary to add that there is no mention of *Figue de Conan*, the supposed title, in Desnos's bibliography and papers.

50 J.G., *Memoirs of Montparnasse.*, 128.

51 Ibid., 135.

52 The annotation is found in Frank and Marian Scott's copy of *Memoirs of Montparnasse*. I have been unable to confirm or discount Glassco's claim.

53 Leon Edel, "Introduction," *Memoirs of Montparnasse*, viii.

54 Leon Edel, "Literature and Journalism: The Visible Boundaries," 17.

55 J.G., *Memoirs of Montparnasse*, 145.

56 Glassco neglects to mention Taylor's extracts in his memoirs. It is unlikely that *Characteristics of the Penroses* is another title for *The Flying Carpet* as there is no sign in the twenty-two pages of extracts of what Glassco describes as the latter novel's 250-pound heroine.

57 Graeme Taylor, "Extract I," 174.

58 J.G., letter to Leon Edel, 3 April 1929, LEP.

59 J.G., "Extract from an Autobiography," 198.

60 Ibid., 208.

61 Graeme Taylor, letter to Leon Edel, 15 April 1929, LEP.

62 J.G., letter to Leon Edel, 17 April 1929, LEP.

63 J.G., *Memoirs of Montparnasse*, 50. The letter that Glassco quotes is not found among his papers; in fact, no correspondence between father and son survives.

64 Ibid.

65 Leon Edel, "Paris Book Chat," *The Montreal Daily Star* (17 August 1929): 6.

66 Ibid.

67 Graeme Taylor, "Dr Breakey Opposes Union," 67.

68 J.G., letter to Leon Edel, 17 April 1929, LEP.

69 J.G., *Memoirs of Montparnasse*, 153-4.

70 Ethel Moorhead, "About Books," *This Quarter* 4 (Spring 1929): 271.

71 Leon Edel, "Paris Book Chat," *The Montreal Daily Star* (3 August 1929): 22.

72 "Callaghan Made Bet Not to Write of Paris," The Star Weekly [Toronto] (18 May 1929): 19.

73 Morley Callaghan, *The Complete Stories, Volume One*, 112.

74 Ibid., 113.

75 Ibid., 118.

76 Ibid.

77 Ibid., 119.

78 Ibid., 120.

79 Leon Edel, *Memories of the Montreal Group*, 10.

80 Morley Callaghan, *The Complete Stories, Volume One*, 116.

81 Ibid., 57. A similar episode is relayed with less subtlety in McAlmon's *The Nightinghouls of Paris*. The manuscript features an editorial note in the author's hand: "omit if this seems censorable" (33).

82 Leon Edel, *The Montreal Daily Star* (2 November 1929): 27.

83 Leon Edel, "A Canadian in Paris," *Ideas*, CBC Radio, 1993.

84 Morley Callaghan, interviewed in "A Canadian in Paris," *Ideas*, CBC Radio, 1993. The line to which Callaghan was referring is found in *North America, Continent of Conjecture* (Paris: Contact Editions, 1929).

85 Its stature was such that in 1958 the story lent its title to a feature film starring John Drainie and narrated by Raymond Massey. Based on four Callaghan short stories – none of which, curiously, was "Now That April's Here" – the project received national coverage and was feted with a lavish black-tie premier. *Now That April's Here*, the motion picture, featured adaptations of the Callaghan stories "Silk Stockings," "Rocking Chair," "The Rejected One," and "A Sick Call," all of which had appeared in *Now That April's Here and Other Stories*. Reviews were poor and the film closed two weeks after its lavish Toronto premiere. *Now That April's Here* was later shown in Hamilton, appar-

ently never to be screened again; Glassco was spared the discomfiture of reading the title on a Montreal marquee.

86 J.G., handwritten draft of *Memoirs of Montparnasse*, first scribbler, JGf.

87 Sanford J. Smoller, letter to the author, 20 November 2008. Though there have been references to the work as a *roman à clef*, I believe Prof. Smoller's description is more accurate.

88 Robert McAlmon, quoted in Sanford J. Smoller, *Adrift among Geniuses*, 205. McAlmon wrote Beach from Theoule, where he was staying when the novel was completed.

89 J.G., letter to Laurie Lerew, 2 August 1964, JGf.

90 J.G., *Memoirs of Montparnasse*, 79.

91 Gore Vidal, "Foreword," in Robert McAlmon, *Miss Knight and Other Stories*, xi–xii. It is worth noting here the accuracy with which McAlmon portrayed the family. Vidal continues: "There is my lecherous great-grandfather, whom he calls 'the gay rakish Mr Dubois,' a widower always on the lookout for rich widows. There is my grandmother, who was so fat that my father never allowed her to visit him at West Point or, later, come to Washington, where he was Director of Air Commerce. McAlmon notes that she is again pregnant at fifty, as indeed she was, to her horror. My Aunt Lorene is called Loraine, Aunt Emma becomes Renee, and the family's sense of fallen grandeur is captured, particularly the endless discussions of how rich the Vidals would be once the Swiss government paid its debt to them for having raised a Swiss regiment to fight for the Spanish king in the war against Napoleon …"

92 Sanford J. Smoller, "Introduction" in Robert McAlmon, *The Nightinghouls of Paris*, xiii.

93 Robert McAlmon, *The Nightinghouls of Paris*, 6.

94 Ibid.

95 Ibid., 14.

96 Ibid., 21.

97 Ibid., 14.

98 Ibid., 82.

99 Ibid., 103.

100 Ibid., 83.

101 Ibid., 128.

102 Ibid., 126.

103 Ibid., 129.

104 Ibid.

105 Ibid., 149.

106 Ibid., 132–3.

107 Ibid., 134.

108 Graeme Taylor, letter to Leon Edel, 12 March 1929, LEp.

109 J.G., Manuscript of *Memoirs of Montparnasse*, sixth scribbler, 34, JGf.

110 Glassco's annotation found in the Scotts's copy of *Memoirs of Montparnasse* identifies Mrs Quayle as "Mrs Margaret Whitney (d. 1939)." On the subject of Mrs Quayle, Glassco's papers both clarify and confuse. While the "Autobiographical Sketch" features a "Mrs Wm. Whitney" and "Mrs Marguerite Lippe-Rosskam," only the latter (as "Peggy") is mentioned in his Intimate Journal. Among the photographic records is an image of an attractive middle-aged woman wearing long leather gloves whom Glassco identifies as Margaret Whitney "taken in Montreal, 1945, on the occasion of our brief reunion." The Intimate Journal contains no mention of this reunion, which according to the annotation addressed to Frank and Marion Scott, would have taken place six years after Whitney's death.

The papers also include a love poem entitled "For Margaret Whitney," which was not published until several years after Glassco's death. As the original title was "Ukyo's Song," named for one of the young homosexual pages in Ken Sato's *Quaint Stories of the Samurais*, it is apparent that the verse was not written with Margaret Whitney in mind. Glassco records March 1926 as the original date of composition, though it should be noted that this predates both his first trip to Paris and the publication of *Quaint Stories of the Samurais*.

111 J.G., *Memoirs of Montparnasse*, 179.

112 Ibid., 238.

113 Lushington-Hayes may very well be the Roland Lushington who penned *The Lost Shepherd*, a novel published in 1934 by the London house of Cobden-Sanderson.

114 J.G., *Memoirs of Montparnasse*, 240.

115 J.G., "The Body Says Goodbye to Love," JGF. The oldest extant draft of the poem, in which Glassco records September 1930 as the original date of composition, is dated 22 November 1963, the date of the Kennedy assassination and the deaths of C.S. Lewis and Aldous Huxley. Here again, Glassco may be having fun with us; a later version of the poem has the date "July '63" scratched out with "Jan. '64" written below. Nevertheless, it seems likely that he worked on the poem in 1963 and 1967. He titled the final version "To W.G.T., from Hospital." Among the other titles considered were: "The Body Takes Leave of Love," "Glassco's Farewell to Everything," "Glassco's Farewell to Love," "Poem to G(raeme) T(aylor)," and "Last Poem." "The Body Says Goodbye to Love" was later incorporated in a longer poem, "The Pit," published in the *The Tamarack Review* 62 (first quarter 1974).

116 J.G., *Memoirs of Montparnasse*, 241. Edmond Sergent (1876–1969) was born in Algeria, the son of a French career soldier. Although he led a successful campaign against tuberculosis in the colony, his main field of interest was in the prevention of malaria. With his brother Étienne he spent nearly five decades researching treatments for the disease. In 1912, Sergent served as the director

of the Institut Pasteur at Algiers, a position he held until politics forced his removal in 1963. He appears to have had no connection with the American Hospital in Paris.

117 Ibid.

CHAPTER THREE

1 J.G., Intimate Journal, 10 February 1935, JGP.

2 The extent of Archibald's reputation is reflected in the honours he received from bodies on three continents, including those presented by the University of Paris and the Société Nationale de Chirurgie de Paris.

3 While Archibald is often described as the first to have done the operation in North America, the achievement belongs to Dr Robert Green Le Conte, who performed the procedure in November 1911 at the Pennsylvania Hospital in Philadelphia. The misperception stems from the fact that Le Conte's operation remained unreported for twenty years.

4 Roderick Stewart, *Bethune*, 24.

5 Fraser Sutherland, interview with the author, 30 June 2003.

6 J.G., Intimate Journal, 26 October 1934, JGP.

7 Ibid., 6 March 1934.

8 Ibid., 28 March 1934.

9 Ibid.

10 Ibid., 10 April 1934.

11 Ibid.

12 Ibid., 26 October 1934. In an earlier entry, dated 17 May 1934, Glassco writes: "finished my little poem to Graeme, which I am afraid will have to be scrapped but for the first stanza – I like the rhythm I used very much."

13 Ibid.

14 Ibid., 28 May 1934.

15 Ibid.

16 Ibid., 17 June 1934.

17 Ibid.

18 Octave Mirabeau, *Le jardin des supplices*, 39.

19 The house, 20358 Lakeshore Road, stands largely unchanged from the summers during which it served as home to Glassco and Taylor.

20 J.G., Intimate Journal, 23 August 1935.

21 Ibid., 15 July 1934.

22 Ibid., 5 July 1934.

23 Coincidentally, when the two Glassco boys were studying at Bishop's College School in the Eastern Townships, David listed as his ambition "To be a farmer" in the school magazine's Christmas 1923 issue. It was a flippant answer from a son of wealth. Buffy Glassco's ambition was "To talk faster."

24 Ibid., 10 February 1935.

25 Ibid.

26 Ibid., 23 August 1935.

27 Ibid., 26 August 1935.

28 These passages, the "Seduction of Adrienne" included, Glassco later destroyed.

29 J.G., "Mr Noad," 280.

30 J.G., Intimate Journal, 23 August 1935, JGP.

31 Ibid.

32 Ibid.

33 Ibid., 15 September 1935.

34 J.G., Memoirs of Montparnasse, 5. In the book, Bydwell, whose full name was Humphrey Burton Bydwell (born 1903), is hidden behind the name "Bertie Ballard."

35 Translated by "John Howard" (Jacob Howard Lewis) as Against the Grain (New York: Boni, 1930), Bydwell's copy was a reprint of the first English-language edition of the novel. It is an abridged version in that it omits Huysmans's preface, the whole of the sixth chapter (in which Des Esseintes picks up a young boy and takes him to a brothel), and the last episode of chapter 9. The book remained in Glassco's library and is now part of the John Glassco collection, W.D. Jordan Library, Queen's University.

36 J.G., Intimate Journal, 9 October 1935, JGP.

37 Oscar Wilde, The Picture of Dorian Gray, 186. Although the title of "the strangest book" is not given in Wilde's novel, it was identified by the author as À rebours in 1895 during the Queensberry trial. The title page of the 1926 Groves & Michaux English language edition, Against the Grain, features the words: "THE BOOK THAT DORIAN GRAY LOVED AND THAT INSPIRED OSCAR WILDE."

38 J.G., The Fatal Woman, ii.

39 J.G., Intimate Journal, 4 July 1934, JGP.

40 George Woodcock, "Private Fantasies: Collective Myths. John Glassco's Decadent Fiction," Tamarack Review 65.

41 J.G., Intimate Journal, 8 January 1936, JGP.

42 Ibid.

43 Ibid.

44 Ibid., 1 April 1936.

45 Ibid., 1 February 1936.

46 Brian Trehearne, Aestheticism and the Canadian Modernists, 115.

47 J.G., Intimate Journal, 15 February 1936, JGP. The final sentence was struck out at a later date.

48 J.G., "Sonnet (On My 24th Birthday)," JGF.

49 J.G., Intimate Journal, 4 April 1936, JGP. Glassco's list of symptoms lengthened the following year with the realization that he'd begun to bald.

50 Ibid.

51 Ibid., 30 July 1936.

52 Ibid.

53 The poem was begun in 1936 under the title "Summer." Abandoned and reworked, it was eventually incorporated into "Ode: The Autumn Resurrection," which was first published in the May 1961 issue of *The Canadian Forum.*

54 J.G., Intimate Journal, 3 September 1937.

55 Ibid., 19 October 1937. Glassco's description of Amélie von Auchemberg continued but was later excised. The relationship ended early in 1938, against Amélie's wishes, when Glassco tired of her.

56 Ibid.

57 Ibid.

58 Ibid., 18 August 1938.

CHAPTER FOUR

1 J.G., *The Deficit Made Flesh*, 16.

2 Kildare Dobbs, "The Great Glassco," 52.

3 J.G., Intimate Journal, undated entry, c. 1939, JGP.

4 Kildare Dobbs, "The Great Glassco," 52.

5 These are the trades listed on Taylor's Canadian Active Service Force attestation paper. Accompanying the description is the claim "Owns show horses." All quotes directly concerning Taylor's military service are drawn from his personnel record held at Library and Archives Canada.

6 J.G., Intimate Journal, 15 October 1940, JGP. The entry is dated incorrectly as "October 15th, 1941."

7 Ibid.

8 J.G., letter to Robert McAlmon, 25 February 1941, RMA.

9 Among those to whom Glassco related the story was Kildare Dobbs, who included the claim in "The Great Glassco," a profile featured in the August 1975 issue of *Maclean's*. The same issue features an early piece on Rough Trade, in which Carole Pope discusses her bisexuality and hopes that the band might one day stage grand production numbers featuring "lots of whips and riding crops, rubber and leather, furs and feathers."

10 Robert McAlmon and Kay Boyle, *Being Geniuses Together*, 356.

11 Sanford J. Smoller, *Adrift among Geniuses*, 267.

12 Kenneth Rexroth, *The Nation*.

13 Richard Ellman, *James Joyce*, 687.

14 J.G., letter to Robert McAlmon, 7 April 1941, RMA.

15 J.G., letter to Robert McAlmon, 5 February 1941, RMA.

16 Ibid.

17 Ibid.

18 J.G., letter to Robert McAlmon, 25 February 1941, RMA.

19 J.G., letter to Robert McAlmon, 4 June 1943, RMA.

20 J.G., letter to Robert McAlmon, 5 December 1941, RMA.

21 J.G., letter to Robert McAlmon, 6 May 1941, RMA.

22 Ibid.

23 The title may have seemed familiar; in his own memoir, Glassco writes that McAlmon was working on a manuscript with this title in 1928, adding that he read the work six months later and found it "exactly like all the others" (*Memoirs of Montparnasse*, 77). Assuming the title of the earlier work to be correct, one might also assume from Glassco's dismissive comment that it was an autobiographical novel consisting of no more than veiled descriptions of actual events. In an annotated copy of *Memoirs of Montparnasse* he gave to Frank and Marian Scott, Glassco recognized *Being Geniuses Together* as a recycled title, yet nowhere in McAlmon's own writing is there mention of a piece of fiction with this name. The novel *Being Geniuses Together* is more likely a phantom; another example of Glassco's subterfuge.

24 J.G., letter to Robert McAlmon, 8 March 1942, RMA.

25 J.G., letter to Robert McAlmon, 26 February 1945, RMA.

26 J.G., letter to Robert McAlmon, 8 March 1942, RMA.

27 Ibid.

28 These and other quotes concerning Taylor's military service are drawn from his personnel record held at Library and Archives Canada.

29 In September 1942, the 22nd Canadian Armoured Regiment was moved to England, where it continued to train. On 21 July 1944, it was deployed to Normandy.

30 J.G., Intimate Journal, 11 August 1942, JGP.

31 Ibid., 2 September 1942.

32 Ibid.

33 Ibid., 11 September 1942.

34 J.G., *The Deficit Made Flesh*, 11-12.

35 J.G., letter to Robert McAlmon, 5 December 1941, RMA.

36 J.G., Intimate Journal, 28 March 1943, JGP.

37 Ibid., 30 April 1943, JGP.

38 Even within the relatively staid atmosphere of wartime publishing in Canada, Longmans, Green & Co. (later Longmans) appeared conservative. This changed little in the postwar era, as evidenced by their decision to publish Marian Engel's 1968 debut novel *Sarah Bastard's Notebook* as *No Clouds of Glory*.

39 J.G., Intimate Journal, 16 September 1943, JGP.

40 Ibid., 28 September 1943.

41 Ibid.

42 In a letter to Robert McAlmon, dated 18 April 1944, Glassco explained the new title:

By the way, I dont [sic] really much care for the title, which is more or less of a hangover from the original (way way back) French version. But the idea is almost untranslatable. BACKWATER is the only really adequate rendering (and the air of the book is pretty stagnant too), but thats [*sic*] dull and cliche-ish. The French gets the three meanins [*sic*] packed into one phrase: the "in arrears" of the straight translation; the "reluctantly and against the grain" of the figurative meaning; and the specialised meaning of "travelling with one's back to the locomotive." I've tried and tried to find something like it in English, but gave up long ago.

Against the grain, one of the meanings related, was the title of the English-language translation of Huysmans's *À rebours* given Glassco by H. Burton Bydwell.

43 J.G., letter to Robert McAlmon, 5 February 1944, RMA.

44 J.G., Intimate Journal, 17 December 1943, JGP.

45 J.G., letter to Robert McAlmon, 18 March 1944, RMA.

46 J.G., letter to Robert McAlmon, 30 September 1944, RMA.

47 John Sutherland, *The Letters of John Sutherland, 1942–1956*. 14.

48 Editorial note, *First Statement* 2:8 (August 1944): 2.

49 John Sutherland, *The Letters of John Sutherland, 1942–1956*, 16.

50 Ibid.

51 Irving Layton, interview with Bill O'Riordan, 30 January 1985, The Irving Layton Collection, Concordia Libraries, Concordia University. Although Layton states that the visit took place in either 1942 or 1943, it would appear that neither year is correct. According to Elspeth Cameron's biography *Irving Layton: A Portrait*, it was not until November 1942 that the poet first met Betty Sutherland, who was to become his second wife. Glassco's earliest letters to John Sutherland were written in 1944. Although the editor does not feature in the Intimate Journal, Glassco mentions Sutherland in a letter to McAlmon, written in summer 1944 (16 August 1944, RMA): "John Sutherland is a very decent chap, about 30, a pretty good drinker too …" It is worth noting that at no point in his reminiscence does Layton mention Taylor's wife, who spent that particular summer living in New York.

52 Ibid.

53 Irving Layton, *Waiting for the Messiah*, 248.

54 Ibid., 236.

55 J.G., letter to Robert McAlmon, 16 August 1944, RMA.

56 John Sutherland, *The Letters of John Sutherland, 1942-1956*, 16.

57 Through Glassco's request to McAlmon, *First Statement* received a poem, "The Clouds," by William Carlos Williams. However, it would appear that Williams withdrew the poem before publication. In a letter to McAlmon, Glassco writes: "Dr Williams may not have liked the mag at all either: he has I understand withdrawn the very good poem he sent them on my request to you." (J.G., letter to Robert McAlmon, 30 September 1944, RMA.)

58 The notes on contributors, featured on the back of the issue reads: "WINGATE

TAYLOR. Wishes to be described as "a farmer in the Eastern Townships of Quebec." [*First Statement*, April-May 1945: 36.]

59 J.G., letter to Robert McAlmon, 13 December 1945, RMA.

60 J.G., letter to John Sutherland, 28 December 1950, Irving Layton Collection, Concordia University.

61 John Sutherland, *The Letters of John Sutherland, 1942-1956*, 169.

62 J.G., letter to Robert McAlmon, 13 March 1945, RMA. Glassco twice writes of the collaborative effort in letters to McAlmon but never mentions a title. There is no work matching this description among Glassco's papers, nor is it mentioned in his Intimate Journal.

63 J.G., letter to Robert McAlmon, 6 March 1943, RMA.

64 Edmund Wilson, "Kay Boyle and *The Saturday Evening Post*."

65 "Pot-Boyler," *Time*, 17 January 1944: 357.

66 Glassco recorded the lyrics on a holograph letter from Ethel Moorehead to Graeme Taylor, dated July 1929:

Sailors don't care,
Sailors don't care
Whether she's dark
Or whether she's fair!
As long as her lily-white bottom is bare
Sailors don't care!

It should be further noted that the phrase "sailors don't care" is not uncommon and was the title of a US film released the year before Lanham's book was published.

67 In 1931, one final Contact Editions title, Nathaniel West's debut, *The Dream Life of Balso Snell*, was published by David Moss and Martin Kamin, two New York booksellers. The use of the imprint was offered by William Carlos Williams, who otherwise had nothing to do with the publication. McAlmon dissociated himself, referring to the work as "an adolescently smart and naughty novel" (Hugh Ford, *Published in Paris*, 88-9).

68 Many of Lanham's early novels, most particularly *The Stricklands* (Boston: Little, Brown, 1939), drew a measure of critical praise but sold poorly. He later enjoyed commercial success as a mystery writer. Lanham died in 1979.

69 While there is the obvious connection between Hart Crane and the character's surname, it is likely that the Guy Hart's name was inspired by Guy Urquhart, a pseudonym Kay Boyle appended to McAlmon's "The Silver Bull," when submitting it to *transition*. The poem appeared in the summer 1928 issue, which also featured Taylor's "Deaf-Mute." Urquhart was McAlmon's mother's maiden name. I am indebted to Sanford J. Smoller for this observation.

There are two interesting coincidences shared between Glassco and Crane. The latter was a friend of Wilbur Underwood, a career officer at the State Department in Washington, DC. Through Underwood, Hart was introduced to a sort of homosexual underground within the diplomatic corps, a group said to have had an expressed admiration of Aubrey Beardsley's *Under the Hill*. Four decades later, Glassco would receive recognition for his completion of the Beardsley classic. His next book, *The English Governess*, would be published under the pseudonym Miles Underwood.

70 Edwin Lanham, *Banner at Daybreak*, 189.

71 Ibid., 157.

72 J.G., letter to Robert McAlmon, 12 December 1943, RMA.

73 Morley Callaghan, *The Complete Stories, Volume One*, III.

74 Robert McAlmon, *The Nightinghouls of Paris*, 25.

75 Ibid., 98.

76 Ibid.

77 Ibid.

78 Ibid.

79 J.G., letter to Laurie Lerew, 2 December 1964, JGf. A dealer in rare books and manuscripts, in 1964 Lerew handled the sale of some Glassco items to McGill and Northwestern University. It was during negotiations with the latter that he asked the dealer to enquire after a McAlmon manuscript entitled "THE SUSCEPTIBLE BOY," adding: "He sent me a carbon here in Foster in 1946 or 1947, which I returned without comment: it ended our friendship" (J.G., letter to Laurie Lerew, 2 December 1964, JGf). Here Glassco is confusing the title of the novel he received with an unpublished novel McAlmon had written when the two were in Paris. The earlier novel, also known as *The Promiscuous Boy* and *My Susceptible Friend, Adrian*, has been lost. Glassco made a second attempt at tracking down the manuscript four years later, asking Kay Boyle whether she might know of its whereabouts (J.G., letter to Kay Boyle, 1 August 1967, JGf).

80 J.G., Intimate Journal, 30 June 1947, JGp.

81 Ibid., 8 June 1947.

82 Ibid., 28 March 1943.

83 J.G., letter to Robert McAlmon, 16 August 1944, RMA.

84 J.G., Intimate Journal, 27 March 1946, JGp.

85 Ibid.

86 J.G., letter to Robert McAlmon, 13 December 1945, RMA.

87 J.G., Intimate Journal, 6 June 1947, JGp.

88 Ibid.

89 Ibid.

90 J.G., "From a Commonplace Book," 61.

CHAPTER FIVE

1 J.G., Intimate Journal, 2 March 1950, JGp.

2 Ibid., 17 February 1948.

3 Likely Amélie von Auchenberg, though possibly the "lame girl" described as an "excellent mistress whom I see once a month, whose caresses I eagerly anticipate & whose company I am quite happy to leave after a single night" (J.G., Intimate Journal, 27 March 1946, JGP).

4 Ibid., 27 March 1948.

5 Ibid., 17 February 1948.

6 Ibid.

7 J.G., handwritten note appended to the Intimate Journal, October 1964, JGP.

8 *Canada Gazette* 1948, 2579.

9 J.G., Intimate Journal, 28 February 1950, JGP.

10 Ibid., 27 March 1948.

11 Ibid., 8 October 1950.

12 Gertrude Stein, *Everybody's Autobiography*, 66.

13 J.G., Intimate Journal, 27 March 1948, JGP.

14 Ibid.

15 J.G., "Town Council Meeting: Undesirable," *The Canadian Forum*; as "Town Council Meeting," the poem was included in *The Deficit Made Flesh* and gives the collection its title: ("You, the eternal deficit made flesh,/ The something over and above the sum/ Allowed by conscience to the home-grown poor …").

16 Ibid.

17 Ann Johansson, letter to the author, 1 March 2005.

18 In later years, Glassco would falsely maintain that he had been mayor of Foster.

19 J.G., *Squire Hardman*, 2.

20 J.G., Intimate Journal, 27 October 1952, JGP.

21 Jay A. Gertzman, *Bootleggers and Smuthounds*, 68.

22 Jay A. Gertzman, letter to the author, 12 October 2006. A friend of H.L. Mencken, Sherwood Anderson, and Ezra Pound, Woodford's greatest contribution to literature was as the author of *Trial and Error: A Dithyramb on the Subject of Writing and Selling* (1933), which has been cited as an influence by Ray Bradbury and Robert A. Heinlein. Among the chapters included are "Masquerade… The Sex Element of Writing," "Clinical Arcana: Liquor, Women and the Writer," and "Excuria: Poetry, Plays and Other Perversions."

23 Originally published privately in 1929, *Flesh and Other Stories* was reissued by the Jack Woodford Press in 1949. The author, Clement Wood, a graduate of Yale Law School, left a magistrate's position in Alabama for a writing career in Greenwich Village. He is known to have written at least 120 books, among them volumes of poetry, novels, and two autobiographies. As versatile as he was a prolific writer, Clement's nonfiction titles include *An Introduction to Philology, A Psycho-analysis of Jesus, Why I Believe in Trial Marriage*, and *Let's Have a Good Time Tonight: An Omnibus of Party Games*. Wood supplemented his often small writer's income through a variety of means: waiting on tables,

acting as secretary to Upton Sinclair, teaching poetry at New York University, serving as dean of the Barnard School for Boys, and, curiously, as a member of the Rockefeller Vice Commission.

24 J.G., Intimate Journal, 27 March 1948, JGP. Glassco added the word "masturbatory" at a later date, most likely in the mid-1960s, when preparing his papers for sale.

25 Ibid., 2 March 1950.

26 J.G., note on photograph, 11 April 1966, JGF.

27 J.G., Intimate Journal, 11 November 1951, JGP.

28 Ibid., 9 July 1954.

29 Ibid., 9 December 1954. Glassco destroyed several passages – perhaps entire entries – dealing with the dancer.

30 Ibid.

31 Ibid. 27 February 1956.

32 "Murder of Family Charged to Drapeau," *The Montreal Star* (17 February 1956): 16

33 J.G., Intimate Journal, 27 February 1956. In an entry dated 15 December 1957, Glassco writes of a third attack and includes further description of the symptoms: "A slight dizziness, to begin with, not definitely unpleasant, but disturbing. A sense of being *divorced* from things around me, physically: an oddness in the *placing* of the floor, the furniture .... Sheer terror over what I *might* do – strangulation, stabbing, braining ...."

This third and, perhaps, final attack became so intense that he asked Elma to leave the house. The act brought considerable relief: "When she was gone half the terror vanished: there was no one to kill."

Although Glassco recognized that his mother had also experienced similar attacks, he clung to a belief that there was no "madness" in his family. In fact, there is evidence that a male relative, a member of the Hamilton Glasscos, suffered from severe mental illness and spent several periods in sanatoriums during the early twentieth century.

34 Pearl Tiberi was born in either 1934 or 1935 (records differ in this account). She died in 1984, never having been married. There is no record that she ever gave birth in the Province of Quebec.

35 J.G., *Selected Poems*, 60.

36 Ibid.

37 Writing of the honour in the 4 March 1956 entry of his Intimate Journal, Glassco neglects to mention the anthology's title and records the publisher incorrectly as "Occidental University." In fact, the book was published by Stanford University Press.

In 1959, he was again included in a Borestone Mountain Poetry Awards anthology; "Utrillo's World" appeared alongside work by Robert Graves, Ted Hughes, Marianne Moore, Sylvia Plath, and May Sarton. Glassco was not the lone Canadian to be recognized; Phyllis Gotlieb, Alden Nowlan, Francis

Sparshott, and Don Geiger were included, as was Miriam Waddington, whose "Elegy for John Sutherland" recalled the late editor of *First Statement* and *Northern Review*.

38 J.G., Intimate Journal, 4 March 1956, JGP.

39 Ibid.

40 J.G., note to Elma Glassco regarding "Deserted Buildings under Shefford Mountain," 4 August 1964, JGP.

41 J.G., "Deserted Buildings under Shefford Mountain."

42 Michael Gnarowski, "People I," in J.G. *Memoirs of Montparnasse*, second edition, 232.

43 J.G., Intimate Journal, 7 November 1956. JGP.

44 Michael Gnarowski, interview with the author, April 2005.

45 J.G., letter to Kay Boyle, 25 March 1969, JGf.

46 "Glassco – Von Colmar," *The Gazette* (21 September 1963): 13.

47 J.G., letter to Elma Koolmer, 7 November 1961, JGP.

48 Alma Baltser, letter to J.G., undated (likely August 1973) JGf.

49 J.G., *The Deficit Made Flesh*, 32. The poem later appeared as "A Devotion; to Cteis" in Glassco's *Selected Poems*.

50 J.G., Intimate Journal, 7 November 1956, JGP.

51 J.G., letter to Kay Boyle, 25 February 1969, JGf.

52 Ibid.

53 J.G., Intimate Journal, 16 September 1960, JGP. Initially, Glassco recorded the year of Taylor's death correctly as 1957 but later changed it to 1956.

CHAPTER SIX

1 J.G., Intimate Journal, 13 November 1960, JGP.

2 David Cobb, "Elegant Pornographer," 10.

3 Ibid.

4 J.G., Intimate Journal, 15 July 1934, JGP.

5 Leon Edel, interviewed in "A Canadian in Paris," *Ideas*, CBC Radio, 1993.

6 F.R. Scott, letter to J.G., 3 November 1957, JGP.

7 J.G., letter to F.R. Scott, 28 November 1957, JGP.

8 Ibid.

9 F.R. Scott, letter to J.G., 23 November 1959, Francis Reginald Scott fonds, Library and Archives Canada.

10 The preface to *Songs of French Canada* is worth quoting at length:

This little collection of English translations of the poetry and folk-songs of French Canada has at least the merit of novelty. That the translations are unequal in quality was perhaps to be expected. That they do not afford much more than a suggestion of the extent, variety, and value of French-Canadian poetry is the misfortune, not the fault, of the editor, whose task was not to select from a large number of translations, but rather to search diligently for a sufficient number to serve his purpose. It is matter of regret that the attempts to render into English verse the poems of such well-known French-Canadians as Louis Fréchette, Octave Crémazie, and William Chapman, to mention no others, have been so few and far between. It is still more unfortunate that no translations whatever could be found of the work of Émile Nelligan or of Pamphile le May, two of the most brilliant French-Canadian poets. (Lawrence Burpee, *Songs of French Canada*, v–vi)

11 David M. Hayne, "Literary Translation in Nineteenth-Century Canada," 38. The bilingual Fréchette booklets were titled *Les excommuniés / The Excommunicated; and, Le drapeau anglais / The British Flag* (c. 1883) and the *Fors l'honneur / All Lost but Honour* (1884).

12 The four Contact Press bilingual collections of poems are: *Eight Poems* by Roland Giguère, *Seven Poems* by Gilles Hénault, *Six Poems* by Paul-Marie Lapointe, and *Nine Poems* by Hector de Saint-Denys-Garneau. Published in Iroquois Falls, Ontario, they range in length from fourteen to twenty-four pages.

13 J.G., letter to F.R. Scott (unsent), 18 October 1966, JGf.

14 J.G., Personal Journal, 1965–1969, 8 May 1966, JGf.

15 In *Memoirs of Montparnasse*, Glassco claimed that his first book, "a sequence of historical sketches with a unifying transvestite motif" (166) entitled *Contes en crinoline*, was published in 1929 by Elias Gaucher, "a fly-by-night publisher" (166) to whom he'd been introduced by a surrealist poet (identified in Frank and Marian Scott's copy as Robert Desnos). No copies of this book, which supposedly appeared under the *nom de plume* Jean de Saint Luc (after the street of his birth), have been found. While Gaucher had been a prolific publisher of erotica in the years preceding the Great War, there is no evidence that he was active during Glassco's time in Montparnasse. Furthermore, the work that Glassco claimed to have referenced in composing *Contes en crinoline, L'écrin du rubis; ou, Les délices des dessous* by Liane de Lauris, was not published until 1932, the year after his return to Montreal. The first mention of *Contes en crinoline* is found in a biographical sketch that accompanied the 1944 *First Statement* publication of "Frogmore's Folly."

Glassco included an anonymous German translation of *Contes en crinoline*, *Märchen en Krinoline*, in at least two self-penned bibliographies. The latter, he claimed had been published in 1931 at Leipzig. A few weeks before his death, when queried by his bibliographer Fraser Sutherland about the books, Glassco described *Märchen en Krinoline* as a "phantom," yet continued to maintain the existence of *Contes en crinoline*, which he described as a slim volume (though he admitted that he'd never seen a copy).

Given Glassco's choice of pseudonym, it is interesting to note that Gaucher pirated works by Mme La Victomtesse de St-Luc, originally published by Auguste Brancart in Amsterdam. The publisher sometimes issued books, such as St-Luc's *Fleurs de chair*, with the deceptive imprint "G. Labaucher, Libraire-Éditeur, Montréal (Canada)." Gaucher also employed the name of a fictitious Montreal publisher in his pirated editions.

16 J.G., *The Deficit Made Flesh*, 50.

17 J.G., Intimate Journal, 27 March 1948, JGf.

18 Ibid.

19 A.J.M. Smith, dustjacket of *The Deficit Made Flesh*. Smith later recycled much of what he had written in "John Stinson Glassco" for *Contemporary Poets of the English Language*.

20 Ibid.

21 On 4 August 1956 Glassco sent Elma holograph copies of "A Devotion" and four of his Eastern Townships poems, to which he added annotations: "The Entailed Farm" ("This is Julia Wheeler's place – you know, just past the cemetery"), "Blighty" ("This is Bill Arnold's place – with the sign!"), "Deserted Buildings under Shefford Mountain" ("Clark Baird's old place in Iron Hill"), and "The Burden of Junk" ("This is me and Arthur Charles who lives (still) beside the farm in Knowlton. The harmonium I saw with my own eyes!"). In an accompanying letter, he described the verse as "my five best poems all now finished" (J.G., letter to Elma Koolmer, 4 August 1956, JGp).

22 Michael Gnarowski, "Introduction," J.G., *Selected Poems with Three Notes on the Poetic Process*, 10.

23 John Robert Colombo, "Three Poets," 95.

24 J.K. Johnstone, review of *The Deficit Made Flesh* and two other works, 45.

25 Louis Dudek, *In Defence of Art*, 162.

26 Milton Wilson, review of *The Deficit Made Flesh*, 65.

27 J.G., Intimate Journal, 23 August 1935, JGp.

28 J.G., letter to Elma Koolmer, 7 October 1961, JGp.

29 Quoted in Philip Lanthier, "An Interview with Doug Jones," 68.

30 Glassco reported these figures in a letter to Brian Brett (21 May 1976, JGf), who was then in the process of publishing the "translation" of *Venus in Furs*. In the same letter Glassco claims to have earned $63 from *The Deficit Made Flesh*. Whether this figure is in addition to his advance or he is simply mistaken is uncertain.

31 *The Penguin Book of Canadian Verse* was a revised, expanded edition of the awkwardly titled *Anthology of Canadian Poetry (English)*. The collection was revised a third time, published during centennial year with three Glassco poems: "Brummel at Calais," "Quebec Farmhouse," and "Utrillo's World."

32 J.G., letter to Elma Koolmer, 10 September 1961, JGp.

33 J.G., letter to Kay Boyle, 10 May 1958, JGf.

34 Kay Boyle, letter to Robert Carleton Brown, 8 August 1958. Robert Carlton Brown III Collection of Bob Brown Papers, Morris Library, Southern Illinois University.

35 J.G., letter to Robert McAlmon, 9 February 1947, RMA.

36 J.G., letter to F.R. Scott, 31 Oct. 1966, JGp.

37 J.G., Intimate Journal, 27 March 1948, JGp.

38 Ibid., 11 November 1951.

39 J.G., "Introduction," Aubrey Beardsley and J.G., *Under the Hill*, 9.

40 Leon Edel, "John Glassco (1909–1981) and His Erotic Muse," 112.

41 J.G., "Introduction," Aubrey Beardsley and J.G., *Under the Hill*, 12.

42 Ibid. The 1967 Award Books edition of Beardsley's work, published as *The Story of Venus and Tannhauser* contains an introduction by Paul J. Gilette, in which it is wrongly claimed that Glassco "incorporates a number of erotic passages which can be found nowhere in the original; in his hands, Beardsley's subtlety is lost completely, as 'penis' becomes 'prick' and euphemism gives way to the vernacular." The false charge injured Glassco greatly; he demanded from Gilette "an acceptable retraction and apology for these false, impudent and defamatory statements, and your publisher's guarantee that any reference to my edition will be omitted from any further printings of your Introduction" (J.G., letter to Paul J. Gilette, 9 May 1968, JGf).

43 Aubrey Beardsley and J.G., *Under the Hill*, 77.

44 Ibid., 76.

45 Ibid., 85.

46 Ibid., 107.

47 Ibid.

48 Ibid., 108.

49 Maurice Girodias, letter to J.G., 30 March 1960, JGf.

50 J.G., letter to Milton Kastello, 4 May 1967, JGf.

51 J.G., letter to F.R. Scott, 9 September 1961, JGp.

52 F.R. Scott, 1968 diary, 2 March 1968, Francis Reginald Scott fonds, Library and Archives Canada.

53 J.G., letter to Donna George, 4 February 1968, JGf.

54 Maurice Girodias, "Introduction," *The Olympia Reader*, 19.

55 J.G., letter to Elma Koolmer, 9 November 1961, JGp.

56 J.G., letter to Maurice Girodias, 28 February 1965, JGf.

57 Michael Gnarowski, "Introduction," J.G., *The English Governess* (Ottawa: Golden Dog, 2000): viii.

58 Dustjacket of *Harriet Marwood, Governess* (New York: Grove, 1967). An argument against Glassco as the hand behind the jacket can be made from the use of the name "Dr Fritz Beobachter." The doctor's name features in blurbs for other Grove Press titles and is rumoured to be the creation of a publisher of fetish art, books, and cartoons.

59 J.G., preface, *Harriet Marwood, Governess* (Toronto: General, 1976): n.p.

60 Ibid.

61 J.G., Intimate Journal, 22 March 1938, JGp.

62 Among the other pseudonymous authors who found outlet with the publisher were James Lovebirch, Lord Kidrodstock, and Lord Birchisgood.

63 Steven J. Gertz, letter to the author, 3 March 2006.

64 Aimé van Rod, *La gouvernante*, 10.

65 Ibid., 90.

66 Ibid., 7–8.

67 J.G., *Harriet Marwood, Governess*, 5.

68 Aimé van Rod, *La gouvernante*, 8.

69 J.G., *Harriet Marwood, Governess*, 6.

70 I refer here to *Harriet Marwood, Governess*. While not divided into chapters, *La gouvernante* employs breaks in the text, some of which correspond to the divisions of Glassco's chapters.

71 Aimé van Rod, *La gouvernante*, 41.

72 J.G., *Harriet Marwood, Governess*, 27.

73 Ibid., 160.

74 J.G., letter to Geoffrey Wagner, 26 October 1966, JGf.

75 The author's copy was acquired after a three-year search from a Parisian bookseller.

76 Morse Peckham, *Art and Pornography*, 18. The back cover of the Black Cat edition of *Harriet Marwood, Governess*, issued fifteen years after Peckham's error, features the claim: "Alongside such classics as *My Secret Life, Pleasure Bound, A Man with a Maid*, and *The Pearl, Harriet Marwood, Governess* takes its place as one of the outstanding works of erotic fiction produced in the Victorian era."

77 Ibid., 78.

78 J.G., letter to F.R. Scott, 18 June 1959, JGp.

79 J.G., Intimate Journal, 13 November 1960, JGp.

80 Ibid.

CHAPTER SEVEN

1 The motto of Glassco's Pastime Press.

2 J.G., letter to Elma Koolmer, 31 March 1961, JGp.

3 J.G., letter to Elma Koolmer, 19 June 1961, JGp.

4 J.G., letter to Elma Koolmer, 25 May 1961, JGp.

5 J.G., letter to Elma Koolmer, 31 July 1961, JGp.

6 A.J.M. Smith, letter to J.G., 25 July 1961, JGf.

7 J.G., letter to A.J.M. Smith, 29 June 1961, JGf. Glassco misidentifies the book as *Confessions of a Dope Fiend*. Published in 1922, the book is generally recognized as Crowley's first novel, though it contains a preface in which the author writes: "This is a true story. It has been rewritten only so far as was necessary to conceal personalities." Crowley's excessive drug use is well documented.

8 J.G., "A Season in Limbo," 427.

9 An alternate, ill-fated version of his experiences was intended for *Maclean's*.

10 J.G. "A Season in Limbo," 429.

11 In *Montreal*, Glassco perpetuates the fantasy: "O childhood streets of Montreal

/ Simpson where I was born / St Luke where I was terrified ..." (25), and yet St Luke Street is recognized as the street of his birth in *Memoirs of Montparnasse*. In the 1950s, St Luke Street became part of de Maisonneuve Boulevard. The northwest corner of de Maisonneuve and St Matthew – once the location of Glassco's birth – is now taken up by an unremarkable commercial building.

12 J.G., "Autobiographical Sketch," JGf.

13 J.G., letter to Elma Koolmer, 15 November 1961, JGp.

14 The only mention of anything sexual in the letter concerned a new orderly: "he is a Lithuanian, has got some kind of crush on me and is making sheep's eyes; yesterday I found him kissing my underwear shorts, really this kind of thing is just another bloody nuisance. If he keeps on with these antics I'm going to threaten to report him to the Head Nurse. Not that I would do a nasty thing like that, but after all there are twenty other men on this floor, many of them younger and presumably better-looking and I don't see why he can't get to work on them." (J.G., letter to Elma Koolmer, 17 November 1961, JGp.)

15 J.G., *Selected Poems*, 65.

16 J.G., *Selected Poems*, 48–9. When first published, in the May 1963 issue of *Delta*, the poem was dedicated to the eccentric French composer Olivier Messaien. The very next month, the poem was reprinted with the dedication to Marion Scott in *Alphabet*. Glassco maintained the Scott dedication in all subsequent appearances.

17 J.G., letter to A.J.M. Smith, 25 July 1962, JGp. Glassco misidentifies Müller's work; the correct title is *An Essay on the Origin of Language*. In the accompanying copy of the poem, Glassco draws attention to the word "Tw'at," and cites: "influence of Layton."

18 J.G., untitled comment on "Catbird" in *How Do I Love Thee*, 8.

19 Gilles Marcotte, "Introduction," Hector de Saint-Denys-Garneau, *The Journal of Saint-Denys-Garneau*, 9.

20 J.G., Intimate Journal, 13 November 1960, JGp.

21 Ibid.

22 Ibid.

23 J.G., "Autobiographical Sketch," JGf.

24 J.G., Intimate Journal, 13 November 1960, JGp.

25 Robert Weaver, "A Talk with Morley Callaghan," 20.

26 J.G., letter to Robert McAlmon, 24 November 1943, RMA. *Strange Fugitive* is the title of Callaghan's first book.

27 Morley Callaghan, letter to J.G., 14 November 1960, JGf.

28 J.G., letter to Kay Boyle, 12 September 1967, JGf.

29 William Barrett, "Subtle Memoirist."

30 Norman Mailer, "Punching Papa."

31 William French. "Hemingway Got the Punchline of This Story."

32 Morley Callaghan, *That Summer in Paris*, 68–9.

33 Ibid., 111.

34 Ibid., 111–12.

35 Ibid., 144.

36 Ibid., 143.

37 J.G., letter to Kay Boyle, 12 September 1967, JGf.

38 Leon Edel, "Literature and Journalism: The Visible Boundaries," 17.

39 Ibid.

40 The failure to recognize the link between Johnny Hill in "Now That April's Here," the "Buffy" of *That Summer in Paris*, and Glassco would continue for many years. Most strikingly, Glassco's name is nowhere to be found in Brandon Conron's *Morley Callaghan* (New York: Twayne, 1966), the first lengthy study of the author, in which the story is discussed in detail.

41 J.G., "Introduction," *English Poetry in Quebec*, 5.

42 J.G., "Quebec Poetry Conference 1963" [Foster Poetry Conference], notes, JGP.

43 Ibid.

44 Michael Gnarowski, interview with the author, 12 April 2005.

45 J.G., "Lines Addressed to a Dozen Young Canadian Poets, after Unwisely Devouring Five Little Magazines at a Sitting," *English Poetry in Quebec*, 99.

46 Seymour Mayne, interview with the author, 20 November 2006.

47 J.G., Personal Journal, 1965–1969, 2 June 1965, JGf.

48 J.G., "Introduction," *English Poetry in Quebec*, 6-7.

49 Sponsored by the Canada Council, the Poets' Conference was attended by Glassco, Earle Birney, Fred Cogswell, Louis Dudek, Michael Gnarowski, Ralph Gustafson, D.G. Jones, Al Purdy, F.R. Scott, A.J.M. Smith, and George Whalley.

50 J.G., letter to A.J.M. Smith, 4 April 1964, AJMSp.

51 J.G, Personal Journal, 1965–1969, 15 June 1965, JGf.

52 Bill Bissett, review of *A Point of Sky*.

53 J.G., letter to Jean LeMoyne, 4 May 1964, JGf.

54 Ibid.

55 J.G., Personal Journal, 1965–1969, 2 June 1965, JGf.

56 Ibid.

57 J.G., letter to A.J.M. Smith, 8 September 1961, JGf.

58 Maurice Girodias, introduction, *The Olympia Reader*, 26.

59 Ibid.

60 The precise number of copies destroyed is unknown. In letters dated 6 September 1965 and 29 September 1966 Girodias writes that 1,600 copies were seized, while his letter of 22 July 1966 states that 1,500 copies were destroyed. All three letters are part of the John Glassco fonds at Library and Archives Canada.

61 J.G., letter to F R. Scott (unsent), 27 October 1966, JGf.

62 Maurice Girodias, letter to J.G., 22 July 1966, JGf.

63 Patrick Kearney, *The Paris Olympia Press*, 269.

64 Maurice Girodias, letter to J.G., 29 September 1966, JGf.

65 J.G., letter to Maurice Girodias, 11 May 1967, JGf.

66 J.G., "Autobiographical Sketch," JGf.

67 Ibid.

68 Ibid.

69 It was Swinburne biographer Jean Overton Fuller who, in 1968, was the first to make the attribution. Ten years later, the case for Milnes was advanced, to great effect, by Ian Gibson in his authoritative and exhaustive study *The English Vice: Beating, Sex and Shame in Victorian England and After*.

70 George Coleman, *The Rodiad*, 7–8.

71 J.G., letter to Geoffrey Wagner, 3 May 1966, JGf.

72 George Coleman [J.G.], epigraph in *Under the Birch*, by Miles Underwood [J.G.], 7.

73 J.G., undated handbill for *Squire Hardman*, JGp.

74 Ibid.

75 J.G., letter to Daryl Hine, 29 April 1971, JGf.

76 J.G., *Squire Hardman*, vi.

77 Ibid.

78 Roderick Haig-Brown, letter to J.G., 28 November 1967, JGf.

79 Iris Murdoch, letter to J.G., undated c. September 1975, JGf. The mutual friend was Geoffrey Wagner.

80 William Cooper, review of *Under the Hill*.

81 Ian Hamilton, review of *Under the Hill*.

82 Alan Pearson, "The Yellow Book Revisited, or a Beardsley Pastiche."

83 Geoffrey Wagner, "How Wild Was Mr Weirdsley?" 549.

84 Philip Core, letter to J.G., 6 August 1967, JGf.

85 J.G., letter to Philip Core, 5 December 1967, JGf.

86 J.G., letter to Philip Core, 14 August 1967, JGf.

87 J.G., letter to Philip Core, 5 January 1968, JGf.

88 The title Glassco used in his excuse was *The Poetry of French Canada in Translation*.

89 Kim Ondaatje, interview with the author, 14 November 2006.

90 Seymour Mayne, interview with the author, 20 November 2006.

91 J.G., letter to Seymour Mayne, 11 March 1971, JGf.

92 J.G., letter to A.J.M. Smith, 24 December 1966, JGf.

93 J.G., Personal Journal, 1965–1969, JGf. Glassco wrote only one other draft of the poem; rechristened "For Elma," it contains only one other change: on line 11, "This blackness" is substituted for "This heartbreak."

94 J.G., marginalia found on the second extant draft of "For Elma," JGf.

CHAPTER EIGHT

1 J.G., Personal Journal, 1965–1969, 18 February 1967, JGf.

2 J.G., letter to A.J.M. Smith, 9 January 1967, JGf.

3 J.G., letter to Ron Everson, 5 January 1967, JGf.

4 J.G., Personal Journal, 1965–1969, 2 May 1967, JGf.

5 J.G., letter to Kay Boyle, 1 August 1967, JGf.

6 J.G., *Montreal*, 27. *Terre des hommes* was drawn from the title of Antoine de Saint Exupéry's 1939 memoir, translated into English as *Wind, Sand and Stars*.

7 Ibid.

8 Robert Choquette, letter to J.G., 12 May 1966, JGf.

9 J.G., letter to Robert Choquette, 12 August 1966, JGf.

10 J.G., letter to Robert Choquette, 27 September 1966, JGf.

11 Louis Dudek, *In Defence of Art*, 68.

12 Ibid., 70.

13 J.G., letter to Robert Weaver, 18 October 1967, JGf.

14 J.G., letter to Leon Edel, 18 October 1967, JGf.

15 Margaret Atwood, interview with the author, 3 May 2005.

16 Ibid.

17 Glassco wrote of this belief in a 1 April 1936 entry in his Intimate Journal: "Well, I have suspected I was getting prematurely aged at 26 …"

18 J.G., Journal, Feb. 25, 1970 to July 5, '75, 25 February 1970, JGf.

19 Margaret Atwood, interview with the author, 3 May 2005.

20 Joseph MacSween, "Sad Crowds Bid Adieu as Fair Gates Close."

21 J.G., *Montreal*, 27.

22 As "Terre des hommes" and "Man and His World," a ghost of the exhibition continued during the summers that followed. It was finally brought to an end in October 1981, nine months after Glassco's death.

23 J.G., Personal Journal, 1965-1970, 3 September 1967, JGf.

24 J.G., letter to Kay Boyle, 1 August 1967, JGf.

25 Kay Boyle, letter to J.G., 22 November 1967, JGf.

26 J.G., letter to A.J.M. Smith, 15 January 1968, JGf.

27 Kay Boyle, letter to J.G., 29 March 1968, JGf.

28 This description appears on the front cover of the 1968 Doubleday edition of *Being Geniuses Together*.

29 In her edition of *Being Geniuses Together*, Boyle claims to have consulted McAlmon's typescript; she notes: "I have frequently substituted McAlmon's undeleted text rather than [*sic*] the edited sections which appear in the Secker and Warburg volume" (xiii). It is worth noting that no typescript matching this description is found among either writers' papers; assuming it exists, its location is unknown.

30 J.G., letter to Kay Boyle, 28 June 1968, JGf.

31 Jean Stafford, "Spirits."

32 Saul Maloff. "Again the Lost Ones."

33 Anthony Powell, "Knocking around the Latin Quarter."

34 In 1923, after Cowley had been arrested for assaulting the *patron* of the Rotonde, McAlmon and others had appeared the next morning at the police station to testify on the American's behalf. The charges were subsequently dismissed, and Cowley was spared what McAlmon believed would have been a six-month jail sentence. The event was covered by McAlmon in the original *Being Geniuses Together*, had been retained by Boyle, but was left unacknowledged in the review.

35 Robert McAlmon and Kay Boyle, *Being Geniuses Together*, 42.

36 Malcolm Cowley, "Those Paris Years."

37 Kay Boyle, letter to J.G., 4 June 1968, JGf.

38 Published in 1963 by Belmont, a New York publisher of cheap massmarket paperbacks, the book holds the distinction of being the first US collection of McAlmon's fiction. It was described on the back cover as a "strange 'lost novel' that takes the reader down dark and unpredictable pathways," but is actually a reprint of the 1925 short-story collection *Distinguished Air: Grim Fairy Tales*, together with "The Highly Prized Pyjamas." The incongruous cover photograph features a pair of bare female legs.

39 J.G., letter to Kay Boyle, 9 July 1968, JGf.

40 J.G., letter to Kay Boyle, 9 September 1968, JGf.

41 Morley Callaghan, *That Summer in Paris*, 65.

42 There was no second printing, nor would there be a paperback edition. Nine years would pass before McAlmon again returned to print, when *A Hasty Bunch* was reissued as part of Southern Illinois University Press' Lost American Fiction series. The new edition featured an afterword by Boyle. Neither this, nor any other edition of *A Hasty Bunch*, is currently in print.

   The reworked version of *Being Geniuses Together* was eventually reissued in 1984 by North Point Press and in 1997 by Johns Hopkins University Press. McAlmon's original continues to exist only in the 1938 Secker & Warburg first edition.

43 J.G., letter to Leon Edel, 9 October 1968, JGf.

44 Kay Boyle, letter to J.G., 3 December 1968, JGf.

45 J.G., letter to Kay Boyle, 2 December 1968, JGf. "Two Old Ladies" was one of too excerpts of *Memoirs of Montparnasse* published in the spring 1969 issue of *The Tamarack Review*. Aside from one reference – as "May Fry" – Kay Boyle is identified by her real name throughout. It is clear within the excerpt that May Fry and Kay Boyle are one and the same person. Glassco corrected this error in his personal copy.

46 Ibid.

47 Kay Boyle, letter to J.G., 6 February 1969, JGf.

48 J.G., letter to Kay Boyle, 25 February 1969, JGf.

49 J.G., letter to Kay Boyle, 19 March 1969, JGf.

50 J.G., typescript of *Memoirs of Montparnasse*, JGf. Glassco later altered the note to read: "All the characters in this book, except those specifically named ..." Neither version of the warning was included in the published work.

51 J.G., *Memoirs of Montparnasse*, 32.

52 Boyle's former husband, Laurence Vail, was hidden under a less complicated disguise. In *Memoirs of Montparnasse* he is the charming Terence Marr, husband to Sally, who is based on Peggy Guggenheim. In fact, Vail and Guggenheim were husband and wife during most of 1929, the year in which they feature in the memoir. With Robert McAlmon, Glassco, Vail, and Guggenheim visit Frank Harris, dine on the Riviera at the Perroquet, take in Nice, and view a blue movie entitled alternately *Der Zeitvertreib Rajahs*, *Les délassements du Rajah*, or *The Rajah's Recreations*. At the time, Nice was one of the most important cities in the distribution of European pornographic films. The scenario Glassco describes is similar to that of a film entitled *Der Raja*, dating from the 1920s. It is interesting to note that in early drafts Glassco records the title of the film he saw as *The Rajah*.

   In 1929, Guggenheim and Vail split. Two years later Vail published his only novel, *Murder! Murder!*, which was a fictionalized account of the marriage.

53 J.G., letter to William Toye, 13 March 1969, JGf.

54 J.G., letter to Kay Boyle, 20 April 1968, JGf.

55 Ibid.

56 Ibid.

57 Sheila Fischman, interview with the author, 20 July 2004.

58 Ibid.

59 Ibid.

60 D.G. Jones, untitled editorial, *Ellipse* 1.

61 J.G. Personal Journal, 1965–1969, 10 June 1968. JGf.

62 Bulimia nervosa was first described in 1979 by Gerald Russell, a consultant psychiatrist at London's Royal Free Hospital. In 1980, it was recognized as an autonomous eating disorder by the American Psychiatric Association.

63 J.G., letter to Kay Boyle, 25 March 1969, JGf.

64 J.G., letter to Milton Kastello, 30 April 1969, JGf.

65 J.G., letter to Kay Boyle, 28 July 1969, JGf.

66 J.G., letter to Kay Boyle, 15 November 1969, JGf.

67 J.G. Personal Journal, 1965-1969, 11 December 1969.

CHAPTER NINE

1 J.G., Personal Journal, 1965–1969, 15 December 1969, JGf.

2 Leon Edel, "Introduction," *Memoirs of Montparnasse*, vii.

3 Ibid.

4 Ibid., vii–viii.

5 Ibid., x.

6 William French. "Pursuing a Dream in Paris Remembered."

7 Margaret Laurence. "Roses and Yew," 80.

8 Arnold Edinborough, "Lessons to Drop-Outs on How to Do Your Own Thing in Style."

9 Malcolm Cowley, "We Had Such Good Times."

10 Ibid.

11 Ibid.

12 J.G., Journal, Feb. 25, 1970 to July 5, '75, 3 July 1970, JGf.

13 It seems likely that Smith was unaware as to the extent of Glassco's work. In 1973, Smith departed from Glassco's line by writing in his anthology *The Canadian Century* that *Memoirs of Montparnasse* had been "completed from contemporary notes." (A.J.M. Smith, ed., *The Canadian Century*, 412).

14 Irving Layton, *Waiting for the Messiah*, 248.

15 Louis Dudek. "A Decadent in Canada in the 1970s? Yes!"

16 Ibid.

17 Ibid.

18 Ibid.

19 Louis Dudek, letter, *The Globe & Mail*, 17 September 1988, D7.

20 Louis Dudek, *Notebooks: 1960–1994*, 231. Dudek continues with brief criticism of Keath Fraser's 1984 essay "Notes Toward a Supreme Fiction," ultimately lumping the author in with Ford and Glassco (232): "What these fanciful writers do not realize is that untruth, or the confusion of untruth and fiction, can be fatal to their survival as writers. We do not read the work of writers we cannot trust. They're tainted meat."

21 Louis Dudek. "A Decadent in Canada in the 1970s? Yes!"

22 Louis Dudek, "Look on the Book as Fantasy."

23 Leon Edel, "Literature and Journalism: The Visible Boundaries," 18.

24 One early and notable exception is Sanford J. Smoller's 1975 biography of Robert McAlmon, *Adrift among Geniuses*, in which the biographer cautions: "Glassco seemed to telescope time, as a novelist might do, for emphasis and structural unity, and thus the chronology is unreliable" (358). Smoller later describes *Memoirs of Montparnasse* as "fictionalized history" (358). It should also be noted that in *A Concise Bibliography of English-Canadian Literature*, published in 1973, Michael Gnarowski lists *Memoirs of Montparnasse* under "Prose Fiction."

25 J.G., Personal Journal, 1965–1969, 2 June 1965, JGf.

26 J.G., as quoted in Stephen Scobie, "The Mirror on the Brothel Wall: John Glassco, *Memoirs of Montparnasse*."

27 J.G., letter to Kay Boyle, 6 February 1970, JGf.

28 J.G., *Memoirs of Montparnasse*, 80.

29 Ibid.

30 Then aged seventy-seven, Bricktop (Ada Smith) was living in Los Angeles. The famous nightclub owner had attracted attention from Hollywood and Cheryl Crawford, co-founder of The Actor's Studio, who was interested in

producing a Broadway musical based on her life. Following Boyle's suggestion, Glassco wrote Bricktop, offering his services. In response, he received a long rambling letter replete with religiosity and crazed, imagined nostalgia. Glassco knew better than to write her again. Bricktop's autobiography, *Bricktop*, did not appear until 1983, the year before her death. It was co-authored by James Hoskins.

31 Kay Boyle, letter to J.G., 19 January 1972, JGf.

32 Mindful of this large number, he considered a number of pseudonyms: Grace Davignon, W.P.R. Eady, Albert Eddy, Nordyk Nudleman, and a near-anagram, S. Colson-Haig. Although he provided all these *noms faux* to John Robert Colombo for *Colombo's Names & Nicknames*, Glassco told Fraser Sutherland that he had never actually used them. Perhaps Glassco meant that the false names were not used in print. S. Colson-Haig, the name that he'd once intended on using for the introduction to *The Temple of Pederasty*, was used in private correspondence of a sexual nature with a transvestite living in the northern Quebec mining town of Chibougamau.

Another bit of hoaxery to which Glassco didn't own up was the appropriation of his first wife's name. After her death he signed at least one letter "(Miss) Elma von Colmar" (J.G., letter to David Lass, 13 May 1974, JGf).

33 Philip Stratford, "Circle, Straight Line, Ellipse," 89.

34 Fred Cogswell, review of *The Poetry of French Canada in Translation*, 104.

35 J.G., "Introduction," *The Poetry of French Canada in Translation*, xix.

36 This politically charged event was held on 27 March 1970 before an audience of nearly two thousand people at Montreal's Théâtre Gésù. Among those who participated were Nicole Brossard, Gérald Godin, Pauline Julien, Michèle Lalonde, Raymond Lévesque, Claude Péloquin, and Denis Vanier. Journalist Jean Basile described the event three days later in the pages of *Le Devoir*: "Cette nuit a été plus qu'un succès : une sorte de triomphe. Sans doute n'y eût-il pas que de la bonne poésie mais ne sait-on pas que la poésie, finalement, prise dans un tel contexte, n'a pas besoin d'être bonne ou mauvaise. En fait, c'est l'acte, l'événement qui sont poétiques."

37 J.G., "To Certain Quebecois Poets," JGf.

38 J.G., letter to A.J.M. Smith, 15 January 1968, JGf. This is just one of many letters in which Glassco writes of "la belle Lalonde." Smith also made frequent use of this affectionate epithet.

39 J.G., "Michèle Lalonde," William Toye, ed., *Supplement to the Oxford Companion to Canadian History and Literature*, 178. Here Glassco might have let his personal feelings influence his public opinion. Writing to Smith three years earlier, Glassco dismisses "Speak White" as "just stupid tubthumping, not a poem at all" (J.G., letter to A.J.M. Smith, 4 December 1970, JGf).

40 J.G., "André Brochu," William Toye, ed., *Supplement to the Oxford Companion to Canadian History and Literature*, 22.

41 J.G., letter to A.J.M. Smith, 22 November 1970, JGf.

42 Ibid.

43 J.G., letter to F.R. Scott, 21 November 1965, JGf.

44 J.G., letter to A.J.M. Smith, 22 November 1970, JGf.

45 J.G., letter to A.J.M. Smith, 4 December 1970, JGf.

46 Ibid.

47 Ibid.

48 In the late 1960s, *Harriet Marwood, Governess* was published in both German and Dutch translations – *Die Gouvernante* (Hamburg: Gala Verlag Gimblt, n.d.) and *Tuchtiging tot Tederheid* (Amsterdam: Uitgeversij De Arbeiderspers, 1969). A Dutch translation of Glassco's completed *Under the Hill, De Venusberg*, was published in 1971 by Uitgeversij De Arbeiderspers.

49 Sheila Fischman, interview with the author, 20 July 2004.

50 J.G., letter to Ken Norris, 2 July 1975, JGf.

51 As P.N. Dedeaux, Wagner published two books with Essex House: *The Nothing Things* and *Tender Buns*. Released in 1969, both were lighthearted, accomplished works of flagellant literature.

52 J.G., letter to Brian Kirby, 11 June 1969, JGf.

53 Ken Sato, *Quaint Stories of the Samurais*, 9. The other Ihara titles from which Sato drew his stories are *Budō denrai ki* (1687), *Buke giri monogatari* (1688), and *Yorozu no fumihō* (1696).

54 Ken Sato, letter to Robert McAlmon, 23 August 1926, RMA.

55 In 1926, McAlmon received the manuscript for *Quaint Stories of the Samurais* courtesy of sexual psychologist Havelock Ellis, forwarded at the request of the "translator." In August 1926, Sato submitted a second manuscript, that of a lengthy original novel entitled *The Yellow Jap Dogs*. While McAlmon considered both submissions for Contact Editions, another Parisian publisher, Standahl et Compagnie, issued a French translation of the "old classic Japanese stories of pederasty," which Sato had undertaken with the aid of a lady friend. The appearance of the Standahl edition placed no pressure on McAlmon, nor did its insignificant reception have any measurable effect on his decision. *The Yellow Jap Dogs* was rejected; it has never been published.

56 Robert McAlmon, in Ken Sato, *Quaint Stories of the Samurais*, title page. McAlmon's relaxed editing style extended to his sales information: "Sold by Edward Tutus [*sic*] at the sign of the Black Manikin."

57 Robert McAlmon, quoted in Hugh Ford, *Published in Paris*, 84. Sato was conscious that his limitations in English were reflected in *Quaint Stories of the Samurais*. In a letter dated 15 February 1929, one month after receiving his copies of the book, he writes McAlmon that a friend "has polished and revised my whole Saikaku stories" (RMA).

58 Ethel Moorhead, quoted in Hugh Ford, *Published in Paris*, 84.

59 In *Memoirs of Montparnasse*, Glassco writes of visiting a Mr Threep at Galignani's bookshop on the rue de Rivoli, a shop that exists to this day. There,

prompted by poverty, he parts reluctantly with inscribed copies of George Moore's *Reminiscences of the Impressionist Painters* and *The Book-Bills of Narcissus* by Richard Le Gallienne – the latter, perhaps tellingly, a novel about a book collector. In *Memoirs of Montparnasse*, Moore's book is incorrectly identified as *Recollections of the Impressionist Painters*. While it is tempting to dismiss the anecdote – Glassco never met Moore – the anecdote may have had some basis in reality as Glassco often turned to bookdealers as a means of supplementing his investments.

60 J.G., letter to Robert McAlmon, 16 June 1947, RMA.

61 Years after McAlmon's friendship with Glassco reached its abrupt end, the US writer resumed a warm and steady correspondence with Ken Sato. Although Sato continued to write after his 1926 return to Japan, it would appear his new work received neither recognition, nor publication. He turned to the theatre and wrote several plays with titles like *The Japanese in America* and *The Jap Family in America*, but these were never staged. *Quaint Stories of the Samurais* and its French translation appear to be his only published titles. Much of Sato's latter correspondence with McAlmon deals with nature, the changes brought about by the US occupation of postwar Japan, and his very real fear of a future war between the United States and the Soviet Union. Though literature is barely mentioned, it is interesting to note that there is one passage relating to a future acquaintance of Glassco: "I just finished 'Two Solitude' [*sic*] by Hugh MacLennan. The author must be a Canadian. The story is about the Canadian English and the Canadian French. It is good, I thought. The characters are depicted quite well and the changes of the Canadian county [*sic*] life is very well written, I felt" (Ken Sato, letter to Robert McAlmon, 18 March 1953, RMA).

62 J.G., "Introduction," *The Temple of Pederasty*, 3.

63 J.G., letter to A.J.M. Smith, 15 January 1962, JGf. It is worth noting that in 1996 an "explicit retelling of Charlotte Brontë's *Jane Eyre*" was published by Blue Moon under the title *An English Education*. The work is credited to P.N. Dedeaux, a pseudonym of Glassco's friend Geoffry Wagner.

64 Ken Sato, *Quaint Stories of the Samurais*, 28.

65 J.G. (Okada Hideki, pseud.), *The Temple of Pederasty*, 35-6.

66 J.G., letter to Maurice Girodias, 14 September 1968, JGf.

67 J.G., letter to Philip Core, 22 October 1968, JGf.

68 J.G., letter to Philip Core, 12 December 1968, JGf.

69 J.G., letter to Brian Kirby, 16 August 1969, JGf.

70 J.G., letter to Harold Straubing, 21 April 1970, JGf.

71 Léonard Trudel, letter to J.G., 21 April 1970, JGf.

72 Douglas Fetherling, *Travels by Night*, 241–2.

73 Ibid., 242. Atwood's "splendidly subtle squib" was "John Glassco's new edition of the Japanese classic, *The Temple of Pederasty*, blends erudition with elegance

and sustains the reader's interest to the end; it is handled with this celebrated editor's habitual grace" (quoted in Fraser Sutherland, *John Glassco: A Personal and Working Library*, 5.)

74 J.G., letter to Daryl Hine, 29 April 1971, JGf.

75 Glassco described himself thus on the title page of a copy that he presented to Michael Gnarowski. With Gnarowski, Glassco was perhaps more open than most; the inscription in his copy of *Squire Hardman* reads:

> For Michael Garowski –
>> to swell his collection of Canadian pseudonyms,
>>> this little item ...
>> With kindest regards
>
> 26/vi/67   John Glassco

76 J.G., letter to A.J.M. Smith, 30 December 1969, JGf. Glassco may not have realized that "Gottfried Wolfgang" is itself a rather faithful translation of Washington Irving's "The Adventure of the German Student," which first appeared in *Tales of a Traveller* (1824).

77 J.G., letter to Ronald Sutherland, 29 November 1969, JGf.

78 J.G., letter to Robert McAlmon, 11 June 1941, RMA.

79 J.G., letter to Milton Kastello, 8 March 1971, JGf.

80 Ibid.

81 J.G., Journal, Feb. 25, 1970 to July 5, '75, 25 February 1970, JGf.

82 Ibid., 18 June 1970.

83 J.G., "Sonnets to A. Ste-C.," JGf. Among the ten other titles considered were *Sonnets for Donathien, Sonnets for Pierre, Flagellation Sonnets, Sonnets to Alan, The Marsyas Sonnets, The Ainger Sonnets*. It would appear that Glassco eventually settled on *The Jupiter Sonnets*.

84 J.G., Journal, Feb. 25, 1970 to July 5, '75, 18 June 1970, JGf.

85 Ibid., 5 March 1971.

86 Alan Hustak, "Interviews Were Broadcaster's Forte."

87 Christy McCormick, letter to the author, 22 January 2009.

88 Joel McCormick, letter to the author, 18 January 2009.

89 Edward O. Phillips, interview with the author, 17 May 2007.

90 Ibid.

91 Ibid.

92 Marion McCormick, quoted in Kildare Dobbs, "The Great Glassco," 52.

93 Joel McCormick, letter to the author, 21 January 2009.

94 J.G., Journal, Feb. 25, 1970 to July 5, '75, 18 September 1971, JGf.

95 Glassco wrote this description on a photograph of himself and Marion taken outside a motel cabin. The image is held in the JGf.

96 J.G., Journal, Feb. 25, 1970 to July 5, '75, 18 August 1971, JGf.

97 Ibid., 24 August 1971, JGf.

98 Ibid., 13 October 1971, JGf.

99 Ibid., 7 November 1971, JGf.

100 J.G., letter to Angela Bowering, 11 November 1971, JGf.

101 On the copyright page, Glassco thanks Smith for his help in choosing and arranging the poems. In fact, Smith's role in these areas was much greater than that of Glassco.

102 J.G., letter to A.J.M. Smith, 16 December 1970, JGf.

103 J.G., Journal, Feb. 25, 1970 to July 5, '75, 24 August 1971, JGf.

104 J.G., letter to A.J.M. Smith, 4 December 1970, JGf.

105 Ibid.

106 J.G., letter to A.J.M. Smith, 19 December 1979, JGf.

107 J.G., *Selected Poems*, 73-4.

108 In fact, it was Marion who took the phone call. Informed by a nurse that "Mrs Glassco" had "slipped away," she initially thought that Elma had somehow escaped from the hospital. "She was so angry at that nurse," recalls Ken Woodman. "'Why do they have to put it that way?' she said" (interview with the author, 5 September 2007).

109 J.G., Journal, Feb. 25, 1970 to July 5, '75, 29 December 1971, JGf.

110 J.G., death notice for Elma Glassco, *The Gazette* (3 December 1971): 43.

111 "No Strings," *Time* (Canadian Edition) (3 April 1972): 11.

112 "Authors Receive Awards," *The Ottawa Citizen* (6 May 1972): 34.

113 Eleanor Wachtel, "Prize and Prejudice." Wachtel provides as examples Marie-Claire Blais's *The Manuscripts of Pauline Archange*, Margaret Laurence's *A Jest of God*, Robertson Davies's *The Manticore*, and Jack Hodgins's *The Resurrection of Joseph Bourne*, winners all; while their respective predecessors, *A Season in the Life of Emmanuel*, *The Stone Angel*, *Fifth Business*, and *The Invention of the World*, had been passed over.

   Coincidentally, in 1964 Al Purdy wrote Glassco that he thought *A Point of Sky* would not win the Governor General's Award for a very similar reason: "In a way this is a bad year for your own book to be coming, on accounta [*sic*] everybody looks at Souster and says look at all the books that guy has written and isn't it about time –?" (Al Purdy, *Yours, Al.*, 82). Purdy's prediction was correct – the award was given to Raymond Souster's *The Colour of the Times*.

114 Ralph Gustafson, letter to J.G., 14 April 1970, JGf.

115 Such is the reputation of *Memoirs of Montparnasse* that it is often assumed to have won the award. The author biography for *The Fatal Woman* states: "John Glassco is a stylist of international reputation and has won the Governor-General's award for both poetry and non-fiction."

116 Al Purdy, *Yours, Al*, 268.

117 J.G. [pseud. Sylvia Bayer], *Fetish Girl*, 9.

118 Ibid., 7.

119 J.G., letter to Philip Nobile, 3 March 1972, JGf.

120 Philip Nobile's book *Intellectual Skywriting* was published in 1974 by New

York's Charterhouse Press. A brief account of his exchange with Glassco – whom Nobile hides behind the name 'Mr Rubber' – appears on page 233.

121 J.G., letter to Margaret Atwood, 29 May 1971, JGf. Responding to Glassco's comment "how revolting about the editor of *Rubber News* being muzzled and fined!" Atwood responded: "what was the editor of R.N. muzzled *with*? That is the question" (letter to J.G., 17 June 1971l JGf).

122 J.G., letter to Milton Kastello, 8 March 1971, JGf.

123 After receiving his BA, Core continued his studies at the Ruskin School of Drawing in Oxford and the Accademia di Belli Arti in Florence. He settled in London, where he achieved notice for his art and as a commentator on the avant-garde. The author of two books, *The Original Eye* and the important *Camp: The Lie That Tells the Truth*, his most moving writing came in the form of obituaries written for *The Independent* about Jean-Michel Basquiat, Robert Mapplethorpe, and others who had died of AIDS. Core himself succumbed to the disease in 1989 at the age of thirty-eight.

124 J.G., letter to Philip Core, 3 August 1972, JGf.

125 Philip Core, letter to J.G., 30 July [*sic*] 1972, JGf. The letter, which could not have been written in July, was almost certainly penned in August – likely 30 August 1972.

126 J.G., inscription dated 20 July 1971, JGf.

127 J.G., inscribed copy of *Fetish Girl*, W.D. Jordan Special Collections Library, Queen's University, Kingston.

128 J.G., letter to Leon Edel, 28 April 1973, JGf.

129 Stephen J. Gertz, letter to the author, 31 July 2006. *Rubber Goddess* was published in 1967 by Corsair Books of Cleveland. Other Lana Preston titles include *Delicious Domineering Doublecross*, *Love's Lash*, and *Sorority Spanks*, among others.

130 J.G., Journal, Feb. 25, 1970 to July 5, '75, 24 August 1971, JGf.

131 Ibid., 14 April 1972, JGf.

132 J.G., "Autobiographical Sketch," JGf.

133 J.G., Journal, Sept. 20, 1975 to Nov. 6, 1979, JGf.

134 J.G., Journal, Feb. 25, 1970 to July 5, '75, 6 August 1971, JGf.

135 Ibid., 2 November 1971.

136 In fact, the collection was not dedicated to Elma, but to Glassco's mother.

137 J.G., Journal, Feb. 25, 1970 to July 5, '75, 28 July 1970, JGf.

138 J.G., letter to A.J.M. Smith, 21 November 1966, JGf.

139 J.G., *Montreal*, 25.

140 As of November 2009, this old chestnut tree was still healthy.

141 J.G., letter to Ken Norris, 25 July 1975, JGf.

142 J.G., letter to Louis Dudek, 1 May 1972, JGf.

143 J.G., letter to Daryl Hine, 13 October 1973, JGf. One year after publication *Montreal* had sold 524 copies. Glassco received a royalty cheque amounting to $75.75, a little over fourteen cents a copy.

144 J.G., letter to Louis Dudek, 19 June 1973, JGf.

145 Douglas Barbour, review of *Montreal*, *The Dalhousie Review*.

146 Joanne Harris Burgess, review of *Montreal* and three other books, *CrossCountry*.

147 Miriam Waddington. "But How Does Glassco Feel about Montreal." *The Globe & Mail*, 17 November 1973: 34.

148 J.G. *Montreal*. 28.

149 Miriam Waddington. "But How Does Glassco Feel about Montreal."

150 J.G., addendum to *Montreal*, JGf.

151 J.G., Journal, Feb. 25, 1970 to July 5, '75, 26 October 1973, JGf.

CHAPTER TEN

1 J.G., "The Heavenly Boy."

2 Unsigned McClelland & Stewart reader's report, 31 March 1959, JGf.

3 Jim Polk, letter to the author, 4 January 2007.

4 J.G., *The Fatal Woman*, i.

5 Ibid, 8. The head office of the Guarantee Company of North America was, indeed, "shaped like a portable gallon can."

6 Ibid., ii.

7 Glassco's new title is drawn from Shakespeare's Sonnet 129: "Th' expense of spirit in a waste of shame/ Is lust in action…"

8 J.G., letter to Sandra Martin, 15 May 1974. JGf.

9 Fraser Sutherland, interview with the author, 30 June 2003.

10 Glassco's found poem is drawn from the final two paragraphs of "'Dead Flies,' Or 'Ye Shall be as Gods,'" the ninth chapter in Frederic William Farrar's *Eric, or Little by Little*. Farrar was headmaster of Marlborough College and dean of Canterbury; his novel was for more than half a century a traditional gift for boys departing for private school. In the author's preface to the 1892 edition, Farrar writes: "The story of 'Eric' was written with but one single object—the vivid inculcation of inward purity and moral purpose, by the history of a boy who, in spite of the inherent nobleness of his disposition, falls into all folly and wickedness, until he has learnt to seek help from above."

11 "Collect Canadian Writers Cards!!" *Northern* Journey, 1 (1971): n.p.

12 Sutherland, who never met Elma, was unaware that the photograph was of Glassco's wife. The picture, sent 15 July 1971, was accompanied by a letter:

Dear Sirs:-

My good friend John Glassco has just told me you have accepted the first chapter of my latest novel *Fetish Girl* and I am delighted.

I understand you would like to use a photograph and to print some kind of introductory-biographical note.

I enclose the photograph. As for the note, here also is a suggested first-person text giving all relevant information and which you can 3rd-person alter, cut, telescope or rearrange as you see fit. Only I must see the final text of whatever note you mean to use, I'm sorry to put you to this extra trouble, but I have to do it.

Yours sincerely

Mrs Sylvia Fenwick-Owen,
1224 Bishop St,
Montreal 107
PQ

P.S. May I beg you to keep my home address quite confidential. Thank you.

(J.G., letter to the editors of *Northern Journey*, 15 July 1971, JGf.)

13 Wil Wigle, "Slow Burn," 17.
14 George Woodcock, letter *Quill & Quire*, 20:6 (July 1974): 2.
15 Rosalie Abella, letter to Fraser Sutherland, 17 January 1974, the Northern Journey fonds, York University Archives and Special Collections.
16 Ibid.
17 Fraser Sutherland, interview with the author, 30 June 2003.
18 Marian Engel, letter to Fraser Sutherland, 20 February 1974, the Northern Journey fonds, York University Archives and Special Collections.
19 J.G., letter to Fraser Sutherland, 14 March 1974, the Northern Journey fonds, York University Archives and Special Collections.
20 J.G., letter to Rosalie Abella, 15 March 1974, the Northern Journey fonds, York University Archives and Special Collections.
21 J.G., letter to Rosalie Abella (unsent), 22 August 1974, JGf.
22 Margaret Atwood, letter to J.G., 8 April 1974, JGf.
23 Ibid.
24 "'Slow Burn' Still Smoldering," *Quill & Quire*, 20:5 (June 1974): 8.
25 George Woodcock, letter. *Quill & Quire*, 20:6 (July 1974): 11.
26 "Editors' Note," *Northern Journey* 4 (June 1974): 6.
27 Advertisement for *Northern Journey* 2-4, *The Globe & Mail* (2 November 1974): 30.
28 *Northern Journey* would cease publication in 1976.
29 Joel McCormick, letter to the authorl 17 January 2009.
30 Roy MacSkimming, "New Book Another Example of Delayed Recognition," *The Toronto Star* (1 November 1974): E14; Kildare Dobbs, review of *The Fatal Woman*, *Maclean's* (November 1974): 116; Peter Buitenhuis, "Style Nestled in the Shadow of de Sade," *The Globe & Mail* (30 November 1974): 40.
31 Louis Dudek, letter to John Glassco, 6 December 1974, JGf.
32 Edward O. Philips, interview with the author, 17 May 2007.
33 J.G., Journal, Feb. 25, 1970 to July 5, '75, 18 December 1974, JGf.

34 Ibid.

35 J.G., "The Poet as Performer Debases His Art. You Hear Him, Not His Poetry."

36 J.G., letter to Geoffrey Wagner, 18 October 1976, JGf.

37 J.G., letter to Henry Beissel, 2 December 1974, JGf.

38 J.G., letter to Henry Beissel, 23 May 1974, JGf.

39 J.G., preface, manuscript of *The Collected Short Stories*, JGf.

40 Ibid.

41 Ibid.

42 Robert McAlmon, *The Nightinghouls of Paris*, 62.

43 Michael Gnarowski, interview with the author, 12 April 2005.

44 Jim Polk, letter to the author, 4 January 2007.

45 J.G., letter to Milton Kastello, c. 1970, JGf.

46 J.G., Journal, Feb. 25, 1970 to July 5, '75, 27 October 1973, JGf.

47 Ibid., 2 November 1972.

48 Ibid., 25 July 1974.

49 F.R. Scott, *Saint-Denys Garneau and Anne Hébert*, 9.

50 J.G., "Introduction," Hector de Saint-Denys-Garneau, *Complete Poems of Saint Denys Garneau*, 17.

51 Eli Mandel, "Saint Denys Garneau? He Goes On Living. He Won't Go Away. Haunted, Self-Conscious."

52 J.G., "Monique Bosco," William Toye, ed., *Supplement to the Oxford Companion to Canadian History and Literature*, 20.

53 Monique Bosco, *Lot's Wife*, 10-11.

54 J.G., Intimate Journal, 23 August 1935, JGp.

55 Brian Brett, interview with the author, 21 October 2006.

56 Chris Scott, "Helter Pelter."

57 Brian Vintcent, review of *Venus in Furs*.

58 J.G., letter to Brian Brett, 14 July 1977, JGf.

59 J.G., "The Art of Pornography," 101.

60 Ibid.

61 Brian Brett, interview with the author, 21 October 2006.

62 J.G., letter to Alan Safarik, 21 September 1978.

63 J.G., Journal – Sept. 20, 1975 to Nov. 6, 1979, 22 June 1976, JGf.

64 Ibid., 25 July 1974.

65 The other titles considered were: *The Judge, The Father, Father and Son, The Master, The Story of J, Translated from the French, Joy and J, Man and Boy, Beyond Guilt and Mourning, Of Guilt and Mourning, The Stripped Man, Marsyas, The Old Sadist*, and *An Old Sadist*.

66 Believe Me, If All Those Endearing Young Charms

Believe me, if all those endearing young charms,
Which I gaze on so fondly to-day,

Were to change by to-morrow, and fleet in my arms
Like fairy-gifts fading away,
Thou wouldst still be adored, as this moment thou art,
Let thy loveliness fade as it will,
And around the dear ruin each wish of my heart
Would entwine itself verdantly still.

It is not while beauty and youth are thine own,
And thy cheeks unprofaned by a tear,
That the fervor and faith of a soul can be known,
To which time will but make thee more dear!
No, the heart that has truly loved never forgets,
But as truly loves on the close,
As the sunflower turns on her god, when he sets
The same look which she turned when he rose!

67 Ibid., 8 September 1976.
68 J.G., Journal, Sept. 20, 1975 to Nov. 6, 1979, 20 September 1975, JGf.
69 Soucy's translation, *Souvenirs de Montparnasse*, was published in 1983, two
    years after Glassco's death. It received little notice.
70 Written by George B. Mair, published by Scottish Exit (now Exit), the book-
    let was the first published guide to euthanasia. It is unlikely that Glassco was
    successful in his attempts to obtain a copy as it was available for purchase only
    to members of right-to-die societies of three months' standing. The publica-
    tion was not among the items in Glassco's library that were offered in 1982
    by The Word Bookshop.
71 J.G., Journal – Sept. 20, 1975 to Nov. 6, 1979, 6 November 1979, JGf.
72 J.G., Journal – Sept. 20, 1975 to Nov. 6, 1979, 29 September 1979, JGf.
73 J.G., note accompanying the final draft of *Those Endearing Young Charms*,
    20 December 1979, JGf.
74 J.G., manuscript for *Those Endearing Young Charms*, final draft, 1, JGf.
75 Ibid., 3.
76 Ibid., 6.
77 Ibid., 7.
78 Ibid., 91–2.
79 J.G., Journal – Sept. 20, 1975 to Nov. 6, 1979, 9 October 1979, JGf.
80 J.G., manuscript for *Those Endearing Young Charms*, final draft, 98, JGf.
81 Ibid., 10.
82 J.G., Journal – Sept. 20, 1975 to Nov. 6, 1979, 13 October 1976, JGf.
83 J.G., letter to A.J.M. Smith, 15 January 1962, JGf.
84 J.G., letter to A.J.M. Smith, 27 October 1964, JGf. Assuming a nine-month
    pregnancy, the time of Glassco's conception would have been mid-March
    1909.

85 J.G., letter to Leon Edel, 12 April 1980, JGf.

86 Leon Edel, letter to J.G., 10 July 1980, JGf.

87 J.G., letter to Leon Edel, 20 July 1980, JGf.

88 The other Canadian novels that have been translated more than once include: Louis Hémon's *Maria Chapdelaine* (1916), translated by W.H. Blake (1921), Andrew McPhail (1921), and Alan Brown (1989); Félix-Antoine Savard's *Menaud, maître-draveur* translated by Alan Sullivan (as *Boss of the River*, 1947) and Richard Howard (as *Master of the River*, 1976); Gabrielle Roy's *Bonheur d'occasion* (1945), translated as *The Tin Flute* by Hannah Josephson (1947) and Alan Brown (1980); and Hubert Aquin's *Prochain épisode* (1965), translated by Penny Williams (as *Prochain episode*, 1967) and Sheila Fischman (as *Next Episode*, 2001). Philippe-Joseph Aubert de Gaspé's *Les anciens Canadiens* (1863) holds a unique position, having undergone translation by four separate hands: Georgiana M. Pennée (as *The Canadians of Old*, 1864); Sir Charles G.D. Roberts (as *The Canadians of Old*, 1890); Jane Bierley (as *Canadians of Old*, 1996); and the Pennée translation was later revised by Thomas Guthrie Marquis and published as *Seigneur d'Hiberville: A Romance of the Fall of New France* (1929).

89 J.G., letter to Michael Gnarowski, 24 July 1980, JGf. Glassco's translation was published in 1982, the year after his death, under the title *Fear's Folly*.

90 J.G., letter to Leon Edel, 20 July 1980, JGf.

91 J.G., letter to Leon Edel, 12 December 1980, JGf.

92 J.G., "The Heavenly Boy."

93 Ralph Gustafson, letter to J.G., 20 December 1980, JGf.

94 Sheila Fischman, interview with the author, 20 July 2004.

95 Michael Gnarowski, interview with the author, 12 April 2005.

96 Stephen Scobie, *McAlmon's Chinese Opera*, 58.

97 Sheila Fischman, interview with the author, 20 July 2004. I am grateful to Sheila Fischman for relating Marion McCormick's account of Glassco's death.

98 J.G., draft of an inscription to Stephen Scobie, dated 2 February 1981, 29 January 1981, JGf.

CODA

1 Fraser Sutherland, interview with the author, 30 June 2003.

2 William Toye, interview with the author, 2 November 2003.

3 Ibid.

Bibliography

The bulk of John Glassco's papers are housed in the John Glassco fonds at Library and Archives Canada, Ottawa, and in the John Glassco papers, Rare Books and Special Manuscripts Division, McGill University Libraries, Montreal. The most significant collection of correspondence not found, either as original or copy, in these two collections is held in the Robert McAlmon Archive, Yale Collection of American Literature, Bienecke Rare Book and Manuscript Library, Yale University. A number of other collections hold correspondence relevant to Glassco and his story; these include Leon Edel papers, Rare Books and Special Manuscripts Division, McGill University Libraries and the Arthur James Marshall Smith Papers, Trent University.

Atwood, Margaret. Letter. *Quill and Quire*, 40.7 (July 1974): 2, 11.

Bailey, Thomas Melville, ed. *The Dictionary of Hamilton Biography*. Hamilton: Dictionary of Hamilton Biography, 1981.

Barbour, Douglas. Review of *Montreal*. *The Dalhousie Review* 53 (Winter 1973–74): 785.

Barrett, William. "Subtle Memoirist." *Atlantic Monthly* (February 1963): 132.

Beach, Sylvia. *Shakespeare and Company*. New York: Harcourt, Brace, 1959.

Beardsley, Aubrey. *The Story of Venus and Tannhauser*. New York: Award, 1967.

– and John Glassco. *Under the Hill*. Paris: Olympia, 1959.

bissett, bill. Review of *A Point of Sky*. *Alphabet* 8 (December 1965–March 1966): 76.

Bosco, Monique. *Lot's Wife* [*La femme de Loth*]. Translated by John Glassco. Toronto: McClelland & Stewart, 1975.

Bricktop [Ada Smith] with James Haskins. *Bricktop*. New York: Antheneum, 1983.

Bruga and J.G. [Euphorian, pseud.]. "Collegiana." *The McGill Daily*, 24 November 1926: 2.

Buitenhuis, Peter. "Style Nestled in the Shadow of de Sade." *The Globe & Mail* (30 November 1974): 40.

Burgess, Joanne Harris. Review of *Montreal* and three other books. *CrossCountry* 3–4 (Fall 1975): 83–4.

Burpee, Lawrence, ed. *Songs of French Canada*. Toronto: Musson, 1909.

Callaghan, Morley. *The Loved and the Lost*. Toronto: Macmillan, 1951.

–*The Complete Stories, Volume One*. Toronto: Exile, 2003.

– *Now That April's Here and Other Stories*. Toronto: Macmillan, 1936.

– *That Summer in Paris*. Holstein, ON: Exile, 2006.

Cameron, Elspeth. *Irving Layton: A Portrait*. Toronto: Stoddart, 1985.

Carpenter, Humphrey. *Geniuses Together: American Writers in Paris in the 1920s*. London: Unwin Hyman, 1987.

Catalogue of Members (2nd ed.). Toronto: League of Canadian Poets, 1980.

Charters, Jimmie "the Barman" (as told to Morrill Cody). *This Must Be the Place: Memoirs of Montparnasse*, with an introduction by Ernest Hemingway, second edition. Edited with a preface by Hugh Ford. New York: Collier, 1989.

Clark, Wayne. "In the Embrace of an Erotic Muse." *Maclean's* 92.51 (17 December 1979): 10–12.

Clarke, F.R.C. *Healey Willan: Life and Music*. Toronto: University of Toronto Press, 1983.

Cobb, David. "Elegant Pornographer." *The Canadian* (21 February 1976): 8–11.

Cogswell, Fred. Review of *The Poetry of French Canada in Translation*. *The Fiddlehead* 88 (Winter 1971): 103–4.

Coleman, George (pseud.). *The Rodiad*. London: Cadell & Murray, 1810 [1898].

Colombo, John Robert. "Three Poets." *The Tamarack Review* 11 (Spring 1959): 95–7.

Cooper, William. Review of *Under the Hill*. *The Listener* (25 August 1966): 283.

Cowley, Malcolm. "Those Paris Years." *The New York Times Book Review* (9 June 1968): 1.

– "We Had Such Good Times." *The New Republic* (25 December 1971): 27–8.

Curry, Ralph L. *Stephen Leacock: Humorist and Humanist*. New York: Doubleday, 1959.

Dau's Society Blue-Book for Montreal. Montreal: Dau, 1898.

Davis, Carroll. "Jazz: A Plea for Tolerance." *The McGill Fortnightly Review*, 2.4 (15 December 1926): 30–1.

de St Jorre, John. *Venus Bound: The Erotic Voyage of the Olympia Press and Its Writers*. New York: Random House, 1994.

Delaunay, Albert. "Edmond Sergent" in *Dictionary of Scienic Biography, Volume XII*. New York: Scribner's, 1975, 315.

Dempsey, Lotta. "Premier Party for Callaghan." *The Globe & Mail*. 12 June 1958. 14.

Djwa, Sandra. *The Politics of the Imagination: A Life of F.R. Scott*. Toronto: McClelland & Stewart, 1987.

Dobbs, Kildare. "The Great Glassco." *Maclean's* 88.8 (August 1976): 48–50, 52.

– Review of *The Fatal Woman*. *Maclean's* 87.11 (November 1974): 116.

Dudek, Louis. "A Decadent in Canada in the 1970s? Yes!" *The Gazette* (7 February 1970): 40.

– *In Defence of Art: Critical Essays and Reviews*. Edited with an introduction by Aileen Collins. Kingston: Quarry, 1988.

– "Look on the Book as Fantasy." *The Globe & Mail* (17 September 1988): D7.

– *Notebooks: 1960–1994*. Ottawa: Golden Dog, 1994.

Ebara, Saikakou [Ihara Saikaku]. *Contes d'amour des samouraïs*. Translated by Ken Sato. Paris: Stendhal, 1927.

Leon Edel. "Book Chat from Paris; News of New Books and Gossip of Litteration." *The Montreal Daily Star* (24 November 1928): 15.

– "John Glassco (1909–1981) and His Erotic Muse." *Canadian Literature* 93 (Summer 1982): 108–17.

– "Literary Revolution: The 'Montreal Group.'" *The McGill You Knew: An Anthology of Memories, 1920–1960*, Edgar Collard, ed. Don Mills, ON: Longman Canada, 1975, 117.

– "Literature and Journalism: The Visible Boundaries." *The Callaghan Symposium*, David Staines, ed. Ottawa: University of Ottawa (1981): 7–22.

– *Memories of the Montreal Group*. St John's, NF: Department of English, Memorial University of Newfoundland, 1986.

– "Paris Book Chat." *The Montreal Daily Star* (3 August 1929): 22.

– "Paris Book Chat." *The Montreal Daily Star* (17 August 1929): 6.

– "Paris Book Chat." *The Montreal Daily Star* (2 November 1929): 27.

– *The Visitable Past: A Wartime Memoir*. n.p.: Biographical Research Center/ University of Hawai'i Press, 2000.

– "The Young Warrior in the Twenties." *On F.R. Scott: Essays on His Contributions to Law, Literature, and Politics,* Sandra Djwa and R. St J. Macdonald, eds. Montreal: McGill-Queen's University Press, 1983, 6–16.

Edinborough, Arnold. "Lessons to Drop-Outs on How to Do Your Own Thing in Style." *The Financial Post* (16 May 1970): 10.

Ellmann, Richard. *James Joyce*. New York: Oxford University Press, 1959.

Entin, Martin A. *Edward Archibald: Surgeon of the Royal Vic*. Montreal: McGill University Libraries, 2005.

Eulenberg, Albert. *Algolagnia* [*Sadismus und Masochismus*]. Translated by Harold Kent. New York: New Era, 1934.

Fetherling, Douglas. *Travels by Night: A Memoir of the Sixties.* Toronto: Lester, 1994.

Fischman, Sheila. "A Night in August." *Matrix* 22 (Spring 1986): 23–27.

Fisher, Neil H. *First Statement, 1942–1945: An Assessment and Index*. Ottawa: Golden Dog, 1974.

Ford, Hugh. *Published in Paris: American and British Writers, Printers, and Publishers in Paris, 1920–1939*. New York: Macmillan, 1975.

French, William, "Hemingway Got the Punchline of This Story." *The Globe & Mail* (12 January 1963): 17.

– "Pursuing a Dream in Paris Remembered. *The Globe and Mail Magazine* (7 March 1970): 16.

Galt, George, ed. *The Purdy-Woodcock Letters: Selected Correspondence 1964–1984*. Toronto: ECW, 1988.

Gertzman, Jay A. *Bootleggers and Smuthounds: The Trade in Erotica, 1920–1940*. Philadelphia: University of Pennsylvania Press, 1999.

Gibson, Ian. *The English Vice: Beating, Sex and Shame in Victorian England and After*. London: Duckworth, 1978.

Girodias, Maurice, ed. *The Olympia Reader: Selections from the Traveller's Companion Series*. New York: Grove, 1965.

Glassco, John. "The Art of Pornography." *Edge* 9 (Summer 1969): 101–13.

– "Aubade." *Delta* 8 (January 1962): 1.

– "Blithe Spirits on the Wing." *The Gazette* [Montreal] (7 June 1980): 79.

– "Canadian Poet." *Aurora: New Canadian Writing 1978*, Morris Wolfe, ed. Toronto: Doubleday, 1978, 57.

– "Ceremony." *The Canadian Forum* (October 1971): 19.

– "'Classy' Lowells Set the Tone fr Boston's Literary Manners." *The Gazette* [Montreal] (2 February 1981): 25.

– "Coleridge Was a Dilettante in Everything but His Poetry." *The Gazette* [Montreal] (30 August 1980): 35.

– [as J.S.G.]. "Collegiana." *The McGill Daily* (27 October 1926): 4.

– [John of Anjou, pseud.] "Collegiana." *The McGill Daily* (10 November 1926): 2.

– [Euphorian, pseud.]. "Collegiana." *The McGill Daily* (17 November 1926): 2.

– [Euphorian, pseud.]. "Collegiana." *The McGill Daily* (8 December 1926): 2.

– "Countess Isabella and the Torturer." *Jewish Dialog* (Summer 1972): 32–41.

– *The Deficit Made Flesh*. Toronto: McClelland & Stewart, 1958.

– "Deserted Buildings under Shefford Mountain." *The Canadian Forum* (July 1956): 39.

– "Donne Procubitus." *The Fiddlehead* 28 (May 1956): 24–5.

– "The Dying Christian to His Body." *The Canadian Forum* (December 1968): 205.

– [Miles Underwood, pseud.]. *The English Governess*. Paris: Ophelia, 1960.

– *The English Governess*, with an introduction by Michael Gnarowski. Ottawa: Golden Dog, 2000.

– "Extract from an Autobiography." *This Quarter* 4 (Spring 1929): 198–210.

– *The Fatal Woman*. Toronto: House of Anansi, 1974.

– [Sylvia Bayer, pseud.] *Fetish Girl*. New York: Venus Library, 1972.

– "For Djuna Barnes on Her 80th Birthday." *A Festschrift for Djuna Barnes on Her 80th Birthday*. Alex Gildzen, ed. Kent, OH: Kent State University Libraries, 1972. n.p.

– "Frogmore and the Fatal Woman." *First Statement* (October–November 19440: 1–10.

– "Frogmore's Fancy." *First Statement* (December 1944–January 19450: 16–22.

– "Frogmore's Folly." *First Statement* (August 1944): 2–7.

– "From a Commonplace Book." *The Tamarack Review* 58 (June 1971): 61–4.

– "From *Montreal*." *CrossCountry* 3–4 (Fall 1975): 71–6.

– [Silas N. Gooch, pseud.]. "Goodnight, Sweet Prince." *Delta* 25 (November 1965): 30.

– [Anonymous]. *Harriet Marwood, Governess*. New York: Grove, 1967.

– *Harriet Marwood, Governess*. Toronto: General 1976.

– "The Heavenly Boy." *Saturday Night* 95.10 (December 1980): 88.

– "Her Goodness, Our Grimace." *Books in Canada* (March 1977): 3–4.

– "It's a Crime! (But, We Do Need the Jobs)." *The Globe & Mail* (11 November 1978): 6.

– "It's Harder Now to Walk These Streets." *The Globe & Mail* (3 April 19760: 39.

– *John Glassco: Selected Poems with Three Notes on the Poetic Process*. Introduced and arranged by Michael Gnarowski. Ottawa: Golden Dog, 1997.

– "'(m)' and '(r)' in 'Revolution 9 Or: A Collage of Letters Written to Alphabet During the Last Nine Years.'" *Alphabet* 16 (September 1969): 34–6.

– "The Marital Sex Education Film." *Ingluvin* 2 (Spring 1971): 25–7.

– "Maxims and Moral Reflections." *Yes* 15 (September 1966): n.p.

– *Memoirs of Montparnasse*. With an introduction by Leon Edel. Toronto: Oxford University Press, 1970.

– *Memoirs of Montparnasse*, second edition, with an introduction and annotations by Michael Gnarowski and the original introduction by Leon Edel. Toronto: Oxford University Press, 1995.

– "Memoirs of Zhivago's Lara." *The Montreal Star* (29 April 1978): C3.

– "Mr Noad." *The Canadian Forum* (March 1953): 277–80.

– *Montreal*. Montreal: DC, 1973.

– [Anonymous]. "Moscow Gold." *The McGill Fortnightly Review*. 2.9–10 (27 April 1927): 80.

– "Most of You Was a Great Smoky Mystery." *The Gazette* [Montreal] (15 April 1978): 1–2.

– "The Music Box." *The Fiddlehead* 20 (Summer 1961): 82–5.

– "The Needham Cemetery." *Queen's Quarterly* 72 (Autumn 1965): 550–1.

– "Never Mind the 10 Best for a Desert Island Here Are the World's Great Bad Books the Kind Thrust upon the Young, Enshrined in Leather and Gold – Nine in All with a Blank for You to Fill In." *The Globe & Mail* (16 April 1977): 25.

– "Nudity and Crudity." *The Montreal Star* (10 October 1970): 65.

– "O Executives, O Commuters." *The Canadian Forum* (August 1964): 107.

– "On Two Canadian Cats." *Mitre* (Spring 1978): 9.

– "Onan; or Little by Little." *Northern Journey* 1 (1971): 76.

– "The Pigtail Man." *Jewish Dialog* (Hannukah 1973): 47–57.

– "The Pit." *The Tamarack Review* 62 (First Quarter 1974): 31–4.

– "The Poet as Performer Debases His Art. You Hear Him, Not His Poetry." *The Globe & Mail* (12 November 1977): 6.

– *A Point of Sky*. Toronto: Oxford University Press, 1964.

– Review of *Barbara* by Frank Newman. *Ingluvin* 1 (1970): 18–20.

– Review of *Earth and High Heaven* by Gwethalyn Graham. *First Statement* (April–May 1945): 33–4.

– "Saisons de l'Avenir." *Ingluvin* 2 (Spring 1971): 24–5.

– "Schlemihl." *Delta* 8 (January 1962): 1.

– [as J.S. Glassco]. "Search." *The McGill Fortnightly Review*. 1.9–10 (22 March 1926): 73.

– "A Season in Limbo." *The Canadian Century: English-Canadian Writing since Confederation*, A.J.M. Smith, ed. [Toronto]: Gage Educational, 1973, 414–40.

– *Selected Poems*. Toronto: Oxford University Press, 1971.

– [George Coleman, pseud.]. *Squire Hardman*. Foster, Quebec: Pastime, 1966.

– "Town Council Meeting: Undesirable." *The Canadian Forum*, June 1952: 67.

– [Hideki Okada, pseud.] *The Temple of Pederasty*. North Hollywood, California: Hanover House, 1970.

– "Turning New Leaves." *The Canadian Forum* (January 1965): 236–7.

– "US Professor Praises Purity of Pornography." *The Montreal Star* (11 July 1970): 5.

– "Ulysses' Sea." *Alphabet* 15 (December 1968): 82.

– Untitled comment on "Catbird." *How Do I Love Thee: Sixty Poets of Canada (and Quebec) Select and Introduce Their Favourite Poems from Their Own Work*. John Robert Colombo, ed. Edmonton: Hurtig, 1970, 8.

– "When We Are Very Old." *Queen's Quarterly* 82 (Summer 1975): 258.

– ed. *English Poetry in Quebec: Proceedings of the Foster Poetry Conference October 12–14, 1963*. Montreal: McGill University Press, 1965.

– ed. *The Poetry of French Canada in Translation*. Toronto: Oxford University Press, 1970.

Gnarowski, Michael. *A Concise Bibliography of English-Canadian Literature*. Toronto: McClelland & Stewart, 1973.

– "Introduction as History." *Eternal Conversations: Remembering Louis Dudek*. Aileen Collins, Michael Gnarowski, and Sonja Skarstedt, eds. Montreal: DC, 2003, 9–31.

– "Notes Towards a Sometime and Probable History of John Glassco." *Reflections: Autobiography and Canadian Literature*. Edited with an introduction by K.P. Stich. Ottawa: University of Ottawa Press, 1988, 1–14.

Gournay, Isabelle and France Vanlaethem, eds. *Montréal métropole, 1880–1930*. Montreal: Les Éditions Boréal, 1998.

Hamilton, Ian. review of *Under the Hill. The New Statesman* (12 August 1966): 235.

Harvey, Jean-Charles. *Fear's Folly* [*Les demi-civilisés*]. Translated by John Glassco. Ottawa: Carleton University Press, 1982.

– *Sackcloth for Banner* [*Les demi-civilisés*]. Translated by Lukin Barette. Toronto: Macmillan, 1938.

Hayne, David M. "Literary Translation in Nineteenth-Century Canada." *Symposium on Translation in Canadian Literature 1982*. Camille R. La Bossière, ed. Ottawa: University of Ottawa Press, 1983, 35–43.

Hazlitt, William Carew. *A Roll of Honour: A Calendar of the Names of over 17,000 Men and Women Who throughout the British Isles and in Our Early Colonies Have Collected Mss. and Printed Books from the XIVth to the XIXth Century*. London: B. Quaritch, 1908.

Hustak, Alan. "Interviews Were Broadcaster's Forte." *The Gazette* [Montreal] (15 January 2004): A8.

Huysmans, J.K. *Against the Grain [À rebours]*. Translated by John Howard. New York: Boni, 1930.

Johnson, Ronald. "Moving with the Movies." *The Globe & Mail* (18 June 1958): 23.

Johnstone, J.K. Review of *The Deficit Made Flesh* and two other works. *Fiddlehead* 40 (Spring 1959): 44–7.

Jones, D.G. Untitled editorial. *Ellipse* 1 (1969): 5.

Kearney, Patrick. *The Paris Olympia Press*. Liverpool: Liverpool University Press, 2007.

Kelly, M.T. "No Puritan, Glassco Had the Gift of Grace." *The Globe & Mail* (7 February 1981): E7.

– "Under Her Thumb." *The Globe & Mail* (4 August 1979): Fanfare 7.

Knoll, Robert E. *Robert McAlmon: Expatriate Publisher and Writer*. Lincoln, NE: University of Nebraska Press, 1959.

Kokotailo, Philip. *John Glassco's Richer World: Memoirs of Montparnasse*. Toronto: ECW, 1988.

Lanham, Edwin. *Banner at Daybreak*. New York: Longmans, Green, 1937.

Lanthier, Philip. "An Interview with Doug Jones." *Matrix*, 22 (Spring 1986): 63–70.

Laurence, Margaret. "Roses and Yew." *The Tamarack Review* 54 (Winter 1970): 77–80.

Layton, Irving. *Taking Sides*. Oakville, ON: Mosaic, 1977.

– *Waiting for the Messiah: A Memoir*. Toronto: McClelland & Stewart, 1985.

Le Gallienne, Richard. *There Was a Ship*. Toronto: Doubleday, Doran & Gundy, 1930.

Lynch, Lucinda. Review of *Complete Poems of Saint-Denys-Garneau*. *The Ottawa Citizen* (18 August 1976): 84.

MacLeod, Wendall, et al. *Bethune: The Montreal Years*. Toronto: Lorimer, 1978.

MacSkimming, Roy. "New Book Another Example of Delayed Recognition." *The Toronto Star* (1 November 1974): E14.

– "Underground Classic Rises from Bondage." *The Toronto Star* (29 January 1976): E16.

MacSween, Joseph. "Sad Crowds Bid Adieu as Fair Gates Close." *Canadian Press* (30 October 1967).

Mailer, Norman. "Punching Papa." *The New York Review of Books*, 1.1 (1 February 1963): 13.

Maloff, Saul. "Again the Lost Ones." *Newsweek* (8 July 1968): 70.

Mandel, Eli. "Saint Denys Garneau? He Goes On Living. He Won't Go Away. Haunted, Self-Conscious." *The Globe & Mail* (20 December 19750: 34.

McAlmon, Robert. *McAlmon and the Lost Generation: A Self-Portrait*. Edited with a commentary by Robert E. Knoll. Lincoln, Nebraska: University of Nebraska, 1962.

– *Miss Knight and Others*. Edited with an introduction by Edward N.S. Lorusso. Albuquerque, New Mexico: University of New Mexico Press, 1992.

– *The Nightinghouls of Paris.* Edited with an introduction by Sanford J. Smoller. Urbana, Illinois: University of Illinois Press, 2007.

– *There Was a Rustle of Black Silk Stockings.* New York: Belmont, 1963.

– and Kay Boyle. *Being Geniuses Together.* New York: Doubleday, 1968.

Mellen, Joan. *Kay Boyle: Author of Herself.* New York: Farrar, Straus & Giroux, 1994.

Merler, Grazia. "Translating and the Creation of Cultural Myths in Canada." *West Coast Review* 2.2 (October 1974): 26–33.

Mirabeau, Octave. *Le jardin des supplices.* Paris: Éditions du Boucher, 2003.

Moorhead, Ethel. "About Books." *This Quarter* 4 (Spring 1929): 264–72.

Morgan, Henry J. *The Canadian Men and Women of the Time: A Handbook of Canadian Biography.* Toronto: Briggs, 1898.

Moodey, Edgar C., and Robert A. Spiers. *Veritas: A History of Selwyn House School, Montreal, 1908–1978.* Westmount, QC: Selwyn House Association, 1978.

Moore, George. *Confessions of a Young Man.* New York: Brentano's, 1920.

Morris, Peter. "Before the Beginning: William Davidson's and Norman Klenman's Now That April's Here." *Take One* 11.38 (July–August 2002): 11–16

Morrison, Flavia. "The Writer Obsessed." *The Montreal Star* (25 September 1976): D4.

Oxley, Allan. "Father Held in Mass Slaying." *The Montreal Star* (14 February 1956): 4.

Pearson, Alan. "The Yellow Book Revisited, or a Beardsley Pastiche." *The Montreal Star* (1 October 1966): Entertainments 4.

Peckham, Morse. *Art and Pornography.* New York: Basic, 1969.

PEW. Letter. *The McGill Daily* (18 February 1927): 2.

Pound, Ezra. *Dk/Some Letters of Ezra Pound.* Edited with notes by Louis Dudek. Montreal: DC, 1974.

– "Paris Letter," *The Dial* (February 1922): 192.

Powell, Anthony. "Knocking around the Latin Quarter." *The London Daily Telegraph* (9 April 1970): 6.

Purdy, Al. *Yours, Al: The Collected Letters of Al Purdy.* Sam Solecki, ed. Madeira Park, BC: Harbour, 2004.

Rexroth, Kenneth. *The Nation* 195.8 (22 September 1962): 195.

Richmond, John. "John Glassco: An Interview." *The Montreal Star* (18 October 1969): Entertainments, 5, 47.

Sacher-Masoch, Leopold von. *Venus in Furs* [*Venus im Pelz*]. Translator unknown. New York: no publisher, 1928.

– *Venus in Furs* [*Venus im Pelz*]. Translated by John Glassco. Burnaby, BC: Blackfish, 1977.

Sadleir, Michael. *Fanny by Gaslight.* London: Constable, 1940.

Saint-Denys-Garneau, Hector de, *Complete Poems of Saint-Denys-Garneau.* Translated by John Glassco. Ottawa: Oberon, 1975.

– *The Journal of Saint-Denys-Garneau*. Translated by John Glassco. Toronto: McClelland & Stewart, 1962.

Sato, Ken. *Quaint Stories of the Samurais*. Paris: [Contact Editions, 1928].

Schwartz, Louis [as L.S.] and J.G. [as J.G.S.]. "Collegiana." *The McGill Daily* (20 October 1926): 2.

Scobie, Stephen. *McAlmon's Chinese Opera*. Dunvegan, ON: Quadrant Editions, 1980.

Scott, Chris. "Helter Pelter." *Books in Canada* (June–July 1977): 15.

Scott, F.R. *The Collected Poems of F.R. Scott*. Toronto: McClelland & Stewart, 1981.

– trans., *Poems of French Canada*. Burnaby, BC: Blackfish, 1977.

– trans., *Saint-Denys Garneau and Anne Hébert*. Vancouver: Klanak, 1962.

Smith, A.J.M. "John Stinson Glassco." *Contemporary Poets of the English Language*. Rosalie Murphy, ed. Chicago: St James, 1970, 423–5.

– ed., *The Book of Canadian Poetry*. Chicago: University of Chicago Press, 1943.

– ed., *The Canadian Century*. Toronto: Gage Educational, 1973.

Smoller, Sanford J. *Adrift among Geniuses: Robert McAlmon, Writer and Publisher of the Twenties*. University Park, Pennsylvania: Pennsylvania State University Press, 1975.

Soucy, Jean-Yves. *Creatures of the Chase* [*Un dieu chasseur*]. Translated by John Glassco. Toronto: McClelland & Stewart, 1979.

Sours, David. "Edwin Lanham." *Dictionary of Literary Biography, Volume 4: American Writers in Paris, 1920–1939*. Detroit: Gale Research, 1980: 244–6.

Souster, Raymond. *Making the Damn Thing Work*. Toronto: Junction, 2001.

Stafford, Jean. "Spirits." *The New York Review of Books* 12.8 (24 April 1969): 28.

Stein, Gertrude. *Everybody's Autobiography*. New York: Random House, 1937.

– *Paris France*. New York: Liveright, 1970.

Stewart, Roderick. *Bethune*. Toronto: New Press, 1973.

Stratford, Philip. "Circle, Straight Line, Ellipse." *Canadian Literature* 49 (Summer 1971): 88–91.

Sullivan, Rosemary. *The Red Shoes: Margaret Atwood Starting Out*. Toronto: HarperCollins, 1997.

Sutherland, Fraser. *John Glassco: An Essay and Bibliography*. Downsview, Ontario: ECW, 1984.

– *John Glassco: A Personal and Working Library*. Montreal: The Word Bookshop, n.d.

Sutherland, John. *The Letters of John Sutherland, 1942–1956*, Bruce Whiteman, ed. Toronto: ECW, 1992.

Tausky, Thomas A. "*Memoirs of Montparnasse*: 'A Reflection of Myself.'" *Canadian Poetry* 13 (Fall/Winter, 1983): 59–84.

Taylor, Graeme. "Deaf-Mute." *transition* 13 (Summer 1928): 172–3.

– "Dr Breakey Opposes Union." *This Quarter* 2.1 (July–August–September 1929): 63–70.

– "Extract I." *This Quarter* 4 (Spring 1929): 171–86.

– "Extract II." *This Quarter* 4 (Spring 1929): 186–92.

– [Hans Mann, pseud.]. "The Flow Will Return." *The McGill Fortnightly Review* 2.9–10 (27 April 1927): 68–9.

– [Jon Grahame, pseud.]. "The Unknown World." *The McGill Fortnightly Review* 2.8 (25 March 1927): 61.

– [as W. Graeme Taylor]. Letter. *The McGill Daily* (12 November 1926): 2.

– [Wingate Taylor, pseud.]. "The Horse-Stall." *First Statement* (April–May 1945): 15–26.

Toye, William, general ed. *Supplement to the Oxford Companion to Canadian History and Literature*. Toronto: Oxford University Press, 1973.

Trehearne, Brian. *Aestheticism and the Canadian Modernists: Aspects of Poetic Influence*. Montreal: McGill-Queens University Press, 1989.

– *The Montreal Forties: Modernist Poetry in Transition*. Montreal: McGill-Queens University Press, 1999.

van Rod, Aimé *La gouvernante*. Paris: Édition Parisienne, 1913.

Vanneste, Hilda M.C. *Northern Review, 1945–1956: A History and an Index*. Ottawa: Tecumseh, 1982.

Vaughan, Walter, and A.P.S. Glassco. *McGill University Centennial Endowment: A Greater McGill*. Montreal: s.n., 1919.

Vintcent, Brian. Review of *Venus in Furs. The Globe & Mail* (30 April 1977): 39.

– Review of *Venus in Furs. Quill and Quire* 44:8 (July 1977): 43.

Wachtel, Eleanor. "Prize and Prejudice." *Books in Canada* (March 1982): 9.

Waddington, Miriam. "But How Does Glassco Feel about Montreal." *The Globe & Mail* (17 November 1973): 34.

Wagner, Geoffrey. "How Wild Was Mr Weirdsley." *The Kenyon Review*, September 1977): 543–9.

Weaver, Robert. "A Talk with Morley Callaghan." *The Tamarack Review* 7 (Spring 1958): 3–29.

Weintraub, William. *City Unique: Montreal Days and Nights in the 1940s and '50s*. Toronto: McClelland & Stewart, 1996.

Whitney, Patricia M. "Darkness and Delight: A Portrait of the Life and Work of John Glassco." PhD dissertation, Carleton University, 1988.

Wigle, Wil. "Slow Burn." *Northern Journey* 3 (October 1973): 13–19.

Wilde, Oscar. *The Picture of Dorian Gray*. London: Ward Lock, 1891.

Williams, William Carlos. *The Autobiography of William Carlos Williams*. New York: Random House, 1951.

Wilson, Edmund. "Kay Boyle and *The Saturday Evening Post*." *The New Yorker* (15 January 1944): 66.

Wilson, Ethel. "Series of Combination of Events and Where Is John Goodwin?" *The Tamarack Review* 33 (Autumn 1963): 3–9.

Wilson, Milton. Review of *The Deficit Made Flesh. The Canadian Forum* 40 (June 1959): 65.

Woodcock, George. *Beyond the Blue Mountains: An Autobiography*. Markham, ON: Fitzhenry & Whiteside, 1987.

– Letter. *Quill and Quire*. 40.7 (July 1974): 2, 11.

– "Literary Worlds and Their Denizens." Canadian Literature 44 (Spring 1970): 67–72.

– *Taking it to the Letter*. Montreal: Quadrant, 1981.

– *The World of Canadian Writing: Critiques and Recollections*. Vancouver: Douglas & McIntyre, 1980.

Credits

p. 87: John Glassco fonds, Library and Archives Canada, reproduction copy number e010767807

p. 90: John Glassco fonds, Library and Archives Canada, reproduction copy number e010767821

p. 102: John Glassco fonds, Library and Archives Canada, reproduction copy number e010767817

p. 103: John Glassco fonds, Library and Archives Canada, reproduction copy number e010767823

p. 129: John Glassco fonds, Library and Archives Canada, reproduction copy number e010767819

p. 135: John Glassco fonds, Library and Archives Canada, reproduction copy number e010767820

p. 139: O'Neil, Montreal, John Glassco fonds, Library and Archives Canada, reproduction copy number e010767822

p. 143: John Glassco fonds, Library and Archives Canada, reproduction copy number e010767810

p. 151: John Glassco fonds, Library and Archives Canada, reproduction copy number e010767808

p. 155: Collection of the author

p. 165: Collection of the author

p. 179: John Glassco fonds, Library and Archives Canada, reproduction copy number e010767812

p. 190: John Glassco Collection, Rare Books and Special Collections, McGill University Library

p. 202: Collection of the author

p. 214: John Glassco fonds, Library and Archives Canada, reproduction copy number PA-188182

p. 225: Micheline Ste-Marie, LAC e010767809

p. 229: John Glassco fonds, Library and Archives Canada, reproduction copy number e010767813

p. 232: Collection of the author

p. 249: Collection of the author

p. 252: John Glassco fonds, Library and Archives Canada, reproduction copy number e010767811

p. 282: Photograph by Gordon Beck

p. 297: Photograph by the author

Index

Barbour, Douglas, 265

Barette, Lukin, 294

Barker, George, 211

Barnard School for Boys, 340n23

Barnes, Djuna, 50, 232

Barrett, William, 182

Basile, Jean, 353n36

Basquiat, Jean-Michel, 358n123

Beach, Sylvia, 46, 70, 241–2, 330n88

Beaconsfield Golf Club, 17–18

Beardsley, Aubrey, 114, 157–9, 193, 201, 244; *Sous la colline et d'autres essays en prose et en vers*, 194; *The Story of Venus and Tannhaüser*, 157; *Under the Hill*, 5–6, 130, 157–9, 172, 179, 193–6, 199–200, 243, 268–9, 283, 286

Beaudelaire, Charles, 93

Beaupré, Jean, 152

Beck, Sir Adam, 318n3

Becket, Samuel, 158

Being Geniuses (Carpenter), 232

Being Geniuses Together (McAlmon): JG's criticisms, 108, 215–16, 221–2; revised by Boyle, 213–20. *See also* McAlmon, Robert: *Being Geniuses Together*

Beissel, Henry, 271, 277

Belmont Books, 350n38

Bennett, R.B., 91

Berton, Pierre, 257; *The Last Spike*, 257

Bertrand, Jean-Jacques, 128

Berys (lover), 136

Bethune, Norman, 80–1

Bierley, Jane, 363n88

Birkett, Herbert Stanley, 25

Birney, Earle, 264, 271, 276, 347n49

Bishop's College School, 24–5, 98, 278, 332n23

Bishopric, John, 276, 292

bissett, bill, 192

Bitch Goddesses, 240

Black Book (Durrell), 158

Blackfish Press, 283, 286

Black Silk Stockings, 240

Blake, W.H., 363n88

Bodley Head, 283

"The Body Says Goodbye to Love," 77

Bonenfant, Joseph, 224

Books in Canada, 284

Borestone Mountain Poetry Awards, 139–40, 340–1n37

The Borestone Mountain Poetry Awards 1955, 139.

Bovey, Wilfred, 41, 323n82, 324n97

Bowering, Angela, 212, 247

Bowering, George, 247

Bowles, Paul, 57

Boyle, Kay, 4, 46–8, 57, 85, 215, 228, 337n69, 350n42; affair with JG, 48, 180; *Avalanche*, 119; commercial success, 118–20; correspondence with JG, 146, 157, 185, 213, 215, 218–26, 234, 338n79, 352–3n30; as ghostwriter of *Relations and Complications*, 46–8, 325n14, 325n15; inscribed copy of *Memoirs of Montparnasse*, 233–4; issues with JG's memoirs, 219–21, 234, 350n45; literary subterfuge, 46–8, 219–20; as model for Dale Burke, 71; as model for Diana Tree, 48, 221; revision of *Being Geniuses Together*, 213–20, 349n29, 350n34

Boyle, Joan, 73, 120

Bradbury, Ray, 339n22

Brancart, Auguste, 342n15

Brandon House Library Editions, 240, 245

Brault, Richard, 46

Brett, Brian, 283–6

Briarcliff Quarterly, 123

Bricktop. *See* Smith, Ada

Brochu, André, 237

Brooke, Bertram, Tuan Muda of Sarawak, 46, 325n12

Brooke, Gladys Palmer, Dayang Muda

Expo 67, 208–9, 211–12, 264

Glassco, Edward David (brother), 14–16, 22–4, 81, 134, 287, 332n23; as investor, 99, 170, 188

Glassco, Elma (1st wife), 142–4, 151, 153, 156, 162, 172–7, 203, 249–50, 263, 272, 283, 340n33, 343n21; appearance, 142–3, 203, 224–6, arrival at Jamaica Farm, 144–5, 203; birthplace, 142; death, 256, 357n108; eating habits, 144–5, 224; family background, 142; illnesses, 145, 203–8, 213–15, 224–6, 249–50, 253–4, 291–2; marriage, 188; as mind-reader, 142; personality, 142; as pornographer, 160; suicide attempt, 208, travels with JG, 157, 159, 170, 208

Glassco, Henry, 9

Glassco, John Girdlestone, 9, 318n3

Glassco, John Stinson: affairs & romances, 48, 51, 75–6, 89, 94, 99, 102, 112, 134–8, 142, 180, 251–5, 334n55, 339n3; appearance, 15, 21, 25, 28–9, 45, 53, 59, 87, 90, 93, 97, 110, 149, 151, 179, 214, 229, 282, 333n49; "attacks," 123–4, 136–7, 340n33; in *Being Geniuses Together*, 213–15; birth, 8, 14; birthplace, 8, 14, 175, 345–55n11; *Byron's Goose*, 140; censored, 193–6, 246; collaborations with Taylor, 58, 89–91, 118, 128, 154, 278–9, 337n62; death, 298; on death, 83, 267, 299; depression, 81–5, 88, 97, 174, 205, 214, 287–9, 292–3, 297; dreams, 97, 134; drinking, 25, 95, 108, 128–9, 137, 192, 206, 287–8; education, 19–21, 24–6, 28, 31–3, 39–40, 324n94; employment, 40, 104, 111, 180; family history, 9–14; as farmer, 103; fears, 6, 83–6, 96, 123–4, 174, 212, 214, 267; fetishism, 89, 94–5, 196, 258–63, 291; finances, 41, 44, 62, 91, 103–4, 109–10, 170–1, 174; funeral, 299–300; as ghostwriter, 47–8, 325n14; heart attack, 288; as horseman, 99, 103, 109–11, 131; inheritance, 16, 41, 81, 88, 91, 99; investments, 99, 103–4, 109, 170–1; as liar, 3, 6, 23; library, 27, 121, 133, 174–5, 186, 194, 323n89, 333n35; literary aspirations, 95, 100, 110, 118, 172, 179, 227; literary influences, 26, 39, 43–4, 84, 93–4, 112, 283; literary rejection, 82, 95, 100, 110, 114, 130, 171, 192–3, 244, 268–9, 279, 283; literary reputation, 130, 154–6, 186, 227; literary subterfuge, 37–8, 47–8, 76, 143, 161, 164–9, 196–9, 228, 230, 232–3, 240–8, 278; 318n11, 325n14, 328n49, 331n110, 335n23, 342–3n15; literary tastes, 43–4, 54, 84, 88, 92–3, 156, 174, 193, 197, 249–50, 282; longing for the past, 88–9, 97; love for Elma, 172, 213, 226, 254; love for Marion, 251, 254–5; love for Sappho, 133–34; love for Taylor, 83–4, 113, 213; marriage to Elma, 144, 188; marriage to Marion, 263, 275; masochism, 94–5, 196, 250, 291; *ménages à trois*, 58–9, 72, 77, 101, 124, 126, 138, 253, 294; as model in fiction, 65, 69–71, 120–3, 181–2, 279, 325n14, 325n16; murderous thoughts, 137, 340n33; nickname, 16; politics, 34, 222–3; political aspirations, 130–2, 141; pseudonyms, 34–5, 143, 160, 175, 239–40, 258, 276, 337–8n69, 353n32; public persona, 227–8, 276, 286; sadism, 250; self-criticism & self-doubt, 6, 82–3, 88, 100, 148–9, 196; as self-publisher, 95, 114, 198–9, 269, 286; sexual encounters, 25, 31, 48, 72, 75, 89, 135, 176–7, 180, 250, 294; sexual fantasies, 32, 75–6, 85, 89, 94–5, 133, 162, 253, 259, 262–3, 287, 292; sexuality, 31–2, 133; speech, 25, 276, 332n23; suicidal thoughts, 226, 288–9, 297; on Taylor's writing, 83, 89, 91; in *That Summer in Paris*, 182–6, 347n40; tuberculosis, 77–84, 97, 110, 172–3, 176, 180; vanity, 97, 212, 333n49; as victim of child abuse, 22–3, 176, 319n26; writing habits, 95, 173–4, 192, 214, 287; writing income, 60, 141, 156, 160, 162–3, 177, 195–6, 257, 282, 343n30

Glassco, John Stinson (works): *The Accomplishments of Cheverel Virtue*, 130; "Anthem for the Centennial of Canadian Confederation," 209–11; *The Art of Pornography* (anthology), 285–6; "The Art of Pornography" (essay), 240, 285–6; *The Augean Stable*, 170; *The Authentic Confessions of Harriet Marwood, an English Governess*, 164; "Autobiographical Sketch," 22, 31, 36, 40, 175–6, 196, 261; "A Ballad on the Death of Thomas Pepys, Tailor," 130; "Belly Dance," 138, 154; "The Black Helmet," 93, 270, 279; "Brummel at Calais," 125; "The Burden of Junk," 154; "The Cardinal's Dog," 154; "Catbird," 177, 258; "A Child in the House," 82; "The Clutch of Circumstances," 218; *The Collected Short Stories*, 278–9; *Complete Poems of Saint-Denys-Garneau*, 280–1; "Conan's Fig," 58, 239; *Contes en crinoline*, 342–3n15; "Countess Isabel and the Torturer," 280; "Dancers," 82; "Day in Autumn," 95; *The Deficit Made Flesh*, 153–7, 179, 191, 227, 263; "Deserted Buildings under Shefford Mountain," 140–1, 149, 154; "Dimensions of Longing," 150; "A Devotion: To Cteis," 145, 153–4; *En Arrière*, 114–15, 117, 130; *The English Governess*, 5, 159–65, 170, 172, 179, 193, 195–6, 198, 200, 246, 258–9, 283, 286; *English Poetry in Quebec*, 189–92, 227; "The Entailed Farm," 154–5; "Euterpe's Honeymoon (Notes on the Poetic Process)," 271; "Extract from an Autobiography," 40–2, 60–1,

112, 130, 231, 301–12; *The Fatal Woman*, 93, 269–71, 276–7, 279, 284, 286; *Fear's Folly*, 363n89; *Fetish Girl*, 5, 143, 258–61, 263, 268, 280; "For Cora Lightbody, RN," 177; "For Elma (My Darling Wife Who Went Mad)," 205–6; "Frogmore and the Fatal Woman," 116; *Frogmore en arrière*, 116; "Frogmore's Fancy," 116; "Frogmore's Folly," 116; "The Fulfilled Destiny of Electra," 269–70; "Gentleman's Farm," 130, 138–9, 154–5; *The Governess*, 163; *Harriet Marwood, Governess*, 5, 15, 132–3, 159, 160, 162–70, 258, 268, 284, 286; "The Heavenly Boy," 295–6; "Jogging Track," 154; *John Glassco: Selected Poems with Three Notes on the Poetic Process*, 5, *The Journal of Saint-Denys-Garneau*, 150, 171–2, 174, 178–9, 191, 227, 281; *The Liberator*, 172, 179; "Lines Addressed to a Dozen Young Canadian Poets, after Unwisely Devouring Five Little Magazines at a Sitting," 189; "Luce's Notch," 175, 192; "Lust in Action," 269–71, 290; "Mairobert," 132, 172, 268–9, 287; "March," 83, 148; *Memoirs of Montparnasse*, 3–5, 40–3, 48, 51–2, 54, 56, 70–1, 74–6, 78, 93, 156, 179–80, 186, 218–22, 227–34, 250, 253, 268–9, 279, 288, 293–4, 298, 301; "Mr Noad," 89; *Montreal*, 212, 264–6, 276, 279; "Morley in Paris," 218; "'Mouse's' First Mouse," 27; "Nobody's Fool," 58; "Ode: The Autumn Resurrection," 192; "Onan; or Little by Little," 271; "One Last Word," 254–5; *Philip Eugene*, 94, 99, 109, 112, 150; "The Pigtail Man," 118, 280; "The Places Where the Dead Have Walked," 175, 255; "The Poet as Performer Debases His Art. You Hear Him, Not His Poetry," 176–7; *The Poetry of French Canada in Translation*, 222–3, 227, 234–5, 237–9, 279, 281; *A Point of Sky* (collection), 27, 191–2, 227; "A Point of Sky" (poem), 175; "Quebec Farmhouse," 192; "Question," 36; "The Rural Mail," 111–12, 154; "Search," 30–1; "A Season in Limbo," 175, 255; *Selected Poems*, 5, 254–8, 268, 279; "Sonnet (On My 24th Birthday)," 97; *Squire Hardman*, 5, 132, 196–200, 268, 286; "Stud Groom," 154; *The Temple of Pederasty*, 240–8, 279, 286; "Thomas à Kempis," 154; *Those Endearing Young Charms*, 280, 286–7, 289–92; "The Three Captains," 89; "To Certain Quebecois Poets," 236–7; "Town Council Meeting: Undesirable," 131, 154; "The Two Linnets," 156; "Two Old Ladies," 218, 221; *Under the Birch*, 195–6, 200; *Under the Hill*, 5–6, 130, 157–9, 172, 179, 193–6, 199–200, 243, 268–9, 283, 286; "Utrillo's World I," 154; *Venus in Furs* (*see Venus in Furs*); "Villanelle," 154, 177; "The Way Back," 85–6, 89, 93, 283; "The Web," 140; "The White Mansion," 154–5; "The Whole Hog," 23, 154–5; "The Wild Canary" 156; "Windmill Point," 123

Glassco, John Thomas, 9

Glassco, Kathleen Mabel Beatrice (mother), 22, 100; affair, 122; "attacks," 340n33; death, 188; finances, 16, 23–4, 99, 134, 170, 188; as "glamour girl," 17–18; inheritance, 16, 188; and JG's rubber fetish, 261–2; marriage, 13–14, 122; as mother, 14–5, 22–3, 25, 27, 31, 41, 78, 81; sexual naïveté, 32; youth, 13

Glassco, William Henry, 9

Globe & Mail, 182, 257, 275, 277, 299;

reviews of JG's work, 192, 228, 266, 281, 284–5

Globe Straw Works, 9

Gnarowski, Michael, 141–2, 188, 248, 279, 294, 300, 347n49, 356n75; final meeting with JG, 297; and *Memoirs of Montparnasse*, 5, 192, 230; as publisher, 265; writings on JG, 5, 154, 227, 352n24

Godin, Gérard, 223, 353n236

Golden Dog Press, 5

Gotlieb, Phyllis, 340n37

"Gottfried Wolfgang" (Borel), 248

Governor General's Awards, 6, 156–7, 181, 256–8, 298, 357n113, 357n115

Governor General's Trophy, 20

Grand Trunk Railway, 9–10, 13

Graves, Robert, 340n37

Grier, Eldon, 189, 230

Grimm, Kenneth, 133

Grove Press, 163, 260

Grove, Frederick Philip, 248

Groves & Michaux, 333n37

Grushenka (anonymous), 161

Guarantee Company of North America, 8, 12, 16, 318n6, 359n5

Guggenheim, Peggy, 54, 180, 232, 351n52

Guilt and Mourning. *See* Glassco, John Stinson (works): *Those Endearing Young Charms*

Gustafson, Betty, 207, 292

Gustafson, Ralph, 117, 130, 207, 272, 277, 292, 347n49; *Anthology of Canadian Poetry (English)*, 156; correspondence with JG, 156, 257, 296; Foster Poetry Conference, 189; *Penguin Book of Canadian Verse*, 156

Haeffely, Claude, 236

Haig-Brown, Roderick, 199

Hallowell, Cecily. *See* Glassco, Cecily Hallowell

Conference, 186–8, 190; *Here and Now*, 117, 257, *Waiting for the Messiah*, 230–1; World Poetry Conference, 211

Leacock, Stephen, 44, 320n38

League of Canadian Poets, 277; *Catalogue of Members*, 277

LeClaire, François, 318n5

Le Conte, Robert Green, 332n3

Ledoux, Urbain J., 327n35

Ledoux, Yvette, 4, 54, 72, 75, 294, 327n35

Lee Furman, Inc., 327n36

Le Gallienne, Eva, 327n34

Le Gallienne, Gwen, 4, 54, 64, 72, 75, 294, 327n34

Le Gallienne, Richard, 327n34

Lehmann, Heinz, 207, 214–15, 291–2

le May, Pamphile, 341–2n10

Le Moyne, Jean, 153, 171–2, 192, 222

Lerew, Laurie, 338n79

Lesage, Jean, 187

Lescarbot, Marc, 235

Levertov, Denise, 211

Lévesque, Raymond, 353n36

Lewis, Jacob Howard, 333n35

Lewis, Wyndham, 106

Lewisohn, Ludwig, 62

Liberal Party of Quebec, 131, 141, 222

Librarie Artistiques et Litéraire, 166

Library and Archives Canada, 260

Lippe-Rosskam, Marguerite (Peggy), 96, 106–7, 120, 136, 180, as model for Mrs Quayle, 75, 331n110

Literary Review, 209

Little Review, 50

"The Locked Door" (McCourt), 118

Lolita (Nabokov), 158

London Daily Telegraph, 216

London Journal (Boswell), 248

Longmans, Green & Co., 112, 114, 143, 268

Lowell, Robert, 211

Lower Canada College, 19, 21, 25

Lucas Medal, 41

Lushington-Hayes, Roland, 77, 96, 331n113

Maccaulay, Colin Campbell, 20, 24, 26, 33

MacCormack, Terrance, 271, 275

Mackenzie, Alexander, 8

Maclean's, 181, 334n9, 345n9

MacLeish, Archibald, 46

MacLennan, Hugh, 195, 355n61

Macmillan of Canada, 171, 182, 294

Macpherson, Jay, 153

MacSkimming, Roy, 276

Madam Bovary (Flaubert), 205

Madame Birchini's Dance (anonymous), 116

Madge (housekeeper), 89

Mailer, Norman, 182

La maîtresse et l'esclave (anonymous), 283

Major, André, 235

Malkine, Georges, 75, 326–7n32

Mandel, Eli, 189–90, 281

Man Ray. *See* Radnitzky, Emmanuel

Manson, Charles, 215

Mao Zedong, 223

Mapplethorpe, Robert, 358n123

Marcotte, Gilles, 178

Marie, Queen of Romania, 34, 321–2n68

Marlborough College, 359n10

Marquis, Thomas Guthrie, 363n88

Martlet, 37

Massey, Raymond, 329n85

Massey, Vincent, 247

Maxwell, Sir John, 321n57

Mayne, Seymour, 189, 204

McAlmon, Bert, 105

McAlmon, George, 105

McAlmon, John Alexander, 48

McAlmon, Robert, 4, 48–50, 54, 65, 104–8, 114–15, 117, 119, 120–1, 123, 181,

243, 249, 278, 326n20, 326n22, 326n26, 330n88, 330n91, 335–6n42, 336n57, 337n62, 337n69, 338n79, 350n34, 350n38, 350n42, 355n61; appearance, 49, 53, 214; *Being Geniuses Together*, 105–6, 213–20; death, 123, 298; as deserter, 48–9, 325–6n19; *Distinguished Air (Grim Fairly Tales)*, 183; drinking, 55, 129; "Extracts from the Politics of Existence," 60; health, 105–6, 123; literary career, 49–50, 57, 60, 105, 123; literary reputation, 49, 216–17, 228, 234; "The Lodging House," 217; marriage, 49; in *McAlmon's Chinese Opera*, 298; in *Memoirs of Montparnasse*, 48, 51–2, 75, 234; "Miss Knight," 217; as model in fiction, 65, 120–1; *My Susceptible Friend, Adrian*, 70; in Nice, 57, 59; *The Nightinghouls of Paris*, 69–74, 88, 121–3, 278–9; *North America, Continent of Conjecture*, 50; *Not Alone Lost*, 105; pseudonyms, 120, 337n69; as publisher, 49–50, 105, 119–20, 241, 354n55, 354n56, 354n57; relationship with JG, 48, 51–2, 62, 67, 69, 75, 104, 123, 180, 293; sexuality, 49, 183; as supporter of JG's writing, 60, 107–9, 114; in *That Summer in Paris*, 183–4, 217; *There Was a Rustle of Black Silk Stockings*, 217; "Unfinished Poem," 60; *Village: As It Happened through a Fifteen-Year Period*, 70

McClelland & Stewart, 153, 171–2, 174, 218–19, 268

McCormick, Christy, 251

McCormick, Joel, 251, 253, 265, 275, 300

McCormick, Marion, 251–5, 258, 265, 274, 277, 288, 292, 295–6, 300, 356n95, 357n108; appearance, 251–2; and JG's death, 298; on JG's past, 253; JG's pornography, 260, 276; and JG's rubber fetish, 262–3; on marriage to JG, 263, 275, 292; travels with JG, 253, 273, 287–8

McCormick, Ted, 251

McGill Daily, 33–7, 96, 251

McGill Fortnightly Review, 29–30, 34, 37–9, 44, 295, 321n59, 324–5n10; JG's contributions, 30–1, 35, 37–8, 322–3n81; and *New Provinces*, 96

McGill University, 18–20, 24, 26, 29, 34–8, 41, 61, 192, 249, 251, 278, 320n38, 323n82, 323n84, 324n97; A.P.S. as student, 9; JG as student, 25, 28, 31–3, 39–40, 278

McGill University Press, 189, 283

McKay, Claude, 51, 326n26

McPhail, Andrew, 363n88

Meagher, Donald, 21

Melzach, Brian, 265

Memoirs of Montparnasse: acceptance, 221–2, annotations and inscriptions, 233–4, 298; composition, 3–4, 86, 93, 192, 220, 228, 230; excerpts in *The Tamarack Review*, 218; influence, 232; introduction, 3, 58, 228; motivation, 180, 186, 293; postscript, 78; prefatory note, 230; publication, 227, 230; reception and reviews, 3–4, 228–9, 231, 257, 268–9; rejection, 192–3; screenplay, 294; translation, 288; working titles, 58. *See also* Glassco, John Stinson (works): *Memoirs of Montparnasse*

"Memoirs of Montparnasse: 'A Reflection of Myself'" (Tausky), 5

Mencken, H.L., 339n22

Merler, Grazia, 281

Messaien, Olivier, 346n16

Metcalf, John, 271

Metropolitan Club, 12

Michener, Norah, 257

Michener, Roland, 257

Middlesex School, 200, 202, 244–5, 259

Millar, Rev'd Dr, 318n4

Sun Life Assurance Co., 40, 323n93
Sutherland, Audrey, 116
Sutherland, Betty, 116, 336n51
Sutherland, John, 115–18, 149, 248, 336n51, 340–1n37; *Other Canadians*, 130
Sutherland, Fraser, 81, 271–5, 299, 328n58, 342n15, 353n32, 359n12
Sutherland, Ronald, 238, 248
Sweetsburg Hospital, 208
Swinburne, Algernon Charles, 197–9, 285, 292; "A Boy's First Flogging at Birchmaster," 197; *The Flogging Block*, 197; *Lesbia Brandon*, 197, 283, 292; "Reginald's Flogging," 197
Symons, Julian, 157

Tamarack Review, 150, 154, 175, 218, 228, 248; 350n45
Taylor, Christina, 28
Taylor, Helen, 28
Taylor, James Hamilton, 28, 146
Taylor, Margaret, 28
Taylor, Samuel J., 28, 74
Taylor, William Graeme, 32–3; 40–4, 46, 48–51, 54–65, 74, 77, 82–92, 98, 116, 133–4, 137–8, 141, 176, 180, 228, 233, 253, 278–9, 293, 322–3n81; "An Afternoon in Luxemburg," 84–5; appearance, 28–9, 53, 59, 87, 129, 135, 214; in *Being Geniuses Together*, 213–15; *Brazenhead*, 117–18, 128–9; Buerger's Disease, 145–6; *Characteristics of the Penroses*, 60; "Deaf-Mute," 56–7, 278–9; death, 146–7, 213; divorce, 127–8; "Dr Breakey Opposes Union," 62–4, 87, 278–9; drinking, 57, 128–9, 148; "Extract I," 60; "Extract II," 60; as "failure," 148; family background, 28; as farmer, 88–9, 98–9, 129, 145, 336–7n58; "the flow will return," 39; *The Flying Carpet*, 56; *The Foundling*, 89; as horseman, 103, 125, 129, 145, 334n5; "The Horse-Stall," 117–18; influence over JG, 86, 108–9, 113–14, 131, 140–1, 147–9; as JG's investor, 98–9, 109–10; literary ambition, 56, 98; literary inspiration, 43–4; literary rejection, 87, 118, 128–9; as literary talent, 29, 55–7, 65, 83; love for JG, 136; marriage to Sappho, 104, 124–5; as *McGill Fortnightly* contributor, 39, 115; military service, 103–4, 106, 109; "Mr Noad," 89–91; as model in fiction, 65, 71, 121–3, 181–2, 279; and the Montreal Group, 96; personality, 29, 67–9, 109, 148; "The Portrait of a Generation," 87, 278; pseudonyms, 39, 118, 336–7n58; sexuality, 32; in *That Summer in Paris*, 182–6; "The Unknown World," 39, 96, 279; "The Volunteer," 84
The Temple of Pederasty: banning, 246; as erotic *collage*, 243–4; illustrations, 244–5; rejection, 244; sales, 248–9. *See also* Glassco, John Stinson (works): *The Temple of Pederasty*
Tennyson, Alfred Lord, 26
Thackeray, William Makepeace, 83
That Summer in Paris (Callaghan): depiction of JG, 182–6; influence on *Memoirs of Montparnasse*, 180, 186, 192, 293. *See also* Callaghan, Morley: *That Summer in Paris*
This Quarter, 46, 50, 60, 62–3, 67, 154, 278, 293, 301
Thomas, Henry, 11
Threep (bookseller), 354n59
Tiberi, Pearl, 138–9, 176, 340n34
Time, 257
Times Literary Supplement, 281
Titus, Edward, 63, 68–9, 183, 354n56
Toklas, Alice B., 54
Toronto Star, 64–5
Torrid Teens, 240
The Torture Garden (Mirbeau), 85–6
Toye, William, 75, 218, 221–2, 248, 294, 300

The White Savannahs (Collin), 96
White Thighs (Trocchi), 161
Whitney, Margaret, 75–6, 180, 331n110
Wickham House School, 19
Wicksteed, Gustavus William, 152
Wigle, Wil, 272–5; "Slow Burn," 272–5
Wilde, Oscar, 47, 333n37; The Picture of
    Dorian Gray, 92
Willan, Healey, 209–11; "Anthem for
    the Centennial of Canadian Confed-
    eration," 209–11
Williams, Penny, 363n88
Williams, William Carlos, 49–50, 57,
    105, 123, 325–6n19, 336n57, 337n67
Wilson, Edmund, 119
Wilson, Ethel, 248
Wilson, Mary Elizabeth (Sappho), 101–
    2, 124, 133, 136, 145, 176, 225, 253, 270,
    336n51; arrival at Windemere; 101;
    divorce, 127–8, as "fatal woman," 129,
    134; marriage, 104
Wilson, Milton, 155, 188–90
Wing, Willis, 192–3
Winnipeg City Hydro, 318n3

With Open Mouth (Van Heller), 161
Wolfe, Humbert, 62
Wolfe, James, 223
Wood, Clement, 133, 339–40n23
Woodcock, George, 3, 94, 272, 274–5,
    284
Woodford, Jack, 132
Woodman, Ken, 251, 292, 357n108
Wordsworth, William, 98, 155–6; "The
    Brothers," 155; "Lines Written a Few
    Miles above Tintern Abbey," 156;
    "Michael," 155; "The Ruined
    Cottage," 155
Workman, William, 318n5
World Poetry Conference, 211
Wreford, James, 156
Wright, Judith, 211
Writers' Union of Canada, 273–5

Yale Law School, 339n23
Yes, 227, 255, 264

Zadkine, Ossip, 157